CROSS-NATIONAL RESEARCH IN SOCIOLOGY

AMERICAN SOCIOLOGICAL ASSOCIATION PRESIDENTIAL SERIES

Volumes in this series are edited by successive presidents of the American Sociological Association and are based upon sessions at the Annual Meeting of the organization. Volumes in this series are listed below.

PETER M. BLAU
Approaches to the Study of Social Structure (1975)

LEWIS A. COSER and OTTO N. LARSEN
The Uses of Controversy in Sociology (1976)

J. MILTON YINGER
Major Social Issues: A Multidisciplinary View (1978)

The above three volumes are no longer in print.

AMOS H. HAWLEY
Societal Growth: Processes and Implications (1979)

HUBERT M. BLALOCK
Sociological Theory and Research: A Critical Approach (1980)

The above two volumes are available from The Free Press.

ALICE S. ROSSI
Gender and the Life Course (1985)

The above volume is available from Aldine Publishing Company.

JAMES F. SHORT, Jr.
The Social Fabric: Dimensions and Issues (1986)

MATILDA WHITE RILEY
in association with
BETTINA J. HUBER and BETH B. HESS
**Social Structures and Human Lives:
Social Change and the Life Course, Volume 1** (1988)

MATILDA WHITE RILEY
Sociological Lives: Social Change and the Life Course, Volume 2 (1988)

MELVIN L. KOHN
Cross-National Research in Sociology (1989)

The above four volumes are available from Sage Publications.

Editor
Melvin L. Kohn

CROSS-NATIONAL
RESEARCH IN
SOCIOLOGY

American Sociological Association Presidential Series

SAGE PUBLICATIONS
The Publishers of Professional Social Science
Newbury Park   London   New Delhi

For information address:

SAGE Publications, Inc.
2111 West Hillcrest Drive
Newbury Park, California 91320

SAGE Publications Ltd.
28 Banner Street
London EC1Y 8QE
England

SAGE Publications India Pvt. Ltd.
M-32 Market
Greater Kailash I
New Delhi 110 048 India

*HM 48
. C 76
1989*

Printed in the United States of America

Library of Congress Cataloging-in-Publication Data

Main entry under title:

Cross-national research in sociology / edited by Melvin L. Kohn.
        p.   cm. — (American Sociological Association presidential
    series)
        Selected papers from the 1987 Annual Meeting of the American
    Sociological Association, held in Chicago, Ill.
        Bibliography: p.
        Includes index.
        ISBN 0-8039-3457-2.   ISBN 0-8039-3458-0 (pbk.)
        1. Sociology—Research—Congresses.   2. Social sciences–
    –Comparative method—Congresses.   3. Cross-cultural studies–
    Congresses.   I. Kohn, Melvin L., 1928–   . II. American
    Sociological Association. Meeting (1987 : Chicago, Ill.)
    III. Series.
    HM48.C76 1988
    301'.072—dc19   88–29529
                                                                   CIP

FIRST PRINTING 1989

Contents

To Robin M. Williams, Jr.—
an exemplar of analytic
incisiveness and humane concern

About the Authors

AARON ANTONOVSKY is Kunin-Lunenfeld Professor of Medical Sociology and Chair of the Department of the Sociology of Health in the Faculty of Health Sciences, Ben-Gurion University of the Negev, Beersheba. He was born in Brooklyn and served in the U.S. Army during World War II. His undergraduate degree is from Brooklyn College; his Ph.D. in sociology, from Yale University (1955). In 1960 he and his wife (a Harvard Ph.D. in psychology) migrated to Israel. He conducted research at Louis Guttman's Israel Institute of Applied Social Research in Jerusalem and taught at the Hebrew University-Hadassah Medical School until 1973, when he moved to Beersheba to help found the community-oriented medical school there. His primary field of research for the past quarter century has been in medical sociology. His two major works in this field are *Health, Stress and Coping* (1979), and *Unraveling the Mystery of Health* (1987), in which what he calls "the model of salutogenesis," with its key concept, the sense of coherence, is put forth.

MARGARET S. ARCHER is Professor of Sociology at the University of Warwick. Her previous publications include *Social Conflict and Educational Change in England and France* (with Michalina Vaughan), the edited volumes *Contemporary Europe: Class, Status and Power*, and *Contemporary Europe: Social Structures and Cultural Patterns* (both with Salvador Giner), *Students, University and Society*, and *The Sociology of Educational Expansion*. Her major works to date are the 800-page *Social Origins of Educational Systems* and the recent book *Culture and Agency: The Place of Culture in Social Theory*. She is a past President of the International Sociological Association's Publications Committee, its Research Committee on Sociology of Education, as well as sometime editor of its journal *Current Sociology*. In 1986 she was elected President of the International Sociological Association.

JANET SALTZMAN CHAFETZ is Professor of Sociology at the University of Houston. Her major research interests are gender theory and gender stratification. She is especially interested in the development of eclectic, middle-range theory. Recent publications include *Sex and Advantage* (1984), *Female Revolt* (1986, with A. G. Dworkin), *Feminist Sociology: An Overview of Contemporary Theories* (1988), and "The Gender Division of Labor and the Reproduction of Female Disad-

9

vantage," (*Journal of Family Issues*, March 1988). That paper, along with one forthcoming, "Gender Equality: Toward a Theory of Change" (in Ruth Wallace, editor, *Feminism and Sociological Theory*), form the basis of a book in progress titled *Stability and Change in Gender Systems: An Eclectic Theory* (Sage 1990).

DONMOON CHO is a doctoral candidate in sociology at the University of Wisconsin, Madison. He is currently working on his dissertation, which deals with the question of working-class formation in the Third World countries. His focus is on the relationship between working-class movements and the state in South Korea, Mexico, and Chile, among others.

TOM COLBJØRNSEN is Professor of Organization Sciences at the Norwegian School of Economics and Business Administration in Bergen, Norway. His recent publications include *Dividers in the Labor Market* (Norwegian University Press/Oxford University Press, 1986) and "Organizing Collective Interests: Explaining Cross-National Variation in Working-Class Formation" (in A. L. Kalleberg, editor, *Research in Social Stratification and Mobility*, Vol. 7, 1988). He is currently doing research on incentives in the labor market and on industrial relations and managerial strategies in service industries.

ANTHONY GARY DWORKIN is Professor and Department Head of Sociology at the University of Houston. He is the author of *When Teachers Give Up* (1985), *Female Revolt* (1986, with Janet S. Chafetz), and *Teacher Burnout in the Public Schools* (1987). His areas of research include minority group relations and the sociology of education. Among his most recent publications are "Fear, Victimization, and Stress Among Urban Public School Teachers" (with C. A. Haney and R. Telschow in *Journal of Organizational Behavior*, 1988), "Inter-Ethnic Stereotypes of Acculturating Asiatic Indians in the United States" (with R. J. Dworkin, in *Plural Societies*, 1988), and "Educational Programs: Indirect Linkages and Unfulfilled Expectations" (with M. D. LeCompte in H. Rodgers, Jr., editor, *Beyond Welfare*, 1988). He and Rosalind J. Dworkin are currently working on a third edition of their race and gender relations book, *The Minority Report*, and he and Margaret LeCompte are completing a book on the structural factors that lead teachers to burn out and students to drop out. He serves as editor of a book series titled "The New Inequalities," published by the State University of New York Press. He is also President of the Southwestern Sociological Association.

DAVID L. FEATHERMAN is John Bascom Professor of Sociology at the University of Wisconsin at Madison. His research focuses on the sociology of the life course and the social psychology of adult development. He coedits an annual series, *Life-Span Development and Behavior*.

CAROLYN HOWE teaches sociology at College of the Holy Cross in Worcester, Massachusetts. She received her Ph.D. in sociology in 1987 from the University of Wisconsin—Madison. She is currently on the editorial board of *Critical Sociology* (formerly *The Insurgent Sociologist*) and an active member of the Marxist Section of the American Sociological Association. She has recently published in the *Review of Radical Political Economics*, *Contemporary Sociology*, and *Current Perspectives in Social Theory*. Her current research interests center on the relationship between gender, ethnicity, and working-class capacities, and she continues to do comparative and historical research on class formation.

MELVIN L. KOHN has been Professor of Sociology at the Johns Hopkins University since 1985, following a long career of research on social structure and personality at the National Institute of Mental Health.

He is the author of *Class and Conformity: A Study in Values* (1969) and of *Persönlichkeit, Beruf und soziale Schichtung* (Personality, Occupation, and Social Stratification) (1981); the coauthor, with Carmi Schooler, of *Work and Personality: An Inquiry into the Impact of Social Stratification* (1983) and of *Praca A Osobowosc: Studium Wspolzaleznosci* (Work and Personality: Study of Their Interrelationships) (1986); and the coauthor, with Kazimierz M. Slomczynski, of *Sytuacja Pracy I Jej Psychologiczne Konsekwencje: Polsko-Amerykanskie Analizy Porownawcze* (The Situation of Work and its Psychological Consequences: Comparative Analyses of Poland and the United States) (1988). He and Slomczynski are presently writing another book on their comparative studies of Poland and the United States, to be published in English by Basil Blackwell. He is a past President of the Sociological Research Association, the Eastern Sociological Society, and the American Sociological Association, and is a Fellow of the American Academy of Arts and Sciences. He is currently a member of the Executive Committee of the International Sociological Association and a member of the U.S.-U.S.S.R. Commission on the Humanities and Social Sciences.

KARL ULRICH MAYER has served (since 1983) as Codirector of the Max-Planck Institute of Human Development and Education and head of its Center on Education, Work, and Societal Development, and is Professor of Sociology at the Free University, Berlin. From 1979 to 1983 he directed ZUMA, the German National Survey Center at Mannheim. Mayer edits the *European Sociological Review*. He is coauthor of *Klassenlagen und Sozialstruktur* (with J. Handl and W. Müller, 1977); "Jobs and

Classes: Structural Constraints on Career Mobility" (with G. Carroll, 1987); and is coeditor of *Event History Analysis and Life Course Research* (with N. B. Tuma, 1989). His research interests include social stratification and mobility, occupational careers and labor markets, and sociology of the life course.

ARTUR MEIER is Professor of Sociology and Director of the Institute of Sociology at the Humboldt University of Berlin, German Democratic Republic, where he received his Ph.D.s in history (1964) and in sociology (1970). Having done research work and lecturing in the field of sociology of education for almost two decades, his theoretical interests and empirical research of late have centered on sociological aspects of new technologies. For the period 1986 to 1990, he is serving as Vice President of the International Sociological Association.

JOHN W. MEYER is Professor of Sociology at Stanford University. He works in the areas of the sociology of education, comparative sociology, and formal organizations, and is involved in cross-national research projects in each of these areas. He is coauthor of *National Development and the World System* (Chicago, 1979), *Environments and Organizations* (Jossey-Bass, 1978), *Organizational Environments* (Sage, 1983), and *Institutional Structure* (Sage, 1987).

STEFAN NOWAK is Professor at the Institute of Sociology of Warsaw University and Head of the Chair of Methodology of Sociological Investigations of this institute. He received his Ph.D. in sociology from Warsaw University in 1958. He has been a visiting professor at Columbia University, the Universities of Chicago, Stockholm, Uppsala, Gotteborg, Lund and Helsinki, and the Center for Advanced Studies in the Behavioral Sciences. He has been a member of the Executive Committee of the Polish Sociological Association since its foundation and served two terms as its president (1976-83). He has also served two terms as a member of the Executive Committee of the International Sociological Association (1974-82). He is Honorary Foreign Member of the American Academy of Arts and Sciences and Foreign Member of the British Academy and the Norwegian Academy of Sciences and Letters. Books he has written include *Studies in the Methodology of the Social Sciences* (in Polish, Warsaw, 1965), *Understanding and Prediction: Essays in the Methodology of Social and Behavioral Theories* (Dordrecht, 1977), *Methodology of Sociological Research* (in Polish, Warsaw, 1976). He has edited *Methodological Problems of Sociological Theories* (in Polish, Warsaw, 1971), *Theories of Attitudes* (in Polish, Warsaw, 1973), *Visions of Man and Society in Scientific Theories and Research* (in Polish, Warsaw, 1984),

Polish Society in the State of Crisis—Transformations of Consciousness and the Variants of Behaviors (in Polish, Warsaw, 1984), *Sociology: The State of the Art* (with T. Bottomore and M. Sokolowska, London, 1982), and *Approaches to Social Theory* (with J. Coleman and S. Lindenberg, New York, 1986).

T. K. OOMMEN is Professor of Sociology at the Centre for the Study of Social Systems, Jawaharlal Nehru University, New Delhi (India). His main interests are social movements, political sociology, professions, and social transformation. Currently he is engaged in a comparative study of nation-states and cultural pluralism. His research papers have appeared in *Comparative Studies in Society and History, Journal of Common Wealth Political Studies, Sociological Bulletin, Social Forces, Asian Survey, Contributions to Indian Sociology, Sociologia Ruralis, Economic and Political Weekly, International Sociology* and in several books edited by outstanding scholars. His important books are *Charisma, Stability, and Change* (Thompson, 1972), *Doctors and Nurses* (Macmillan, 1978), *Social Transformation in Rural India* (Vikas, 1984), *Social Structure and Politics* (Hindustan, 1984), and *From Mobilization to Institutionalization* (Popular, 1985). Winner of two prestigious awards, V.K.R.V. Rao Prize in Sociology for 1981 and G. S. Ghurye Award in Sociology and Social Anthropology for 1985, he was University Grants Commission National Lecturer in Sociology for 1985-86. An Associate Editor of *International Sociology*, he was the Secretary-General of the XI World Congress of Sociology held in New Delhi in August 1986. Currently he is a member of the Executive Committee of the International Sociological Association.

CHARLES RAGIN is Professor of Sociology at Northwestern University. His publications include articles in major journals on ethnic national resurgence (e.g., "Ethnic Political Mobilization: The Welsh Case" in *American Sociological Review*), international inequality (e.g., "Structural Blockage: A Cross-National Study of Economic Dependence, State Efficacy, and Underdevelopment" in *American Journal of Sociology*), and comparative methodology (e.g., "Theory and Method in Comparative Research: Two Strategies" in *Social Forces*). His recent book on strategies of comparative research (*The Comparative Method: Moving Beyond Qualitative and Quantitative Strategies*, University of California Press, 1987) explores techniques of holistic, qualitative comparison and formalizes basic features of comparative and historical research. Current research includes work on mass-based political responses to austerity programs in Third World debtor countries and further work on comparative methodology, especially the problem of linking causal complexity and outcome complexity.

BRYAN R. ROBERTS is Professor of Sociology and C. B. Smith, Sr., Chair in U.S.-Mexico Relations at the University of Texas at Austin. He spent 22 years in the Department of Sociology of the University of Manchester, specializing in comparative social structure, development, and urbanization, carrying out field research in Guatemala, Peru, Mexico, and Spain. His publications include *Organizing Strangers* and *Cities of Peasants*.

ANDRZEJ RYCHARD is Assistant Professor in the Laboratory of the Sociology of Organization in the Institute of Philosophy and Sociology of the Polish Academy of Sciences. Born in Gdansk in 1951, he graduated from Warsaw University in 1974, received his doctorate in sociology in 1978, and his doctor habilitatus in 1987. His research interests concern the relations between the state and the economic system and the influence these relations exert on social structure. He has conducted research on sociopolitical conflict in Poland, sociology of economic reforms, and sociology of medical institutions. His recent books are *Power and Interests in the Polish Economic System* (in Polish, Warsaw University, 1987) and *Poles 84: Dynamics of Conflict and Consensus* (coauthor and coeditor, in Polish, Warsaw University, 1986). Some of his representative English-language publications are *The Social and Political Preconditions for and Consequences of Economic Reform in Poland* (The Vienna Institute for Comparative Economic Studies, Working Paper no. 143, Vienna, 1988), "Legitimation and the Stability of the Social Order," in *Crisis and Transition: Poland of the 80s* (J. Koralewicz, I. Bialecki, and M. Watson, editors, London, Berg, 1987), and "Politics, the Economy and Society: How They Interrelate," in *The Polish Dilemma: Views from Within* (L. S. Graham and M. K. Ciechocinska, editors, Boulder and London, Westview Press, 1987).

KAZIMIERZ M. SLOMCZYNSKI teaches at the Institute of Sociology, University of Warsaw, Poland. He has written extensively on class structure and social mobility and on the methodology of sociological research. His books include: *Socio-Occupational Differentiation and Its Correlates* (1972, in Polish), *Investigations on Class Structure and Social Mobility in Poland, 1945-1975* (with W. Wesolowski, 1977), *Occupational Scales* (with G. Kacprowicz, 1979, in Polish), *Occupational Status and Its Relation to Education* (1983, in Polish), *Work Conditions and Psychological Functioning: Comparative Analyses of Poland and the United States* (with M. L. Kohn, 1988, in Polish). Among volumes he edited are two anthologies of Polish sociological research: *Class Structure and Social Mobility in Poland* (with T. K. Krauze, 1978) and *Social Stratification in Poland: Eight Empirical Studies* (with T. K. Krauze, 1986). Currently he is the principal investigator of a large-scale project on social structure and mobility in Poland sponsored by the Polish Academy of Sciences.

MAGDALENA SOKOLOWSKA has been at the Institute of Philosophy and Sociology, Polish Academy of Sciences, for 25 years. She is Professor and Head, Department of Sociology of Health and Medicine. A pioneer in medical sociology in eastern Europe, she earned her physician's certificate (M.D.) and the degree Med.Sc.D. at Medical School in Gdansk (1949 and 1951), Master of Public Health at Columbia University in New York (1960), docent degree in sociology at the Polish Academy of Sciences in Warsaw (1965), and full professorship in sociology (1987). From 1978 to 1982 she served as Vice President, International Sociological Association. She is a member of Regional Health Development Council, World Health Organization, Regional Office for Europe. From 1982 to 1987 she was President of the European Society of Medical Sociology established in 1982. She is dr.h.c. of the University in Helsinki (Finland, 1986) and dr.h.c. of the University of Siegen (F.R.G., 1987). She has published articles and books in Poland and abroad devoted to the discipline of sociology of medicine, the social aspects of illness and disability, and the position of women in society. She is author of the critical reports on health and health care of the Polish population. Her recent interests include empirical research on the role of family in caring for its sick member and analyses of nonformal mechanisms aimed at meeting the social and health needs of Polish society.

KEN'ICHI TOMINAGA is Professor of Sociology at the University of Tokyo, from which he also received his Ph.D. in 1966. He has been a visiting scholar at the University of Illinois, Harvard University, Australian National University, Ruhr-Universität Bochum, and the U.S. National Institute of Mental Health. His published books in Japanese include *A Theory of Social Change* (1965), *Dynamics of Industrial Society* (1973), *Economic Sociology* (editor, 1974), *Social Stratification in Japan* (editor, 1979), *Modern Social Scientists* (1984), *Principles of Sociology* (1986), *Social Structure and Social Change* (1987), and *A Turning Point of the Japanese Industrial Society* (1988). His current research interests include social change, modernization theory, social stratification, organization theory, economic sociology, and the history of sociological thought.

DONALD J. TREIMAN is Professor of Sociology at the University of California at Los Angeles. He is the author of *Occupational Prestige in Comparative Perspective* (1977) and the coeditor (with Ann R. Miller, Pamela S. Cain, and Patricia Roos) of *Work, Jobs, and Occupations: A*

Critical Review of the Dictionary of Occupational Titles (1980). His principal fields of interest are comparative stratification and mobility, and research methods.

WLODZIMIERZ WESOLOWSKI is Professor of Sociology at the Institute of Philosophy and Sociology, the Polish Academy of Sciences, Warsaw. He is the author or editor of a number of works on social stratification, including *Classes, Strata and Power* (1979) and *Social Mobility and Social Structure* (with Bogdan Mach, 1982); on social development in comparative perspective, including *Social Structure and Change: Poland and Finland. Comparative Perspective* (edited with Erik Allardt, 1978) and *Marksizm a procesy rozwoju spolecznego* (Marxism and Processes of Social Development) (editor, 1979); and on sociological theory, including his recent essays on Max Weber ("Weber's Concept of Legitimacy: Limitations and Extensions," forthcoming in *Sisyphus— Sociological Studies*). He has been Visiting Professor at the University of East Anglia, the University of Stockholm, Cornell University, and the University of Konstanz, and has been a Foreign Scholar at the (U.S.) National Institute of Mental Health. His works have been translated into English, German, Italian, Japanese, and other languages. He is a Foreign Honorary Member of the American Academy of Arts and Sciences.

ERIK OLIN WRIGHT is Professor of Sociology at the University of Wisconsin, Madison, and Director of the A. E. Havens Center for the Study of Social Structure and Social Change. For the past decade he has been coordinating a cross-national project on class structure and class consciousness that currently involves replicated social surveys in eleven countries, with four additional countries planning surveys in the future. His most recent book is *Classes* (London, Verso, 1985).

KAM-BOR YIP is a graduate student in the Department of Sociology of the University of California at Los Angeles.

Introduction

One of the few real prerogatives of being President of the American Sociological Association is the opportunity to choose the theme of the annual convention that concludes one's presidency. This theme governs only part of the academic program of an annual ASA convention; most of the topics discussed are much the same from one convention to the next, and properly so. The theme, nonetheless, is what makes any particular convention unique. The "thematic sessions" organized around the president's chosen theme focus sociological attention, at least for the duration of that one convention, on some one issue or substantive or methodological problem that the particular president deems to be especially important. I chose "cross-national research in sociology."

For me, this was a highly valued opportunity. I am—I might as well admit it from the start—a bit of a missionary on the subject of cross-national research; I think that there is much to be gained from investigating whether what we learn from research in any one country holds true in other countries as well. I am also a bit of missionary about the desirability of our creating a truly international sociology. As I wrote in my initial announcement of the theme for the 1987 ASA Convention, in words addressed to U.S. sociologists but with a message that I believe is applicable to sociologists everywhere:

In the years immediately following World War II, the United States enjoyed a dominant position in world sociology: Sociology had been largely destroyed on the continent of Europe by the Nazis and had not yet developed to any marked degree in many parts of the world. In the following years, partly as a result of the European nations' re-importing their own sociologies back from the United States, partly as a result of sociologists everywhere learning from our sociology, partly as a result of indigenous developments, sociology developed rapidly, not only in the countries where it had been well-established before the War, but in many other countries as well. Today, U.S. sociology no longer holds a hegemonic position, but instead is part of a flourishing world sociology. I believe that this is a development to be applauded and encouraged. U.S. sociology and U.S. sociologists have much to learn from the sociologies and sociologists of other countries.

Even more important, we have much to learn from explicitly comparative cross-national research. The time has long passed, if it ever existed, when it is sensible to generalize from findings based on studies done entirely within the United States, without asking whether our findings are descriptive only of the U.S. or would apply as well to other developed countries, to other Western countries, to other capitalist countries, to other countries in general.

U.S. sociologists are coming to understand and appreciate the importance of cross-national research and the value of keeping abreast of sociological research done by our colleagues in other countries. Yet, in my opinion, we are still a bit parochial. The time is ripe to impress on U.S. sociology—not just on the area specialists and those already engaged in cross-national research, but upon U.S. sociology in general—the value of cross-national research and of seeing our country in comparative perspective.

I hoped that by choosing cross-national research as the Convention theme and by inviting scholars from many countries to participate, I could advance both causes. I believe that I succeeded.

This book is an effort to continue those missionary endeavors, on a smaller scale but with perhaps more enduring effect. From the nearly 100 pertinent papers presented at the convention, I have selected a much smaller set that I believe best illustrate the uses, the problems, and the possibilities of cross-national research. As editor of the volume, I have had the unusual luxury of being able to (and also the painful necessity of having to) choose from a far larger number of first-rate papers than could possibly fit into one volume.

CRITERIA OF SELECTION

It may help the reader's understanding of the book to know what criteria I employed.

First, of course, was the criterion of quality, the same criterion that I employ in evaluating manuscripts for sociological journals. As editor of a book, I could be a bit more subjective in my judgments of what was not only competent but also exciting, for this was after all to be *my* book; but in any case my foremost criterion was that I thought the paper to be of first-rate quality. (I must admit, though, that never before have I had to make judgments that so stretched the limits of my expertise.)

Second, to serve my purpose of advancing explicitly comparative research, I selected only those papers that either actually do comparative research, using systematically comparable data from two or more countries, or that discuss issues directly pertinent to the conduct of such research. I decided not to include some very appealing papers that I deemed only implicitly comparative, including several that used analyses of some country other than the United States (most often, Japan) to demonstrate that conclusions drawn from studies done only of the United

States would lead to erroneous conclusions. Such studies are often very valuable, but I regard them as the first step in comparative inquiry; and I had at hand sufficient papers that took what I regard as the pivotal second step of actually using comparable data from two or more countries.

Third, with some ambivalence, I decided not to include papers addressed only to showing that two nations (most often, once again, the United States and Japan) are different in some respect or other, with no explanation of the difference save the residual explanation that they have different histories or cultures. I wanted more by way of social-structural analysis. We are, I think, well beyond needing to demonstrate that nations and cultures differ; it is time to explain these differences.

Having decided on these criteria, I deliberately did not invoke a number of other criteria that I might have used.

I did not give preference to authors from the United States or from anywhere else. It happens that more than half of the authors are from countries other than the United States, the roster including scholars from the Federal Republic of Germany, the German Democratic Republic, Great Britain, India, Israel, Japan, Norway, and Poland. To my disappointment, we do not have any contributions from Latin America, from Africa, from any of the Third World except India; but this failure was not for lack of trying.

I did not give preference to comparisons of particular nations. Inevitably and appropriately, many of the comparisons involve the United States; but some do not or do so only incidentally, as in comparisons of capitalist and socialist countries.

I certainly did not give preference to any particular methodology, for I strongly believe that there are no superior or inferior types of methodology, only methodologies more or less appropriate to the analytic task, more or less competently and imaginatively employed. Nor did I give preference to the reporting of primary or of secondary analyses, both of which can be useful; and we have some diversity here.

I did give some preference to broad discussion of the theoretical and methodological issues in cross-national research. I did not, however, give preference to research in any particular subject matter, knowing full well that this would mean a disproportionate number of studies of social stratification, social class, and kindred subjects; but if that is where a disproportionate amount of the best cross-national research is being done these days, so be it. I was pleased, nonetheless, to find splendid examples of cross-national research on such other topics as education, health, women's movements, the labor force, political legitimization of the state, industrialization, and even conceptions of Christendom.

TYPES OF CROSS-NATIONAL RESEARCH

A book about "cross-national research" had better be explicit about what is meant by the term. It is useful as well to delineate the principal types of cross-national research—as I see them.

The broadest possible definition of "cross-national research" is any research that transcends national boundaries. This definition is somewhat ambiguous, though, because many studies of single societies are implicitly cross-national, in that the investigators interpret their findings by contrasting what they learn about the country they actually study with what is known or is believed to be true about some other country or countries. I prefer to restrict the term "cross-national" to studies that are *explicitly* comparative, that is, to studies that utilize systematically comparable data from two or more nations.

In restricting the term to explicitly comparative studies, I do not mean to belittle the importance of studies that are only implicitly comparative. Such studies contribute importantly to our understanding; witness, for example, the distinguished series of studies of American society by foreign observers, beginning with Alexis de Tocqueville's *Democracy in America*. Consider, too, studies in which the selection of some one country is particularly appropriate for testing a general proposition—as in Kelley and Klein's (1981) use of the Bolivian revolution of 1952 to test their theory that "radical revolutions" inevitably lead to an increase in inequality, or Chirot and Ragin's (1975) use of the Romanian peasant rebellion of 1907 to test competing interpretations of the intensity of peasant rebellions. And consider, finally, those pivotal studies—Stephen Bunker's (1985) *Underdeveloping the Amazon* is a particularly good example—where some country or region of a country is selected for study precisely because it exemplifies a more general social phenomenon. I leave such research out of my purview not because it is unimportant, but because to include it would make the bounds of "cross-national" so large and so ambiguous that it would be difficult to say what, other than research focused single-mindedly on a particular country, is not cross-national.

Within the large genre of research that is explicitly comparative, I would further distinguish four types of cross-national research of somewhat differing intent. The four types are those in which nation is *object* of study, those in which nation is *context* of study, those in which nation is *unit of analysis*, and those that are *transnational* in character.[1] Although these four types of research shade into one another, their purposes are distinguishable and their theoretical implications somewhat different.

In the first type of cross-national research, where nations are the *object* of study, the investigator's interest is primarily in the particular countries studied: how Germany compares to the United States, France to the Soviet Union, or India to Pakistan. Alternatively, the investigator may be interested in comparing particular institutions in these countries: the social security systems of the   United States and Australia, the educational systems of the German Democratic Republic and the Federal Republic of Germany. At their best, as in the systematic comparisons of Finland and Poland by Erik Allardt, Wlodzimierz Wesolowski, and their collaborators (1978), such studies can lead to well-informed interpretations that apply far beyond the particular countries studied. What distinguishes such research, though, is its primary interest in understanding the particular countries. In this research, one wants to know about Finland and Poland for their own sakes; the investigator does not select them for study just because they happen to be useful settings for pursuing some general hypothesis.

By contrast, this book will focus on cross-national studies in which, to borrow from Erwin Scheuch's (1967) apt phrase, nation is *context*. In such research, one is primarily interested in testing the generality of findings and interpretations about how certain social institutions operate or about how certain aspects of social structure impinge on personality. In Burawoy and Lukacs's (1987) comparison of a U.S. machine shop with a Hungarian machine shop, for example, their primary interest is not in the United States and Hungary for their own sakes, nor certainly in the particular machine shops, but in these machine shops as exemplifying the relative efficiency of capitalist and socialist industrial enterprises.

Admittedly, it may be difficult to differentiate research in which nation is object from research in which nation is context. When Robin Williams (1985) studies the use of threats in US/USSR relations, he clearly is interested in the United States and the Soviet Union both for their own sakes and as exemplifying superpowers in a nuclear age; there is no way of separating the two purposes. It is nevertheless generally useful to

[1.] I make no claim that this classification is theoretically superior to other classifications of cross-national research, only that it serves my analytic purposes better than others do. By comparison to Tilly's (1984) well-known classification, my "nation as object" category corresponds roughly to his "individualizing comparisons"; my "nation as context" category encompasses both his "universalizing" and his "variation-finding comparisons"—what he sees as two distinct *strategies* of research I see as attempts to interpret two distinct types of *findings;* my "nation as unit of analysis" category is ignored in his classification; and my "transnational" category may be a little broader than his "encompassing comparisons," which are limited to studies that see nations as components of encompassing international systems. (For other useful classifications of cross-national research, see Hopkins and Wallerstein 1967; Marsh 1967; Elder 1976; Nowak 1977; see also Hill 1962.)

distinguish between research whose primary purpose is to tell us more about the particular countries studied and research whose primary purpose is to use these countries as the vehicles for investigating the contexts in which social institutions operate.

The latter domain includes such diverse studies as Theda Skocpol's (1979) comparative analysis of revolution; and also, from quite a different theoretical perspective, Michael Burton and John Higley's (1987) analysis of the conditions under which competing elites settle their differences in grand political compromises; Donald Treiman's (1977) analysis of the stratification systems of the industrialized world; William Form's (1976) study of the complexity of industrial technology, workers' skill levels, and the quality of workers' social interactions; Janet Chafetz and Anthony Dworkin's (1986) analysis of the determinants of the size and range of ideologies of women's movements throughout the world; and my colleagues' and my comparative research on social stratification and psychological functioning in Poland, Japan, and the United States (Slomczynski, Miller, and Kohn 1981; Naoi and Schooler 1985).

It is also useful to differentiate research where nation is context from two other types of cross-national research. In the first, where nation is the *unit* of analysis, investigators seek to establish relationships among characteristics of nations qua nations. In such research, one no longer speaks of countries by name, but instead classifies countries along one or more dimensions—their gross national product, or average level of educational attainment, or position along some scale of income inequality. A prototypic example is Bornschier and Chase-Dunn's (1985) analysis of the relationship between the penetration of national economies by transnational corporations and the hypothesized long-run stagnation of those economies. Other pertinent examples are Blumberg and Winch's (1972) analysis of the relationship between societal complexity and familial complexity; and Ellis, Lee, and Petersen's (1978) test of the hypothesis that there is a positive relationship between how closely adults are supervised in a society and the degree to which parents in that society value obedience for children.

What distinguishes research that treats nation as the unit of analysis is its primary concern with understanding how social institutions and processes are systematically related to variations in national characteristics. Such analyses need not treat each nation as a homogeneous entity, but may study intranation institutions and processes, as Meyer, Hannan, and their colleagues (1979) have done in their analyses of national development. Nor need research that treats nation as unit of analysis assume that each nation exists in an international vacuum. As Bornschier and Chase-Dunn (1985, p. 65) put it,

We do not contend that nation-states are closed systems. A unit of analysis does not need to be a closed system. When we compare individuals or schools we know that these units interact with one another and are parts of a larger social context. The unit of analysis in comparative research is any unit in which the process of interest is known to operate.

In distinguishing research that treats nation as the unit of analysis from research that treats nation as the context for analysis, we are again dealing with gradations, not sharp differences. As will become evident later in this book, attempts to understand cross-national differences sooner or later require one to search for the pertinent dimensions that differentiate the nations qua nations. One can, in fact, argue that research in which nation is treated as context is simply a way station to more general analyses in which the pivotal distinguishing characteristics of nations become variables in the analysis. In principle, as Rokkan (1964), Przeworski and Teune (1970), Hopkins and Wallerstein (1967), and Chase-Dunn et al. (1982) all argue, one can and should convert descriptive differences between countries into analytic variables. I have no quarrel with this objective, only a belief that in many fields of sociological inquiry there is much to learn from research in which nation is treated as context before we are ready to translate "nations" into "variables."

Research that treats nations as the unit of analysis requires that one be able to discern which of the many differences between countries are the pertinent analytic variables; that one be able to formulate meaningful hypotheses at the appropriate level of abstraction; and—if one is ever to test such interpretations—that one have at hand or have the potential to collect data from a sizable sample of countries. It also requires much better data than are generally available in multination data sources. I hope that a book about cross-national research written ten or twenty years from now will be able to focus much more on such research than I believe is warranted today.

And then, finally, there are studies that treat nations as components of larger international systems. Borrowing a term from economists and political scientists who have studied corporations (and I hope not distorting their usage of the term), I call this "transnational" research. Immanuel Wallerstein's (1974, 1980) analysis of the capitalist world-system and Fernando Cardoso and Enzo Faletto's (1979) analysis of dependency and development in Latin America are prominent examples. We are at a rather early stage in the development of appropriate methodologies for transnational research (Meyer and Hannan 1979; Chase-Dunn 1979; Chase-Dunn, Pallas, and Kentor 1982). Even now, though, transnational research has proved its importance by demonstrating that the nations we compare in all types of cross-national research are not isolated entities but are systematically interrelated.

In selecting the papers for this book, I was delighted to be able to include several fine studies in which nation is treated as "context," that is, where the object of the analysis is to ascertain whether similar or dissimilar processes occur in diverse nations. I would have liked to include more studies of other types as well, studies in which characteristics of nations are systematically related to processes that occur within nations; and studies in which *intra* national processes are seen in context of each nation's position in larger *inter* national structures. Such studies are being done, but not in any great number and they are not necessarily ready for publication at just the time that an editor would like to have them. I am pleased, though, at being able to include a few particularly fine examples of such research.

ORGANIZATION OF THE BOOK

Although the organization of an edited volume is generally of greater interest to the editor than to any reader, making the basis of that organization explicit may help orient the reader to what the editor had in mind.

My rationale for the first part of the book is the most self-evident: this is a set of papers dealing with general theoretical and methodological issues in cross-national research. I am pleased that the first two papers are by authors from whom I have learned much in my efforts to broaden my own knowledge about cross-national research. I do not agree with everything that Stefan Nowak and Charles Ragin say in these essays; but I greatly respect their thoughtful presentations—in this volume as in their past writings—of positions based on long experience and profound understanding of the research literature.

Their perspectives, as you soon will see, are quite different, albeit complementary rather than in conflict. Nowak is concerned with the fundamental issue of the utility of cross-national research (and of research generally) for generating and testing social theory. He comes to some rather startling conclusions, including the paradoxical conclusion that cross-national research is especially useful where theory is poorly formulated—as is generally true in the social sciences. Ragin is concerned about the gap between intensive studies of a very few societies and extensive studies of many societies—and the disturbing implications of this gap for sociological theory. He provides a penetrating analysis of the reasons for this gap and offers thoughtful suggestions for bridging it.

My own chapter, rather less ambitious than Nowak's or Ragin's, addresses the question of the utility of cross-national research for social theory from still another perspective. I have for some years been deeply involved in one specialized program of cross-national research. I use this opportunity to review that research, mainly to ask what lessons there may be in these studies that might be germane to cross-national research more generally.

The second part of the book is devoted to two chapters in which I take particular delight, in part because I find the very existence of these papers so surprising. The authors, Wlodzimierz Wesolowski and Ken'ichi Tominaga, are the sponsors of the Polish and Japanese studies on which my own cross-national research on the psychological concomitants of social stratification is based. Yet, their chapters have nothing to do with this research, nor even with their own considerable research on the sociology of social stratification. Instead, in recent years both men have focused their scholarly attention on theoretical work in the tradition of Max Weber. It struck my fancy that two of the hardest-nosed quantitative analysts in the world, Wesolowski and Tominaga, went back to Weber for inspiration. Perhaps because of their expertise as empirical investigators, their approach to Weber goes considerably beyond exegesis and amplification: they *use* Weber, in highly imaginative ways, as an aid in dealing with concrete problems. They have thereby demonstrated, as no amount of preaching could have done, the continued vitality of the work of the father of cross-national research in sociology.

Most of the remaining chapters—more than half of the book—use nation as the "context" for inquiry. These analyses investigate whether social processes that occur in one nation or one type of nation are similar to or different from social processes that occur in other nations or other types of nations. There are many ways one could divide these papers into parts of a book: by subject matter, by methods employed, by countries compared; it really doesn't much matter.

Because I want to emphasize the relevance, even the essentiality, of cross-national inquiry for *all* fields of sociology, I preferred not to group the chapters by subject matter: For my purposes, the subject matter of each individual chapter is almost incidental to its main purpose for being in the book, namely, that it illustrates the value of cross-national inquiry in dealing with some sociologically important issue, whatever the particular issue may be. And I did not want to organize the parts according to whether the analyses were primarily quantitative or primarily qualitative, for I strongly believe that this is not a distinction to be emphasized; in the best sociological research, one uses whatever method or methods are most appropriate to the theoretical task at hand. Nor, certainly, did I want to organize parts by the criterion of which particular countries are compared, for that would result in a banal duality: studies in which the United States is one of the countries involved, in contrast to all other cross-national comparisons.

I decided, instead, to group these chapters into three parts, an admittedly arbitrary grouping but one that serves my heuristic purposes: one set of chapters that do intensive primary analyses of data collected by the investigators themselves, another set that do intensive secondary analyses of existing data or of previous primary analyses; and a third set that differ from the others primarily in being extensive analyses of much larger numbers of countries. I regard this as an ad hoc classification, of no intrinsic merit. I make this division simply to illustrate the theoretical utility of *both* primary and secondary cross-national studies and of *both* intensive and extensive modes of inquiry.

The part on intensive primary analyses begins with Kazimierz Slomczynski's analysis of the psychological effects of status inconsistency in the United States, Japan, and Poland. Slomczynski resurrects Gerhard Lenski's well-known and oft-tested hypothesis—a hypothesis that has always seemed to me to be theoretically appealing but that rarely seemed to be confirmed by the data. By using new and more powerful methods of analysis, Slomczynski shows that the theoretical appeal of Lenski's hypothesis was justified: Although the psychological effects of status inconsistency are not large, they are consistent for all three countries—suggesting that the hypothesis is valid for both capitalist and socialist societies, as well as for Western and non-Western societies.

Then Artur Meier asks whether educational systems, in particular the systems of vocational training, are essentially the same in all socialist societies, based as these societies are on the same formal blueprint. By comparing the vocational training systems, and the transitions from school to work, of the German Democratic Republic and the Soviet Union, he demonstrates that historical and cultural differences have a decisive importance for how social institutions function, in socialist as in capitalist societies. It is a useful lesson, one that is too often overlooked even by analysts who well understand the importance of history and culture in comparing advanced capitalist countries, but who nevertheless treat socialist societies as if they were all of a piece.

The third chapter in this part, by Erik Olin Wright, Carolyn Howe, and Donmoon Cho, compares the class structures of two advanced capitalist societies, the United States and Sweden. Focusing on two of the most advanced capitalist societies gives them theoretical leverage for being able to delineate not only the essential similarities in the class structures of advanced capitalist societies but also some pivotal differences in the class structures, and in the consequences for class identification, in these two economically similar yet politically quite distinct nations.

In the final chapter of this part, Karl Ulrich Mayer, David Featherman, Kevin Selbee, and Tom Colbjørnsen nicely illustrate the utility of combining historical and statistical analyses. By comparing German to Norwegian history, they are able to formulate hypotheses as to the ways in which mobility processes should be similar and the ways in which they should be different in the Federal Republic of Germany and Norway today. They then test these hypotheses rigorously with statistical analyses of data from carefully selected cohorts in the two countries.

The part of the book devoted to intensive secondary analyses begins with Margaret Archer's trenchant critique of educational sociology, analyzing in detail its failure to deal with educational systems qua systems. Because educational sociologists have neglected the serious study of educational systems—research that must of necessity be cross-national—each investigator has unwittingly assumed that the educational system of his or her own country is typical of educational systems generally. Archer demonstrates that this is certainly not the case; she then examines the consequences of neglecting cross-national differences in educational systems by critically assessing analyses of education by noted French and British scholars, each of whom treats the educational system of his own country as if it were prototypic of educational systems throughout the world. As an antidote, she provides a comprehensive analytic scheme for the cross-national analysis of educational systems.

Magdalena Sokolowska and Andrzej Rychard follow with observations about the "alternative" system of health care in socialist Poland, extending their analysis to consider the conditions that give rise to "alternativeness" in other institutions as well. Although Poland provides a particularly good setting for such an analysis, they recognize that their understanding will gain insight and richness by persistently asking which of these conditions are unique to the economic and political situation of Poland, which are shared with other socialist societies, and which are more generally true of industrialized societies. They thereby provide a model for examining their own society that U.S. sociologists might well emulate.

T. K. Oommen then provides a fascinating analysis of ethnicity that is at once cross-national, cross-cultural, and historical. He contrasts the "young" United States (Oommen generously ascribes to the United States a 500-year history and still considers this country to be "young") with the ancient society of India. The phenomena that he discusses—ethnicity, nationality, cultural pluralism, and kindred phenomena—are quite familiar to both U.S. and Indian sociologists, as well as to sociologists in many other countries. These familiar phenomena take on quite a new light, however, when systematically compared from a perspective that only considerable distance in both history and culture can afford, a perspective enriched by Oommen's consistent mastery and clear explication of the essential sociological concepts.

I have set aside a separate part of the book for two chapters that differ from many of the preceding chapters mainly in that they are based on a particular strategy of data collection and analysis—the use of information from all countries for which such information is available. The two analyses, which I regard as among the best of their genre, represent two quite different stages in what I see as basically the same research process.

Aaron Antonovsky, intrigued and perplexed by a doctors' strike in Israel, wondered what he could learn from similar phenomena in other countries. To this end, he searched for accounts of even remotely similar occurrences in any country. The data are incomplete, sparse, and unreliable; Antonovsky is properly tentative about his conclusions and his interpretations. Yet, from these data he has fashioned an ingenious interpretation, which provides the basis for a highly plausible set of hypotheses, worthy of being pursued in further cross-national inquiry.

Janet Chafetz and Gary Dworkin also rely on whatever information is available from whichever countries such data can be secured. In contrast with Antonovsky's preliminary efforts, though, Chafetz and Dworkin present us with the end result of several years of research. They have collected and assessed a considerable body of information about women's movements and countermovements throughout the world. Here they summarize and reassess their evidence, bringing it together into one consistent interpretation of both feminist movements and countermovements.

These two analyses, one highly preliminary and one a final report on a major research program, each illustrate the great utility of thinking about sociological problems in worldwide perspective.

I have reserved the sixth and final part of the book for three chapters that go beyond treating nations as *contexts* for the analysis of *intra* national processes, to deal with countries (in one way or another) as themselves having characteristics that can be classified and even quantified.

Bryan Roberts compares labor markets in Britain, Spain, and Mexico— an endeavor not essentially different in methodology from that of several of the preceding chapters, *except* that Roberts uses these three nations as exemplars of three positions in the world economy: core, semiperiphery, and periphery. His analysis demonstrates the utility of seeing nations not just as individual entities but as interrelated in the larger international system. His analysis thereby provides a bridge from studying nation as context to systematically considering the influences of the larger international structure on what we have generally thought of as purely intranational processes.

Donald Treiman and Kam-Bor Yip in a low-key style do something quite dramatic: They advance from treating nations as named entities to instead *classifying* nations along sociologically meaningful dimensions, and then systematically relating those national characteristics to intranational processes, in this case, mobility processes. The models are simple, perhaps requiring further amplification in subsequent analysis. Yet, the very simplicity of the models well illustrates their interpretive power. I see this analysis as a prototype of what cross-national research will more and more attempt to do in the years to come.

In the final chapter of the part and the book, the always intellectually audacious John Meyer sees the West not only as an international system but as one of many international systems that have existed in human history. Never afraid to ask the large questions, he wonders about the distinctiveness of this particular world-system; and, as usual, he provides thoughtful and provocative answers.

I hope I have whetted your appetite to read on. Remember, though, that what we offer here is more akin to a wine tasting than to a full-course dinner. These chapters do not exhaust what one could say about cross-national comparative analyses in any of the subjects dealt with, nor do they exhaust the range of sociological topics for which cross-national analysis can be and is being fruitfully applied, nor, for all their diversity, do they utilize all the pertinent methods that can be and have been employed in cross-national inquiry. What I mean to illustrate in this selection of chapters is that cross-national inquiry adds to our understanding of social process, all social process, everywhere.

ACKNOWLEDGMENTS

I would like to give my most heartfelt thanks to the members of the 1987 ASA Program Committee, who (among their other tasks) planned the thematic sessions and selected the speakers. The members of the committee were Joan R. Acker, Michael T. Aiken, Theodore Caplow, David R. Heise, Cora B. Marrett, Albert J. McQueen, Alejandro Portes, Theda R. Skocpol, Ruth A. Wallace, Everett K. Wilson, and Mayer N. Zald.

Our ability to invite scholars from other nations to participate in the thematic sessions of the 1987 ASA Convention was greatly facilitated by grants in support of the travel expenses of those scholars (mainly from Eastern Europe and the Third World) who could not raise such funds locally. Our principal benefactor was the National Science Foundation. We received welcome support too from the North East Asia Council (in support of Japanese scholars), the International Research and Exchanges Board (in support of scholars from Eastern Europe), the Smithsonian

Institution (in support of a scholar from India), and the Ford Foundation (in support of a scholar from Brazil).

I want also to thank Reva Rolnick and Pam Skalski for their competent and uncomplaining assistance in typing and retyping several of the papers by foreign scholars that required extensive stylistic editing.

Finally, I want to express my appreciation to the John Simon Guggenheim Memorial Foundation, which provided me a Fellowship that greatly facilitated my ability to edit this volume.

—Melvin L. Kohn

REFERENCES

Allardt, Erik and Wlodzimierz Wesolowski, eds. 1978. *Social Structure and Change: Finland and Poland—Comparative Perspective.* Warsaw: Polish Scientific Publishers.

Blumberg, Rae Lesser and Robert F. Winch. 1972. "Societal Complexity and Familial Complexity: Evidence for the Curvilinear Hypothesis." *American Journal of Sociology* 77:898-920.

Bornschier, Volker and Christopher Chase-Dunn. 1985. *Transnational Corporations and Underdevelopment.* New York: Praeger.

Bunker, Stephen G. 1985. *Underdeveloping the Amazon: Extraction, Unequal Exchange, and the Failure of the Modern State.* Urbana: University of Illinois Press.

Burawoy, Michael and Janos Lukacs. 1987. "Mythologies of Work: A Comparison of Firms in State Socialism and Advanced Capitalism." *American Sociological Review* 50:723-37.

Burton, Michael G. and John Higley. 1987. "Elite Settlements." *American Sociological Review* 52:295-307.

Cardoso, Fernando Henrique and Enzo Faletto. 1979. *Dependency and Development in Latin America.* Berkeley: University of California Press.

Chafetz, Janet Saltzman and Anthony Gary Dworkin. 1986. *Female Revolt: Women's Movements in World and Historical Perspective.* Totowa, NJ: Rowman & Allanheld.

Chase-Dunn, Christopher K. 1979. "Comparative Research on World-System Characteristics." *International Studies Quarterly* 23:601-23.

Chase-Dunn, Christopher K., Aaron M. Pallas, and Jeffrey Kentor. 1982. "Old and New Research Designs for Studying the World System: A Research Note." *Comparative Political Studies* 15:341-56.

Chirot, Daniel and Charles Ragin. 1975. "The Market, Tradition and Peasant Rebellion: The Case of Romania in 1907." *American Sociological Review* 40:428-44.

Elder, Joseph W. 1976. "Comparative Cross-National Methodology." Pp. 209-230 in *Annual Review of Sociology.* Vol. 2, edited by Alex Inkeles. Palo Alto, CA: Annual Reviews.

Ellis, Godfrey J., Gary R. Lee, and Larry R. Petersen. 1978. "Supervision and Conformity: A Cross-Cultural Analysis of Parental Socialization Values." *American Journal of Sociology* 84:386-403.

Form, William H. 1976. *Blue Collar Stratification: Autoworkers in Four Countries.* Princeton, NJ: Princeton University Press.

Hill, Reuben. 1962. "Cross-National Family Research: Attempts and Prospects." *International Social Science Journal* 14:425-51.

Hopkins, Terence K. and Immanuel Wallerstein. 1967. "The Comparative Study of National Societies." *Social Science Information* 6:25-58.

Kelley, Jonathan and Herbert S. Klein. 1981. *Revolution and the Rebirth of Inequality: A Theory Applied to the National Revolution in Bolivia.* Berkeley: University of California Press.

Marsh, Robert M. 1967. *Comparative Sociology: A Codification of Cross-Societal Analysis.* New York: Harcourt, Brace & World.

Meyer, John W. and Michael T. Hannan, eds. 1979. *National Development and the World System: Educational, Economic, and Political Change, 1950-1970.* Chicago: University of Chicago Press.

Naoi, Atsushi and Carmi Schooler. 1985. "Occupational Conditions and Psychological Functioning in Japan." *American Journal of Sociology* 90:729-52.

Nowak, Stefan. 1977. "The Strategy of Cross-National Survey Research for the Development of Social Theory." Pp. 3-47 in *Cross-National Comparative Survey Research: Theory and Practice,* edited by Alexander Szalai and Riccardo Petrella. Oxford: Pergamon.

Przeworski, Adam and Henry Teune. 1970. *The Logic of Comparative Social Inquiry.* New York: Wiley-Interscience.

Rokkan, Stein. 1964. "Comparative Cross-National Research: The Context of Current Efforts." Pp. 3-25 in *Comparing Nations: The Use of Quantitative Data in Cross-National Research,* edited by Richard L. Merritt and Stein Rokkan. New Haven, CT: Yale University Press.

Scheuch, Erwin K. 1967. "Society as Context in Cross-Cultural Comparisons." *Social Science Information* 6:7-23.

Skocpol, Theda. 1979. *States and Social Revolutions: A Comparative Analysis of France, Russia, and China.* Cambridge: Cambridge University Press.

Slomczynski, Kazimierz M., Joanne Miller, and Melvin L. Kohn. 1981. "Stratification, Work, and Values: A Polish-United States Comparison." *American Sociological Review* 46:720-44.

Tilly, Charles. 1984. *Big Structures, Large Processes, Huge Comparisons.* New York: Russell Sage.

Treiman, Donald J. 1977. *Occupational Prestige in Comparative Perspective.* New York: Academic Press.

Wallerstein, Immanuel. 1974, 1980. *The Modern World System.* 2 vols. New York: Academic Press.

Williams, Robin M., Jr. 1985. "The Use of Threats in US/USSR Relations." Pp. 1-32 in *Research in Social Movements, Conflicts and Change.* Vol. 8. Greenwich, CT: JAI.

Part I
Conceptual and Methodological Issues in Cross-National Research

1

Comparative Studies and Social Theory

Stefan Nowak

THE GAP BETWEEN THE AMOUNT OF BROAD SOCIOLOGICAL DATA AND THE PRESENT STATE OF SOCIAL THEORY

I would like to focus in this chapter on the analysis of the relations between comparative social studies and the development of social theory. This is one of the crucial problem areas in contemporary sociology; this relation seems to be far from satisfactory and there seems to be an essential "gap" between large parts of present social theory and comparative verificational studies.

Sociology is—or at least it was supposed to be, according to the intentions of its founding fathers—a theoretical science, that is, a nomological discipline, which tries to establish laws and theories about societies and other social phenomena and processes. It was also meant to be an empirical (as opposed to a speculative) science, which is able not only to formulate some explanatory principles about the social world but also to test the empirical validity of its laws and theories. To the degree that these laws were often (not to say usually) meant to be valid for broad spaciotemporal regions of the social world (even mankind in general), their verification usually involved the use of data from various areas of time and space—in principle from more than one society. Today we call such studies "comparative."

For many classical writers, the notion of "comparative" sociological study would sound redundant. Sociology *had* to be "comparative," almost by definition. And it was comparative, when we look at the scope of interest of our founding fathers, who studied all societies for which they were able to find any data that seemed to be relevant for the theories they tried to substantiate (see Robert Merton's "Introduction" in Marsh 1967).

Then, in the "empiricist period" in the history of sociological research, work in comparative sociology decreased for several decades, because the development of the "empiricist" orientation, typical of the last fifty years of sociological studies, aimed toward direct, standardized assessment of various social facts. This trend led to research questions dealing more and more with facts and relationships within the boundaries of one society, one culture, or one social system, with the validity of findings or generalizations from such studies confined to the boundaries of one national state.

Despite the rapid development of monocultural or monosystemic standardized studies, broadly valid questions and hypotheses did not disappear from sociology. They were sometimes stimulated by the old theoretical tradition and sometimes they emerged independently of that tradition. In any case, these hypotheses required proper empirical validation.

In response to this need, the "comparative" research orientation reemerged after World War II within the standardized research orientation. Sociologists began to use the term "comparative sociology" to denote research that transcends the limits of one society in one period of its history, that is, research that is cross-national or cross-cultural or cross-historical. There has since been a great deal of explicitly comparative research in sociology. The book by Marsh, *Comparative Sociology*, published in 1967, had a bibliography of more than 1,100 comparative studies. Fifteen years after his original volume, Marsh published with J. M. Armer another review of comparative research (Armer and Marsh 1982). This time the material had to be systematized in 12 substantive review papers (plus one on methodology), all written by invited specialists, and the joint bibliography of these papers—now representing a much shorter period—was probably even longer than in the first book.

To these studies we should also add all those studies about particular societies, or conducted within one society and dealing with its lower-level units and their characteristics and changes, that have a "comparative verificational potential," that is, that provide data useful for the verification of theories of broad spaciotemporal validity.

Moreover, the methodological self-awareness of contemporary social research is growing, particularly with respect to the verificational use of "comparative" studies in the test of broad social theories. (See, e.g., Nowak 1961, 1976a, b, c, 1977; Moore 1961; Andreski 1956; Scheuch 1966; Przeworski and Teune 1970; Vallier 1971; Szalai and Petrella 1977; Kohn Chapter 3, this volume.)

Finally, it seems that the importance of the development of theory is more and more strongly accepted in contemporary sociology, which might suggest that the results of comparative studies would be welcomed by theorists now more than ever.

In such a situation, one could expect a rapid development of theory in sociology and one might expect sociology to be a theoretically flourishing discipline. There seems to be rather general agreement, though, that sociological theory is in rather bad shape today. This opinion is addressed both to a fairly broad range of so-called approaches to theory construction in sociology and also to what we can find in sociological textbooks and monographs under the title of "sociological theories." It would be rather useless to quote all those according to whom contemporary sociological theory is in the state of a "deep crisis." Of all those who have explicitly expressed this view (to which I also adhere), let me quote only Jonathan Turner, who wrote: "Much of what is labelled sociological theory is, in reality, only a loose clustering of implicit assumptions, inadequately defined concepts, and a few vague and logically disconnected propositions" (Turner 1978, p. 13; see also Mennel 1981, p. 2).

If the amount of empirical data about social reality, particularly data provided by the rapid development of "comparative sociology," seemed to promise well-formulated, consistent, broadly applicable, and—what is crucial here—empirically tested theories of society, we are still waiting for the realization of this promise. We must conclude that there still (see Merton 1967) seems to exist a "gap" between what is termed "theory" in sociology and empirical social research. Either sociological theory does not stimulate its own verificational studies or the studies themselves are not contributing sufficiently to the verification of theories.

The main goal of this chapter is to look into some of the causes of this gap, and to suggest some ways of closing them, or at least of making them narrower.

In my opinion, the main source of these problems is to be found in the present state of social theory, rather than in the present state of research methodology. Large areas of what is regarded as "sociological theory" are formulated in ways that make empirical verification of hypotheses or theorems difficult or even impossible. No wonder that such theories are not able to stimulate sufficient comparative verificational research or to draw proper supportive (or falsifying) conclusions from the results of studies that ought to be relevant for assessing the theories.

For this reason, I deal in this chapter primarily with the problems and difficulties of proper theory: that is, of the testable, generalizable, and connectable formulation of various social theories within different "styles of theorizing" (see Nowak 1977, 1986).

IMPLICIT-FALSIFICATIONIST AND EXPLICIT-EXPLORATORY COMPARISONS IN INDUCTIVE VERIFICATION OF SOCIAL THEORIES

There has been a long dispute in sociology as to whether "comparative" studies should be distinguished as a special category of research (see, e.g., Ragin 1982). Whatever conclusion one reaches about the necessity of distinguishing a special category of "comparative" studies, we should be aware that when comparative research is applied to the verification of social theories (either to theories characterizing societies as entities or to theories characterizing particular subsocietal units) the use of comparisons is determined by the rules of inductive logic.

Here Mill's famous "canons" of induction tell us only to compare the values of two sets of theoretical variables—the "independent" and the "dependent" ones—under several sets of accompanying conditions: either possibly identical (the "canon of only difference") or possibly diversified (the "canon of only agreement"). These canons say nothing about the spaciotemporal origins of the data nor whether these data should be taken from one social system or from many such systems.

Unfortunately, induction in sociology poses some special problems, because in the social sciences we are studying a multilevel reality with various patterns of distribution and variation of phenomena from different levels in space and time. Some patterns of variation make necessary the use of data, "comparative" in the sense specified above, taken from different systems, different cultures, or from different epochs in human history.

When we want to generalize about the events or processes occurring in the "units" located at a high level of social integration (e.g., about nations, societies, states, or cultures) or at the level of different epochs in the history of such "high-level units," the need for a broad, "comparative" research perspective seems obvious.

But, even when our theory deals primarily with the characteristics of social units at a "subsocietal" level (from individual human beings, through small groups, to local communities or subnational institutions), we may need cross-systemic comparisons. There are at least two reasons why this is so:

Within the boundaries of any one society, we may be not able to find a sufficient range of the values of variables characterizing such units, or the whole range of configurations of the values of these variables required by the inductive canons.

Even when the range of variation of the units of the given category within one particular society seems to represent a sufficient range of values of the theoretically pertinent variables, generalizations formulated or substantiated in a monocultural study often turn out to be "nonreplicable" in other societies. Investigators have had to limit their generalizations to "historical generalizations" valid for one society only.

Unless we think that there are some special, "mystical," scientifically nonanalyzable properties related to particular subareas of the time and space of social reality, and responsible for certain mechanisms working only in some special "historical locations," we have to assume that our "historically limited" theory is at best incomplete. Time-space limits of validity of such historical generalizations are substitutes for some unknown factors, the empirical variation of which is correlated with the boundaries of particular societies, systems, or cultures—within some of which our theory "works," while in other societies the theory "does not work." These unknown factors may be

(1) some "analytical," "structural," or "global" characteristics of the societies or cultures (see Lazarsfeld and Menzel 1972), empirically equivalent to the historical limits of the validity of the generalizations: These characteristics—being the properties of whole societies or their cultures—by definition cannot have intrasystemic variation and therefore their relevance for the tested relationship cannot be discovered or proved through intrasystemic comparative analysis (see Nowak 1961); or

(2) they are defined as the lower-level characteristics of the lower-level units so that in principle, from a strictly logical point of view, they could also have intrapopulation variation. But, it empirically happens that in each of the particular populations only one value of this lower-level variable is represented, even when their subsystemic variation does not constitute a logical impossibility.

Suppose that we find empirically that a certain lower-level relationship works only in a Roman Catholic country and not in a Protestant one. If we think that the influence of the church as an *institution* is responsible and that one of the countries is dominated by the Catholic church, while the other is dominated by a Protestant church, this influence is then characteristic of the whole society. We have, then, a typical two-level hypothesis. The situation is conceptually and theoretically quite different if we think that the *religious beliefs* of the people are responsible for the "historical" limits of validity of such a finding, even if each of these countries is completely monoreligious at the time of our study. This is, then, a one-level hypothesis. We can even in some future study try to test such a hypothesis in a monosystemic research design, but for that we must wait until some Protestants immigrate to a Roman Catholic country or vice versa. Then we can check the validity of such a one-level hypothesis with two independent variables. Until this happens, unfortunately, these two cases are inductively indistinguishable.

The basic rules of multilevel inductive strategy in sociology can be summarized as follows: If you have an intrapopulation relationship established in only one population, try to extend its validity by testing other populations of the same level. If such "replication" works, it means that at least those system-level variables on which these populations differ are irrelevant for the lower-level relationship. If such replication fails at some border between some populations, we try to apply Mill's canons of inductive logic, to see what is similar in the populations that provide similar results and what is different about those populations that provide different results.

I have thus described a research strategy that is both inductive, increasing step by step the degree of empirical validity of a theory, and also exploratory, because the research delivers answers clarifying the meaning of the tested hypothesis. This clarification is provided both with respect to the degree of historical validity of the hypothesis and with respect to providing information about subsystemic and systemic variables that should be included in the formulation (see, e.g., Inkeles and Smith 1974). Therefore, such an inductive (some call it "inductionist") strategy in sociological studies is not only a confirmatory but also an exploratory method.

But, we should not forget the possibility of also applying as a test of our theories a Popperian, that is, a "deductionist," or falsificationist, research strategy. Under this strategy, which is, of course, implicitly comparative, we begin our study with a broad hypothesis (if possible, a hypothesis that is intended to be universally valid) or theory formulated in a complete manner (i.e., specifying all relevant variables for its mechanisms, both from the subsystemic and from the systemic level). Because such theory claims to be true for an entire class of objects or events within the limits of its intended validity, we are entitled to test it on any particular case to which it applies. Therefore, any intrasystemic study conducted in a society to which the theory is intended to apply makes a good case for the verification, or rather, according to Popper, for the rejection of such a hypothesis. To our science belong only those theories that we were not able to falsify, even when we tried to do so.

One can give quite a few examples of studies, sometimes sociological studies, more often social psychological, of "monosystemic" data that played an essential role in testing a hypothesis, the limits of validity of which were much broader than the population on which it had been tested (see, e.g., Lipset et al. 1956). These studies were then "implicitly comparative" in the Popperian sense.

Unfortunately for the social sciences, the falsificationist strategy is most efficient in those sciences where the theory can be completely spelled out before we undertake its verification. This includes the specification of the role of both lower- and higher-level variables, as well as the limits and conditions of the theory's validity. Only under such an assumption can the falsificationist strategy be fruitfully applied; under those conditions, it is much more efficient (and requires much less effort and cost) than the inductionist strategy.

When we cannot assume that the hypothesis we want to test is completely formulated, we have to apply the inductive-exploratory strategy, which combines discovering the relevant variables of the theory with the process of its confirmation and the extension of its historical validity (see, e.g., Jacob et al. 1971). Unfortunately, such situations are much more frequent in our discipline at its present stage of development. Therefore, the importance of an explicitly comparative research strategy—inductionist and exploratory at the same time, stressing the importance of cross-national, cross-cultural, and cross-historical studies—constitutes another indirect evidence of the weakness of our theories.

PROBLEMS WITH TESTABILITY AND
PRECISENESS OF
"GENERAL SOCIOLOGICAL THEORIES"

Those who more or less agree with the opinion exemplified by the quotation from Turner usually accept what is sometimes called a "propositional" notion of "theory." According to this notion, the term "theory" should refer to possibly unambiguous sets or systems of laws, or to broad lawlike generalizations, integrated on the basis of a common unifying principle, with clearly stated topological and (or) historical conditions of their validity. Such laws or generalizations should be empirically testable and supported by satisfactory inductive evidence. They can be used for explanations (and sometimes also for predictions) of phenomena to which the theory applies within the limits of the theory's explicit applicability. This is the notion of theory that I would like to support in this chapter.

As we know, not all students of social reality regard the formulation of such theories as possible. To them we can say only that quite a few systems of propositional generalizations have been formulated about various social phenomena, some of which look quite satisfactory from the point of view of the above standard. For some of these generalizations, we are also able to show quite strong inductive supporting evidence. For those who would like to pursue such an idea of social theory, as I would,

it is enough to demonstrate that nomothetic systems of explanatory generalizations can sometimes be formulated in the social sciences.

Unfortunately, many constructions that are labeled "sociological
theories," especially those that are called "general theories" or "general
theoretical approaches" to the explanation of social reality, fall far short
of these standards. In Turner's book, for example, we find functionalism,
conflict theories, exchange theorizing, the interactionist perspective, various phenomenological approaches to society, and finally structuralism as
examples of "theories," to all of which his opinion applies. Many years
earlier, Merton (1967) called some of these constructions "total systems
of sociological theory." He stressed their basic untestability, and proposed
replacing them, at least for the time being, with more readily testable
"theories of the middle range."

If such an evaluation of these "theoretical systems" or "approaches" is
correct, then one might think that instead of trying to improve such
theories, it might be better to forget them. However great the temptation
to do so, I think that it would constitute a serious intellectual loss for
sociology not to use in our contemporary theorizing the explanatory ideas
about social reality that we can find in the "classical" and "neoclassical"
theoretical approaches—despite all their weaknesses.

Some of these approaches contain theoretical concepts (or even vague
notions) of great explanatory potential, that is, they denote a property of
an object about which either a great number of laws dealing with a certain
domain or a few laws of powerful explanatory potential referring to this
domain may be formulated. Concepts like "social class," "social role,"
and "reference group" are good examples. In such cases, one should make
explicit all laws applying to the object, phenomenon, or process to which
such a notion refers, and then bring some internal logical order into the
sets of such propositions. Here the abstract notion constitutes the unifying
principle of the theory.

In some other situations, we find these unifying principles in certain
explanatory mechanisms, postulated by some "general social theories."
These mechanisms may constitute a potential set of starting assumptions
for a well-formulated propositional theory. They are often denoted by
such terms as "homeostasis," "exchange," "conflict," "purposive behavior," "principle of rationality," or "binary structural oppositions." All of
these are examples of such explanatory mechanisms, describing at least
partially, and usually without sufficient specification of the conditions to
which their validity is limited, such ways of influencing some social
phenomena by other social phenomena, on the basis of which entire
theoretical systems may be built.

These ideas (whatever their ambiguity) usually have a fairly high
degree of generality and abstractness and, therefore—if properly reformu-

lated and supplemented by proper specification of scope, limits, and conditions of validity—might have fairly broad applicability to the explanation of social events, phenomena, and processes, and different domains of social life. In some cases, they may be applied to the explanation of some more specific mechanisms, described by less general and less abstract social theories, which are built in many specialized subdomains of sociological inquiry. Nevertheless, even a brilliant explanatory notion, principle, or mechanism does not yet make an empirically testable system of propositional generalizations. The numerous shortcomings of most "general social theories" as seen from this point of view can be briefly summarized as follows (see Nowak 1986):

(1) The concepts of many such explanatory approaches are not sufficiently clearly defined. This applies both to the "social units" (in particular, to the specification of their level or levels) to which each of these theories applies and to which it does not apply, and also to the properties of such units, denoted by the theoretical variables of such theory. If a theory should refer to several levels of social reality at the same time, involving the joint action of both "subsystemic" and "system-level" variables, these joint actions are not explicitly defined to a degree sufficient to make their meanings understandable to all. In many cases, such joint actions are not defined at all. Moreover, system-level variables are often substituted by their time-space coordinates, or by proper names of societies in which the theory "works," or by reference to the data on the basis of which the variables have been constructed.

As a consequence, neither the domain of intended validity of the theory nor the subsystemic and systemic conditions of this validity are known. Needless to say, such theory is basically untestable, because we do not know which sequences of events confirm it and which contradict it. With respect to the unclear meaning of system-level variables, such formulation of theories does not give us guidance for the proper selection of the systems necessary for inductive-falsificationist confirmation of a comparatively tested theory. We are bound to use an exploratory-inductive strategy.

There is one problem that should be especially stressed here. If we assume that comparative studies aim toward the verification of broadly valid, not to say universally valid, theories, additional stress must be put upon the requirement that the concepts of such theory be defined. These concepts must be so explicitly defined that we know which objects, phenomena, and processes are dealt with by the theory in each society (or better, in all societies) to which the theory is intended to apply. We may still face further problems, such as how we can identify those objects in practical research operations in different cultural or systemic contexts, but at least we must be completely clear as to what are we looking for in different cultures or systems.

The objects themselves must be so specified so that in comparative educational research, for example, we know what is and what is not a "school." The properties of particular units may be absolute (in which case they cannot differ in various national settings) or they may be relative (in which case they may be equivalent in various settings, where they bear the same relation to the same or equivalent criterion variables). In the latter case, a whole set of relational equivalences can be distinguished, from causal through functional, cultural, and structural, and each of them might be relevant for other theoretical mechanisms (see Nowak 1976c). Until those concepts are so formulated that they can apply to all cultures and systems, and constitute a sufficient premise for the choice of indicators in those systems, the domain of applicability of theory is not clear enough for cross-national testing.

(2) The second problem is the exact meaning of the relationships between the phenomena (variables) denoted by the broadly valid concepts (or referred to by the terms) of the theory. In many cases, they are not specified clearly enough; we often don't know whether the relationships postulated by the theory are supposed to be general, statistical, or, in both cases, what is the shape of such relations, and their strength. They also may only be existential relationships ("x and y may be related so and so," or "occur sometimes jointly"). Then we don't know whether they are synchronic (structural) or diachronic and, if diachronic, whether they postulate a causal relation between the independent and the dependent variables.

An additional problem here is the precise specification of the exact substantive meaning of the explanatory mechanisms postulated by the given theory, that is, specification of the nature of causal or structural connections to which the theory refers (homeostasis, conflict, exchange, and so on) so that the proper conditional derivation of other laws and generalizations of theory is possible.

Whatever their formal and substantive nature, these relations may be universal or historical. If historical, what is the historical scope of their intended validity? And then, the crucial thing: To which historically or theoretically specified conditions is the validity of the mechanisms postulated by the given theory limited? Only by knowing these limits can we know where a theory may, and where it may not, be tested, and where different theories can be used jointly for the explanation of the same phenomena.

(3) The concepts referring both to the phenomena (variables) of a theory and the relationships among these phenomena may be easily direct-

ly observable, or observable only with serious difficulty, or not observable at all. In the last two situations we face the problem of operationalization of the theory, that is, to choose proper indicators of variables and of relationships connecting these variables. Until we solve this problem, the theory cannot be regarded as testable. But we should be aware that "operationalization" cannot replace the cross-culturally valid explicit "nominal" definitions of concepts, because the specification of strictly empirical relations cannot replace the theoretical characterization of the substantive nature of the mechanisms connecting theoretical variables.

(4) Finally, theories may also have serious problems in their internal consistency, with a lack of a logical, deductive pattern of coherence between different propositions or of nondeductive patterns of internal structure. The ideal for a deductive theory is to make it axiomatic, but many weaker forms of such systematizations are also possible. We may, for example, present a theory of social interactions, deriving its hypotheses from the postulates of "operant conditioning" or from the "postulate of rationality." Such theories may be called "vertical," because they stratify their laws by logically deriving some of these laws from other, more general or more fundamental laws.

Other theories may have a nondeductive structure, but they may still be quite consistent internally. This is the case when we present all causes of the same effect in the theory and relate these causes to each other—in an additive or interactive, direct or indirect, manner—as, for example, in a path diagram. Such theories may be called "horizontally ordered" theories, because none of their laws is more fundamental than the others. In some theories, both "horizontal" and "vertical" patterns can be jointly applied. One of the consequences of internal inconsistency is that even when particular laws or generalizations of the theory are clear and testable, we are not able to derive empirical predictions from the whole unordered set of such propositions.

PROBLEMS WITH GENERALITY AND "CONNECTABILITY" OF SUBSTANTIVE THEORIES FORMULATED IN SPECIALIZED SUBDOMAINS OF SOCIOLOGY

"General theoretical systems" are not the only source of theoretical knowledge about social phenomena. The general picture of "social theory" presented above requires some modification because there are many empirical generalizations that have been formulated and validated during many decades of sociological studies. Many of these were either discovered or tested in comparative studies.

Unfortunately, these empirical generalizations are rarely presented in our theoretical monographs, courses, or textbooks. Instead, we teach them in courses on "family," "industrial organization," "values," "political behavior", or "local communities." Or we present them in collections of papers on "comparative sociology," instead of classifying them by their topical subjects, in the same way that we might present other unrelated piles of generalizations under the titles of "survey sociology," "content analysis sociology," and the like. We thereby contribute to the unjustified impression that there is very little general, empirically substantiated, theoretical knowledge about social phenomena in our discipline.

Implicitly and explicitly comparative studies of modern sociology have established many well-documented generalizations. Some of these deal with abstractly defined phenomena ("social roles," "reference groups"), but this is rather rare. Most of the theories tested systematically on a cross-national basis refer to some "natural social objects" ("family," "school," "village," "city"), the meaning of which is specified by the everyday experiences of the members of the studied populations and is defined in the way that these people see and define them. These usually empirically well-substantiated intrasystemic and intersystemic generalizations about various social phenomena or processes, constituting theories of particular subdomains of specialized social inquiry, should be regarded as an intrinsic part of social theory. Much of what has been said about the state of social theory with respect to "general systems" does not apply to these empirical generalizations of specialized domains of sociological study.

In a way, we have two kinds of theories in sociology: One of them formulates potentially powerful explanatory principles, or delineates phenomena or objects having a strong explanatory potential for broad areas of reality, but that are poorly formulated and either untestable in their present form or require serious efforts at systematic verification. Then we have the sets of empirical generalizations. These generalizations and theories of specialized sociology are not perfect either. Their concepts should be more explicitly defined, the relationships involved better characterized, and the conditions of their intended validity more clearly spelled out. Moreover, many of these specialized theories constitute loosely interrelated "bunches" of generalizations, sometimes called "inventories of theoretical propositions." They usually develop in isolation from what is ordinarily regarded as "theory" in sociology, developing a kind of empirically embedded theory of their own. It is important for many of them to bring some internal consistency into the structure of their propositions. One can apply deductive patterns for the systematization of some of them, while the structure of others will have to be nondeductive. Many of these specialized theories are of a fairly low level of abstraction and have a low degree of generality. Because many of the concepts have been defined in terms of everyday language, their "connectability" to other broader and more general, more abstract theories is decreased.

It is more likely that "general theories" that start from an "explanatory mechanism" and try to derive its consequences for various kinds of objects, phenomena, or conditions will belong to the deductive patterns of theory construction. When we try to systematize the totality of generalizations about a certain "social object," it is less likely that we will be able to order them into a logically coherent deductive structure. But this does not mean that we cannot bring any order even into a set of laws of a fairly low level of abstractness. We can order, for example, the different causes of the stability or change of the given "object" according to rules (the prototype for which can be found in path analysis), or we can order various functional connections between the elements of a given complex system, connecting them by causal loops, feedbacks, and so on. Finally, we should be aware that in many theories some fragments can be deductively ordered, while nondeductive rules will have to be applied for other fragments.

When we want to treat both empirical generalizations and theories based upon explanatory principles as intrinsic parts of one, slowly emerging, more comprehensive structure of theoretical sociology, then the question arises: How should particular theories dealing with various phenomena and objects be related to each other within this theoretical structure?

In every science we have generalizations and laws of various degrees of generality and abstractness. Some of the less general laws are derivable from (explained by) some more general and more abstract, more elementary laws and theories, and we should try to find such explanatory connections between theories of different degrees of generality. For other, less general regularities we will not be able to find, at least at the moment, "explanatory correspondents." There would be nothing peculiar to theoretical sociology if it were to include propositions of various levels of generality and abstractness.

Trying to establish this "vertical" deductive-explanatory pattern of correspondence between different theories is important for several reasons. First, the application of a more general mechanism to the explanation of some less general regularity increases our understanding of this regularity and sometimes may suggest hypotheses about the nature of missing factors. Alternatively, generalizations that have been previously tested, especially in cross-national, cross-historical, or cross-cultural studies, may constitute serious evidence for validating some more abstract theories with which they have been deductively connected. Such instances create the possibility of finding indirect but broad empirical validation for these more abstract or more general theories, the weak side of which is often the lack of systematic empirical evidence of their validity.

The crucial thing here is to find rules of correspondence connecting concepts and mechanisms of the explained—that is, less abstract—theory with those of the explaining—that is, more abstract—theory. In some cases, we can relate the less abstract theory to only one more general theory and explain it in this way. In other cases, we have to use several more general and more fundamental theories jointly in order to explain laws and regularities established empirically in a substantive subdomain of social inquiry. By doing this, we also increase the empirical validity of more abstract theories, that is, of "general theoretical systems."

GENUINE AND SPURIOUS SYSTEM-LEVEL VARIABLES IN THEORIES TESTED IN CROSS-SYSTEMIC STUDIES

To demonstrate how the precise formulation of a theory is important for the choice of the proper, adequate, and economical research strategy, let us look at the problem of the proper conceptualization of those elements of the theory that are crucial in the choice of a proper comparative strategy of verification, namely, the "system-level" variables. These system-level variables—as any other independent variables—may exert their additive or interactive impact upon the "subsystemic" phenomena and relationships to which our theory refers; or these system-level properties may have no impact on these relationships at all. For the latter kind of hypothesis, no comparative study is needed, provided that all essential values of the lower-level variables are represented in our population, or can be created there by experimental manipulations.

If the lower-level relationship is additively dependent upon a system-level variable, still the "subsystemic" part of the hypothesis can be tested on any intranational sample and does not require comparative study. On the other hand, a comparative study may turn out to be necessary for the "unmasking" of such hypotheses, where the theorist wrongly assumed the additive impact of higher-level variables, when in fact the impact is interactive. Now suppose that a system-level variable is interactively influencing a lower-level relationship. Interaction may mean here any modifying impact of system characteristics upon a lower-level relationship: it may be a catalyst for a conditional relationship, a multiplicative factor for the intensity of this relation, or it may change the direction or shape of the relationship. Here the verification of our hypothesis involves the observation of the behavior of subsystemic relations in various populations characterized by various values of the system variable, and in comparisons of different subsystemic relationships in those systems.

In the falsificationist, implicitly comparative approach, this seems, at least in principle, a simple problem, because we can derive the properties of the subsystemic relations for each particular system, so that any, for example, national sample can be checked against the theory.

When applying an inductionist strategy, we should explicitly compare different systems, differing on the values of system variables believed to be responsible for the "historical limits" to the generality of the relationships. If more than one characteristic of the systems (e.g., nations) has an impact upon variables or relationships from a lower level, then the number of systemic cases we need for proper comparisons increases accordingly. Practically, this increases the energy and cost involved in such verification and it also may happen that, for example, the population of nations or cultures could be exhausted before we find all appropriate combinations of values of the tested system variables (see Ragin 1982).

We may meet another barrier here, namely, the syndromatic character of covariation of systemic variables. Within one society the investigator finds "too many agreements," but between societies "too many differences" (see Nowak 1961).

In some cases, instead of trying to find systemic similarities or differences, we may be able to eliminate some system-level variables from our theory, changing them into subsystemic variables. This operation (especially important in the case of an interactive impact of such variables) is equivalent to the transformation of a "two-level hypothesis" into a one-level hypothesis, testable in a "noncomparative" manner provided that we find sufficient variation of relevant subsystemic variables within the boundaries of a single population.

To say that a variable plays the role of a systemic condition for lower-level relations is equivalent to saying that it plays the role of a contextual variable for the lower-level relationships. Such variables function as contextual factors in lower-level relationships when their additive, or interactive (modifying), impact on this relationship comes "from above" in a uniform way and with equal strength upon all members of the given population. It has then, by definition, a constant value for all members of this collectivity. We may obtain on the basis of strictly logical premises other values of the given contextual variable only when we move in our observations to other collectivities. It is irrelevant whether at the collectivity level the variable constituting such a contextual factor for a lower-level relationship has been previously defined, with respect to properties of lower-level units, as "analytical," "structural," or "global" (see Lazarsfeld and Menzel 1972).

When we suppose that what was initially regarded as a higher-level variable acts in reality within the boundaries of one system or society in a differentiating way, we should change the meaning of the corresponding concept, stressing its noncontextual character. Assuming that in the test of this hypothesis we may find, or may create by experimental manipulations, the instances of intrasystemic variation of both independent variables, this may make cross-national comparisons unnecessary for the test of the hypothesis. To give the most simple example: We often suspect that national culture is a relevant system-level factor for a certain, cross-nationally tested relationship, and compare societies markedly different in their cultures. But do we really think that the culture acts only as a nondifferentiating overall context of human thinking and behavior, having the same impact on all members of the given society with respect to the tested regularity?

In fact, "culture" (understood usually as an "analytical" variable at the national level) may refer to the values of individuals or of small groups. These values are usually internalized to different degrees by different members of society, and the differences are then relevant for the tested hypothesis. If so, we should specify which cultural values seem to be involved as additive or modifying lower-level factors. Then we might be able to observe empirically variations in the degree of acceptance of these values within one society, without undertaking a labor-consuming and expensive cross-national study. Such an understanding of the theoretical function of "culture" transforms this concept from a systemic property of an entire collectivity into a noncontextual lower-level characteristic of the members of this society—the degree to which they accept some specified cultural values. In a similar way, we may transform the meaning of other system-level variables, for example, the "dominant religion of the society," which has been treated as a contextual variable in the study of many subnational relationships, for example, in the study of political behavior. Suppose that we come to the conclusion that the theoretically relevant variable here is the probability of being in direct and intense social contact with people of a particular religious denomination. Until now, we have been able to measure this probability only at the collectivity level. But we can also think of ways of finding intrasystemically differentiated indicators, measuring their different intensities at the individual level.

Many intranational studies have demonstrated that contextual variables (such as the famous "climate of opinion" variable, or "average IQ" in a class of high school students) do really operate, both additively and interactively, on certain subsystemic relationships. These contextual characteristics are then acting jointly with corresponding noncontextual characteristics of lower-level units. We know this from Coleman's (1961) studies of education, which show the combined impact of individual IQ and the average IQ of a school class; and from empirical studies of relationships between religion and political behavior, which have shown that religion acts both as a contextual variable and as an absolute characteristic of community members. We may justifiably expect the occurrence of similar phenomena at the national level.

PROBLEMS IN DEFINING MEANINGFUL AND OPERATIONALIZED CONCEPTS FOR BROADLY VALID AND COMPARATIVELY TESTABLE HYPOTHESES AND THEORIES

The proper "operationalization" of theoretical concepts is an obviously necessary condition for testing any theory, unless the theory itself has been formulated in strictly observational language, something that is a rare exception in the social sciences. Let me discuss here another, seemingly quite opposite, category of problems: hypotheses or theories in which, instead of a properly defined concept, we only have indicators related to scientific terms, devoid of any theoretical meaning. This kind of situation is an "empiricist legacy" in sociological theorizing, coming from the early period of standardized empirical studies, and it may be met often in generalizations emerging from empirical studies.

Concepts need indicators. But these indicators may be definitional, or inferential, or empirical, being in the last two cases definitionally external to the indicated properties (see, e.g., Nowak 1962). Therefore, "the properties of observation" don't have to be identical with the "properties of inference," either in intranational or in cross-national studies.

Even some of the earliest comparative studies applying standardized methods saw the danger of too rigorous an operationist approach, and tried to find what was later termed "functional equivalence" of different indicators in different systems for the same broadly valid concepts. But attempts to find "equivalent" indicators for concepts are meaningless unless we are able to say to what theoretically understood entity these indicators are supposed to be equivalent. Only through explicit definitions of theoretical concepts, supplemented by the definitional or nondefinitional relations between these concepts and their indicators (identical or different in different systems), and also by information about the validity of each indicator for the given concepts in each particular system, can we relate the data from broad comparative studies to the theories they are supposed to test.

Trying to define these concepts, we should first remember that in sociology we are usually interested both in the observable and in the subjective side of social reality. Most existing theories, both classical and newer theories (phenomenology, symbolic interactionism, structuralism, ethnomethodology), and many "empirical generalizations" about natural social objects are formulated in terms of concepts that refer to both the objective and the subjective aspects of social phenomena.

The difference between concepts and their nondefinitional indicators becomes even more apparent when we see that even the formal, logical-definitional character of concepts and their indicators does not have to be identical. To give the most simple example of a concept referring to the collectivity level: "Social integration" is a typical "structural" concept at the collectivity level, understood in terms of certain relationships among the members of a given collectivity. But we measure it by such indices as Durkheim's "suicide rate," which is a typical "analytical property" at the level of human aggregates.

In cross-national study, the empirical relationships between concepts and their indicators may be different for different populations, and even the indicators may be quite different; therefore, for nondefinitional indicators, the inference from research data to theoretical processes is always problematic. For each population, we must establish as accurately as we can the pattern and the degree of empirical correspondence between the indicators used to measure cross-nationally valid concepts—what is often called the validity of the indicators for the concept. But then we must agree that the degree of confirmation of our hypothesis may be different for different populations. The "overall credibility" of a hypothesis may then be a "weighted average" of all our intranational results.

The crucial problem of empirical studies is how to connect by strict—logical or empirical—rules of correspondence the subjective, cultural side of social facts with their observable indicators, so that the researcher can move in his or her study in both directions: from concepts to their indicators, and back from indicators to concepts again. Different solutions to this problem have been proposed in the sociological literature. Some of them have a rather logical character (see Nowak 1976, pp. 48-69), while others use various statistical rules of inference (see Blalock et al. 1970; Costner 1969; Heise and Bornstedt 1970).

Another solution that seemed to avoid the dangers of radical operationalism was the application of various psychometric techniques, both for the specification of meaning and for the operationalization of concepts of intranationally and cross-nationally tested hypotheses (see Przeworski and Teune 1970, part II). In psychometry these techniques were meant to measure dispositions such as intelligence or some personality traits, free in their meaning from any additional inferential "surplus meanings," for example, introspectively observable inner experience of people or culturally defined meanings of social facts. Psychologists applying these techniques for identifying these strictly dispositional properties did not necessarily treat them as completely identical with the behavior they are thought to produce. Nevertheless, the only inferential meaning of any concept measured this way is that such clusters of items constitute both its definition and its operationalization. The clusters of correlated answers to psychometric tests were in fact definitional indicators, that is, operational definitions of some dispositional characteristics, void of any other theoretical meanings, even when labeled as "theoretical constructs."

This might have worked in some areas of psychology. It could have worked also in some domains of social studies that used concepts similar to those used by psychologists, that is, strictly dispositional properties of individuals or groups without additional reference to their socially or culturally meaningful side, for example, "intellectual flexibility" (see Kohn and Schooler 1983) or "group syntality" (see Cattell, 1955). But, in most sociological studies, variables so defined were understood (initially even by the authors of the study) to include many introspective or culturally meaningful notions, which played an essential role both in the formulation of hypotheses and in the choice of indicators. Unfortunately, the indicators replaced these never explicitly stated meanings not only in the research itself but also in the interpretation of the results. In this way, "humanistic" components of these theories were lost at the stage of operationalization and never regained (see Nowak 1976c).

When applying this psychometric, operationalist philosophy of research, some investigators thought that their generalizations were dealing with the "theoretical constructs" that they had in mind, when in fact they were actually making generalizations about relationships between the syndromes of observable indicators. Instead of concepts that are rich in potential theoretical implications, but requiring that they be supplemented (not replaced) by proper observable indicators, empirical sociologists used a kind of psychometric jargon, from which it was almost impossible to return to meaningful understanding and explanation of social phenomena and to rich explanatory theories.

WHAT IS THEORY ABOUT?

Monotheoretical Phenomena and Multitheoretical
Vectors in Comparative Studies

Formally correct definitions are necessary but not sufficient conditions for good theoretical concepts. Also crucial, when we formulate a hypothesis or theory, is the specification of fruitful concepts denoting the phenomena, events, or objects to which the theory should apply. Concepts are fruitful when they permit us to grasp adequately the nature of uniform mechanisms governing the domain of reality to which the theory is addressed.

In general, this is the problem of "what theory is about," or, in other terms, the problem of the specification of the meaning of the concepts, denoting proper "theoretical entities," categorizing or classifying the phenomena from the given domain in such a way that adequate, sufficiently general, and empirically confirmable theory can be formulated about each particular class. Thus, for example, in "prescientific" medicine, illnesses were categorized by the parts of the body in which they occur. Now we know that these were not adequate principles for the proper classification and conceptualization of illnesses. Instead, we classify them by their etiology, because only on such a basis can we build adequate explanatory theories. Once we have these theories, we can explain particular pain located in the body of a sick person by its proper causes and sometimes we can even heal the human body. We may say that the reconceptualization of medicine meant the application of such rules, which correspond to Mill's principle of "uniformity."

I think that this also is one of the central problems for contemporary social theory: the problem of specifying and defining adequate "theoretical entities," that is, the problem of defining classes of objects, events, processes, or properties in a way that corresponds to the principle of general uniformity.

Many theories and generalizations refer to some "naturally existing and socially important objects." It may turn out in the future that we were lucky and some of these objects can be explained by one single explanatory mechanism. This would imply that the term denoting such objects constitutes a theoretically fruitful concept. But, in other cases, we may be less lucky, and some "naturally existing" and "socially defined" objects of a certain class, even though they are socially important for the members of the given society, may turn out not to be "theoretical entities," explainable by one theoretical mechanism. Then, of course, we cannot formulate a broad, adequate, verifiable theory, referring to all objects belonging to such a naturally defined class.

The more complex are the objects or phenomena in which we are interested, and the more they correspond to common-language categories—which usually means that they are in all their complexity socially relevant for the members of the population who perceive and define them—the less likely it is that such natural social objects will be explainable by a single explanatory theory. This does not mean that they are not explainable theoretically. It means that it is not possible to formulate a single, consistent, and confirmable theory about them. Many real, naturally distinguishable objects, phenomena, and processes of the social world are such "multitheoretical objects," and the mechanisms of their functioning, behavior, and change cannot then be explained by a single law or theory.

This does not mean that they are "irregular" or "unexplainable." It means that the mechanisms governing their functioning and change should be understood as multitheoretical "vectors," composed of several more fundamental mechanisms, each of them explainable by another explanatory theory. If we formulate a single theoretical hypothesis (or a set of hypotheses belonging to one theory) to deal with such objects in all their complexity, either we completely fail in our attempts to find confirmatory results or, at least, our hypothesis will have a significant number of exceptions. We should remember that the mechanisms described by each of these theories, which jointly determine the shape of the given "vector," act only under some "catalyzing" or modifying conditions, and do not operate in other conditions. It may also happen that certain conditions determine in a differentiating manner the scope of influence of a particular theoretical mechanism on the objects of the given class and, therefore, the degree of applicability of the given theory for different objects of the class. If these conditions occur in a syndromatic manner, the entire vector will still behave regularly on a broad cross-national scale.

The empirical occurrences of the conditions determining, catalyzing, or modifying the degree of applicability of different composite mechanisms of such multitheoretical vectors do not have to be correlated. Therefore, in different complex objects of the same "naturally distinguishable" class, different sets of mechanisms may operate, or at least the scope of applicability of each of them may be different in different cases. To give a simple example: Both conflict and consensus mechanisms operate in all political systems, making these two approaches valid in a complementary manner for all societies because they are components of a two-dimensional theoretical vector. But we have to use these two theoretical approaches in various proportions, when, for example, comparing and explaining composed vectors of political processes in Switzerland and in Lebanon. That is why so many hypotheses applied to some political processes on a broad comparative scale fail to be verified.

Comparative, cross-historical, cross-cultural, or cross-national studies often aim at the discovery of broad, possibly universally valid regularities applying to such complex objects. The more complex are the objects of study, the more independent from each other are the antecedent conditions of particular composite mechanisms of the given vector corresponding to the mechanisms that govern them, and the more diversified the societies in which we find such vectors, the more likely are these studies to fail in such verification-exploratory attempts.

REFERENCES

Andreski, Stanislav. 1956. *The Uses of Comparative Sociology*. Berkeley: University of California Press.

Armer, Michael and Robert Marsh, eds. 1982. *Comparative Sociological Research in the 1960s and 1970s*. Leiden: E. J. Brill.

Blalock, Hubert M., M. S. Caryll, F. Wells, and Lewis F. Carter. 1970. "Statistical Estimation with Random Measurement Error." In *Sociological Methodology, 1970*, edited by Edgar F. Borgatta and George W. Bornstedt. San Francisco: Jossey-Bass.

Cattell, Raymond. 1955. "Types of Group Characteristics." In *The Language of Social Research*, edited by Paul F. Lazarsfeld and Morris Rosenberg. New York: Free Press.

Coleman, James S. 1961. *Adolescent Society*. New York: Free Press.

Costner, H. L. 1969. "Theory, Deduction and Rules of Correspondence." *American Journal of Sociology* 75(September): 245-263.

Heise, David R. and George W. Bornstedt. 1970. "Validity, Invalidity and Reliability." In *Sociological Methodology, 1970*, edited by Edgar F. Borgatta and George W. Bornstedt. San Francisco: Jossey-Bass.

Inkeles, Alex and David H. Smith. 1974. *Becoming Modern: Individual Change in Six Developing Countries*. Cambridge, MA: Harvard University Press.

Jacob, P. et al. 1971. *Values and the Active Community*. New York: Free Press.

Kohn, Melvin L. and Carmi Schooler. 1983. *Work and Personality*. Norwood, NJ: Ablex.

Kohn, Melvin L., Kazimierz M. Slomczynski, and Carrie Schoenbach. 1986. "Social Stratification and the Transmission of Values in the Family." *Sociological Forum* 1: 73-102.

Lazarsfeld, Paul F. and Herbert Menzel. 1972. "On the Relations Between Individual and Collective Properties." In *Continuities in the Language of Social Research*, edited by Paul F. Lazarsfeld, Ann Passanella, and Morris Rosenberg. New York: Free Press.

Lipset, Seymour M., Martin Trow, and James S. Coleman. 1956. *Union Democracy: The Internal Politics of the International Typographical Union*. Glencoe, IL: Free Press.

Marsh, Robert. 1967. *Comparative Sociology: A Codification of Cross-Societal Analysis*. New York: Harcourt, Brace & World.

Mennel, Stephen. 1981. *Sociological Theory, Uses and Unities*. London.

Merrit, Richard L. and Stein Rokkan, eds. 1966. *Comparing Nations: The Use of Quantitative Data in Cross-National Research*. New Haven, CT: Yale University Press.

Merton, Robert K. 1967. "Introduction." In *Comparative Sociology: A Codification of Cross-Societal Analysis*, edited by Robert M. Marsh. New York: Harcourt, Brace & World.

———. 1967. *On Theoretical Sociology*. New York: Free Press.

Moore, Frank W. 1961. *Readings in Cross-Cultural Methodology*. New Haven, CT: HRAF.

Nowak, Stefan. 1961. "General Laws and Historical Generalizations in the Social Sciences."
    Polish Sociological Bulletin 1-2.
———. 1962. "Correlational, Definitional and Inferential Indicators in Social Research and
    Theory." *Polish Sociological Bulletin* 3-4.
———. 1976a. "Comparative Social Research and Methodological Problems of Sociological
    Induction." In *Understanding and Prediction: Essays in the Methodology of Social and
    Behavior Theories*. Dordrecht, Holland: D. Reidel.
———. 1976b. "Concepts and Indicators in Humanistic Sociology." In *Understanding and
    Prediction: Essays in the Methodology of Social and Behavior Theories*. Dordrecht,
    Holland: D. Reidel.
———. 1976c. "Meaning and Measurement in Comparative Studies." In *Understanding and
    Prediction: Essays in the Methodology of Social and Behavior Theories*. Dordrecht,
    Holland: D. Reidel.
———. 1977. "The Strategy of Cross-National Survey Research for the Development of
    Social Theory." In *Cross-National Comparative Survey Research—Theory and Practice*,
    edited by A. Szalai and R. Petrella, in collaboration with S. Rokkan and E. Scheuch.
    Oxford: Pergamon.
———. 1986. "Style teoretyzowania w socjologii wspolczesnej" [Styles of theorizing in
    contemporary sociology]. *Kultura i Spoleczeustwo* (Warszawa) 4.
Przeworski, Adam and Henry Teune. 1970. *The Logic of Comparative Social Inquiry*. New
    York: Wiley-Interscience.
Ragin, Charles C. 1982. "Comparative Sociology and Comparative Method." In
    Comparative Sociological Research in the 1960s and 1970s, edited by Michael Armer
    and Robert M. Marsh. Leiden: E. J. Brill.
Scheuch, Erwin. 1966. "Cross-National Comparisons Using Aggregate Data: Some
    Methodological Considerations." In *Comparing Nations, the Use of Quantitative Data in
    Cross-National Research*. New Haven, CT: Yale University Press.
Szalai, Alexander and Riccardo Petrella, in collaboration with S. Rokkan and E. Scheuch,
    eds. 1977. *Cross-National Comparative Survey Research—Theory and Practice*. Oxford:
    Pergamon.
Turner, Jonathan. 1978. *The Structure of Sociological Theory*. Homewood, IL: Dorsey.
Vallier, Ivan, ed. 1971. *Comparative Methods in Sociology—Essays on Trends and
    Applications*. Berkeley: University of California Press.

2

New Directions in Comparative Research

Charles Ragin

DIVIDED INTELLECTUAL LABOR?

Imagine a frequency distribution showing the number of empirical studies conducted by comparative social scientists in the last quarter century plotted by sample size. The plot would show that there were many studies with samples of one or two or three cases. (Of course, studies with samples of one are only implicitly comparative.) There would be a sharp drop-off in the number of studies with sample sizes in the middle range— from five or so to about thirty cases, and then at about forty or fifty cases the number of studies would increase with increasing sample size. This upward pattern would continue up to sample sizes approaching the universe of observations—all relevant macro-social units.

Is there anything natural about this U-shaped relation between number of studies and sample size? Do comparative social scientists ask questions that can best be answered with only one or two or three cases or with many, but not with an intermediate number? The simplest explanation of this distribution is that it is very difficult to do in-depth research on more than a few cases. As a result, many scholars study only a select few. Those who study many cases, by contrast, rely on cross-national data compendia (such as those compiled by the World Bank and the United Nations) and take advantage of the substantial supply of information on virtually the universe of nations available in these handbooks. Thus the U-shaped plot of number of studies by sample size results in part from the practical demands of comparative research.

While these demands certainly encourage the curvilinear pattern, the distribution of studies by sample size also reflects decisions that investigators make regarding difficult methodological and theoretical issues. These issues overlay practical considerations.

The first such issue concerns the competing goals of comparative social science. According to this reasoning, there are basically two kinds of comparative social scientists—those interested in understanding or interpreting one or a small number of cases and those interested in general questions relevant to large numbers of macro-social units. In the introduction to this volume, Kohn describes comparativists in the first set as interested in nations as objects of study. Conceived in this way, the gulf between small-N and large-N research results from two competing goals of comparative social science—to explain major patterns of macro-social variation and to interpret important or significant historical outcomes or processes in specific cases. Many engaged in the two kinds of study might accept this explanation of the distribution of studies by sample size. Some who do small-N studies, for example, readily accept the label *area study* for the kind of work they do, and many who do large-N studies readily embrace the label *cross-national study* for the kind of work they do.

But does this way of dividing and describing intellectual labor in comparative social science tell the whole story? Some who do small-N research argue that they are not interested in the cases themselves (i.e., simply as cases), but in broad theoretical issues. They argue further that the work they do is as social scientific as the work of the large-N researchers. After all, both large-N and small-N researchers are trained as social scientists and are interested in many of the same basic theoretical questions. Those who do large-N studies try to provide answers to these questions that are extensively correct, embracing many observations; those who do small-N studies try to provide answers that are intensively correct, embracing one or a small number of observations in a detailed and holistic way. The large-N researcher justifies findings by demonstrating their generality in a very direct and visible way; the small-N researcher justifies findings by showing their correctness or completeness relative to other aspects of the case or cases in question. Further, those who do small-N studies sometimes go to great lengths to argue that the few cases examined in an investigation are the *best* cases to study for a given question, or that these cases are the *most representative* of the general process in question, or that they are the *most decisive* relative to the theoretical issues at hand (see, e.g., Bendix 1978; Lipset 1963; Moore 1966; Smelser 1959). Some go as far as to argue that their cases, while few, represent the *universe* of relevant observations of a theoretically important phenomenon (e.g., Skocpol 1979). Kohn argues that this second kind of small-N research involves using nations as contexts.

Thus, while it may be tempting to relegate small-N researchers to a case-study role—seeing them as area specialists who examine specific cases because of their intrinsic value or who check the generality of the broad statements made by large-N researchers—this simple way of dividing comparative social science contradicts the reality of a community of researchers with many common theoretical interests. There are at least two ways of attacking basic theoretical issues in comparative social science, two ways of testing general arguments—one empirically extensive, the other empirically intensive.

These two explanations of the U-shaped relation between number of studies and sample size essentially give two reasons why some researchers are interested in specific cases—because individual cases are intrinsically interesting or because they are especially relevant to theoretical questions. There are other forces at work, however, that reinforce this distribution of studies by sample size. Primary among these is the fact that social scientists have a limited repertoire of research methods, a repertoire that pushes them toward studying either few cases or many.

Small-N researchers study cases as wholes and compare whole cases to other whole cases. That is, they study configurations of structures and events and try to unravel complexity by comparing configurations. This holistic approach to cases becomes unwieldy when the number of cases is greater than a mere handful. The unraveling of the web of similarities and differences that exists among eight cases—a feat attempted by Barrington Moore, Jr., in *Social Origins of Dictatorship and Democracy*—is cause for great acclaim in comparative sociology. One source of the difficulty is the simple fact that the number of comparisons that must be addressed increases geometrically as the number of cases increases: number of comparisons $= [(N)(N - 1)]/2$. It is difficult, if not impossible, to analyze all the relevant similarities and differences that exist among many cases, especially when these similarities and differences are understood holistically, as is usually the case in intensive comparative research. This explains the tendency to keep the number of cases to a minimum in such studies.

By contrast, large-N, cross-national research follows mainstream social science in the application of multivariate statistical methods to large data sets. Here the problem is the opposite of that faced by small-N researchers. Large-N researchers in comparative social science are often frustrated by a scarcity of cases. For statistical techniques to work well, many cases are necessary. Thirty is usually too few, and if the investigation calls for the examination of interaction effects, the entire universe of countries is too small. This accounts for the common tendency among large-N researchers (1) to cast a very broad net—to include every possible case in a study—and (2) to restrict their analysis to simple additive models.

These methodological limitations are generally not recognized as such because of biases in many existing theoretical perspectives. This is the fourth explanation of the U-shaped distribution and is an adjunct to the second and third explanations. The basic argument is that until recently the limitations of research methodologies in comparative social science have not been apparent because most macro-social theories are biased against recognition of diversity and causal heterogeneity. From the time of Comte, the tendency to array societies along one or a small number of dimensions and to search for one or a small number of basic causal processes has pervaded social science. With the exception of Weber and portions of Marx, the tendency to try to reduce societal variation to a small number of variables was common among classical social theorists. Among modern theories, it is apparent in the evolutionary theories of both Parsons and Lenski, in modernization theory, in convergence theory, and in some strands of dependency and world-systems theories. Nisbet (1969) presents a version of this same criticism very forcefully in *Social Change and History*; Tilly (1984) elaborates similar arguments. This theoretical bias in favor of ignoring diversity is reflected in existing methodologies. These techniques—both large-N *and* small-N—tend to obscure diversity, usually as part of an effort to assert or demonstrate generality.

There are few who would quarrel with the idea that a tried-and-true way to achieve generality is by studying many cases (i.e., conducting an extensive, large-N study). This way of demonstrating generality, however, obscures diversity in a very direct and profound way. In quantitative cross-national studies, cases lose their identities as they are disaggregated into variables. Relations between variables are studied, not similarities and differences among whole cases. Typically, a single model applicable to all cases is fit to the data, resulting in a univocal answer to the research question. It is still possible to address diversity among cases, but diversity becomes defined in terms of deviations from a specific prediction model. And even this timid route to diversity is too rarely traveled. Thus large-N studies are biased toward univocal answers to research questions. Univocal answers, in turn, are highly compatible with nomothetic macro-social theories.

It is less conventional to argue that the intensive study of a small number of cases also might obscure diversity. Before making this argument, it must be admitted first that many who do small-N studies are interested in the cases themselves (i.e., as objects) and that these investigators contribute to social scientists' knowledge and understanding of diversity. Many small-N studies (especially those by sociologists), however, often are designed in a way that minimizes this aspect of their contribution. Whenever an investigator argues that a small set of cases (including a set with only one member) is the *most relevant* to a particular question, or is *highly typical* of the broader category of cases relevant to a specific theory, or is *theoretically decisive*, or *embraces the universe* of relevant observations, or is justified through some other elaborate theoretical rationale, essentially he or she is trying to make the case that the intensive study of this case or small set of cases provides a direct route to testing the theory in question. When case selection is justified in this way, the individuality and historical specificity of the cases themselves (despite their small number) become less relevant. Many authors of case studies, in fact, present their results as universally relevant (e.g., a test of a theory of ethnic political mobilization based on a single case). From a statistical point of view, this practice is ludicrous because a sample of one is no basis for generalization. From the standpoint of research design, however, it is acceptable because the most important cases for testing theory have been selected for intensive examination.

What does this have to do with the gulf between small-N and large-N research? The problem is that the greater the number of cases selected for intensive study, the lower the probability that the investigator will find theory-confirming uniformity among the cases. In short, with more cases, the likelihood of encountering unmanageable diversity (i.e., unmanageable from the perspective of nomothetically oriented theories) increases. Thus, keeping the degree of diversity (i.e., the number of cases) in intensive studies to a minimum maximizes the likelihood of a univocal answer to a research question. Investigating only a single case *ensures* an univocal answer. Theoretical pressures toward nomothetic answers to research questions (i.e., bias against recognition of diversity), therefore, reinforce the tendency to study few cases.

What has been described so far is a set of pressures—in addition to the practical problem of knowing many cases intimately—that push research designs in comparative social science toward the two extremes of sample size—very small or as large as possible. These pressures include (1) the competing goals of comparative social science; (2) the dichotomy between the two ways of demonstrating theoretical arguments, intensive and extensive; (3) the limited repertoire of analytic techniques available to social scientists; and (4) the consistency of these limitations with theoretical biases favoring nomothetic generality at the expense of knowledge and appreciation of diversity. The main consequence of these pressures is a bifurcated subdiscipline, a division of labor between those who know a few cases well and those who know a lot about broad patterns of cross-national covariation. Despite all the possibilities for creative symbiosis between intensive and extensive investigation, little actually takes place.

The basic premise of this chapter is that new directions in comparative research over the next several decades will involve greater attention to the gulf between intensive and extensive research and more creative effort to bridge this gulf. This argument is explored from several vantage points.

First, the basis for anticipating efforts to bridge the gulf are explored, and then possible foundations for building this bridge are explored. Finally, I discuss some practical problems in linking intensive and extensive research.

BASIS FOR ANTICIPATING NEW
EFFORTS TO BRIDGE THE GULF

The current gulf between the two general styles of comparative research is great. It might be more reasonable to anticipate a widening gulf and greater differentiation between the two types rather than more bridging efforts. Why not anticipate separation into two subdisciplines? Alternately, it might be more reasonable to predict the demise of one of the two types. Intensive researchers might become frustrated with their feeble efforts to generalize; extensive researchers might become frustrated with the gap between their variables, on one hand, and actual cases and empirical phenomena and processes, on the other. There are several good reasons to anticipate bridging efforts, however, and these reasons extend beyond the commonplace observation that it is good sociological practice to attack a research question from a variety of perspectives and to use different methods.

First, recall the argument presented above that the gulf is in part a legacy of the dominance of nomothetic macro-social theory. It is clear that in the last decade comparative social scientists, all types, have shown greater and greater dissatisfaction with such theories. This dissatisfaction is part of a long-term trend that began with a rejection of Parsons in the 1960s and has continued through the present in attacks on evolutionary theory, modernization theory, convergence theory, developmental theory, and more recently in attacks on some versions and strands of Marxist theory, dependency theory, and world-systems theory (e.g., for ignoring the state or for treating it in simplistic ways; see Evans, Rueschemeyer, and Skocpol 1985). Tolerance for theories that push nomothetic ideas has declined dramatically. By contrast, the popularity of theories that provide tools for the analysis of diversity and causal complexity has increased. There is a renewed interest in Weber and in Weberians (not the Parsonsian version) and in other historically oriented theorists (see, e.g., essays in Skocpol 1984).

Second, there is more interest in phenomena that are historically situated or historically emergent. In part this stems from the realization that all sociological work is historical. A survey of residents of the United States in 1988 is no less historically or culturally situated than a survey of residents of France in 1788. The present interest in historically situated phenomena, however, goes beyond this simple acknowledgment of historicity, and concerns problem selection. Historians have long used historical and cultural *significance* as guides in problem selection. Until recently, other social scientists, sociologists especially, have avoided studying phenomena that are tightly circumscribed by time and place. Today, however, the idea that singular, large-scale events and processes (e.g., the emergence of a system of social welfare, the decline of a social movement) should be understood both sociologically *and* historically— on their own terms—has won wider acceptance.

Among those engaged in the study of historically situated phenomena, there is a continuum from sociology to journalism, with history in the middle. The different activities on this continuum are all directed toward interpreting events; they differ in the degree to which social science theory plays a part in interpretation and in the degree to which the importance of theory is recognized. The interpretation of events by sociologists is clearly theory-driven and is recognized as such; at the other end of this dimension, interpretation by journalists usually is not consciously theory-driven at all. Because of their clear attention to theory— which typically carries with it attention to comparative cases and issues of generalizability—sociologists have a special contribution to make to the analysis and interpretation of historically situated phenomena. Theoretically oriented investigation of such phenomena requires research strategies that are sensitive both to context (and, therefore, intensive in nature) and to broad, theoretically relevant patterns and relationships (and, therefore, extensive in nature). This highlights the importance of bridging research strategies that focus on cases and those that focus on general patterns of relationships.

The third basis for anticipating more bridging efforts is a modest trend toward efforts by social scientists to reach broad audiences, including nonacademic audiences. Generally, these audiences are not interested simply in dimensions of macro-social variation and patterns of covariation among structural variables. They are interested in social scientific interpretation of historically and culturally significant processes and outcomes; they seek new perspectives on common origins and common destinies. The market for abstract social science has declined among fellow academics, students, and the general public, and sociologists have published more work of an interpretive or historical nature (e.g., Paul Starr's *The Social Transformation of American Medicine*). This trend has been encouraged by the decline of purely academic publishing and the increased pressure on scholars to write for wider audiences.

Another trend that has contributed to the search for wider audiences is the fact that social scientists have become less bashful about admitting that moral, political, and other social concerns have an impact on problem selection. It is less common today for social scientists to assert that theory alone dictates problem choice. Social scientists study things that matter to them and to their audiences. After all, as Weber (1949) argued eloquently, it is not wrong to let your values influence your choice of research question as long as they do not dictate the answer. Writing for wider audiences involves more attention to historically situated phenomena, to political context, and to matters of wide public concern, and less attention to generic features of social phenomena and processes. As previously argued, attention to context encourages intensive investigation. At the same time, such work becomes more connected to social science theory when analysis and interpretation draw on a knowledge base provided by extensive investigation.

The fourth and final basis for anticipating more efforts to bridge intensive and extensive work in comparative social science is that social scientists in the United States have become more aware of the uniqueness of the United States and of the fact that any study that focuses exclusively on the United States is limited. The theoretical perspectives of the 1950s and 1960s (e.g., convergence theory, evolutionary theory, structural-functional theory, and modernization theory) were highly compatible with a world dominated by a single country. To simplify a great deal, these perspectives argued that there was a universal modern culture (as exemplified by U.S. society) and that all countries were moving in the direction of that culture. Thus implicit in the work of many social scientists was the idea that the United States presented the rest of the world a likely path of future development and that the study of the United States, therefore, had universal relevance.

The realities of the late twentieth century challenge this view as essentially anticultural, ahistorical, and elitist. The United States, while still an advanced country, has declined in importance in the world economy and is less dominant militarily and politically as well. This new awareness of the altered geopolitical context not only demands more attention to other countries by U.S. social scientists, but also argues in favor of contextualizing the results of all research whether or not it is explicitly comparative. In short, it makes intensive work on the United States (or any other country) seem incomplete in the absence of background knowledge of cross-national variation and of global patterns and trends.

To summarize: Changes in the discipline, in problem selection, in audiences, and in the geopolitical context of U.S. social science have challenged sociologists to pay more attention to cross-national diversity, to address historically situated social phenomena, and to contextualize their findings. These changes argue in favor of greater efforts to bridge intensive and extensive work—to find new ways to bring the two styles of comparative work together.

BUILDING THE BRIDGE

I. The Unity of Comparative Social Science

The identification of key elements that link different kinds of comparative social science is central to the task of bridging them. What characteristic features define comparative social science? One way to address this question is first to provide a comprehensive scheme that systematically elaborates different types of comparative work and then to identify the most basic commonality.

Various scholars have proposed different schemes for describing types of investigations included under the heading of comparative social science. They range from the simplistic dichotomy presented here (intensive versus extensive study; also called case-oriented versus variable-oriented; see Ragin 1987) to elaborate schemes embracing multiple and overlapping categories (see, e.g., Skocpol and Sommers 1980). Intermediate between these two is the one proposed by Kohn in the introduction to this collection, which focuses less on research strategies per se (e.g., "variation-finding," as in Tilly 1984) and more on general types of comparative investigation.

Kohn's scheme has four main categories and one minor. The four main categories include two labeled here as intensive: countries as objects and countries as contexts. In the first, cases are selected and studied because they are intrinsically interesting; in the second they are chosen for specific theoretical purposes. His third major category is studies with countries as the unit of analysis, which overlaps well with the extensive, variable-oriented category discussed here. (In this discussion I use the term cross-national to describe studies that use countries as the unit of analysis.) His fourth major category is transnational, a clear nod to world-systems theory and other global perspectives and to the possibility that these approaches may entail special methods (see, e.g., Bach 1977; Bergesen 1980). Kohn, however, does not address this fourth major category in any detail and simply emphasizes his favorite, countries as contexts. The minor category is the case study, which is slighted by Kohn because it is not explicitly comparative. The case study qualifies as an intensive strategy according to the logic of the present discussion.

These five categories can be arrayed along a single dimension, with case study at one end and cross-national and the ambiguous category transnational at the other. There is substantial overlap between this unidimensional representation of Kohn's scheme and the intensive-extensive dichotomy. The most troublesome category is the transnational because many studies inspired by transnational perspectives are, in fact, intensive case studies or comparative case studies, and other studies are

TABLE 2.1: Types of Comparative Research

N of Cases	Explanatory Statements Cite:		
	Intrinsic Qualities of Cases	General Features of Cases	Features of a Larger Unit Formed by Cases
One	1. Geertz (1960)	4. Dumont (1970)	7. Chirot (1976)
Several	2. Bendix (1978)	5. Moore (1966)	8. Moulder (1977)
Many	3. Collections of case studies (e.g., Lipset and Rokkan 1967)	6. Most pre-1975 quantitative cross-national work in sociology	9. Most post-1975 quantitative cross-national work in sociology

cross-national. Recognition of this anomaly is probably one of the reasons Kohn devoted little attention to this category.

Arraying types of comparative work only according to sample size is unsatisfactory for present purposes because this representation conflates two dimensions. The first dimension is *number of cases* and has three positions: one case, several cases, and many cases. The second dimension concerns the *nature of explanatory statements.* Explanations may cite intrinsic features of cases, general features of cases, or features of the larger unit or system that cases constitute (e.g., the world economy). Studies that use countries as objects typically cite intrinsic features; those that use countries as contexts or as the unit of analysis typically cite general features; and those that are transnational cite features of a larger system. The cross-tabulation of these two dimensions as trichotomies results in nine logically possible types of comparative work, shown in Table 2.1. Cell 2 is identical to Kohn's countries as objects category; cell 5 is his countries as contexts category; cells 6 and 9 represent his countries as the unit of analysis category (my cross-national category); and cells 8 and 9 form his transnational category. Cells 1, 4, and 7 all fit Kohn's case-study category. Differentiating three types of case studies brings some clarity to the mixed bag that this category embraces. Table 2.1 also helps to clarify the transnational category by treating it as a type that is defined by the nature of the explanatory unit, not by any special research style or strategy. Of course, Table 2.1 constitutes only one of many ways to differentiate types of comparative social science. It is useful for present purposes because it presents different types of intensive and extensive research in a way that incorporates and elaborates the major categories of Kohn's scheme. Table 2.1 also presents examples of each of the nine types of comparative research.

At first glance it seems that there is little that might unify these different kinds of work. Cell 1 contains intensive case studies using intrinsic qualities of countries in explanatory statements; cell 9 contains large-N, cross-national studies using features of transnational systems in explanatory statements. There is a major commonality across all nine types, however, that is apparent when these nine types are contrasted with other kinds of social science. *Characteristics of macro-social units appear in explanatory statements in all nine types.* This is a key, unifying feature of comparative social science (see also Ragin 1982, 1987).

This unity is not apparent at first glance. The middle column of Table 2.1 shows studies that are the modal comparative work according to standard treatments (e.g., Przeworski and Teune 1970) because general features of countries appear in explanatory statements. The other two columns contain studies that seem to deviate substantially from this norm. An individualizing case study, for example, might conclude that "the outcome of the Russian Revolution reflects Russian culture," and thus cite intrinsic qualities of a single macro-social unit. At the opposite corner of Table 2.1, a cross-national study might conclude that "countries in the semiperiphery of the world economy experience high levels of labor unrest during periods of hegemony and labor peace in the core," and thus cite characteristics of a larger unit—the world-system—in explanatory statements, and not characteristics of the units in question. These two deviating types of explanation, however, can be reconceptualized in a way that enhances their compatibility with the modal type.

Explanations that cite intrinsic features of cases usually cite unique configurations. Russian culture (the hypothetical explanation of the outcome of the Russian Revolution), for example, is a *unique* combination of *general* cultural elements. Identical cultural elements exist in other countries in different combinations. Thus Russian culture may be intrinsic to Russia and unique, but it can be compared and contrasted with other cultures as one among many possible configurations of general cultural elements. In this light, an important task for the comparativist is to specify precisely the cultural configuration—the special combination of general cultural elements—that make up Russian culture. This provides the primary avenue for the identification of relevant comparative cases. An accumulation of studies of the different cultural forces shaping different political outcomes (conducted by the same investigator or by different scholars) would provide a basis for advancing social scientific knowledge about the effect of culture on political outcomes, despite the fact that each study, in isolation, might be an individualizing case study.

Explanations citing features of larger systems (e.g., the world economy) also can be reconceptualized in a way that makes them more compatible with explanations citing general features of countries. In the transnational example presented above, the explanation cites hegemony and labor peace in core countries (temporally bound phenomena) and semiperipherality of countries (a structural state specific to some countries) as factors explaining high levels of labor unrest in some countries. *Semiperipherality* is a theoretically defined configuration of conditions; it is an ideal type. Countries vary in the *degree* to which they conform to this ideal type (most do not conform) and, among those that do conform, in the *way* that they conform (i.e., they may conform in different ways and for different reasons). In other words, semiperipherality is a general feature of countries that is manifested in varying degrees and in qualitatively different ways. Thus it can be conceived as a general feature expressed in a variety of empirical configurations and can be used as a basis for assessing the relation between level of labor unrest and semi-peripherality (degree and type) during periods of hegemony and labor peace in core countries. This treatment of semiperipherality allows the translation of a transnational explanatory statement into a more conventional explanatory statement—into the modal type in Table 2.1.

Of course, this way of thinking about structural position in the world economy does not carry with it the theoretical idea of a dynamic world-system, but it is a perfectly acceptable usage of the theoretical concept for purposes of empirical investigation. In fact, to carry out a test of the argument (about the occurrence of high levels of labor unrest in the semiperiphery), it would be necessary to operationalize semiperipherality in a way that allowed assessment of the degree to which different countries qualify as *semiperipheral* and the different ways they qualify. Thus ways of thinking and associated operations that follow the dictates of modal comparative social science are central to the research agenda of transnational perspectives.

This reconceptualization of explanations citing intrinsic qualities of countries and of explanations citing transnational phenomena provides a metatheoretical basis for unifying comparative social science. All types of comparative social science in Table 2.1 contribute to a knowledge base that uses general features of countries in explanatory statements. This reconciliation of different kinds of comparative work provides a way to bridge them in the realm of methodology because it highlights the importance of systematic analysis of similarities and differences among countries.

II. Methodological Issues

The methodological gulf between intensive and extensive comparative work is wide. Intensive, case-oriented work typically examines many causal and outcome variables in different configurations in a limited number of cases (e.g., the social origins of democracy in Great Britain, France, and the United States), while extensive, variable-oriented work typically examines only a few variables across a large number of cases (e.g., several measures of economic dependency and development in all underdeveloped countries). To bridge different kinds of comparative social science, it is necessary to develop methodological tools that preserve the intensity of the case-oriented approach, especially its attention to combinations and configurations of causal conditions, when examining many cases. This synthesis combines the strengths of the two approaches and provides as well a way to travel the middle road between generality and complexity (see Ragin and Zaret 1983).

Is it possible to be broadly comparative without disaggregating countries into variables and then focusing only on relations among variables? Is there a methodology appropriate for analyzing systematic similarities and differences among many cases (i.e., more than a mere handful) that allows preservation of the integrity of cases as separate, meaningful, interpretable wholes? The basic problem is to implement methods and strategies that bring some of the logic and character of intensive, small-N research to investigations with larger numbers of cases.

Relevant features of small-N, intensive research that should be preserved in broadly comparative studies include the following:

(1) Their attention to cases as wholes, as configurations of parts. In small-N studies the different parts of a whole (e.g., different characteristics of a country) are defined in relation to each other—in terms of the whole they form. For example, an aspect of a country's political system (e.g., its multiparty character) is understood *in the context of* other features of the country (e.g., its ethnic diversity). This way of approaching cases is not the same as using one aspect to account for another (e.g., as in using degree of ethnic diversity to explain why a multiparty system exists in some countries but not in others). It is a matter of interpretation: Having a multiparty system conveys and signifies different things about a political system depending on whether or not ethnic diversity exists.

(2) Their attention to qualitative outcomes. Small-N studies typically address specific qualitative changes in specific contexts. In some studies the qualitative changes are dramatic (e.g., countries with social revolutions); in others the changes emerge gradually through time (e.g., countries experiencing similar historical transformations of certain institutional arrangements). Often the boundaries of an investigation are set by the universe of relevant qualitative changes (e.g., a study of the causes of postindependence military coups in sub-Saharan Africa).

(3) Their attention to causal conjunctures. Explanations of qualitative changes typically cite *combinations* of conditions—causal conjunctures. The classic example of this kind of explanation is Weber's explanation of

the conditions that combined to give rise to rational capitalism in the West. John Stuart Mill called this type of causation *chemical* because qualitative change emerges from a *combination* of causal agents.

(4) Their attention to causal heterogeneity. In small-N research a typical finding is that different causes combine in different and sometimes contradictory ways to produce roughly similar outcomes in different settings. Barrington Moore, for example, showed how different but comparable conditions combined to produce democratic institutions in Great Britain, France, and the United States. There is no presumption that the same causal factors operate in the same way in all contexts. The effect of any particular causal condition depends on the presence and absence of others, and several different conditions may satisfy a general causal requirement—they may be causally equivalent at a more abstract level. For example, according to Moore (1966) either a civil war or a social revolution may constitute a "revolutionary break with the past," one of the conditions necessary for the emergence of democratic institutions.

(5) Their attention to "deviant" cases and concern for invariance. There is no such thing as error in small-N studies; investigators try to account for *every* case in their attempt to uncover patterned diversity. Cases may deviate from common patterns, but these deviations are identified and explained. Thus, conclusions are not stated in probabilistic terms, and nothing is relegated to the error vector. The goal of unraveling patterned diversity mandates careful attention to cases that deviate from common patterns and gives them a special place in the investigation (e.g., as exceptions that elaborate and embellish general findings).

Most of these features of small-N research are antistatistical. This is obvious for the fifth feature listed above, which argues that probabilistic statements and error vectors usually are not permissible. The other four features are antistatistical in the more limited sense that they structure a research dialogue that is relatively hostile to the world of statistical methodology.

The first feature, for example, argues in essence that no value on any variable (be it categorical or interval) can be understood in isolation, but only in the context of the values of other relevant variables. This principle wreaks havoc on most measurement procedures because it suggests that apparent similarities (e.g., the category *countries with multiparty political systems*) may be epiphenomenal. Most statistical analyses assume that the meaning of a category or a value of a variable is the same across all cases.

The second feature, which asserts an interest in unraveling how causes fit together to generate qualitative change, presents problems for statistical methods to the extent that negative instances of qualitative change are difficult to identify. How large is the set of negative cases of social revolutions? In small-N research it is common to study causal similarities and differences among only positive instances. In statistical parlance this amounts to selecting on the dependent variable (a sin to be avoided) or, worse yet, to using a dependent variable with no variation (a practical impossibility).

The third argues that causes rarely operate in a simple additive fashion; rather, they usually combine and intersect to produce change. In the world of statistical methods, causal combinations are assessed through analysis of statistical interaction. But the most used and most popular statistical techniques are additive, and quantitative researchers are often warned to remove interaction from their models by transforming variables. Interaction models present difficult estimation and specification issues, especially when the number of observations is modest, as is usually the case in cross-national research.

The fourth feature extends the idea of causal conjunctions by arguing that *different* combinations of causes may produce the same outcome. That is—in statistical terminology—there may be several relevant interaction models for a given outcome. The only way to uncover this kind of causal complexity is through techniques that assume maximum causal complexity (i.e., saturated interaction) at the outset and then work backward toward simpler models. Most tests for interaction, however, work from the bottom up—testing second-order interactions, then third-order, and so on. If many causal conditions are relevant, saturated interaction creates an indecipherable mountain of multicollinearity. Also, in most cross-national investigations there are simply too few cases to permit starting with saturated interaction and then working backward toward simpler models.

Thus it is difficult to preserve these five measures of intensive work in a multivariate statistical framework. An alternate framework is available through the logical analysis of configurations of similarities and differences using Boolean algebra, the algebra of logic (see Ragin 1987). Boolean methods of logical comparison represent each case as a combination of causal and outcome conditions. These combinations can be compared with each other and then logically simplified through a bottom-up process of paired comparison. Computer algorithms developed by electrical engineers in the 1950s provide simple techniques for simplifying this type of data (see, e.g., Roth 1975; Mendelson 1970). The data matrix is reformulated as a "truth table," and simplified in a way that parallels the minimization of switching circuits (see Ragin 1987). These minimization procedures mimic case-oriented comparative methods but accomplish the most cognitively demanding task—making multiple comparisons of configurations—through computer algorithms (see Drass and Ragin 1988).

Consider a simple illustration. Skocpol's *States and Social Revolutions* examines six countries and six main causal factors, as shown in Table 2.2.

TABLE 2.2: Simplified Representation of Skocpol's *States and Social Revolutions*

	Conditions for Political Crisis				Conditions for Peasant Insurrection		Social Revolution
	BA	*LL*	*AE*	*IP*	*AC*	*LP*	*SR*
France	1	1	0	1	1	1	1
Russia	1	0	0	1	1	1	1
China	1	1	0	1	1	0	1
Prussia/Gm. 1807	1	0	1	1	0	0	0
Prussia/Gm. 1848	1	0	1	0	0	0	0
Japan	1	0	0	1	0	0	0
England	0	1	1	0	0	0	0

NOTE: BA = bureaucratic, absolutist state; LL = landed commercial class with political leverage; AE = agrarian economy: transition to capitalist agriculture; IP = international pressure (at least moderate); AC = agrarian class structure: agrarian sector composed mainly of peasant smallholders; LP = local politics: peasant communities are relatively autonomous; and SR = social revolution. 1 = Present; 0 = Absent

(This table is based on Skocpol 1979, pp. 155-57; an alternate treatment is provided by Nichols 1986.) From a statistical point of view, this data matrix does not offer many analysis possibilities because there are too few cases relative to the number of independent variables. An additional complication is Skocpol's explicitly combinatorial approach: For social revolution to occur, conditions for political crisis must be combined with conditions for peasant insurrections. This implies an interaction model, which would require even more cases. (A complete test of a model with six-way interaction requires estimation of 64 coefficients.)

Skocpol argues that conditions for political crisis coincide with conditions for peasant insurrection in each of the three positive cases of social revolution but not in the negative cases. As Nichols (1986) has noted, her argument operates at the relatively abstract level of these two macro-variables (state breakdown and peasant insurrection), not at the level of specific conditions. Application of the indirect method of difference (Mill [1843] 1967; Ragin 1987) to combinations of conditions in Table 2.2 leads to the conclusion that there are four necessary conditions for social revolution: a bureaucratic authoritarian state, an incomplete or absent transition to capitalist agriculture, international pressure, and an agrarian sector composed mainly of peasant smallholders. The three positive cases all share this combination, and none of the negative cases displays it.

This "reanalysis" of Skocpol at the level of conditions provides results consistent with her main argument concerning the two macro-variables (state breakdown and peasant insurrection); the conjuncture of these four

TABLE 2.3: Data on Conditions for Social Revolution Drawn from 16 Hypothetical Cases

	Conditions for Political Crisis				Conditions for Peasant Insurrection		Social Revolution
	BA	LL	AE	IP	AC	LP	SR
1.	0	1	1	1	0	1	1
2.	0	1	1	1	1	1	1
3.	1	0	0	1	1	0	1
4.	1	1	0	1	1	1	1
5.	1	0	0	1	1	1	1
6.	1	1	0	1	1	0	1
7.	1	1	1	1	0	1	1
8.	1	1	1	1	1	1	1
9.	0	0	0	1	0	0	0
10.	1	0	1	1	0	0	0
11.	1	0	1	0	0	0	0
12.	1	0	0	1	0	0	0
13.	0	1	1	0	0	0	0
14.	0	0	1	0	0	1	0
15.	0	0	0	0	0	0	0
16.	0	0	1	1	1	0	0

NOTE: BA = bureaucratic, absolutist state; LL = landed commercial class with political leverage; AE = agrarian economy: transition to capitalist agriculture; IP = international pressure (at least moderate); AC = agrarian class structure: agrarian sector composed mainly of peasant smallholders; LP = local politics: autonomous peasant communities; and SR = social revolution. 1 = Present, 0 = Absent

conditions provides an image compatible with historical evidence, as well. If crude statistical methods had been applied to the data, however, and conditions examined one at a time, then a much more parsimonious conclusion would have been reached: that countries with agrarian sectors composed mainly of peasant smallholders experience social revolutions. Clearly, this explanation is unsatisfying from the perspective of both theory and historical evidence—despite its consistency with the evidence in Table 2.2 and its parsimony.

The pattern of Table 2.2 is clear enough; no special procedures are needed to unravel causal complexity. Assume for the moment, however, that Skocpol had eight positive and eight negative cases and that they displayed the combinations of values shown in Table 2.3. Application of the indirect method of difference to the data in this table does not culminate in a single cause or causal conjuncture distinguishing positive from negative cases. The single condition shared by all the positive cases (international pressure) is also found in some of the negative cases. This indicates that there are probably multiple combinations of conditions that result in social revolution. But what are they?

There are several ways to proceed at this point, and different ways of proceeding produce different results. These different results follow from alternate treatments of the 48 logically possible combinations of causes that do not appear in the table. There are 64 logically possible combinations of 6 dichotomies; only 16 appear in the table. If it is assumed that social revolution could not occur in any of the 48 missing combinations, then the table is reduced to a relatively simple logical equation. Using notation from Table 2.2, with uppercase indicating presence and lowercase indicating absence, the logical equation is

$$SR = BA*ae*IP*AC + LL*AE*IP*LP$$

The equation states simply that there are two combinations of conditions that result in social revolution: (1) a bureaucratic absolutist state, a failed or absent transition to capitalist agriculture, international pressure, and an agrarian sector composed mainly of peasant smallholders; and (2) a landed commercial class with political leverage, a successful transition to capitalist agriculture, international pressure, and relatively autonomous peasant communities.

Systematic holistic analysis of cases as configurations of causes and outcomes is the essence of case-oriented comparative work. When the number of cases and configurations is great, it is a cognitively demanding task, especially in the absence of algorithms to aid the researcher. The formalization of holistic comparative methods sketched here (and explained in detail in Ragin 1987) allows the preservation of essential features of case-oriented work in the analysis of many cases and provides an important methodological bridge between intensive and extensive work. It brings some of the intensity of case-oriented work to extensive investigation. Furthermore, this technique of holistic comparison is highly compatible with a comparative social science oriented toward examination of general features of cases and thus complements metatheoretical arguments presented above concerning the unity of comparative social science.

THE DECADES AHEAD

The creative bridging of intensive and extensive comparative work can take many forms; only a few lines have been sketched here. A key part of the bridging effort is the task of linking case studies. This can be accomplished in several ways. A single researcher can try to achieve familiarity with a range of cases and then attempt to link them in the course of the investigation. This might be termed the *Max Weber* model of comparative work because in-depth knowledge of many cases is required. An alternate way to accomplish this linking is for a single scholar to take on the role of synthesizer and rely on the expertise of country and area specialists. This might be termed the *project* model of comparative work because it requires the involvement of a large number of scholars as consultants in a single project. A third way to link case studies is through more intense and more regular interaction among scholars applying similar models or ideas to different cases. This third model, which might be termed the *collective* model, requires the prior coalescence and ascendance of a relatively small number of guiding questions or research agendas. Isolated scholars working on similar issues applied to different countries could meet to examine commonalities across sets of cases.

If the examination of each case is considered a separate analysis, then comparative analysis can be seen as a type of meta-analysis. The three different ways of linking case studies just described lay out different ways of performing meta-analysis: (1) by a single scholar in isolation, (2) by a single scholar assisted by country and area specialists, and (3) by a group of scholars working as equals. The current organization of academic labor discourages the first and third approaches. The first is discouraged because universities as organizations (1) encourage greater and greater specialization (knowing more and more about less and less) and (2) have reward structures that tend to favor short-term projects. The third is unlikely because social scientists, like other academics, are in constant competition with each other and seek to establish individual reputations and niches. Therefore, they are forever trying to separate their research agendas from each other. The second vehicle for performing meta-analysis (the project model) is the most feasible. It requires the financial support of universities, foundations, or other funding agencies, however.

The linking of intensive and extensive work is the key to a healthy and vibrant comparative social science. Bridging these two kinds of work provides a way to comprehend differences and similarities among many cases in a coherent framework and also allows preservation of the integrity of cases as configurations of meaningfully related parts.

REFERENCES

Bach, Robert. 1977. "Methods of Analysis in the Study of the World Economy: A Comment on Rubinson." *American Sociological Review* 42:811-14.

Bendix, Reinhard. 1978. *Kings or People: Power and the Mandate to Rule.* Berkeley: University of California Press.

Bergesen, Albert. 1980. "From Utilitarianism to the World-System: The Shift from the Individual to the World as a Whole as the Primordial Unit of Analysis." Pp. 1-12 in *Studies of the Modern World-Systems*, edited by A. Bergesen. New York: Academic Press.

Chirot, Daniel. 1976. *Social Change in a Peripheral Society: The Creation of a Balkan Colony*. New York: Academic Press.

Drass, Kriss and Charles Ragin. 1988. *QCA: Qualitative Comparative Analysis*. Evanston, IL: Northwestern University, Center for Urban Affairs and Policy Research.

Dumont, Louis. 1970. *Homo Hierarchicus: The Caste System and Its Implications*. Chicago: University of Chicago Press.

Evans, Peter B., Dietrich Rueschemeyer, and Theda Skocpol. 1985. *Bringing the State Back in*. New York: Cambridge University Press.

Geertz, Clifford. 1960. *The Religion of Java*. London: Free Press, Collier-Macmillan.

Lipset, Seymour Martin. 1963. *The First New Nation: The United States in Comparative and Historical Perspective*. New York: Basic Books.

Lipset, Seymour Martin and Stein Rokkan. 1967. *Party Systems and Voter Alignments*. New York: Free Press.

Mendelson, Elliot. 1970. *Boolean Algebra and Switching Circuits*. New York: McGraw-Hill.

Mill, John Stuart. [1843] 1967. *A System of Logic: Ratiocinative and Inductive*. Toronto: University of Toronto Press.

Moore, Barrington, Jr. 1966. *Social Origins of Dictatorship and Democracy: Lord and Peasant in the Making of the Modern World*. Boston: Beacon.

Moulder, Frances. 1977. *Japan, China, and the Modern World Economy: Toward a Reinterpretation of East Asian Development ca. 1600 to ca. 1918*. New York: Cambridge University Press.

Nichols, Elizabeth. 1986. "Skocpol on Revolution: Comparative Analysis vs. Historical Conjuncture." *Comparative Social Research* 9:163-86.

Nisbet, Robert. 1969. *Social Change and History: Aspects of the Western Theory of Development*. New York: Oxford University Press.

Przeworski, Adam and Henry Teune. 1970. *The Logic of Comparative Social Inquiry*. New York: Wiley-Interscience.

Ragin, Charles. 1982. "Comparative Sociology and the Comparative Method." Pp. 102-20 in *Comparative Sociology in the 1960s and 1970s*, edited by M. Armer and R. Marsh. Leiden: E. J. Brill.

———. 1987. *The Comparative Method: Moving Beyond Qualitative and Quantitative Strategies*. Berkeley: University of California Press.

Ragin, Charles and David Zaret. 1983. "Theory and Method in Comparative Research: Two Strategies." *Social Forces* 61:731-54.

Roth, Charles, 1975. *Fundamentals of Logic Design*. St. Paul: West.

Skocpol, Theda. 1979. *States and Social Revolutions: A Comparative Analysis of France, Russia, and China*. Cambridge: Cambridge University Press.

———, ed. 1984. *Vision and Method in Historical Sociology*. New York: Cambridge University Press.

Skocpol, Theda and Margaret Sommers. 1980. "The Uses of Comparative History in Macrosocial Inquiry." *Comparative Studies in Society and History* 22:174-97.

Smelser, Neil J. 1959. *Social Change in the Industrial Revolution: An Application of Theory to the British Cotton Industry*. Chicago: University of Chicago Press.

Starr, Paul. 1982. *The Social Transformation of American Medicine*. New York: Basic Books.

Tilly, Charles. 1984. *Big Structures, Large Processes, Huge Comparisons*. New York: Russell Sage.

Weber, Max. 1949. *The Methodology of the Social Sciences*. New York: Free Press.

3

Cross-National Research as an Analytic Strategy

Melvin L. Kohn

In this chapter, I discuss some of the uses and some of the dilemmas of cross-national research. I argue that cross-national research is valuable, even indispensable, for establishing the generality of findings and the validity of interpretations derived from single-nation studies. In no other way can we be certain that what we believe to be social-structural regularities are not merely particularities, the product of some limited set of historical or cultural or political circumstances. I also argue that cross-national research is equally valuable, perhaps even more valuable, for forcing us to revise our interpretations to take account of cross-national differences and inconsistencies that could never be uncovered in single-nation research.

My thesis is that cross-national research provides an especially useful method for generating, testing, and further developing sociological theory. As with any research strategy, cross-national research comes at a price: It is costly in time and money; it is difficult to do; it often seems to raise more interpretive problems than it solves. Yet it is potentially invaluable and, in my judgment, grossly underutilized.

AUTHOR'S NOTE: *I am indebted to my collaborators in cross-national research: Carmi Schooler, Kazimierz M. Slomczynski, Joanne Miller, Carrie Schoenbach, Atsushi Naoi, and (some years ago) Leonard I. Pearlin; to the sponsors of the Polish and Japanese studies: Wlodzimierz Wesolowski and Ken'ichi Tominaga; and to colleagues who have critiqued one or another version of this chapter: Stephen G. Bunker, Christopher Chase-Dunn, Andrew J. Cherlin, Bernard M. Finifter, William H. Form, Jonathan Kelley, Janet G. Kohn, Tadeusz Krauze, John W. Meyer, Joanne Miller, Jeylan T. Mortimer, Alejandro Portes, Carrie Schoenbach, Carmi Schooler, Theda Skocpol, Kazimierz M. Slomczynski, Katherine Verdery, and Wlodzimierz Wesolowski.*

I shall illustrate the uses and dilemmas of cross-national research by scrutinizing the body of cross-national research I know best, namely, my own, my rationale being William Form's (1979) cogent observation that "probably no field has generated more methodological advice on a smaller data base with fewer results than has [cross-national] comparative sociology." Using my research as a source of illustrations makes it possible to discuss the issues concretely. I review this research in sufficient detail to highlight its accomplishments and its failures, my concern being only in part with the substance of the research for its own sake; I also want to extrapolate from this concrete example, to make some more general observations. Finally, I discuss some fundamental issues about the conduct of cross-national research. In so doing, I bring in studies dealing with quite different substantive problems from those that I have addressed in my own research, and using quite different methods, to see whether my conclusions apply as well to a much broader range of studies.

ESTABLISHING THE GENERALITY OF
RELATIONSHIPS AND
THE LIMITS OF GENERALITY

Many discussions of cross-national research (Ragin and Zaret 1983 is a thoughtful example) contrast two research *strategies*—one that looks for statistical regularities, another that searches for cultural or historical differences. I prefer to pose the distinction, not in terms of research strategies, nor of methodological preferences, nor even of theoretical proclivities toward "transhistorical" generalizations or "historically contextualized knowledge," but in terms of interpreting the two basic types of research *findings*—similarities and differences. Granted, investigators' theoretical and methodological preferences make it more or less likely that they will discover cross-national similarities; granted, too, what can be treated as a similarity at one level of analysis can be thought of as myriad differences at more detailed levels of analysis. Still, the critical issue is how to interpret similarities, and how to interpret differences, when you find them.

Finding cross-national similarities greatly extends the scope of sociological knowledge. Moreover, cross-national similarities lend themselves readily to sociological interpretation; cross-national differences are much more difficult to interpret. As Kazimierz Slomczynski, Joanne Miller, and I argued (albeit a little too categorically) in our first comparative analysis of the United States and Poland (1981, p. 740):

Insofar as cross-national analyses of social structure and personality yield similar findings in the countries studied, our interpretation can ignore whatever differences there may be in the cultures, political and economic systems, and historical circumstances of the particular countries, to deal instead with social-structural universals. But when the relationships between social structure and personality differ from country to country, then we must look to what is idiosyncratic about the particular countries for our interpretation.

The first half of this formulation asserts that when the relationship between social structure and personality is the *same* in two or more countries, then the unique historical experiences of each country, their distinctive cultures, and their particular political systems are not of focal importance for interpreting the relationship. The formulation does *not* assert that history, culture, and political context have been irrelevant in shaping social structures, but that the resultant social structures have a cross-nationally consistent impact on people. The explanation of this impact should be sought in terms of how people experience the resultant social structures, rather than in the historical or cultural processes that shaped those structures.

Admittedly, this may not always be the best interpretive strategy. Apparent similarities can mask profound differences; what seems to call for a unitary interpretation may actually require entirely different explanations. Nevertheless, I believe that where we find cross-national similarities, the most efficient strategy in searching for an explanation is to focus on what is structurally similar in the countries being compared, not on the often divergent historical processes that produced these social-structural similarities. Social-structural similarities may have been brought about by very different historical processes and yet have essentially similar social and psychological consequences.

The second half of the formulation directs us to interpret cross-national *differences* in terms of historical, cultural, political, or economic idiosyncrasies. Przeworski and Teune (1970) argued that what appear to be cross-national differences may really be instances of lawful regularities, if thought of in terms of some larger, more encompassing interpretation. I agree, but I also believe that developing such interpretations is an immensely difficult task. A necessary first step is to try to discover which of the many differences in history, culture, and political or economic systems that distinguish any two countries are pertinent to explaining the differences we find in their social structures or in how these social structures affect people's lives. I do not contend that cross-national differences cannot be lawfully explained—quite the contrary—but only that the lawful explanation of cross-national differences requires more explicit consideration of historical, cultural, and political-economic particularities than does the lawful explanation of cross-national similarities.

Ultimately, the distinction between cross-national similarities and differences breaks down, and the issues cannot be so simply and neatly dichotomized. Nonetheless, it is a useful way to think about these issues. Therefore, I shall discuss the two types of cross-national research findings separately, beginning with cross-national similarities. I use the U.S.–Polish and U.S.–Japanese comparisons that my collaborators and I have carried out as my principal illustrations both of cross-national similarities and of cross-national differences, my substantive concern in this part of the chapter being the relationship between social structure and personality. The conclusions I draw are by no means limited to this substantive area.

CROSS-NATIONAL SIMILARITIES

Over the course of three decades of research in the United States, Carmi Schooler and I, in collaboration with Joanne Miller, Karen A. Miller, Carrie Schoenbach, and Ronald Schoenberg, have intensively studied the psychological impact of social stratification—by which we mean the hierarchical distribution of power, privilege, and prestige (Kohn 1969; Kohn and Schooler 1983). We interpret the consistent relationships that we have found between social stratification and such facets of personality as values, orientations to self and others, and cognitive functioning as the product, in large part, of the intimate relationship between social stratification and particular job conditions. People of higher social-stratification position (as indexed by educational attainment, occupational status, and job income) enjoy greater opportunities to be self-directed in their work—that is, to work at jobs that are substantively complex, free from close supervision, and not highly routinized. The experience of occupational self-direction, in turn, is conducive to valuing self-direction, both for oneself and for one's children, to having self-conceptions and social orientations consonant with such values, and to effective intellectual functioning. It is even conducive to seeking out opportunities for engaging in intellectually active leisure-time pursuits (K. Miller and Kohn 1983). All this is true both for employed men and for employed women (J. Miller, Schooler, Kohn, and K. Miller 1979; Kohn and Schooler 1983; Kohn, Slomczynski, and Schoenbach 1986).

Structural-equation analyses of longitudinal data have enabled us to confirm even that part of the interpretation that posits a causal impact of job conditions on personality (Kohn and Schooler 1978, 1982; Kohn and Schoenbach 1983). These analyses show the relationships to be reciprocal, with job conditions both affecting and being affected by personality. Moreover, analyses of housework (Schooler, Kohn, Miller, and Miller 1983) and of education (K. Miller, Kohn, and Schooler 1985, 1986) demonstrate that the experience of self-direction, not only in paid employment, but also in housework and schoolwork, decidedly affects people's self-conceptions, social orientations, and cognitive functioning. The interpretation has considerable generality.

In the absence of appropriate cross-national evidence, though, there would be no way of knowing whether this (or any other) interpretation applies outside the particular historical, cultural, and political contexts of the United States. No analyses based solely on U.S. data could tell us whether the relationships between social stratification and personality are an integral part of the social-stratification system typical of industrial societies, or are to be found only in the United States, or only in countries that have capitalist economies, or only in countries characterized by Western culture, with its purportedly higher valuation of self-direction. Replications of our research by colleagues in other countries (for a review, see Kohn and Schooler 1983, chap. 12), particularly the comprehensive replications that have been carried out by our Polish and Japanese colleagues (Slomczynski et al. 1981; Naoi and Schooler 1985), have made possible tests of the generality of the U.S. findings and of the validity of our interpretation. In the main, these findings are highly consistent with those for the United States, thus greatly enlarging the power of the interpretation.

Of pivotal importance here are the Polish–U.S. comparisons, particularly the comparative analyses of men, for whom the Polish study contains more complete occupational data. The principal issue to which these analyses are addressed is the specificity or generality of the U.S. findings about the linkages of social stratification to job conditions, and of job conditions to personality. Are these linkages specific to the economic and social structures of capitalist society, or do they obtain as well in socialist society?

We have found, for Poland as for the United States, that higher social-stratification position is associated with valuing self-direction, with holding social orientations consonant with such a value—namely, a nonauthoritarian, open-minded orientation, personally responsible standards of morality, and trustfulness (Slomczynski et al. 1981)—and with effective intellectual functioning (Slomczynski and Kohn 1988). We have further found a strong reciprocal relationship, for Poland as for the United States, between social-stratification position and occupational self-direction (Slomczynski et al. 1981). Finally, insofar as possible with cross-sectional data, we have shown for Poland, too, a causal impact of occupational self-direction on values, social orientations, and intellectual functioning (Slomczynski et al. 1981; Kohn et al. forthcoming). Self-direction in one's work leads to valuing self-direction for one's children, to having a more open, flexible orientation to society, and to effective intellectual functioning. The lack of opportunity for self-direction in one's work leads to valuing conformity to external authority for one's children, to viewing social reality as hostile and threatening, and to diminished intellectual flexibility. The effects of social stratification on job conditions, and of job conditions on personality, are much the same in socialist Poland as in the capitalist United States.

This does not mean that these processes are necessarily the same in all socialist and all capitalist societies, but it does mean that the U.S. findings are not restricted to capitalist countries. There is solid evidence, instead, that the interpretive model developed for the United States applies to at least one socialist society.

The United States and Poland, of course, are both Western societies. Are the processes similar in non-Western societies? The Japanese study provides an excellent test of whether our interpretation of the U.S. and Polish findings applies as well to a non-Western industrialized society. In the main, the findings for Japan are markedly consistent with those for the United States and Poland. Social-stratification position is related to values, to social orientations, and to cognitive functioning in the same way, although perhaps not to quite the same degree, as in the United States and Poland (Kohn et al. forthcoming). Occupational self-direction has markedly similar effects on psychological functioning in Japan as in the West (Naoi and Schooler 1985). Thus, despite pronounced cultural differences, and despite the sharper division between the primary and secondary sectors of the economy in Japan, the linkages of social stratification to occupational self-direction, and of occupational self-direction to personality, are much the same in Japan as in the United States and Poland. The U.S. and Polish findings are not limited to Western society. Here, again, a single cross-national comparison yields immense benefits for our ability to test the generality of a set of empirical relationships and their interpretation.

Moreover, because the United States, Poland, and Japan are such diverse societies, the set of three studies provides prima facie evidence that the psychological impact of social stratification is much the same, and for much the same reasons, in all industrialized societies. Admittedly, negative evidence from research in any industrialized society would require a modification of this hypothesis or a restriction of its generality. Admittedly, too, the interpretation speaks only to existing societies. We can say nothing from this evidence as to whether it would be possible for there to be an industrialized society in which one or another link in the explanatory chain is broken—a society with a less pronounced system of social stratification; a society in which social-stratification position is not so intimately linked with opportunities for occupational self-direction; even a society where occupational self-direction has less impact on personality. Nevertheless, the Polish and Japanese studies do tell us that in decidedly diverse societies—arguably, in all industrialized societies— social stratification is associated with values, social orientations, and cognitive functioning, in large part because people of higher position have greater opportunity to be self-directed in their work.

In studying social stratification, I am, of course, dealing with a feature of social structure that is notably similar in all industrialized societies (Treiman 1977). I would like to extend the argument a bit, to suggest that even where some feature of social structure is not "identical" in all the countries being compared but only "equivalent," it is still possible to find cross-nationally consistent relationships between contemporaneous social structure and personality. More than that, it is still appropriate to interpret these consistent relationships in terms of contemporaneous social structure, however much that feature of social structure has been shaped by the particular histories and cultures of those countries.

My illustration here comes from our analysis of position in the class structure and personality in the United States, Japan, and Poland (Kohn et al. forthcoming). For all three countries, we have adapted the same basic idea to the particular historical, cultural, economic, and political circumstances of the country—the idea being that social classes are to be distinguished in terms of ownership and control of the means of production, and control over the labor power of others. (For Poland, where *ownership* of the means of production is not a primary desideratum of class, *control* over the means of production and over the labor power of others is our primary criterion of class position.) The guiding hypothesis is that, in all three countries, those who are more advantageously situated in the class structure are more self-directed in their values and orientations, and are more intellectually flexible, than are those who are less advantageously situated. Our further hypothesis, paralleling what we have learned for social stratification, is that in all three countries the explanation lies mainly in the greater opportunities for occupational self-direction enjoyed by those who are more advantaged in class position. The hypotheses, then, are simple extrapolations to social class from what we have consistently found to be the psychological impact of social stratification; the new element is the much greater country-to-country variability of class structures than of stratification systems.

Both hypotheses are confirmed. All three countries can be meaningfully thought to have class structures; class position has similar effects on cognitive functioning, values, and orientation in all three countries; and class affects these facets of psychological functioning for essentially the same reason—because of the intimate relationship between position in the class structure and opportunities afforded for occupational self-direction. Hence, to extrapolate, it is no bar to structural interpretation that social structures have been shaped by distinctly different historical processes.

CROSS-NATIONAL DIFFERENCES

Interpreting differences, as I said earlier, is where things become much less certain and much more difficult. The key, of course, is the truism that, if consistent findings have to be interpreted in terms of what is common to the countries studied, then inconsistent findings have to be interpreted in terms of how the countries—or the studies—differ. This truism, unfortunately, gives no clue as to which of the many differences between countries or between studies lies at the heart of the differences in findings. Prudence dictates that the first hypothesis one entertains is that the inconsistent findings are somehow a methodological artifact. As Bernard Finifter (1977, p. 155) noted,

> There is a curious inconsistency in the way researchers interpret results from attempted replications when discrepancies crop up. Failure to reproduce a finding in the *same* culture usually leads the investigator to question the reliability, validity, and comparability of the research procedures used in the two studies for possible method artifacts. But failure to corroborate the same finding in a *different* culture often leads to claims of having discovered "cultural" differences, and substantive interpretations are promptly devised to account for the apparent differences.

Issues of method. The most fundamental methodological issue is whether the concepts employed in the analyses are truly equivalent. Stefan Nowak (1976, p. 105) posed the issue with characteristic clarity:

> How do we know we are studying "the same phenomena" in different contexts; how do we know that our observations and conclusions do not actually refer to "quite different things", which we unjustifiably include into the same conceptual categories? Or if they seem to be different, are they really different with respect to the same (qualitatively or quantitatively understood) variable, or is our conclusion about the difference between them scientifically meaningless? (See also Almond and Verba 1963, pp. 57-72; Scheuch 1967, 1968; Smelser 1968; Nowak 1977; Marsh 1967; Armer 1973)

The issue is so complex that a thorough treatment would require quite another essay. In this chapter, instead, I simply assume equivalence of concepts and go on to consider more mundane methodological differences.

In principle, methodological differences between studies could produce either consistent or inconsistent findings (Finifter 1977). Still, when one finds cross-national similarities despite differences in research design, even despite defects in some of the studies, it is unlikely that the similar findings were actually produced by the methodological differences. Substantive similarity in the face of methodological dissimilarity might even argue for the robustness of the findings. But when one finds cross-national differences, then dissimilarities and defects in research design make for an interpretive quagmire—there is no way to be certain whether the apparent cross-national differences are real or artifactual.

To obviate the possibility that differences in findings are merely an artifact of differences in method—in the nature of the samples, in the meaning of the questions asked, in the completeness of data, in measurement—one tries to design the studies to be comparable, to establish both linguistic and conceptual equivalence in questions and in coding answers, and to establish truly equivalent indices of the underlying concepts (Scheuch 1968). Edward Suchman (1964, p. 135) long ago stated the matter with elegant simplicity: "A good design for the collection of comparative data should permit one to assume as much as possible that the differences observed . . . cannot be attributed to the differences in the method being used." Unfortunately, one can never be certain. The best that is possible is to try to establish damage control—to present whatever evidence one can that methodological incomparables are not so great as to explain the differences in findings. Short of that, it remains a gnawing doubt.

My colleagues and I have written extensively about the technical issues in achieving true cross-national comparability, particularly those involved in interviewing and in index construction (J. Miller, Slomczynski, and Schoenberg 1981; Slomczynski et al. 1981; J. Miller et al. 1985; Kohn et al. 1986). So, too, have many other scholars (see, in particular, Nowak's chapter in this volume; Scheuch 1968; Przeworski and Teune 1970; Armer 1973; Elder 1976; Kuechler 1987). Therefore, I do not discuss these issues further in this chapter. Instead, I assume comparability of methods (as well as comparability of concepts) and go on to the equally perplexing *substantive* issues in interpreting cross-national differences.

Substantive interpretations of cross-national differences. Finding a cross-national difference often requires that we curtail the scope of an interpretation, by limiting our generalizations to *exclude* implicated variables or relationships or types of countries from a more encompassing generalization. Ultimately, though, we want to *include* the discrepant findings in a more comprehensive interpretation, by reformulating the interpretation on a more general level that accounts for both similarities and differences. Thus, although the discovery of cross-national differences may initially require that we make a less sweeping interpretation, in time and with thought it can lead to more general and more powerful interpretations.

I wish that I could offer from my research an example of a powerful reinterpretation derived from coming to terms with cross-national differences. Instead, I can only share with you my dilemma in still not fully understanding some differences that I have been struggling to understand for some years. I may not thereby convince you that discovering cross-national differences necessarily leads to new understanding, but I shall certainly convince you that the discovery of such differences forces one to question generalizations made on the basis of studying only one country. To illustrate, I use the most perplexing cross-national inconsistencies that we have found in the U.S.–Polish–Japanese comparisons (Kohn et al. forthcoming).

Quite in contrast to our consistent findings about the relationship of social stratification to other facets of personality, we have found a decided inconsistency in the relationship between social stratification and a principal underlying dimension of orientations to self and others—namely, a sense of well-being *versus* distress.[1] In the United States, higher stratification position *decreases* feelings of distress (r = −0.18); in Japan, there is virtually no relationship between social stratification and feelings of distress (r = −0.01); and in Poland, higher stratification position *increases* feelings of distress (r = +0.15). The magnitude of the correlation is not great in any country, but the inconsistency in direction of relationship is striking. This is similar for social *class*: In the United States, members of more advantaged social classes, managers in particular, have a greater sense of well-being; members of less advantaged social classes, blue-collar workers in particular, have a greater sense of distress. In Poland, quite the opposite: It is the managers who are more distressed, the blue-collar workers who have a greater sense of well-being. In Japan, as in the United States, managers have a strong sense of well-being, but it is the *white*-collar—not the blue-collar—workers who are most distressed.

---

[1] Second-order confirmatory factor analyses demonstrate that there are two underlying dimensions to the several facets of orientation to self and society indexed in our studies: (1) *Self-directedness of orientation*, which implies the beliefs that one has the personal capacity to take responsibility for one's actions and that society is so constituted as to make self-direction possible, is reflected in not having authoritarian conservative beliefs, in having personally responsible standards of morality, in being trustful of others, in not being self-deprecatory, in not being conformist in one's ideas, and in not being fatalistic. (2) *Distress* is reflected in anxiety, self-deprecation, lack of self-confidence, nonconformity in one's ideas, and distrust. (See Kohn and Schooler 1982, 1983, chap. 6.)

Why don't advantageous positions in the stratification and class systems have cross-nationally consistent effects on the sense of distress? On one level, this question is readily answered: Our analyses show that stratification and class matter for psychological functioning primarily because people of more advantaged position have greater opportunity to be self-directed in their work. But we find, in causal models of the reciprocal effects of occupational self-direction and distress, that although occupational self-direction has a statistically significant effect (negative, of course) on the sense of distress for the United States and Japan, it has no effect at all for Poland. This is in marked contrast to the cross-nationally consistent effects of occupational self-direction on intellectual flexibility, values, and self-directedness of orientation. One can, in fact, incorporate the cross-national inconsistency into an encompassing generalization: Where occupational self-direction has cross-nationally consistent effects on psychological functioning, so too do social stratification and social class; where occupational self-direction fails to have consistent effects, stratification and class also have inconsistent effects.

On another level, though, the question persists: *Why* doesn't occupational self-direction ameliorate distress in Poland, as it does in the United States and Japan? Moreover, occupational self-direction does not provide as effective an explanation of the relationships of stratification and class with distress in *any* of the three countries as it does for their relationships with other facets of personality in *all* three countries. Given the rather substantial effect of occupational self-direction on distress for the United States, we might well expect a higher correlation of social stratification with distress than the −0.18 that we actually do find. We should *certainly* expect a higher correlation than the −0.01 that we actually do find for Japan. We should expect *no* relationship, not a positive relationship, for Poland. Clearly, more than occupational self-direction is involved in explaining the relationships of stratification and class to distress. My formulation, which implies that occupational self-direction, and therefore also stratification and class, would have an impact on feelings of distress consistent with its impact on values, self-directedness of orientation, and cognitive functioning, must be revised.

It is not at all certain from the evidence at hand, though, whether the interpretation requires minor revision or extensive overhaul. I am reasonably certain that the cross-national differences are not merely a methodological artifact, for example, in the conceptualization or measurement of distress. In particular, the cross-national differences are found, not only in analyses using the "higher-order" concept, distress, but also in analyses using the "first-order" concepts, notably self-confidence and anxiety. The issues are substantive, not methodological.

In any reformulation, it is essential that we not lose sight of the fundamental principle that any explanation of cross-national differences must also be consistent with the cross-national similarities. To be valid, any explanation has to explain why we find cross-national inconsistencies only for the sense of distress, not for values, for self-directedness of orientation, or for cognitive functioning. Explanations so broadly framed as to lead one to expect Polish or Japanese men of more advantaged position to value conformity for their children, to have a conformist orientation to self and society, or not to be intellectually flexible could not be valid. Nor would it make any sense to explain the findings in terms of a weaker linkage of social stratification or of social class to occupational self-direction in Poland or in Japan than in the United States, or in terms of occupational self-direction being any less important for Polish or Japanese men than for U.S. men.

As I see it, there are at least five ways that my interpretation might be reformulated:

The simplest reformulation would be to limit the scope of the interpretation to exclude the sense of distress; for as yet unknown reasons, an interpretation that does apply to cognitive functioning, to values, and to self-directedness of orientation seems not to apply to the affective realm. This reformulation simply curtails the scope of my interpretation, until such time as we are able to develop a more general interpretation that incorporates the cross-national differences along with the cross-national similarities.

A second type of reformulation would posit that the psychological mechanisms by which job conditions affect distress may be different from those by which job conditions affect cognitive functioning, values, and self-directedness of orientation. Such a reformulation might or might not emphasize job conditions different from those that I have emphasized; it certainly would posit different *processes* by which job conditions affect personality. Mine is a learning-generalization model: People learn from their job experiences and apply those lessons to nonoccupational realms of life (Kohn forthcoming). One could argue that the inconsistent effects of occupational self-direction on the sense of distress raise questions as to whether a learning-generalization model applies to this facet of personality. Perhaps, instead, one should employ some other model of psychological process—a "stress" model is the obvious candidate—for understanding the effects of job on the sense of distress. The "stress" model posits that job conditions affect personality, in whole or in part, because they induce feelings of stress, which in turn have longer-term, off-the-job psychological consequences, such as anxiety and distress. Clearly, "stress" is a plausible link from job conditions to distress. But I think the evidence for a "stress" model, even when applied only to anxiety and distress, is less than compelling (Kohn forthcoming); moreover, positing different mechanisms for different facets of personality would be, at best, inelegant.

A related possibility, one that is much more to my liking, retains the learning-generalization model but expands the range of pertinent job conditions. This reformulation begins with the U.S. finding that job conditions other than those directly involved in occupational self-direction are more important for distress than for other facets of personality (Kohn and Schooler 1982, 1983, chap. 6). *Some* of these job conditions are related to stratification and class, and thus might explain the effects—or lack of effects—of stratification and class on distress. The crux of this reformulation is the hypothesis that the effects of these other job conditions on distress may be at odds with, and perhaps more important than, those of occupational self-direction.

We have some pertinent, albeit limited, evidence that lends credence to this possibility (Kohn et al. forthcoming). In the United States, for example, job protections (such as seniority provisions in union contracts) ameliorate distress. Nonetheless, the very people who at the time of our interviews enjoyed the greatest job protections—the blue-collar workers—were also the most distressed. Blue-collar workers were distressed *because* they lacked opportunities for occupational self-direction and *despite* the job protections that many of them, particularly union members, enjoyed. Occupational self-direction and job protections seem to have countervailing effects—which may account for the relatively modest relationships of both social stratification and social class with distress, even in the United States.

For Japan, we find that believing that one works under pressure of time, and believing that people in one's occupation are at risk of being held responsible for things outside of their control, are both related to distress. Although these findings may merely reflect a propensity of distressed people to overestimate the pressures and uncertainties of their jobs, it is at least a plausible hypothesis that such job conditions do increase distress. Our causal models suggest as well that either education itself or job conditions related to education increase distress. The countervailing effects of occupational self-direction, education, and other job conditions correlated with them both may help explain why stratification and class have so little net effect on distress in Japan.

For Poland, we lack the data to test whether *manual workers'* low levels of distress result from their extraordinary job protections. We do, however, have one fascinating bit of information that may help explain what it is about the conditions of life experienced by Polish *managers* that makes them more distressed than members of other social classes, quite in contrast to the situation of managers in the United States and Japan. We find that one segment of the Polish managerial class is particularly distressed—those managers who are not members of the Polish United Workers (Communist) party. There are too few nonparty managers for this finding to be definitive, but I think it suggestive that the nonparty managers have decidedly higher levels of distress, compared not only to managers who are members of the party, but also compared to members of any other social class, party members or not. The implication, I think, is that being a nonparty manager in the Polish system of centralized planning entails uncertainties, risks, and insecurities—greater than those experienced by managers who are members of the party, and greater than those experienced by managers in the less centralized systems of capitalist countries. The Polish system may hold these managers responsible for accomplishments they have neither the leeway nor the resources to achieve. By the same token, the U.S. and Japanese systems may lead managers to feel more in control of the conditions of their lives than they really are.

Our evidence suggests, then, that not only does occupational self-direction fail to have the cross-nationally consistent effect on distress that it has on other facets of psychological functioning; but, also, that other job conditions associated with stratification and class may have countervailing effects. What is lacking is adequate information about these other job conditions.

A fourth type of reformulation would take greater account of the processes by which people attain their occupational positions and of the meaning these positions have to them. Slomczynski, Miller, and I (1981) speculated at length about the implications of post-World War II historical developments that resulted in differences between the United States and Poland in structural mobility, job-selection processes, and the symbolic importance attached to class position—differences that might explain why social stratification bears a different relationship to distress in the two countries. These speculations still seem to me to be plausible and they are certainly potentially testable. One could similarly point to differences between Japan and the West in the structure of industry—particularly in the sharper division in Japan between primary and secondary sectors of the economy—that might be pertinent to explaining why stratification has so little relationship to distress in Japan, and why Japanese white-collar workers are more distressed than are members of other social classes.

Finally, one could broaden the scope of the interpretation even more, by taking account of conditions of life other than those involved in job and career. It might be, for example, that cross-national differences in family structure, or in religious belief, or in whether the urban population is primarily rural in origin, or in "national culture" bear on the sense of distress. The pivotal questions, though, are not whether family, religion, rural origins, or culture account for differences in Polish, Japanese, and American men's sense of distress, but whether such nonoccupational conditions help explain why *social stratification* and *social class* bear different relationships to the sense of distress in Poland, Japan, and the United States.

We do not have the evidence in hand to test any of these interpretations. Each type of reformulation (other than simply limiting the scope of the interpretation to exclude distress) would require a different type of data. To test a "stress" formulation would require more information about psychological process, including information both about the relationship between objective job conditions and the subjective sense of "stress" in one's work, and about the relationship between job stress and off-the-job distress. Similarly, to test any other model of psychological process would require data directly pertinent to that formulation. To test the hypothesis that job conditions other than those involved in occupational self-direction help explain the relationships of social stratification and social class to distress would require that we obtain much fuller information in all three countries about those job conditions thought to be productive of a sense of distress. To test the hypothesis that different processes of educational and occupational attainment account for the differential effects of stratification and class on the sense of distress would require information of yet another type: historical information about the impact of changes in the educational and occupational structures of Poland, Japan, and the United States since World War II as they impinged on particular cohorts of Polish, Japanese, and American workers. And then, finally, to test the rather vaguely formulated hypothesis that nonjob conditions explain the cross-nationally inconsistent relationships of both class and stratification with distress would require information about the interrelationship of stratification and class with these other lines of social and cultural demarcation, in all three countries.

In any case, on the basis of presently available evidence, I still do not have a fully adequate explanation of why social stratification and social class have cross-nationally inconsistent effects on the sense of distress. Perplexed though I am, I value the cross-national evidence for making clear wherein my interpretation applies and wherein it does not, thus defining what is at issue. Were it not for the Polish and Japanese findings, there would have been little reason to doubt that my interpretation applies, albeit not quite as well, to the sense of distress, just as it clearly does to values, to self-directedness of orientation, and to cognitive functioning.

SOME GENERAL CONSIDERATIONS

I can now address some more general issues about cross-national research that I deliberately deferred until I had offered some concrete examples. These remarks are primarily addressed to research in which—to use the terminology I employed in the Introduction to this volume—nation is treated as the "context" for analysis.

(1) In whose interest is cross-national research? This seemingly innocuous question contains a range of serious ethical and professional issues. At its worst, as in the infamous Camelot affair (Horowitz 1967), cross-national research has been used in the service of political oppression. In a less dramatic way, cross-national research has too often been a mechanism by which scholars from affluent countries have employed scholars in less affluent countries as data-gatherers, to secure information to be processed, analyzed, and published elsewhere, with little benefit either in training or in professional recognition for those who collected the data (Portes 1975; Scheuch 1967). These are complex issues, in which surface appearances may be misleading. But, certainly, the history of cross-national research has not been entirely benign.

Past sins and mistakes notwithstanding, cross-national research need not be employed in the service of academic or other imperialism. My own research is again illustrative. As a matter of historical record, it was not I but Wlodzimierz Wesolowski (1975, p. 98) who proposed the Polish–U.S. comparative study. He did so for precisely the same reason I found the prospect so attractive when he suggested it to me: to see whether the U.S. findings would apply to a socialist society. The study was funded and carried out by the Polish Academy of Sciences, who thought the issues important for Polish sociology and Polish society. The extension of the U.S.–Polish comparison to encompass Japan came about because Ken'ichi Tominaga, his Japanese colleagues, and the Japanese universities and foundations that funded this research were as interested as were the Americans and the Poles in seeing whether these phenomena are similar in that non-Western society.

The opportunities for genuine cross-national collaboration today—when there is a thriving, highly professional sociology in many parts of the world—are much greater than they were only a few years ago. Today it is quite possible, and advantageous for all concerned, for sociologists of many countries to collaborate effectively. The theoretical and policy issues to be addressed in cross-national research can be—in principle, ought to be—equally important for sociologists of all the countries concerned.

(2) Is cross-national research distinctly different from research that compares social classes, or ethnic groups, or genders, in a single

country? I see cross-national research as one type of comparative research. In many discussions, though (see, for example, Armer and Grimshaw 1973), the term "comparative research" is treated as synonymous with cross-national research, as if the only possible comparison were international comparison; this I regard as hubris on the part of the internationalists. In other discussions (e.g., Hopkins and Wallerstein 1967), the term "comparative" is used more broadly and "cross-national" is limited to what I consider to be only one type of cross-national research, transnational research. And in still other discussions (e.g., Ragin 1982), comparative research is seen as that particular type of cross-national research where "society" is used as the explanatory unit. These varying usages seem to me to impede meaningful discourse. I think it best to use the commonsense meanings of both "comparative" and "cross-national."

My own research shows that cross-national research is no different in principle from other comparative research, although in practice it is likely to be more complex, especially as one tries to interpret cross-national inconsistencies. What makes it worth distinguishing cross-national research from other types of comparative research is that a much broader range of comparisons can be made—comparisons of political and economic systems, of cultures, of social structures. Any comparisons we make within a single country are necessarily limited to the one set of political, economic, cultural, and historical contexts represented by that particular country. I simply cannot imagine any study of the psychological impact of class and stratification done entirely within the United States that could have extended the scope of our knowledge, or the power of our interpretation, as greatly as did the Polish and Japanese studies.

(3) Why put the emphasis on cross-national? Why not cross-cultural or cross-societal or cross-systemic? Doesn't the term, "cross-national," ascribe a greater importance to the nation-state than it deserves? I use the term "cross-national" mainly because "nation" has relatively unambiguous meaning. Cross-cultural can mean anything from comparing subcultures within a single nation, for example, comparing Mexican American and Anglo American subcultures in the Southwest region of the United States, to comparing very large groupings of nations that share broadly similar cultures—as in William Goode's (1963) comparative analyses of historical changes in family patterns in "the West," Arabic Islam, Sub-Saharan Africa, India, China, and Japan. Similarly, as Charles Tilly (1984) cogently argues, it is extremely difficult to define what is a "society." And the term, cross-systemic, is so vague as to have little research utility.

I do not think that this usage of "nation" necessarily implies anything about the importance of nation—or the nation-state—as such, any more than "cross-cultural" implies (or, at any rate, should imply) that "culture" is the explanatory desideratum. Furthermore, we learn something about the importance or lack of importance of the nation-state by discovering which processes transcend national boundaries and which processes are idiosyncratic to particular nations or to particular types of nations. In choosing which nations to compare, sometimes we do mean to compare nation-states; how could Theda Skocpol (1979) have done differently in her analyses of revolutions? When we deal with governments, laws, and legally regulated institutions, the nation-state is necessarily a decisive context. But sometimes we use nation as a way of comparing cultures; in this case, we would choose nations with distinctly different cultures, for example, by comparing the United States to Japan, not the Federal Republic of Germany to Austria. Sometimes we mean to compare political and economic systems, as in comparing the United States and Japan to Poland, or—if one wanted to minimize cultural differences while contrasting political systems—in comparing the German Democratic Republic to the Federal Republic of Germany. Cross-national research is flexible, offering the advantage of making possible multiple types of comparison within one general analytic framework.

This flexibility, it must be recognized, comes at a price: When one finds cross-national differences, it may not be clear whether the crucial "context" that accounts for the differences is nation or culture or political or economic system (Scheuch 1967). Still, one can at least try to assess which of these contexts might logically be pertinent to explaining a particular cross-national difference. And, for many types of research, one can then proceed to design new studies to differentiate among the contexts.

(4) How many nations are needed for rigorous cross-national analysis, and how should they be chosen? For some purposes, particularly when using secondary data to establish cross-national generalities, it is desirable to include all countries for which pertinent data can be secured. Thus Alex Inkeles's pioneering paper, "Industrial Man" (1960), gained considerably from its demonstration that the relationship between social stratification and many facets of values and beliefs is consistent for a wide array of countries. Seymour Martin Lipset's argument, in "Democracy and Working-Class Authoritarianism" (1959), that the working class is more "liberal" than the middle class on economic issues, but illiberal on issues of civil liberties and civil rights, was the more forceful because he marshalled evidence from several countries. Donald Treiman's (1977) comprehensive analysis of the similarity of social stratification systems throughout the industrialized world effectively utilized data from many countries and was enriched as well by information about the historical past. Alejandro Portes and Saskia Sassen-Koob (1987) demonstrated anew the usefulness of a broad comparative sweep, in showing that, contrary to

all theoretical belief, the "informal," "underground" sector of the economy is not merely a transitional phenomenon of Third World development, but is instead a persistent and integral part of the economies of even advanced capitalist nations. In doing secondary analyses, it is highly advantageous to utilize data from all countries for which pertinent information can be secured.

Moreover, even in collecting primary data, there can be considerable advantage to assessing the consistency of findings across a range of nations, cultures, and political systems, as Inkeles and Smith showed in *Becoming Modern* (1974) and as Erik Olin Wright and his colleagues are demonstrating anew, in a very different type of research endeavor, in their multination studies of social class.

Yet, it is expensive, difficult, and time-consuming to collect data in many countries. We rarely are able to collect reliable data about enough nations for rigorous statistical analysis. Nor are we ordinarily able to study many countries in sufficient depth for intensive comparison. It is not necessarily true that the more nations included in the analysis, the more we learn. There is usually a trade-off between number of countries studied and amount of information obtained. In this trade-off, investigators can certainly disagree about the relative importance of number of countries and depth of information. And the same investigator might make different choices for different substantive problems. By and large, though, I would opt for fewer countries, more information.

My own preferred strategy is the deliberate choice of a small number of nations that provide maximum leverage for testing theoretical issues. One might begin with a study in one country, with subsequent extensions of the inquiry to other countries, as my collaborators and I have done. Alternatively, one can select pivotal countries that provide maximum opportunity to test some general hypothesis, as Theda Skocpol (1979) did in selecting France, Russia, and China for her study of the causes and consequences of social revolutions, or as John Walton (1984) did in selecting the Philippines, Colombia, and Kenya for his comparative analysis of national revolts in underdeveloped societies. Whether one starts with one country and then extends the inquiry to others, or begins with a small set of countries, does not seem to me to be crucial. Either way, the deliberate choice of a small number of countries for *systematic, intensive study* offers maximum leverage for testing general propositions about social process.

How, then, does one decide which countries to compare? The only rule of thumb I know is that cross-national research is maximally useful when it can resolve a disputed question of interpretation. It follows that what is a strategic comparison at one stage of knowledge may be overly cautious or overly audacious at another.

Were I to embark on a new comparative study today, the considerations would be quite different from what they were when I began my earlier cross-national studies, mainly because of what we now know from the Polish and Japanese studies, and because of new interpretive problems that have arisen from these studies. It would now be useful to study another socialist country and another non-Western industrialized country. It would also be useful to study a less than fully industrialized country, I think preferably (for the nonce) a capitalist country with a predominantly Western culture, perhaps a Latin American country. The possibilities for fruitful comparison do not shrink as one learns more, but actually grow.

The choice of countries should always be determined by asking whether comparing these particular countries will shed enough light on important theoretical issues to be worth the investment of time and resources that cross-national research will certainly require (Galtung 1967, p. 440). One must always ask: If I find cross-national consistencies, will this particular cross-national comparison extend the scope of my interpretation enough to have made the venture worthwhile? And if I find differences, will this particular cross-national comparison shed light on crucial interpretive problems? Cross-national research is always a gamble; one might as well gamble where the payoff is commensurate with the risk.

(5) What are the costs of doing cross-national research? If, as I have argued throughout this chapter, the advantages of cross-national research are considerable, so too are the costs. These costs are considerably greater than most investigators realize, great enough to make a rational person think twice about doing cross-national research when it is not needed or when it is premature.

Securing funds is always problematic, even (as in my own research) when financial support is obtained in the countries that are participating in the research. This, however, is only the first and by no means the most serious difficulty. Establishing collaborative relationships that can be sustained and will develop throughout the course of what can be counted on to be difficult research is much more problematic (Hill 1962; Sarapata 1985). Both the greatest benefits and the most difficult problems of cross-national research come from the collaborative relationships. If a good collaboration is like a good marriage, rewarding yet difficult, then a good cross-national collaboration is akin to a cross-cultural marriage that manages to succeed despite the spouses living much of the time in different countries, sometimes with considerable uncertainty about passports, visas, and the reliability and timeliness of mail delivery, and despite working in different institutional settings with conflicting demands and rewards. And still, it's far preferable to the alternatives. More than that, without good collaboration, many types of cross-national research are simply not possible.

The methodological pitfalls are another set of obstacles to good cross-national research; I have touched on some of them earlier in this chapter. It would be hard to exaggerate the amount of time, thought, and analysis that must go into the effort to achieve comparability of methods, concepts, and indices. There are also issues in the standards of research employed in different countries. Sometimes these issues become acutely problematic when one least expects them. As a simple yet telling example: The reason why we do not have Polish data about some of the job conditions that may be pertinent to distress is that the survey research specialists at the Polish Academy of Sciences refused to include questions about job conditions that did not meet their criteria of objectivity in a survey for which they were professionally responsible. Even when we appealed to them that cross-national comparability required their repeating the defects of the earlier U.S. study, they would not yield. They were as zealous in imposing their justifiable, yet irrelevant professional standards as were the clearance officers of the U.S. Department of Health, Education, and Welfare, and of the Office of Management and the Budget, in imposing their not nearly so justifiable requirements.

And still, there are yet more difficult problems—problems of interpretation. Particularly when one finds cross-national differences, an expert knowledge of all the countries is essential—a knowledge most easily achieved, of course, by collaborators who have expert knowledge of their own countries (see Kuechler 1987). Even when such collaboration exists, though, sharing knowledge, interpreting within a common framework, even having enough time together to think things through at the crucial junctures, do not come easily.

Unless one has a good reason why research *should* be cross-national, it generally isn't worth the effort of making it cross-national. Operationally, this means that one should do cross-national research either when a phenomenon cannot be studied in just one country (for example, the causes of revolutions) or else when some phenomenon has been well substantiated in one country and the next logical questions have to do with the limits of generality of what has been learned. In principle, but rarely in practice, it may be worth embarking on a cross-national study of a less well researched problem if you have good a priori reason to believe that important theoretical issues can be more effectively addressed by conducting the research in more than one country. I remain a strong proponent of cross-national research, but I would not wish to mislead anyone into thinking that its very considerable advantages do not come at equally considerable cost.

(6) Finally, to return to a question that has pervaded this chapter: What role does history play in cross-national interpretation? In posing this question, I most decidedly do not mean to cast doubt on the utility of historical analysis as a method for doing cross-national research. I regard the persistent debate about the relative merits of historical and quantitative methods in cross-national research as a wasteful distraction, addressed to a false dichotomy.[2] Each method is appropriate for some research purposes and inappropriate for others. Best of all, as Jeffery Paige (1975) demonstrated in his analysis of the relationship between agricultural organization and social movements in 70 developing nations, is to combine the two. My question concerns not historical analysis as method but history as explanation. At issue, of course, are the competing merits of idiographic and nomothetic explanation. I can hardly do justice to this complex question in the closing paragraphs of this chapter, but I would at least like to point out that the issues are somewhat different when analyzing cross-national similarities from what they are when analyzing cross-national differences.

As I have argued throughout this chapter, the interpretation of cross-national *similarities* should not focus on the unique historical experiences of each of the countries. One seeks to discover, instead, social-structural regularities that transcend the many differences in history, culture, and experience that occur among nations. This is true even in inquiries—Walton's (1984) *Reluctant Rebels* is a good example—in which the evidence is mainly historical but the analysis searches not for historical idiosyncrasies but for historical commonalities. The intent in all analyses of cross-national similarities is to develop generalizations that transcend particular historical experiences in a search for more general explanatory principles. In short, the method may be historical; the interpretation should be sociological.

In a broader sense of history, of course, cross-national analysis—just as any other type of sociological analysis—cannot be ahistoric, even when much about history is only implicit in the interpretation (Sztompka 1986). To compare the impact of social stratification on personality in the United States and Poland, for example, assumes that we are comparing industrialized states that have shared much of Western history. That one is a

---

[2.] The methodological debate takes place on two levels: the type of analysis used *within* each nation and the type of analysis used for *comparing* nations. I see nothing of value in the first part of the debate; one uses whatever methods are appropriate to the task. The second part of the debate deals with real issues, for example, the meaningfulness of using "samples" of nations, the utility of statistical tests when basing one's analysis on the entire set of existing countries, and the difficulties of having to test multiple interactions on a necessarily small number of "cases" (see, e.g., Ragin 1982). This literature, despite its antiquantitative bias, offers some useful cautions.

capitalist state and the other a socialist state can be viewed, depending on how you read the broad sweep of history, as a comparison of different economic-political systems or as a comparison of different levels of political development. In either case, even though history is not treated explicitly, historical considerations are certainly there implicitly. And when one compares fully industrialized to partially industrialized societies, historical issues are, necessarily, at least implicit. Nevertheless, in interpreting cross-national similarities, history need not be at the forefront of attention.

In interpreting cross-national *differences*, by contrast, historical considerations cannot be merely implicit; history must come to the forefront of any interpretation. For example, after demonstrating remarkable parallels in both the causes and the consequences of the French, Russian, and Chinese revolutions, Skocpol (1979) had to explain differences, particularly in revolutionary outcomes, in terms of historically unique circumstances. Similarly, when I find that social stratification and social class do not have the same impact on the sense of distress in the United States, Poland, and Japan, I have to look to the separate historical developments of the three countries, to try to discover what might explain the inconsistent findings. I maintain, though, that even in interpreting cross-national differences explanation cannot consist merely in explicating pertinent historical differences. The object is not an understanding of history just for history's sake, but the use of history for understanding more general social processes. The interpretation must be historically informed, but sociological interpretations, even of cross-national differences, are quintessentially transhistorical.

REFERENCES

Almond, Gabriel A. and Sidney Verba. 1963. *The Civic Culture: Political Attitudes and Democracy in Five Nations.* Princeton, NJ: Princeton University Press.
Armer, Michael. 1973. "Methodological Problems and Possibilities in Comparative Research." Pp. 49-79 in *Comparative Social Research: Methodological Problems and Strategies,* edited by Michael Armer and Allen D. Grimshaw. New York: John Wiley.
Armer, Michael and Allen D. Grimshaw, eds. 1973. *Comparative Social Research: Methodological Problems and Strategies.* New York: John Wiley.
Elder, Joseph W. 1976. "Comparative Cross-National Methodology." Pp. 209-30 in *Annual Review of Sociology.* Vol. 2, edited by Alex Inkeles. Palo Alto, CA: Annual Reviews.
Finifter, Bernard M. 1977. "The Robustness of Cross-Cultural Findings." *Annals New York Academy of Sciences* 285:151-84.
Form, William H. 1979. "Comparative Industrial Sociology and the Convergence Hypothesis." Pp. 1-25 in *Annual Review of Sociology.* Vol. 5, edited by Alex Inkeles. Palo Alto, CA: Annual Reviews.
Galtung, Johan. 1967. *Theory and Methods of Social Research.* Oslo: Universitetsforlaget.

Goode, William J. 1963. *World Revolution and Family Patterns*. New York: Free Press.

Hill, Reuben. 1962. "Cross-National Family Research: Attempts and Prospects." *International Social Science Journal* 14:425-51.

Hopkins, Terence K. and Immanuel Wallerstein. 1967. "The Comparative Study of National Societies." *Social Science Information* 6:25-58.

Horowitz, Irving L. 1967. *The Rise and Fall of Project Camelot*. Cambridge: MIT Press.

Inkeles, Alex. 1960. "Industrial Man: The Relation of Status to Experience, Perception, and Value." *American Journal of Sociology* 66:1-31.

Inkeles, Alex and David H. Smith. 1974. *Becoming Modern: Individual Change in Six Developing Countries*. Cambridge, MA: Harvard University Press.

Kohn, Melvin L. 1969. *Class and Conformity: A Study in Values*. Homewood, IL: Dorsey. (2nd ed., 1977, published by the University of Chicago Press)

―――. Forthcoming. "Unresolved Issues in the Relationship Between Work and Personality." In *The Nature of Work: Sociological Perspectives,* edited by Kai Erikson and Steven P. Vallas. New Haven, CT: Yale University Press.

Kohn, Melvin L., Atsushi Naoi, Carrie Schoenbach, Carmi Schooler, and Kazimierz Slomczynski. Forthcoming. "Position in the Class Structure and Psychological Functioning: A Comparative Analysis of the United States, Japan, and Poland." *American Journal of Sociology.*

Kohn, Melvin L. and Carrie Schoenbach. 1983. "Class, Stratification, and Psychological Functioning." Pp. 154-89 in *Work and Personality: An Inquiry into the Impact of Social Stratification*, by Melvin L. Kohn and Carmi Schooler. Norwood, NJ: Ablex.

Kohn, Melvin L. and Carmi Schooler. 1978. "The Reciprocal Effects of the Substantive Complexity of Work and Intellectual Flexibility: A Longitudinal Assessment." *American Journal of Sociology* 84:24-52.

―――. 1982. "Job Conditions and Personality: A Longitudinal Assessment of Their Reciprocal Effects." *American Journal of Sociology* 87:1257-86.

―――. With the collaboration of Joanne Miller, Karen A. Miller, Carrie Schoenbach, and Ronald Schoenberg. 1983. *Work and Personality: An Inquiry into the Impact of Social Stratification*. Norwood, NJ: Ablex.

Kohn, Melvin L., Kazimierz M. Slomczynski, and Carrie Schoenbach. 1986. "Social Stratification and the Transmission of Values in the Family: A Cross-National Assessment." *Sociological Forum* 1:73-102.

Kuechler, Manfred. 1987. "The Utility of Surveys for Cross-National Research." *Social Science Research* 16:229-44.

Lipset, Seymour Martin. 1959. "Democracy and Working-Class Authoritarianism." *American Sociological Review* 24:482-501.

Marsh, Robert M. 1967. *Comparative Sociology: A Codification of Cross-Societal Analysis*. New York: Harcourt, Brace & World.

Miller, Joanne, Carmi Schooler, Melvin L. Kohn, and Karen A. Miller. 1979. "Women and Work: The Psychological Effects of Occupational Conditions." *American Journal of Sociology* 85:66-94.

Miller, Joanne, Kazimierz M. Slomczynski, and Melvin L. Kohn. 1985. "Continuity of Learning-Generalization: The Effect of Job on Men's Intellective Process in the United States and Poland." *American Journal of Sociology* 91:593-615.

Miller, Joanne, Kazimierz M. Slomczynski, and Ronald J. Schoenberg. 1981. "Assessing Comparability of Measurement in Cross-National Research: Authoritarian-Conservatism in Different Sociocultural Settings." *Social Psychology Quarterly* 44:178-91.

Miller, Karen A. and Melvin L. Kohn. 1983. "The Reciprocal Effects of Job Conditions and the Intellectuality of Leisure-Time Activities." Pp. 217-41 in *Work and Personality: An*

Inquiry into the Impact of Social Stratification, by Melvin L. Kohn and Carmi Schooler. Norwood, NJ: Ablex.

Miller, Karen A., Melvin L. Kohn, and Carmi Schooler. 1985. "Educational Self-Direction and the Cognitive Functioning of Students." *Social Forces* 63:923-44.

————. 1986. "Educational Self-Direction and Personality." *American Sociological Review* 51:372-90.

Naoi, Atsushi and Carmi Schooler. 1985. "Occupational Conditions and Psychological Functioning in Japan." *American Journal of Sociology* 90:729-52.

Nowak, Stefan. 1976. "Meaning and Measurement in Comparative Studies." Pp. 104-32 in *Understanding and Prediction: Essays in the Methodology of Social and Behavioral Theories*. Dordrecht, Holland: D. Reidel.

————. 1977. "The Strategy of Cross-National Survey Research for the Development of Social Theory." Pp. 3-47 in *Cross-National Comparative Survey Research: Theory and Practice*, edited by Alexander Szalai and Riccardo Petrella. Oxford: Pergamon.

Paige, Jeffery M. 1975. *Agrarian Revolution: Social Movements and Export Agriculture in the Underdeveloped World*. New York: Free Press.

Portes, Alejandro. 1975. "Trends in International Research Cooperation: The Latin American Case." *American Sociologist* 10:131-40.

Portes, Alejandro and Saskia Sassen-Koob. 1987. "Making it Underground: Comparative Material on the Informal Sector in Western Market Economies." *American Journal of Sociology* 93:30-61.

Przeworski, Adam and Henry Teune. 1970. *The Logic of Comparative Social Inquiry*. New York: Wiley-Interscience.

Ragin, Charles. 1982. "Comparative Sociology and the Comparative Method." *International Journal of Comparative Sociology* 22:102-20.

Ragin, Charles and David Zaret. 1983. "Theory and Method in Comparative Research: Two Strategies." *Social Forces* 61:731-54.

Sarapata, Adam. 1985. "Researchers' Habits and Orientations as Factors Which Condition International Cooperation in Research." *Science of Science* 5:157-82.

Scheuch, Erwin K. 1967. "Society as Context in Cross-Cultural Comparisons." *Social Science Information* 6:7-23.

————. 1968. "The Cross-Cultural Use of Sample Surveys: Problems of Comparability." Pp. 176-209 in *Comparative Research Across Cultures and Nations*, edited by Stein Rokkan. Paris: Mouton.

Schooler, Carmi, Melvin L. Kohn, Karen A. Miller, and Joanne Miller. 1983. "Housework as Work." Pp. 242-60 in *Work and Personality: An Inquiry into the Impact of Social Stratification*, by Melvin L. Kohn and Carmi Schooler. Norwood, NJ: Ablex.

Skocpol, Theda. 1979. *States and Social Revolutions: A Comparative Analysis of France, Russia, and China*. Cambridge: Cambridge University Press.

Slomczynski, Kazimierz M. and Melvin L. Kohn. 1988. *Sytuacja Pracy I Jej Psychologiczne Konsekwencje: Polsko-Amerykanskie Analizy Porownawcze* [Work Conditions and Psychological Functioning: Comparative Analyses of Poland and the United States]. Wroclaw: Ossolineum.

Slomczynski, Kazimierz M., Joanne Miller, and Melvin L. Kohn. 1981. "Stratification, Work, and Values: A Polish-United States Comparison." *American Sociological Review* 46:720-44.

Smelser, Neil J. 1968. "The Methodology of Comparative Analysis of Economic Activity." Pp. 62-75 in *Essays in Sociological Explanation*. Englewood Cliffs, NJ: Prentice-Hall.

Suchman, Edward A. 1964. "The Comparative Method in Social Research." *Rural Sociology* 29:123-37.

Sztompka, Piotr. 1986. "The Renaissance of Historical Orientation in Sociology."
     International Sociology 1:321-37.
Tilly, Charles. 1984. *Big Structures, Large Processes, Huge Comparisons*. New York:
     Russell Sage.
Treiman, Donald J. 1977. *Occupational Prestige in Comparative Perspective*. New York:
     Academic Press.
Walton, John. 1984. *Reluctant Rebels: Comparative Studies of Revolution and
     Underdevelopment*. New York: Columbia University Press.
Wesolowski, Wlodzimierz. 1975. *Teoria, Badania, Praktyka. Z Problematyki Struktury
     Klasowej* [Theory, Research, Practice: Problems of Class Structure]. Warszawa:
     Ksiazka i Wiedza.

Part II
Max Weber's Enduring
Pertinence for
Cross-National Research

4

Legitimate Domination in Comparative-Historical Perspective: The Case of Legal Domination

Wlodzimierz Wesolowski

There are two sources of the continual reinterpretation of every classical sociological theory. The first is "unresolved issues" that stem from the very internal logic of a given theory and were poorly developed or even unnoticed by its creator. The second is changing social reality. In the case of Max Weber's theory, both of these sources play a role in the continual reinterpretation of his thought.

It has been widely acknowledged that Weber's sociological theories provide a fine basis for cross-national comparison. This chapter is an attempt to utilize Weber's notion of domination for comparative research. It is clear, however, that, in attempting to apply Weber's concept of "legitimate domination" (*Legitime Herrschaft*) to the classification and understanding of contemporary political systems, both the limits of Weber's conceptualization and the present-day dynamics of politics make a revision and expansion of his formulations necessary.

There have been and still are lively discussions of how Weber's three types of legitimate domination (traditional, charismatic, and legal) should be understood. Are these three types universal tools of analysis? Do they exhaust the arrangements for a conceptual classification and historical analysis of all known state systems? Often implied in these questions are other possible typologies that would either replace or supplement the typology suggested by Weber. I shall not go into these options here, for I am interested primarily in the applicability of Weber's three models of legitimate domination to explaining contemporary political systems.

More specifically, I am looking for the possibility of applying Weber's concept of domination to state-socialist systems. Anticipating my conclusions, I shall say two things at the outset. Thus far, Weberians have understood the political systems of the Soviet Union and the countries of Eastern Europe as special variants of charismatic domination or special variants of traditional domination. Here I argue that these systems can better be understood as a special variant of legal domination.[1]

A FEW GENERAL QUESTIONS

Weber defined legitimate domination as

the situation in which the manifested will (command) of the ruler, or rulers, is meant to influence the conduct of one or more others (the ruled) and actually does influence it in such a way that their conduct to a socially relevant degree occurs as if the ruled had made the content of the command the maxim of their conduct for its very own sake. Looked at from the opposite end, this situation will be called obedience. (1968, p. 946)

Reflecting as it does the general "methodological" principle of Weber's "interpretive sociology" (*verstehende Soziologie*), human actions are treated as being guided by the subjective meaning ascribed to those actions. The task of sociology then is to unveil these meanings. From the point of view of citizens, it is *belief* in legitimacy that gives subjective meaning to their behavior and makes obedience to the ruler meaningful.

Legitimacy maxims (which form the background of the legitimacy beliefs of individuals) are part of a larger cultural order or civilization complex. In this sense, they are extraindividual, that is, "structural" or supraindividual, phenomena. Yet, in Weber's work, both the structural and the individual-action approaches are always present. "Interpretive analysis" looks at structures as generated and maintained by individual actions. In tune with this, I look at legitimate domination from the perspective of individual motives, orientations, and attitudes by speaking of "legitimating convictions," or the lack of them. "Maxims" become the object of

[1] The first step toward such an interpretation of the Soviet system was made in the well-known book *The Soviet Political System,* by Alfred G. Meyer (1965).

analysis as internalized convictions that lead to a definite action or withdrawal from action.[2]

An important general methodological question arises here, if we wish to apply Weber's typology to state-socialist political systems. Weber thought of legitimate domination as composed of three sets of phenomena: (1) the real structures of power, encompassing, at least, the "highest authority" and the "administrative apparatus"; (2) power struggles going on within these structures; and (3) the legitimacy maxims suggested to the population by the ruling circles as well as the popular legitimacy convictions generated by these maxims. Characterizing all three sets of phenomena as an integrated complex, Weber nevertheless suggested that "legitimacy beliefs" are a decisive factor in distinguishing among types of domination.

Such a methodological elevation of legitimacy beliefs (popular convictions) to a primary position in the whole complex of domination has clear disadvantages for historical research. It presents a scholar with the dilemma: Should he or she abandon the "Weberian approach" in all cases where there is no evidence of a popular belief in legitimacy maxims—even where preliminary considerations suggest the existence of the "typically Weberian" pattern of real structures of power, struggles within those structures of power, and propagation of maxims to the masses? A more negative than positive answer to this question seems advisable. Such an answer, however, demands a clearly explicated modified approach.

My proposed modification consists in dissociating (1) real structures of power, (2) legitimacy claims in the form of maxims, and (3) popular legitimacy-conferring convictions. The implication then is that one should distinguish between domination and legitimate domination. The structures of a given ("Weberian") type of domination and legitimacy maxims can exist without the population coming to accept the claims of legitimacy.

This distinction is particularly relevant for the study of contemporary forms of legal domination, although it might also be useful in the study of traditional and even charismatic types of domination. One should not exclude the possibility that, for example, some "pretensions" to charisma do not result in willing, uncritical obedience or that some forms of routinized charisma, contrary to appearances, have ceased to be perceived by the population as an incarnation of a good form of public power. There

---

[2.] For the general elaboration of the concept of legitimacy as it is understood in the Weberian literature, see Weber (1956, 1968), Bendix (1962), Habermas (1979), Luhmann (1983), Mommsen (1974), Kielmansegg (1971), Rigby (1982), Stallberg (1975), and Wesolowski (1989).

exist "pretended" forms of legitimate domination, disintegrated forms, and crippled forms. These alternative forms of domination may all be relatively stable and may thus demand Weberian-style analysis.

The analytical approach suggested in this chapter has one important methodological advantage. It does not force the analyst to invent and attribute to the population some kind of legitimacy belief notwithstanding serious doubts as to whether such a belief actually exists.[3]

Another general problem requiring consideration is the range of phenomena to which legitimacy beliefs refer. Weber's definition of the content of legitimacy beliefs was very scanty or "abstract." The central legitimating beliefs he described were belief in "sacred tradition," belief in the exceptional personal qualities of a leader, and, finally, belief in the validity of enacted law. In his analyses of concrete societies and various subtypes, Weber sometimes expanded these characteristics somewhat. Basic to all his analyses, however, is his insistent concern with what legitimatizes the demand for, and the demonstration of, *obedience*.

It seems that contemporary studies of what convictions confer legitimacy must be divested of Weber's reductionism. For in the second half of the twentieth century, legitimacy beliefs have broader grounds and functions. They are conducive, after all, to cooperation with government agencies or to the withdrawal of such cooperation. They also foster acceptance or rejection of mediation by state institutions in intergroup or interorganizational disputes. Thus legitimacy convictions are relevant not only for obedience but also for other kinds of political bonds within the state.

[3.] The distinction between domination and legitimated domination has been used in some analyses, although this distinction has not been conceptually elaborated and presented as a modification and extension of Weber's position. Thus Jowitt (1983) discussed the power structure of the Soviet Union without reference to the legitimation problematique. His analysis is Weberian in style, as is evident in many direct references to Weber's work and terminology. Jowitt calls the *institutional framework* of the Soviet Union "charismatic-traditional." Lowenthal (1974) stresses structurally conditioned difficulties in gaining "long-run legitimacy" by the one-party system of the Soviet type in modern society. His methodological position is close to mine. He (1974, p. 353) writes: "In fact, for modern societies there is no long-run alternative to legitimacy based on institutional procedures. Of the two types of legitimacy listed by Max Weber—traditional and charismatic legitimacy—the first does not apply to modern conditions and the second does not apply to the long run. There remains Weber's rational-legal type of legitimacy." Lowenthal says that, under rational-legal domination, it is necessary for well-qualified people to be selected for the political elite and for decisions made by that elite to reconcile group interests. Lowenthal believes, however, that the plausibility of satisfying these two conditions by present political arrangements in the Soviet Union is weak.

I think that, in contemporary society, belief in legitimacy is a result of a psychological process that involves several subprocesses. In this overarching process, the subprocesses are, first, evaluation of fundamental aspects of political arrangements; second, the set of social values reflected in governmental policy; and third, the performance of government in its administrative and coordinating functions. It may happen that, in individual cases, one subprocess is paramount while others are of secondary importance.

SUBTYPES OF LEGAL DOMINATION

Weber defined legal domination as "resting on enactment; its pure type is best represented by bureaucracy. The basic idea is that laws can be enacted and changed at pleasure by a formally correct procedure" (Weber 1956, Hlb. 2, p. 531; for an English translation, see Etzioni 1961, p. 4).

He also said that "legal authority can be exercised in a wide variety of different forms" (1968, p. 219). He did not, however, systematically describe any specific variants. What he did do was make some remarks on possible subtypes. For example, he said that both an authoritarian subtype and a democratic subtype of legal domination are possible. He maintained that legal domination can be "imposed" or "agreed upon." These formulations suggest the possibility of distinguishing a democratic and nondemocratic subtype of legal domination, both based on "enacted law" and bureaucratic administration.

In a great variety of modern, industrialized countries, the bureaucracy and enacted law play a decisive role in the daily process of ruling or, in Weberian terms, in the "routine" of ruling. Formally speaking, socialist countries are governed by parliaments and by the governments that these parliaments appoint. The governments evoke "legality" as the basis of their legitimacy. The bureaucracy is at least formally treated as a means for executing programs formed outside of it, namely, by the legislature. The bureaucracy is expected to be impartial and to make its decisions on the basis of law.

Drawing from Weber's remarks, one could distinguish three subtypes of legal domination: *postabsolutist*, *democratic*, and *posttotalitarian*.

The postabsolutist subtype was constructed mainly from the analytical knowledge supplied by Weber himself and is based on the prototype of Germany of the Bismarck period and up to the time of World War I.

The democratic subtype was constructed from sociological studies of Western Europe and the United States today.

The posttotalitarian subtype is based on the Soviet Union and the countries of Eastern Europe.[4]

In Tables 4.1, 4.2, and 4.3, I have summarized the similarities and differences among the three subtypes of legal domination. The first table indicates the arrangements of political institutions and political principles operative in the three subtypes. Table 4.2 specifies some qualitative and quantitative differences between bureaucracies in the three subtypes. Table 4.3 summarizes differences in legitimacy claims and gives a provisional assessment of which claims are recognized and which are refuted by the population.

[4.] The most popular position today seems to be the characterization of the Soviet system as "traditional domination." This argument refers to the conscious allusion to tradition in public life and also the revival of traditional values in the private lives of citizens (e.g., appeals of the authorities to strengthen the family as well as the high value of the family in the consciousness of individuals). It is also argued that the socialist revolution of 1917 is presented in the mass media as the fundamental "tradition" on which the entire edifice of Soviet life today is based. Finally, it is stated that relations between the government and officials, and between officials and clients, have taken on a patrimonial character (Feher 1982; Murvar 1985).

I believe that the first and second arguments miss the point. The first has no application at all to government-citizen relations. The second is a misunderstanding. The traditional justification of power says that "it was always so" from time immemorial. This unchangeability makes tradition inviolable: "Kings always ruled." One cannot argue in the same way that "the government always came from a revolution of the people." On the other hand, the third argument makes an important observation: In fact, public relations in the countries of state-socialism, first of all in the Soviet Union, take on features of personal relations. Yet, this is too little on which to base a claim that the political system is becoming one of "traditional domination."

Another position that is taken in the secondary Weberian literature talks about a goal-rationality type of domination in the Soviet Union and Eastern Europe (Rigby 1982). This position is somewhat closer to reality than the previous ones. The aim of carrying out a substantive social program, that is, a particular version of economic development and a particular doctrine of social justice, was an important aspect of social policy in the countries of state-socialism. The legitimacy claim of the rulers also appeals to this program. These substantive programs, however, are losing their importance in confrontation with the requirements of efficiency and the necessity of securing the existing power structure.

There is still another way of characterizing the political systems of the countries of state-socialism. It has been borrowed from Weberian as well as non-Weberian typologies. For example, it has been applied by Feher, Heller, and Markus (1983). They argue that the present political system of the Soviet Union has to be characterized as totalitarianism that uses the traditional justification of legitimacy claims as an auxiliary support. Such a typology transcends the boundary of Weberian study.

TABLE 4.1 Aspects of Political Arrangements in Three Subtypes of Legal Domination

Aspects of Political Order	Subtypes		
	Postabsolutist	Democratic	Posttotalitarian
Supreme authority (the "ruler")	imposed	elected	imposed
Citizens' freedoms	introduced (in *statu nascendi*)	assured	uncertain
Formation and scope of governmental policy	(a) formed at the top (b) small in scope	(a) formed in the political process (b) small in scope	(a) invented at the top (b) all-encompassing
Political conflicts	primary importance: within the political elite secondary importance: within the society	between social groups and within the political elite, of equal importance	(a) open political struggle: nonexistent (b) latent conflict: ruling-ruled (c) restricted struggle: within the political elite

TABLE 4.2 Aspects of Bureaucracy in Three Subtypes of Legal Domination

Aspects of Bureaucracy	Subtypes		
	Postabsolutist	Democratic	Postotalitarian
Competence	high	high or medium	low
Efficiency	high	high or medium	low
Lawfulness	high	high	low
Accountability	high	high	low
Interactions with political bodies	conflict and cooperation	conflict and cooperation	(a) top level: fusion (b) middle level: irrelevant
Manipulative inclinations	high	medium	medium or high
Self-assertive attitude	high	medium	low
Ethics of reliability	high	medium	low
Prestige	high	medium	low

TABLE 4.3 Legitimacy Claims and Legitimacy Convictions (recognition of legitimacy) in Three Subtypes of Legal Domination

Aspects of Legitimacy Claim	*Postabsolutist*	*Subtypes* *Democratic*	*Posttotalitarian*
Rule through enacted law	reasonableness of the law (accepted)	humanized instrumentality of the law (accepted)	steering and coordinating function of the law (questioned)
Bureaucratic administration and coordination	functional efficiency (accepted)	functional efficiency (irrelevant)	global societal utility (refuted)
Political arrangements			
(a) principal foundations of the power structure	constitutional monarchy (accepted)	institutions of representative democracy (accepted)	the hegemony of one party (refuted)
(b) purpose served	continuity/modernity complex of value (accepted)	democratic process in the place of substantive values (accepted)	substantive justice (accepted with reservations; growing doubts)

Obviously, we all know that some of the similarities between East and West are superficial. Some of the real features of socialist bureaucracy would have been a surprise to Weber. The most important commonly known differences appear in the real operations of political institutions and in their relations to the society. One cannot forget that police and special military corps serve as an important instrument for keeping the population under control and—if necessary—liquidating outbursts of dissatisfaction or independent political actions. This is why my subtype for socialist countries retains in its name the adjective "totalitarian." No matter what other ways totalitarian regimes use, they do not eliminate those structural features of domination I am referring to in my subtypology. Aside from the general premises, my reasons for placing East and West in the same overall category result from observations of historical change.

In the Soviet Union there is a steady decline in the role of ideology in the process of ruling, as well as a tendency to abandon, though grudgingly and gingerly, totalitarian principles of forceful indoctrination and direct political control of all aspects of social life. In instructing people in how they should behave, the government nowadays appeals to legal obligation rather than to ideological motivation.

We are presently observing an inclination toward economic and political reforms by the leadership of the Soviet Union. The announced departure from the command system in the management of the economy will increase the status of general rather than specific legal regulations. This will also mean a depoliticization of the economy.

Here I wish to mention Poland, in order to call attention to a somewhat different element: the legitimacy claim. Since 1944, that is, since the Communist party came to power in Poland, two elements have always been present in propaganda. The first emphasizes the revolutionary nature of the changes introduced in economic and social life. The second suggests that the new government has been installed "legally" and operates in the majesty of the law.

POLITICAL ARRANGEMENTS

The political institutions of the *postabsolutist* state formed gradually into a rather tangled configuration. They included the institution of the emperor as sovereign; the institution of the "chancellor," whose ministers are appointed from among the highest aristocracy, the politically dominant stratum; and, finally, the institution of the parliament, to which deputies are elected by "qualified voters" or the entire adult population. In the postabsolutist state, however, the parliament has limited influence on the actual process of ruling the country and on the concrete shape of government policy. The emperor and his cabinet have the most power. The sovereign of the state is unquestionably imposed on the population, since he is not appointed by any political institution or elected by any political community. The government is authoritative, and the bureaucracy is a trustworthy instrument of the sovereign. Policy is made "at the top" by a narrow political elite, which is under the powerful influence of the privileged classes. Reforms expanding the range of the government's interests are very limited.

The political conflicts that appear in this system vary. Those that have a direct impact on the process of governing take place within a narrow power elite. Conflicts between the system of rule and the aspirations of the population are not yet fully developed, though they already begin to manifest themselves in demonstrations, "revolutions," and the like.

From the point of view of the citizen, the major advance of the postabsolutist state over absolutist and feudal systems is the introduction of the civil and political rights of the individual. This means, among other things, the safeguarding of personal liberty and also the possibility—although limited—of participating in political life.

The political institutions of the *democratic* system, as a rule, evolved from the postabsolutist system. At the base of this transformation was the recognition that the society is sovereign.

As a result, legal guarantees of civil liberties become powerful and effective. The "rulers" are elected or "agreed upon," in Weberian terminology. In a democratic system, the formulation of policy takes place in a complicated network of horizontal and vertical bargaining and negotiations between organized groups (parties, interest groups) and between political leaders and the masses. The program of the government is generated both from below and from above. But, whatever its direction, the government's program must gain the acceptance of a majority of the population in a rather complicated political process.

From a broader historical perspective: Pressure from below expands the policy of the government, while large areas are still left to the unrestrained initiative of the citizens. The most spectacular case of this expansion of government activities was the emergence of the "welfare state" in the 1950s and 1960s.

In the *posttotalitarian* political system, all of the political institutions typical of the Western democratic systems formally exist. The relations among these institutions, however, differ substantially from what they are in democratic states. The sovereign is the Communist party, whose power was imposed on the society. The political system is characterized by two formally separate centers of the highest power: the Political Bureau of the party and the Presidium of the Government. The government is formally responsible to the Parliament. There are also two parallel hierarchical bureaucracies, those of the party and the government. At the decision-making top, the personnel of the Political Bureau and the Presidium of the Government largely overlap. Although there are many trivial conflicts between the two bureaucracies, they act in concert when there is any threat that they will be subjected to the influence of society. They form an interlocked apparatus controlling all areas of social life without being controlled from the outside.

The political program of the government is formulated at the top of interlocked hierarchies. It is, in effect, an "invented" program that is, after all, based on a narrow elite's knowledge of the so-called laws of social development and this elite's desire to bring about rapid economic growth and social progress. By the elite's assumption, this is a program for everything and everybody. It covers all areas of social life and is supposed to stimulate and organize the actions of all citizens. In this sense, this program is a continuation of the thinking typical of the totalitarian system. Departures from this kind of thinking occur only slowly.

An open political struggle over governmental program and appointments to official positions does not exist. What are accepted, though, are disputes among and within branches of the economy over the division of state funds for new investments, for employee wages, and for subsidies.

There is, however, a latent conflict between the rulers and the ruled over the very shape of the political system. This latent conflict manifests itself in several ways. Its visible signs are large demonstrations and outbursts of dissatisfaction. The most spectacular manifestation was the crisis in Poland in 1980-81.

Legal guarantees of civil liberties exist, but they are limited. The most limited of these liberties are freedom of association and freedom to conduct open political struggle. Guarantees of personal liberty can be annulled for opponents of the existing political system.

In the first table, one can quickly identify the specific features of each subtype and similarities and differences among the subtypes.

BUREAUCRACY

Bureaucracy should be considered both a critical element of each of these individual political arrangements and an autonomous element in typologies of legitimacy. It is in this area, however, that Weber's definitions need to be refined most. Weber, after all, generalized the features of the administrative machines and of the bureaucrat in *all* "modern" states, apparently irrespective of their variations and possible divergent developments. His definition of bureaucracy came directly from his experience with and vision of the bureaucracy he knew best—that of Bismarckian Germany. From a twentieth-century perspective, his definition of bureaucracy is relevant only for the postabsolutist subtype.

In that subtype, or, at least, in the Bismarckian case that serves as its referent, the bureaucracy is both competent and efficient. Recruitment to its echelons is based on education and expert knowledge. Employment in bureaucracy offers a lifetime career. The work of the "office" is based on a carefully laid out legal code and, with this legal code, is very predictable. This reduces uncertainty in everyday relations between state administration and ordinary citizens. Voluntarism in making official decisions is excluded.

As the bureaucracy is subservient to the sovereign and not really hampered by democratic principles, these bureaucrats demonstrate a strong sense of themselves and of their need to be reliable and responsible for the system. At the same time, this leads them to manipulate the policy that they help design and administer to their own institutional interests. Bureaucrats know how to make political use of information. Collecting data and preparing official reports serve as a basis for manipulative influence, which is sometimes successful, on political bodies. Declaring information a "state secret" helps them in manipulating or limiting public opinion.

At the same time, they develop a strong "sense of duty" and high standards of performance—a specific code of reliability and accountability. In this sense, they are bearers of high professional ethics. This feature helps to establish the relatively high prestige of an "official" (bureaucrat) among the citizenry.

A description of bureaucracy in the *democratic* subtype centers on features that are clearly distinct from the features of the postabsolutist subtype or Bismarckian "model." In the democratic subtype, there are strong centers of political power generated from the society (parliament, political parties, interest groups, and local governments) that seriously limit or eliminate the claim of the bureaucracy to dominate policymaking and policy-implementing processes. Effectively, the complex structure of democratic states does what Weber thought only a plebiscitarian leader could do—it successfully checks the bureaucracy. The government bureaucracy is controlled by political bodies, although the bureaucracy also influences those same political bodies by collecting and classifying information and by direct attempts at manipulation. This is not enough for the bureaucracy to accumulate power, because there are also others who gather information.

The existence of civil society not subordinated to the bureaucracy or to other centers of authoritarian power (such as the "emperor"), then, has at least two consequences for democratic systems. Autonomous groups exist and they are capable of evaluating social needs and generating knowledge and programs of collective action. Moreover, a political struggle goes on among groups to implement particular programs.

Group cohesiveness, self-assertiveness, and the prestige of the state bureaucracy are lower in the democratic subtype than in the postabsolutist subtype. Several factors contribute to this. First and foremost, the state authority has been deprived of its aureole of "superior" origin and importance. Second, bureaucracy implements rather than creates policy. Third, new social groups with high competence and great prestige emerge and attract the attention of the public: natural scientists, managers of industry, men of ideas, and idols of entertainment. New groups have not pushed into the shadow professional groups with long-standing and high prestige, such as medical doctors or lawyers, but they have pushed the "officers of the state" to a relatively lower position. The functional importance and social visibility of officials somehow have been diminished.

In the environment of the democratic state, there are also private firms with their own management structures. In many respects, such firms are very attractive employers. These "business bureaucracies" do things that are considered more important for the well-being of society than what the state administration does. This also minimizes the importance of the state administration in public opinion.

There are no private bureaucratic organizations in state-socialist societies, that is, in the *posttotalitarian* subtype. Nationalization of the economy in the form of state ownership brings about both the submission of the economy to the control of state power and the expansion of the bureaucratic mode of operation throughout the whole economy, services included. Because almost all kinds of public activities are put under state control and the state is bureaucratically organized, the monopolistic power position of bureaucracy is thus firmly established.

Weber clearly foresaw this kind of globalization of the bureaucratic mode of operation under state-socialism as well as the monopolistic power position of bureaucracy. He could not, however, foresee particular characteristics of bureaucracy under state-socialism.

Actually, as previously noted, there are formally two separate structures of bureaucracy in the posttotalitarian subsystem, the state and the party bureaucracies, although their close association makes this distinction one of secondary importance. Although formally separated, they both have the same general aim of directing and overlooking all types of social activity; moreover, they have parallel organs that "do the same thing," so ministries have equivalent "divisions" within the apparatus of the Central Committee of the Communist party; finally, they, in fact, act as an interlocking network of control over the society. Two separate hierarchies, those of the government and the party, merge at the top, forming one ruling elite.

There are frictions between the two apparatuses, party and government; but, in relation to the society, they are highly integrated and act accordingly. In a sense, they can be conceived of as a double-checking device. If one apparatus fails to control the society, the second still works. And, there is, in the long run, the growing bureaucratization of the party, which once was much more ideologically oriented and at least pretended to be something more than a mechanism of group rule. Today the difference between the governmental "official" and the party "apparatchik" is hardly detectable, either in mentality or in style.

What are the characteristic features of this huge "socialist officialdom," as seen particularly among governmental officials?

The universal application of bureaucratic administration in production, services, and culture has led to an enormous increase in the number of bureaucrats. This was not, however, accompanied by a corresponding concern for the competence of the bureaucracy. For example, if higher education is required for a position, this is largely a formal requirement involving little more than having a diploma. More important than that diploma is a political recommendation (the so-called *nomenklatura* system). This recommendation, in fact, is decisive in the staffing of higher positions, including managerial positions in industry. It actually lowers the functional efficiency of managerial cadres.

Another important factor in the bureaucracy's operation is the intrusion of changing directives into its everyday functioning. Hence, legal regulations are complemented by instructions given over the telephone or at briefings. Quite often, instructions force officials to circumvent the law. This depreciates the relevance of legal rules for the actual performance of duties. At the same time, there is a proliferation of laws that, today, is criticized even in the official press. For instance, in the Polish newspaper *Zycie Warszawy*, July 24, 1987, it was reported that in Poland, which has a uniform penal code, civil code, and work code, more than 429 statutes, 2,216 "implementation decrees," and 7,500 regulations issued by the ministries are in force. What the newspaper did not report was that almost every statute in Poland is continually revised and the regulations of the ministries change from year to year.

The inflation of law has very significant consequences. The accountability and predictability of the actions of the state administration are greatly reduced. The citizen suffers from this, as does the state as a whole, because one bureaucratic agency is unable to predict the decisions of another bureaucratic agency. In every case, several different legal regulations can be applied. This leads to uncertainty and even to elements of chaos in relations among specialized bureaucracies. Their subjection to supreme control by the power center does not remove this semichaos. Rather, the chaos consumes enormous amounts of time for "mediating" among the specialized bureaucracies and forces the power center to make Solomon-like decisions.

There is also a tendency toward "secrecy." Weber did observe that the collection of information and its elaboration in synthetic reports by bureaucrats goes hand in hand with their manipulation of this information so as to allow them to force through their own preferred options. In posttotalitarian systems, bureaucracies take advantage of this possibility just as Weber predicted. The monopoly of information is closely guarded. Such manipulation of information often serves to mislead public opinion and protect the power interest of the top bureaucratic echelons. Above all, the biased reports and news aim at improving the image of the political system.

The relations of the bureaucracy with political bodies take a very specific form in the posttotalitarian subsystem, with the political "fusion" of the dominant Communist party and governmental bureaucracies. Legislative bodies are subordinated to party directives and the subsequent programs of the government. Thus the party and government bureaucracies control the legislative bodies, both central and local.

Because independent social associations do not exist, the most elementary conditions for the interaction of the bureaucracy with various social groups are not met. Thus there is no impact of the outer world on the bureaucracy.

The entire set of conditions in which officials have to work is detrimental to the development of an ethic of accountability and responsibility. The bureaucratic setting is also detrimental to fostering a feeling of one's own importance, something that normally would produce pride and a self-assertive attitude.

An official learns from his own experience that the top administrative decisions are bent to the requirements of the moment and to others' incidental pressures. Quite often, "particular reasons" are given priority over the universal rules of the application of the law. This means a biased interpretation of status. An official has to manipulate the law under pressure "from above" and such pressures do not breed self-esteem. Particular criteria applied in making decisions at the "top" tend to develop into completely personal criteria at the lower levels of the administrative hierarchy. In this way, pure and simple corruption has developed. Changeability and biased interpretation of law turn into moral relativism.

An official knows how real power is distributed. So, he is arrogant when dealing with anyone dependent on him. But, he shows compliance when confronted with a superior. Members of the society are aware of manipulations by officials. As a consequence of this and other features of bureaucracy, the popular image of the upper- and middle-rank bureaucrat is negative. Professionals receive much higher social recognition than even top-rank officials. The lowest-rank officials are so numerous and so poorly paid that they are seen as part of the population; they are needed but unrewarded cogs in the bureaucratic machine.

The posttotalitarian "officialdom" presents the case in which a strong power position in bureaucratic structures is accompanied neither by high self-esteem nor by high social prestige.

LEGITIMACY

There are three possible bases for the claim of legitimacy and its recognition or refutation: rule through enacted laws, bureaucratic administration, and political arrangements (see Table 4.3).

The postabsolutist subtype bases its appeal on the idea of law. The system of law is portrayed as a foundation of social order and a key mechanism regulating the relations between the citizen and the state and among citizens. Stability and impartiality of law or, as Weber termed it, implementation "without regard to person," are considered the most important aspects of a lawful order. The general philosophical idea of law in this subtype is that certain characteristics of man and fundamental conditions of his collective existence have been "discovered" in the law through reason. Personal liberty and equality before the law are conceived as the "rights of man," grounded in reason. In this case, the general idea of the "reasonableness" of the law finds expression (see Schluchter 1981), as do nascent democratic ideals.

But these ideas of reasonableness and democratic rights also allow for the law to be changed. Necessary adjustment to social change or to desired new social arrangements are accepted as a source of amendments and refinements of status and regulations. The lawmaking process is not yet democratic, however. It is confined to a rather narrow elite of jurists, higher public officials, and selected politicians. In Bismarckian Germany, the Reichstag (parliament) voted only a limited number of laws, because the majority of issues were under the jurisdiction of the separate states within the German Reich. Even more important, the Reichstag was deprived of "legislative initiative"; proposals for new laws normally came from the government.

In the democratic subtype, the idea of reasonableness of the law does not disappear, although the "democratic" elements are strengthened in the general perception of the role of law and its use. First, the new laws are formed in a complex democratic process in which negotiations and mediations of group interests are carried out. Politicization of the lawmaking process is accepted as a necessary and positive aspect of social life. Second, law is uniformly conceived of as a vehicle for introducing various

social policies that are recognized as desirable. Third, the law is seen as
an instrument in the realization of an extended list of human rights. The
law thus is given a quality of what may be termed "humanized instrumentality."

In the posttotalitarian subtype, the law also is treated instrumentally
but the nature of this instrumentality is different. The law is used by the
ruling elites as a convenient tool for "organizing" society according to
their "new design." In the economy, market mechanisms are replaced by
legal regulations. Law is also used as a powerful tool for steering people
into various types of economic and social activity. In short, for the ruling
circles, the law is the most useful device for implementing both their
global ideas and specific, detailed plans, including the five-year economic
plan and annual economic plans. Such utilization of the law is presented
to the population, on one hand, as "lawful action" that by its nature
demands compliance. On the other hand, it is presented as the basis for
legitimizing the substantive goals of governmental actions, according to
the formula: what was enacted in legal procedures must be legitimate.

Moreover, the rulers appeal to the law as an instrument protecting
"normal" life against the threat of outbursts of social dissatisfaction.
"Normalization" was, in this way, a governmental slogan in Poland after
the imposition of martial law. The rulers appealed to law in trying to
portray their state as "the same as others" and "the same as always" and
thus they justified their coercive actions.

On a broader basis, the appeal to reasonableness in the postabsolutist
system and the appeal to the human instrumentality of the law in the
democratic system are accepted by the population, but the appeal to the
"organizing" and steering qualities of the law in the posttotalitarian
regime does not result in real legitimating support for the rulers. This is
because organization and control by means of the law cum bureaucracy
are not perceived by the population as bringing benefits to them. Furthermore, people realize that they are being manipulated when they hear
assertions that "our state is the same as others" or that its laws must be
accepted.

Do "political arrangements" contribute to the creation of a legitimacy
belief? Weber does not directly relate legitimacy belief to political
arrangements. Even in his time, however, political arrangements did contribute to the creation of legitimacy belief in the postabsolutist system.
The main features, in these cases, were the existence of the emperor,
constitution, and parliament. In legal-political terminology, this was a
"constitutional monarchy." Its acceptance played a part in the creation of
a "legitimacy belief."

Political arrangements in democratic rule can be globally defined as
"representative democracy." I believe that such arrangements also gain

legitimacy because people see them as politically "functional" and morally "good."

In the posttotalitarian subtype, on the other hand, the foundation of political arrangements is the hegemony or "the leading role" of the Communist party. All evidence suggests that this legitimacy claim is widely rejected. Of course, various conscious or subconscious manipulations occur, so that legitimating positions can be fabricated—especially for the sake of appearances. In some countries, too, delegitimating thoughts may be repressed and pushed into the subconscious. In Poland, rejection of "the leading role of the party" is not, however, repressed by many people.

What about the social programs generated in different power structures? In the postabsolutist system, the formation of specific programs is weak. The government wavers between the desire to continue traditional arrangements in social life and the pressure to consider partial social reforms. The value of tradition and the value of modernity coexist as the basis for specific governmental goals. Such an attitude of the rulers—if it is transformed into a legitimacy claim—gains the support of the majority of the people.

The democratic subtype only partly realizes its own substantive goals. Most generally, one can say: Popular opinion is that government ought to be guided by the preferences of the society. Because the preferences of various groups differ, however, agreement is reached on a more basic question, the procedures for setting goals. This is the democratic process. It is legitimate and, as a consequence, every set of goals negotiated in that process is legitimate. Concrete goals are replaced by the principles for arriving at such goals.

Obviously, every democratic state today espouses certain concrete social goals. I do not believe, however, that it is the concrete goals, as such, that legitimate the governments. Rather, convictions about the appropriateness of the democratic way of choosing goals are more important for legitimacy-granting processes. This is why conflict among interest groups may coexist with legitimating convictions.

In the posttotalitarian subtype, the government uses a specific substantive program as the basis for its claim of legitimacy. Expressed as a slogan, this program pretends to realize the interests of the working people, their social advancement, and general social justice.

In the initial period of rule in the Soviet Union and the socialist governments of Eastern Europe, the substantive program on which the elite sought to base its legitimacy met with a positive reaction among some groups of the population. This program embraced land reform, industrialization, and diminishing social differences among classes. The process of consolidating legitimacy on a substantive basis was blocked, however, because of a decline in the efficiency of the system as a whole, a failure to carry out promises, and the determination by a narrow elite of what specific policies were in the interest of the population. Today, at least in Poland, the elite has shifted its legitimacy claim to the thesis of allegedly realized social justice and governmental protection of "economically weak" groups. These claims are not supported by the population. Severe limitations of political liberty seem to destroy the potentially positive impact of social policy on legitimating thought.

When the legitimacy claim is based on the role of the bureaucracy in the contemporary state, it appeals to what is called functional efficiency. In all likelihood, Weber and his countrymen in Germany at the beginning of the twentieth century had this type of efficiency in mind. In contemporary democratic states, however, governments cannot base their legitimacy on the efficiency of the bureaucracy, in part because antibureaucratic conceptions and grass-roots antibureaucratic attitudes would undermine faith in such a claim for legitimacy. The main reason, however, would be that bureaucratic efficiency would not be equated with legitimacy. Besides, bureaucracy does not dominate all areas of life. Its relevance for the question of legitimacy is limited.

In the countries of the posttotalitarian subtypes, the "socialist organization of society" is portrayed as a great novelty and achievement, and its most universal and pervasive incarnation is the state bureaucracy. Those officials who carry out their duties poorly are distinguished as not being part of the "socialist organization of society" and are called bureaucrats. In a hidden, indirect way, it is suggested that socialist bureaucratic administration is the bearer not only of efficiency but also of something more—a "global utility for the society." It is alleged that such an administration carries out organizing and controlling functions, and stimulates economic and social development. It manages almost all the economy. It implements the social program of the government. It also "teaches" state discipline to young cadres of the intelligentsia.

The legitimacy claim refers to this beneficial function of the state administration. This claim fails to be actualized in positive convictions of people. The reason is the commonly perceived inefficiency of the bureaucracy as an organizer and animator of human actions as well as the exclusion of this bureaucracy from social control. The legitimacy claim behind the supposed beneficial functions of the state apparatus is rejected by the population.

In short, the postabsolutist bureaucracy *contributes* to the legitimacy belief; the democratic bureaucracy is *irrelevant* for the formation of the legitimacy belief; and the posttotalitarian bureaucracy *does not bring expected legitimating results.*

To conclude: How are particular aspects of the legitimacy claim recognized by the population? It would seem that, in the postabsolutist subtype, the legitimacy claim is recognized in all specified aspects; in the democratic subtype, some aspects are irrelevant and some are accepted; and in the posttotalitarian subtype, none of the specified aspects generates legitimacy belief.

REFERENCES

Bendix, Reinhard. 1962. *Max Weber: An Intellectual Portrait.* Garden City, NY: Anchor, Doubleday.

Etzioni, Amitai, ed. 1961. *Complex Organizations: A Sociological Reader.* New York: Holt, Rinehart & Winston.

Feher, Ferenc. 1982. "Paternalism as a Mode of Legitimation in Soviet-Type Societies." In *Political Legitimation in Communist States,* edited by T. H. Rigby and Ferenc Feher. New York: St. Martin's.

Feher, Ferenc, Agnes Heller, and Gyorgy Markus. 1983. *Dictatorship over Needs: An Analysis of Soviet Societies.* Oxford: Basil Blackwell.

Gerth, H. H. and C. Wright Mills, eds. 1958. *From Max Weber: Essays in Sociology.* New York: Oxford University Press.

Habermas, Jürgen. 1979. *Communication and the Evolution of Society.* Boston: Beacon.

Jowitt, Ken. 1983. "Soviet Neotraditionalism: The Political Corruption of a Leninist Regime." *Soviet Studies* 35:275-97.

Kielmansegg, Peter. 1971. "Legitimitat als analitische Kategorie." *Politische Vierteljahresschrift* 12:367-401.

Lowenthal, Richard. 1974. "On 'Established' Communist Party Regimes." *Studies in Comparative Communism: An International Interdisciplinary Journal* 7:335-58.

Luhmann, Niklas. 1983. *Legitimation durch Verfahren.* Frankfurt am Main: Suhrkamp.

Meyer, Alfred G. 1965. *The Soviet Political System.* New York: Random House.

Mommsen, Wolfgang J. 1974. *The Age of Bureaucracy: Perspectives on the Political Sociology of Max Weber.* New York: Harper & Row.

Murvar, Vatro. 1985. "Patrimonialism, Modern and Traditionalist: A Paradigm for Interdisciplinary Research on Ruleship and Legitimacy." In *Theory of Liberty, Legitimacy and Power: New Directions in the Intellectual and Scientific Legacy of Max Weber,* edited by Vatro Murvar. London: Routledge & Kegan Paul.

Rigby, T. H. 1982. "Introduction: Political Legitimacy, Weber, and Communist Mono-Organizational Systems." In *Political Legitimation in Communist States,* edited by T. H. Rigby and Ferenc Feher. New York: St. Martin's.

Rigby, T. H. and Ferenc Feher, eds. 1982. *Political Legitimation in Communist States.* New York: St. Martin's.

Schluchter, Wolfgang. 1981. *The Rise of Western Rationalism: Max Weber's Developmental History.* Berkeley: University of California Press.

Stallberg, Friedrich W. 1975. *Herrschaft und Legitimatat: Untersuchungen zu Anwendung und Anwendbarkeit zentraler Kategorien Max Webers.* Meisenheim am Glan: Verlag Anton Hain.

Weber, Max. 1956. *Wirtschaft und Gesellschaft.* Hlb. 1, 2. Tübingen: Mohr.

———. 1968. *Economy and Society: An Outline of Interpretive Sociology.* Vols. 1-3. New York: Bedminster.

Wesolowski, Wlodzimierz. 1989. "Weber's Concept of Legitimacy: Limitations and Continuations." In *Sisyphus—Sociological Studies.* Vol. 6. Warsaw: Polish Scientific Publishers.

5

Max Weber and the Modernization of China and Japan

Ken'ichi Tominaga

HEGEL, MARX, AND WEBER ON ORIENTAL SOCIETY OF THE NINETEENTH CENTURY

Since the time when European thinkers of the nineteenth century became seriously interested in Asia, Europeans have thought of Asia in terms of *stagnation* and *despotism*. Words like "Asian" (or "Oriental") stagnation and despotism express such a view.

Hegel, saying in his *Vorlesungen über die Philosophie der Geschichte* that world history goes from East to West, divided world history into four developmental stages: Orient, the Greek World, the Roman Empire, and the Germanic World. In these stages, Asia is the beginning; Europe is the end of world history. This is to say that the position of Asia in the development of the world remains always in a more primitive stage than the classical antiquity of Europe. In Hegel's mind, China has not changed, has not progressed, despite the alternation of dynasties, because it lacks the contrast of "objective being and subjective movement." As China is the empire of absolute equality but of no freedom except for the emperor, the mode of reign must inevitably be despotism (Hegel, *Werke* 12, 1970, pp. 133-57).

Marx started from accepting Hegel's interpretation of world history. When Marx presented the conceptualization of Asiatic, ancient, feudal, and modern bourgeois modes of production as successive epochs of economic formation of the society (*ökonomische Gesellschaftsformation*) in the preface of *Zur Kritik der politischen Ökonomie*, we see here again that Asia appears only once in the history of the world—as the most primitive stage, prior to the classical antiquity of Europe. This means that in Marx's mind Asia remains always primitive throughout the course of history.

On the other hand, Marx distinguished three stages of the forms of possession in his manuscript, "Formen, die der kapitalistischen Produktion vorhergehen" in *Grundrisse*: Asiatic possession, classical-ancient possession, and Germanic possession. It seems clear that these categories, adding the fourth form, capitalist possession, run parallel to the four categories in the preface of *Zur Kritik*. What Marx designated by the name of the Asiatic form of land possession is the state in which the family or its extended form, the clan, is the unit of land ownership, the individual being embedded in the community (Marx, in Marx-Engels, Werke 42, 1982, pp. 383-95). The particular part of Asia connoted by Marx's word, "Asiatic," however, cannot be identified. What Marx fragmentarily referred to in his contribution to the *New York Daily Tribune*, in letters addressed to Engels, and in *Das Kapital* as examples of "Oriental despotism" are mostly examples from India. It seems that he did not specifically study China.

Then comes the name of Max Weber. His study of China in *Konfuzianismus und Taoismus* and of India in *Hinduismus und Buddhismus*, both collected in three volumes of essays, *Gesammelte Aufsätze zur Religionssoziologie* (hereafter abbreviated as *GAzRS*), are the first, and perhaps still the best, works written by the Westerners on Asia that clearly apply the theoretical framework of comparative sociology. Weber, being a century younger than Hegel and half a century younger than Marx, stood in a far more advantageous position for being able to make extensive use of the accumulation of Asian studies achieved by nineteenth-century Europe. We must also notice, though, that Weber, before beginning his specific studies of Asia, had constructed a sociology of religion, a sociology of domination, and an economic sociology as theoretical frameworks for the comparative study of East and West. These theoretical frameworks gave his Asian studies an unprecedented high level.

Both of Weber's Asian studies have the title of "religious" study, because his macro-sociological analysis has as its micro base a theory of action in which the "practical motives" (*praktische Antriebe*) of human social action, including economic action, are sought in religious ethics (*GAzRS*, I, p. 238). But Weber's study of religion is not simply a study of religion. Weber's sociology of religion has a close internal relation with his sociology of domination and his economic sociology. We should give thought to Weber's often-repeated central thesis that the most rationalized form of economic action is capitalism, which in turn is inseparably connected with the social structure of modern bureaucratic organization as the most rationalized form of domination. This is to say that his *GAzRS* cannot be separated from his other monument, *Wirtschaft und Gesellschaft* (hereafter abbreviated as *WuG*). In the latter, too, Weber analyzes Asian society, including a fragmentary but especially suggestive comparison of the social structures of traditional China and of Tokugawa Japan.

The purpose of my analysis is, first, to examine the theoretical frameworks of Weber's sociology of domination and his economic sociology, in relation to his sociology of religion, from the standpoint of the analysis of Asian society, and, second, to endeavor to do some comparative study of the modernization of China and Japan by making use of a conceptual scheme derived from Weber's work.

WEBER'S THEORY OF MODERNIZATION

Weber's object of study in his *Konfuzianismus und Taoismus* is the social structure of premodern China. But when he studied traditional societies, whether in his sociology of religion, his sociology of domination, or his economic sociology, he always gave thought to the contrast between Occident and non-Occident. Contemporary Occidental societies are the modernized societies. In selecting, therefore, non-Occidental premodern societies as his subject of study, his purpose was to investigate the possibilities for modernization of non-Occidental societies by comparing them with the premodern stage of Occidental societies. That is, Weber's sociology of religion, sociology of domination, and economic sociology always have a latent common theme of modernization.

Weber asked himself, at the opening paragraph of *Vorbemerkung* in *GAzRS*, the basic question: "What linkage of circumstances should be attributed to the fact that on the ground of Western civilization, and here only, cultural phenomena have appeared which—as at least we like to think—lie in a line of development having *universal* significance and validity?" He answered it by presenting the long list of items that were alleged to exist "only in the Occident" (*nur im Okzident*) as follows (*GAzRS*, I, pp. 1-12):

— sciences in the developmental stage we now recognize as universally valid;
— the strictly juristic scheme and mode of thought of the Roman law, and of the Western law that belongs to that school;
— rational harmonious music;
— the rational use of the Gothic vault;
— the press and periodicals;

— the rational and systematic operation of specialized sciences, with trained and specialized personnel;
— the trained official, the pillar of both the modern state and of the modern economy;
— *Ständestaat* (as distinguished from the patriarchal state);
— parliaments of periodically elected representatives;
— the state in general, in the sense of political association with a rationally ordained constitution, rationally ordained law, and an administration oriented to rationally enacted rules or laws, administered by trained officials;
— capitalist economic action as one that rests on the expectation of profit by the utilization of opportunities for exchange, that is in (formally) peaceful chances of profit;
— capital calculation;
— the rational capitalistic organization of (formally) free labor;
— the separation of household and business; and
— rational bookkeeping.

After the long enumeration of these and other related items, he mentions "the specific nature of rationalism of Western culture" as a kind of summary statement. Rationalism, of course, can be conceived of on various specific levels, but Weber emphasizes "rationalism in the life-style" as a general factor in the human attitude. And he maintains that religion is the most important factor in the formation of the life-style. Thus a last item is added:

— rationalism in the life-style as related to rationalization of religion.

Weber listed the above items rather promiscuously, but we may be able to put them in a logical order by thinking of them in terms of four dimensions:

(1) *scientific spirit* as the motive of scientific-technological modernization— among the above items, "sciences" and "the rational and systematic operation of specialized sciences" belong to this dimension;
(2) *spirit of capitalism* as the motive of economic modernization—among the above items, "the capitalist economic action," "capital calculation," "rational capitalistic organization of free labor," and "the separation of household and business" belong to this dimension;
(3) *spirit of democracy* as the motive of political modernization—among the above items, "*Ständestaat* (as distinguished from the patriarchal state)," "parliaments," and "the state in the sense of political association" belong to this dimension; and

(4) *spirit of rationalism* as the motive of sociocultural modernization—among the above items, "the strictly juristic scheme," "rational harmonious music," "the Gothic vault," "the press and periodicals," "the trained official," and "rationalism in the life-style as related to rationalization of religion" belong to this dimension.

Among these four dimensions, dimension 2 and dimension 3 are the subject of his economic sociology and sociology of domination, respectively. And all the considerations of dimensions 1 to 3 are merged into dimension 4, which is the subject of his sociology of religion, thus together constituting his huge system of modernization theory. Weber asserted, among other things, that the last item, above, in dimension 4, "rationalism in the life-style," expresses the human attitude of living that underlies all the items he enumerated. Weber saw the root of this factor, which determines the attitude of living, in religion. While religion is, in essence, concerned with the irrational aspect of the human mind, modernization rationalizes this realm of essential irrationality. According to Weber, there are two measures of the degree of rationalization of religion. One is the degree to which it is liberated from magic; the other is the degree to which the relation between the god and the world is systematically integrated. Weber observed that ascetic Protestantism promotes the rationalization of both, whereas Confucianism still has many irrational elements (*GAzRS*, I, pp. 512-16).

Almost 70 years have passed since Max Weber published these writings in 1920, during which time the world has changed drastically. While Weber mentioned repeatedly that the above items are "only in the Occident," they are now no longer limited to the Occident, but are shared by several non-Occidental societies, most conspicuously Japan. It is true that these non-Occidental societies did not produce them as their own invention, but accepted them through cultural diffusion. Nevertheless, if we define the modernization of a nation by the degree to which everyone in the nation is able to enjoy the above items, it would be safe to say that modernization is no longer confined to the West, and that non-Western nations now bear the burden of developing these items still more. Japan stands on this side. At the same time, however, we must say that Weber's "only-in-the-Occident" proposition is still not outdated, to the extent that many of his items are not yet shared by many developing nations in the world. China still stands on this side.

In this chapter, I compare the social structures of China and Japan. While Weber's references to China are extensive, his references to Japan are fragmentary. But even in these fragments he had a clear recognition of the very contrasting nature of the two countries in terms of their social structures. Comparative analysis needs a set of conceptual tools. Thus we start from the investigation of Weber's theoretical framework.

WEBER'S SOCIOLOGY OF DOMINATION AND ECONOMIC SOCIOLOGY

An important feature of Weber's sociology of domination and economic sociology lies in the construction of a typology of social and economic structures. He developed two such typologies, one for the analysis of premodern social structure, one for the analysis of modern social structure. The former is a combination of the types of traditional structures of domination (patriarchalism, patrimonialism, and feudalism) and of non-market structures of the economy. The latter is a combination of the bureaucratic structure of domination and the capitalist structure of the market. Using these typologies, Weber investigates the conditions of the transition from premodern to modern sets of structures. In this way, both his sociology of domination and his economic sociology are linked to the theory of modernization.

What is specifically important in our context is that Weber's conceptualization of traditional society is constructed not as a single type but as pluralistic types. Weber's central thesis is that the social structure of traditional societies is highly diversified. This diversity is expressed in terms of a continuum of which patrimonialism and feudalism, two models of domination, constitute the two extreme poles.

Patrimonialism consists of social relations in which father-son relations in the patriarchal family are as if extended to nonblood lord-vassal relations. The patriarchal family is that type of stem family or extended family in which the family head (the patriarch), the oldest man, has despotic power over family members but family members have a feeling of *Pietät* toward the family head. When this father-son relation is transformed into a lord-vassal relation, it is called *Tischgemeinschaft*—a monarch's single "household" in which all the land and people are owned by the monarch. In patrimonialism, however, the lord and the vassals are geographically separated, so that *Tischgemeinschaft* is disorganized but the *Pietät* relation is maintained. As all the land and people belong to the monarch in the patrimonial state, he can assign the obligation of *Leiturgie* (corvée and tax) to all of them. The dispatched vassals, being patrimonial bureaucrats, are paid prebend (*Pfründe*) from the monarch's household, an individually appropriated but noninheritable allowance in kind or in rent (*WuG*, 5. Aufl., p. 136).

Feudalism is, in contrast to patrimonialism, a mode of decentralized domination in which vassals are themselves independent small lords who have their own fiefs, and in which the central lord, king, has only a limited power over these vassals. Feudalism is characterized by many small-scale lords who own the land and people by inheritance. They make a contract of lord-vassal relation with the king for mutual security, which takes the form that the king nominally invests them with the fief as *Lehen* for protecting them, in exchange for the small lords' rendering vassal homage to the king. But vassals have no *Pietät* feeling toward the king. The king's power is so limited that he cannot assign the *Leiturgie* to land and people under the hands of his vassals. Unlike *Pfründe*, the allowance paid to the vassals from the monarch's household, *Lehen* is inherited by vassals as appropriation, independent of the monarch's household. This is the decisive difference between patrimonialism and feudalism (*WuG*, 5. Aufl., pp. 625-30).

Patrimonialism and feudalism are the two opposite poles of the types of traditional domination in the stage of agricultural society.[1] But while patrimonial domination was formed in ancient times (an early period of the agricultural stage) and has existed all over the world extensively and enduringly up to modern times, feudalism as *Lehen*-system in the pure type existed only in the medieval age (a later period of the agricultural stage) and geographically in Western Europe. Outside of Europe, Japan is, as was systematically depicted by Jacobs (1958), the only country that had feudalism akin to the European type. But Weber argued that the Japanese feudal system was not perfectly the *Lehen*-type, because while the relations between *bakufu*- and *tozama*-daimyos were close to *Lehen*-type, *fudai*-daimyos, who were the kinship or retainers of, and had a subordinate relation with, the shogun had a strong feeling of *Pietät* toward the shogun (*WuG*, 5. Aufl., p. 629).

The problem of whether patrimonialism and feudalism are facilitative of or detrimental to the development of capitalism is central to us. While what Weber mentions on this point is fragmentary and somewhat equivocal, his essential thesis can be summarized:

Patrimonialism tends to be detrimental to, rather than facilitative of, capitalist development, because patrimonial bureaucrats, who take the role of tax-collection contractors, and who stand between the monarch and the people, tend to produce "politically oriented capitalism" rather than market-oriented capitalism (*WuG*, 5. Aufl., p. 117). On the other hand, patrimonial bureaucracy is not as rationally and objectively (*sachlich*) operated an organization as is modern bureaucracy, because as

---

[1] There are many varying combinations within the two poles of patrimonialism and feudalism. Weber offers a list of such classifications. But we need not enter into these details here.

patrimonial bureaucrats are subordinated to the monarch they tend to be affected by his arbitrariness. For example, it is typical for patrimonial bureaucrats to be promoted or to lose their positions overnight through the monarch's arbitrariness. Such arbitrariness hinders rational development by preventing "calculability" (*Berechenbarkeit*). Patrimonial bureaucracy, moreover, has no specialization of jobs nor guarantee of functional autonomy (*WuG*, 5. Aufl., pp. 596-98, 650-52).

Feudalism, on the contrary, tends to be facilitative of, rather than detrimental to, capitalist development, because feudalism, as it is based on a decentralized administration based on small districts (unlike patrimonialism, based on centralized administration on a national scale), "minimizes the necessity of bureaucracy," so that there is no group of bureaucrats who take the role of tax collectors. In feudalism, moreover, vassals establish independent status (*Stände*), which is not affected by the monarch's arbitrariness. Furthermore, in contrast to patrimonialism, where all wealth concentrates on the monarch's household, feudalism makes it possible to raise the middle strata, because of the economic independence of the citizens. Weber maintains that the reason why the development of modern capitalism occurred first in Britain can be explained by the fact that the domination by patrimonial bureaucracy was minimized in Britain (*WuG*, 5. Aufl., pp. 625-53).

WEBER ON CHINESE SOCIETY

Weber's view of China, in one respect, reflects the common view of European intellectuals, as represented by Hegel and Marx. In this view, China, in contrast to the West, is the society of no development. The "only-in-the-Occident" proposition expresses this view. It argues from the Western standard that China could not attain modernization because China lacked specific elements that existed in the West. Indeed, Weber's *Konfuzianismus und Taoismus* is full of such propositions as "China lacked . . ." (*Es fehlte . . . in China*), ". . . did not exist in China" (. . . *existierte in China nicht*), and ". . . was hindered by lack of . . ." (. . . *ist durch das Fehlen des . . . gehemmt worden*).

In another respect, however, it must be emphasized that Weber's view of China is fundamentally different from such conceptualizations as Hegel's "beginning of the World history" or Marx's "Asiatic mode of production." Although he asserted that China has been a stagnant society for over 2,000 years since the Qin (221 to 207 B.C.)-Han (202 B.C. to 221 A.D.) dynasties, Weber correctly recognized that there had been development in China in its own way. Although he acknowledged that China had been dominated by despotism, he recognized that it is an error to apply such a loose concept as "Oriental despotism" to all of Asia, bundling China, Japan, Islam, and others, and that the Asian countries have their distinct social structures. These recognitions were possible because Weber had already established his theoretical framework of comparative sociological analysis.

From Weber's analysis of traditional China, I think it is possible to extract five important factors that differentiate China from Europe:

(1) Patrimonialism as contrasted to feudalism. The social structure of China started as sib feudalism in the Zhou dynasty in ancient times (ca. 1122-256 B.C.), a different system from the feudalism of medieval Europe, and then moved to a patrimonial bureaucratic system in the Qin-Han dynasty.

Feudalism under the Zhou dynasty was not based on the system of *Grundherrschaft* in the Western sense. Instead, it was a system in which the members of the patrilineal kinship group (sib) of the king are given the official *Lehen* corresponding to hereditary family rank (*GAzRS*, I, pp. 314-15). The Emperor Shi Huang Di, after he united the whole of China (221 B.C.), ceased to divide the land to give his kinship the *Lehen*, and established a centralized bureaucratic system of office hierarchy. Thus sib feudalism terminated and people outside of the monarch's sib group became qualified to be promoted as bureaucrats. The whole land and people were the emperor's patrimonium and were governed directly by him through his bureaucratic system. This can be interpreted as the common pattern of the ancient bureaucratic empire similar to the Roman Empire. The decisive difference between China and Europe, however, is that while Europe moved to *Lehen*-feudalism in the Middle Ages, China continued to be a patrimonially unified despotic state for 2,000 years until the end of Qing dynasty in 1912. This would basically explain why China has been so stagnant despite the high level of civilization in ancient times.

(2) The sib group (zongzu) *in rural villages.* In China, the sib (*Sippe*), which disappeared entirely in medieval Europe, developed highly in rural villages, especially in the Song dynasty (960-1279) up to modern times.[2] While in the ancient Zhou dynasty its development was limited only to the kinship of the king, the sib system called *zongzu* became universal among farmers in the Song dynasty and thereafter; it was connected with the religious function of ancestor worship as well as with the self-governing function of the maintenance of village peace.

[2.] It was in South China that *zongzu* (sib) fully developed. Olga Lang, who visited rural villages of Guangdong and Fuzhou provinces in 1936, reported the strongly organized big sibs (Lang calls them clans) that developed ancestor temples, owned large amounts of farmland, administered schools, and owned stores and pawnshops. In Central and North China, contrary to the South, sibs were already declining at that time, either no longer existing or existing but functioning minimally without sib property (Lang 1946, pp. 173-80).

Zongzu in China was the patrilineal and exogamous kinship group, headed by a leader elected from among the patriarchs, and known by its close union of blood ties. *Zongzu* had not only an ancestral hall where a general meeting was held twice a year but also common property, usually farmland, for getting rent; a genealogical chart listing all the sib members' names, classified by generations from a founder up to the present; and sib precepts for conducting strong self-government, self-defense, and mutual aid. Weber emphasized above all that the strong self-government and self-defense of the sib "from below" firmly prevented the permeation of the lower reach of patrimonial-bureaucratic administration "from above."[3] This means that successive Chinese dynasties had been characterized, despite centralized despotism, by very weak administration and jurisdiction, so people could not get governmental services, public peace could not be maintained, and daily life suffered from social unease. The *zongzu* system was a kind of functional substitute for administration that grew naturally from the functional requirement of coping with these situations. Conversely, the firm self-government of *zongzu* created an apathetic attitude in the people toward the state, making the continuation of the emperor's despotism possible over 2,000 years. In this sense, the strong *zongzu* tie was one of the important sources of the stagnation of Chinese society (*GAzRS*, I, pp. 375-90).

(3) The guild organization (hanghui) *in cities.* In cities, unlike the villages, the sib was not developed; the guild was the functional equivalent of the sib. Weber, while emphasizing that Chinese cities lacked the citizens' self-government of medieval European cities, stresses that the guild organizations firmly kept the regulation of the economic life of the city in their hands.

The *hanghui* had millions in fortune and in many cases invested them in the land. While the *hanghui*, unlike the medieval European guilds that were guaranteed liberties by governments through "charters," were spontaneous associations without government sanction, they often had absolute jurisdiction over their members. They controlled all the economic

---

[3.] On the relation between the despotic state and the village self-government in China, Morimitsu Shimizu gave this sociological explanation: The village is *Gemeinschaft*, forming human cooperation that embraces the entire person, while the state is *Gesellschaft*, particularistic and specific. Therefore, custom, mores, tradition, social authority, and the like cannot be created by the state, and their origin lies in the village community. In the traditional Chinese state, politicians had been devoted only to the maintenance of the national defense and to collection of taxes, demanding submissiveness by the people without making any effort to cooperate with them. Thus almost all indispensable items for cooperative life in the village, such as engineering, economy, police, water, sanitation, education, and religion, could never be provided by the state. Chinese villagers had to develop a system of self-government (Shimizu 1939, pp. 104-14, 251-59).

matters that had important meaning for their members: measures and weights, standards of currency, street maintenance, control of credit, cartels. The *hanghui* levied not only taxes from their members but also entrance fees and securities from new members. They also arranged play and took care of funerals for poor members. While in China the city had no right of self-government, guild organizations virtually achieved self-government (*GAzRS*, I, pp. 290-96).

(4) *The literati[4] as the traditional ruling class.* The ruling class in China had consistently for 2,000 years been the literati (*Literatenstand*). While patrimonialism existed all over the world—in ancient Egypt, Turkey, India, ancient Rome—patrimonial structure in China had a different feature from these others in that the literati had dominated it.

The literati, unlike the clerics of Christianity or Islam, Jewish rabbis, Indian Brahmans, or the priests of ancient Egypt, were educated in secular ("layman") learning (*Laienbildung*). Their prestige was based not on magical charm, but on knowledge of writing and literature (*Schriftgelehrtentum*). Their status was not hereditary but achieved by a long series of selection mechanisms known as the classical system of national examinations (*keju*). By passing an examination at the appropriate level, they secured a government post at that rank, and became members of the hierarchy of patrimonial bureaucracy, of which the emperor was the top. The examination being a bitter struggle for achieving the status of the ruling class, a unified system of the orthodox doctrine was required. This was the Confucian doctrine.

(5) *The role of Confucianism.* Confucianism was a nonreligious religion or a "religious ethics." Weber calls it "layman religion" (*Laienreligion*). There was no prophet nor priest in China. The cult of Confucianism, being entirely nonorgiastic, was exercised by men of political power; this was the role of the literati as patrimonial bureaucrats. In this sense, the patrimonial state in traditional China was, as Weber suggested, a "church state" (*Kirchenstaat*) in which the Emperor was the pontifex (*GAzRS*, I, pp. 311-12, 396-401). Weber admits the similarity of the literati with the Indian Brahmans, who were also the stratum of aristocratic knowledge and training, but emphasizes the important difference in that the Brahmans had no "governmental career" nor any connection with the temporal power of the emperor (*GAzRS*, II, pp. 136-39).

We need to consider the relationship between the importance of *zongzu* as the blood tie in traditional China and the role of Confucianism as the

---

[4.] The literati are sometimes likened to the English gentry, and in Chinese-Japanese *shenshi* (*shinshi*) or *shitafu* (*shitaifu,*). The top grade was called *jinshi*, the title of those who passed the highest stage of the national examination.

2,000-year spiritual background of traditional China. This relationship seems to be twofold:

On the one hand, that Confucianism was secular knowledge, and as such accessible to anyone through training, made it possible to separate the patrimonial bureaucracy decisively from the ascriptive status of blood tie. It was a great paradox of traditional China that the hierarchical order of the patrimonial bureaucracy at its top was separated from the blood principle of *zongzu*, which continued to restrict people's lives through ancestor worship, sib property, and sib precept. It was Confucianism that made this paradox possible. Confucianism in this respect stands out in sharp contrast to Hinduism, which produced the caste system. Weber, too, observed the rational and antitraditional character of Confucianism in this respect (*GAzRS*, I, pp. 396-99).

On the other hand, however, the role performed by Confucianism as the spiritual background of the patrimonial bureaucracy throughout 2,000 years of the history of China was, of course, its traditionalism, that is, the system of beliefs that supported the traditional social structure. Weber expresses this by saying that Confucianism presupposes "the ethics of unconditional affirmation of and adaptation to this world" (*GAzRS*, I, p. 515). Confucian ethics did not include the motivation to reshape (*umgestalten*) this world, as did the Puritan ethics that produced "mighty and pathetic tension against this world" (*GAzRS*, I, p. 513). Confucian ethics are the ethics of patriarchal family relations on the basis of which the son must have a feeling of *Pietät* toward his father. Thus Weber concludes:

> The content of the duties of a Confucian Chinese was always and everywhere *Pietät* toward concrete, living or dead people, who are closely connected to him through given order, and was never toward a supermundane God, and therefore never toward sacred "thing" or "idea." . . . The great achievement of ethical religions, above all of the ethical and ascetic sects of Protestantism, was to break the sib band, and to establish the superiority of belief- and ethical way-of-living-*Gemeinschaft* against blood-*Gemeinschaft*, even to a larger extent against the family. (*GAzRS*, I, p. 523)

Modernization can only be achieved by going beyond the closed blood-*Gemeinschaft* of kinship relations. In the Occident, the Puritan ethic provided motivation to do so, because it emphasized *Pietät* toward a supermundane God. In China, the Confucian ethics failed to provide motivation to do so, because *Pietät* always remained within the order of blood relations. Here is, we may say, the basic reason why Confucianism could not surpass traditionalism.

CHINA AND JAPAN: A COMPARATIVE
SOCIOLOGY OF MODERNIZATION

We have extracted from Weber's analysis five sociological factors that characterize the traditional society of China: patrimonial bureaucracy, sib system, urban guild, the literati, and Confucianism. When we examine these items from the perspective of modernization, we realize that each had the effect of making Chinese society adhere to traditionalism, hindering modernization.

(1) We have already mentioned Weber's point that the patrimonial bureaucracy tends to produce "politically oriented capitalism" and not to facilitate modern market-oriented capitalism. This gives insight into why, in the Republic of China after the Xinhai Revolution (1911), the natural growth of private entrepreneurs was blocked by the development of a limited number of bureaucratic capitalists and *maiben* (comprador) capitalists, who were in governmental jobs and formed a *zaibatsu* family.[5] They made up an early monopoly peculiar to late-coming industrialization, and hindered the growth of free market capitalism of the middle-class type.

(2) We have already seen that the sib group *zongzu*, characteristic of Chinese society, had grown under the Song dynasty up to modern times, while the sib or clan disappeared in Europe during the Middle Ages. Generally speaking, as blood group kinship declines, functional groups (organizations) grow in the process of modernization. When strong blood groups continue to exist, as in China, social relations that accumulated within the kinship group do not readily diminish. This would prevent the growth of functional groups and hence modernization itself. For example, there is a tendency in China, as is seen in "sib industry" (*Sippengewerbe*), pointed out by Weber, for what would otherwise be functional groups to be connected with blood groups. In such a case, industrial technology

[5.] The Chinese word *maiben* (comprador), when it originated at the time of the Ming Dynasty, meant the merchants who provided the court with goods, then after the Opium War, it came to refer to those Chinese who, being employed by a foreign (Western) commercial firm situated in China, took the role of the agent. Western merchants needed *maiben*, as they could not enter into confident relations with Chinese, nor could they be familiar with Chinese commercial habits, which differed in each local market. Above all, in the development of the Westernization movement after the 1860s, Western-oriented bureaucrats came to be closely connected with compradors, because they needed compradors for the process of importing Western technology, capital, and products. Thus compradors, starting from their early role of agents employed by Western firms, had grown to become independent big businessmen through their association with bureaucratic-capitalist as well as military leaders. See, for example, Huang et al. (1982).

tends to be confined within the inherited secret. This would hinder modernization and industrialization.

(3) What is true for the rural sibs can be applied as well to the urban guilds, *hanghui*. Guilds, of course, are not blood groups, but occupational groups. But sibs and guilds are similar in that both are closed and do not admit new entrants from outside. As we have seen, Chinese guilds, unlike European and Japanese guilds, were spontaneous associations without government sanction, so they were politically powerless. But they had a strongly closed nature, because in addition to occupational similarity they were limited to people of the same province (Shimizu 1939, pp. 35-40). Because of this closedness as well as political powerlessness, guilds in China could not take the lead in the process of modernization.

(4) It is well known that the literati, who continued to be in the orthodox ruling position during 2,000 years' history of patrimonial bureaucracy, could not become the innovators in the modernization of China. First, although the literati achieved their status not by family background but by success in the severe selection process,[6] the content of the national examinations demanded only knowledge of literature, and did not demand professional qualification based on scientific knowledge. Second, the national examinations required not only long preparation but also waiting time. The *zongzu* of the candidate gave financial help for covering these costs. It was, therefore, an important condition for success that wealthy *zongzu* invested a lot of money in helping talented youth among the sib members.[7] Third, patrimonial bureaucrats, being the tax-collection contractors of the emperor, had many chances for accumulating wealth by exploiting their official status (*Amtsausbeutung*). They then could contribute to the increase of the sib's property by investing the accumulation

[6.] Robert Marsh, who statistically analyzed the family background and careers of mandarins of the Qing Dynasty (1644-1912), concluded that, although the chance was opened to sons of commoners, it was actually the 2% of elite families who produced 65% of *jinshi*, whereas the 98% of commoner families produced 35% of them. But he added that once a person successfully qualified for *jinshi*, chances for promotion were not influenced by family background (Marsh 1961, pp. 124-39, 186-90).

[7.] Income from the sib property (mainly farm rent for tenancy) was used for expenditures functionally necessary for the maintenance of *zongzu*. In Morimitsu Shimizu's historical study of the institution of the sib property, the expenditure for *zongzu* of Fan, known as the founder of the institution in the age of the North Song Dynasty (960-1127), were (1) provision of rice to all the sib members, (2) subsidies for funeral and marriage expenses, (3) educational and travel expenses for those among the sib youths who took *jinshi* examinations, (4) administration costs of the sib school for children, and (5) expenses for ancestral worship ceremonies and for maintenance of the sib temple and tombs (Shimizu 1949, pp. 64-72, 145-53). The larger the size of the sib property per its population, the larger the expenditure for each item, so that a youth who belonged to a rich *zongzu* could enjoy a financial advantage in taking the *jinshi* examination.

in land after retirement. In this way, the examination actually had an inseparable connection with sib. Weber called such bureaucrats' accumulation of wealth through exploitation of the official post "internal-political booty capitalism" (*innerpolitischer Beutekapitalismus*) (GAzRS, I, p. 375). Such booty capitalism produced an extreme gulf between big landowners and poor tenant farmers.

(5) The spiritual aspect of the traditionalism in the 2,000 years of China is, essentially, Confucianism. Weber, asking himself what the essence of Confucianism is, gave four components to his answer: Confucianism is (a) ethics; (b) inner-worldly morality of laymen (*innerweltliche Laiensittlichkeit*); (c) adaptation to this world, to its orders and conventions; and (d) a tremendous code of political maxims and rules of social propriety for cultured men of the world (*GAzRS*, I, p. 441). While all these items are appropriate for characterizing Confucianism, it must be noted that the most important point is the limitation of the inner-worldly order to the blood-related society. Only Puritanism, Weber argued, has carried through the complete demystification of the world (*Entzauberung der Welt*), whereas Confucianism has still left untouched the tradition of irrational elements. After the Xinhai Revolution, many Chinese intellectuals came to reject Confucianism, having instead sought the doctrine of the reform of inner-worldly order in Marxist thought imported from the West. Confucianism could not in the end produce the motivational force to change the traditional society from within.

Our next step is to apply these five dimensions to Japan. While Weber did not develop a systematic analysis of Japanese society, he made several fragmentary references to it in *WuG*, which shows that he had insight into the differences between the social structures of traditional society in China and Japan. In the following, going considerably beyond Weber's own analysis, I compare China and Japan, using Weber's principles as the framework for my analysis.

(1) Medieval Japan, unlike traditional China, was not a patrimonial society. In contrast to traditional China, in which patrimonial bureaucracy had dominated for 2,000 years since the Qin-Han dynasty, in Japan feudalism had dominated for 700 years, from the beginning of the Kamakura period to the end of the Tokugawa period (1192-1868). Corresponding to the sib feudalism of China before 221 B.C., Japan before the Taika Reform in 645 was a society of the clan system. Corresponding to the formation of patrimonialism in China after 221 B.C., Japan after the Taika Reform became a despotic, patrimonial type of empire, the institutional basis of which Japan learned from Tang China (618-906). In Japan's transformation from ancient patrimonialism to feudalism, however, Japanese social structure decisively parted from the Chinese. It is true that, as Weber emphasized, Japanese feudalism cannot exactly be iden-

tified with *Lehen*-feudalism of Europe. This is especially true for the relation between shogun and the *fudai*-daimyos of the Tokugawa period, in which the *fudai*-daimyos were strongly connected with shogun by the *Pietät* feeling. Moreover, the Tokugawa shogunate was engaged in state administration through the *bakufu* bureaucracy, composed of *fudai*-daimyos and other direct retainers of shogun (*hatamoto* and *gokenin*), whose structure was different from that of the feudalism Weber depicted as "minimizing the requirement of bureaucracy." Furthermore, the emperor system, the institutional derivative of the ancient despotism, continued to exist in Japan all through the feudal ages. The legitimacy of the shogunate power had its roots in the institutionalized charisma of the emperor, in the sense that the shoguns were nominally appointed by the emperor. In these respects, we cannot deny that Japanese feudalism had a more or less patrimonial background. Despite these differences, however, Japanese social structure was much closer to that of Europe than to that of China, in the sense that the land and the people were divided into pieces possessed by feudal lords (*daimyos*), and that the shogunate, the central power, could not assign *Leiturgie* to daimyos' territory.

(2) The blood-tie group was not so strong in Japan as in China. In contrast to traditional China in which *zongzu*, the firmly structured sib group, was widely developed, there existed in Japan another type of kinship system called *dozoku*.[8] While both *zongzu* and *dozoku* are kinship groups bound together by the consciousness of common ancestors through patrilineal descent, usually characterized by the name of sib, they differ from one another in the following respects:

(a) While *zongzu* in China was based on a system of exogamy and as such exercised a strong control as sib over the members, *dozoku* in Japan did not. Correspondingly, in China a husband's *zongzu* did not accept his

---

[8.] The comparison between Japan's *dozoku* and China's *zongzu* is a very interesting and important research subject. The two have been studied by different researchers, however, so that a comparative perspective has not been achieved. On this point, it is important to note that Kizaemon Aruga, one of the central figures in the study of *dozoku*, emphasizing the existence of nonblood branch families, asserted that *dozoku* is something other than the kinship. Aruga's point of emphasis was placed on the Japanese uniqueness of *ie* and *dozoku*, having the effect of diverting interest to the comparison of *dozoku* with kinship groups of other societies (Aruga 1971, pp. 28-52). While Seiichi Kitano, who took a different point of view in the study of *dozoku*, opposed Aruga's emphasis on Japanese uniqueness, he maintained, as Aruga did, that *dozoku* is not kinship (Kitano 1976, pp. 12-14). In my opinion, however, the existence of the nonblood branch families does not prevent us from regarding *dozoku* as a form of kinship, as they actually have had the fiction of the blood relation. It was Yuzuru Okada who defined Japan's *dozoku* clearly as a form of patrilineal kinship group (Okada 1959, pp. 25-38). By following his lead, we can compare Japan's *dozoku* to China's *zongzu*, which is another form of patrilineal kinship group.

wife, who retained a different surname from her husband's, whereas in Japan the wife became a member of her husband's *dozoku* by marriage.

(b) While *zongzu* in China had a physical base in sib property, usually farmland, and the rent that came from this property was an important source of income for the common use of the sib, the *dozoku* in Japan had no such common economic base. There was nonmonetary mutual help (for example, farm work) among *dozoku* members, but no monetary gift as in China, where, as I argued earlier, a youth could get financial help from the sib for the national examination.

(c) While *zongzu* in China had an ancestral temple, a genealogical chart, and sib precepts, as we already observed, the *dozoku* in Japan had none of them.

(d) While *zongzu* in China had no distinction of head-family versus branch-family, because the Chinese inheritance system was based on an equal division, so that the head of *zongzu* was selected from the sib members by criteria of social class status, reputation, and seniority,[9] *dozoku* in Japan consisted of the linkage of head-family versus branch-family, so that the head of *dozoku* was always fixed on the patriarch of the head-family.

(e) While *zongzu* in China conducted strong internal self-government and self-defense, and even developed jurisdiction for sib members, *dozoku* in Japan never had such functions.

Each of these five differences tells us that *zongzu* in China was a far more strongly institutionalized organization than *dozoku* in Japan.

[9.] According to Olga Lang (in her survey of Guangdong and Fujian provinces), *zongzu* in South China had two sets of leaders: the clan elders and the clan executives. At the time of her survey (1937), the real power shifted from the former to the latter (Lang 1946, pp. 175-76). Contrary to that, according to the Japanese research group of the South Manchuria Railway Company (in a survey of Hebei and Shandong provinces), *zongzu* in the North China had only one leader: the sib head. At the time of this survey (1940-1942), the sib head was usually chosen from the oldest generation of the sib members, and from the eldest men among the oldest generation. The power of the sib head varied case by case. Where the power of the sib head was great, he intervened in each family's decisions about marriage, adoption, division of property, and so on, and took the role of mediator in conflicts among sib members. Where the power of the sib head was small, he had only the nominal status of being invited to marriage and funeral ceremonies and was given the place of honor (Niida 1952, pp. 82-93). Japan's *dozoku* differs from China's *zongzu* in that in the former branch families were dependent on the head family under the rule of primogeniture, whereas in the latter, because of lack of the rule of primogeniture, there is no head-branch distinction. It is the group in which the membership (or family) order is determined in advance in head-branch terms. The head family is always one and fixed, and branch families are connected with the head family by *Pietätbeziehung*. From this point of view, we can characterize *dozoku*, as was clearly stated by Kitano, as a form of *Patrimonialismus* in Weber's definition (Kitano 1976, pp. 23-29). Japan's *dozoku* had no word for "sib head" (*zokucho*) because it was always fixed on the head of the head family (*honke no kacho*).

(3) Guild organizations in Tokugawa Japan were subordinate to the feudal power and could not survive the Meiji era. Parallel to the development of guilds in traditional Chinese cities, trade and craft associations called *kabunakama* developed in the cities of Tokugawa Japan. *Kabunakama*, similar to Chinese *hanghui*, were closed groups, which advanced the interests of the group members in restricting the numbers of *kabu* (shares) and excluding new entrants. There were two differences between Chinese guilds and Japanese guilds: While Chinese guilds were spontaneous independent groups without government sanction, Japanese guilds received the approval of the *bakufu* or *han* government; and while Chinese guilds had a rural background in that they organized people of the same province, Japanese guilds had no such background. The former character of Japanese guilds resulted in the subordinate relation to the feudal political power of *bakufu* and *han*, and prevented them from forming a politically independent power for the self-government of the city as a community. The result of the latter character of Japanese guilds was that they were less enduring than Chinese ones. These observations explain why in Japan guild organizations quickly disappeared when the feudal power was disorganized after the Meiji era began.

(4) Japanese society never developed an intellectual ruling class equivalent to the Chinese literati. Although there was the formation of a court nobility of Fujiwara under the ancient despotism, the development of patrimonial bureaucracy was limited in Japan because the importation of Chinese-type centralized administration was not fully fixed in the Heian period (784-1192). In the feudal ages, beginning with the formation of the Kamakura shogunate, warriors became the ruling class, and the *bakufu* bureaucracy was also organized by samurais. Therefore, there was no possibility of the formation of literati, organized as a distinct social class, as in China. In contrast to the patrimonial state of China in which wealth was concentrated in the emperor's household and the retired literati could become big landlords, accumulation of wealth in the hand of samurais in Japan was limited. In the Tokugawa period (1603-1868), the financial situation of the *bakufu* and *han* deteriorated after the eighteenth century, and the warrior class became impoverished. The rural villages of this age consisted of relatively equal-sized independent farmers, except for a few subordinated tenants in underdeveloped areas, and there were no big landowners. The rapid increase in large-scale absentee landowners began only after the Meiji Restoration. Warriors in the feudal system in Japan were separated from the land, so that there was no possibility for them to become landowners.

(5) The role of Confucianism in Japan was to some extent different from that in China. The Tokugawa shogunate designated Confucianism as

the official learning, so that samurai youths were taught it in the schools of *bakufu* and *han*. The ruling class in Tokugawa Japan, however, was not the literati but the warriors, so that the Confucianism that was originally the thought of literati in China changed its nature in Tokugawa Japan into an ethics of teaching warriors the modus vivendi. The intention of the Tokugawa shogunate to designate Confucianism as the official learning was, of course, to legitimize the hierarchical order of the *bakufu* and *han* regime by Confucian ethics. Actually, however, the development of Confucianism in Tokugawa society did not necessarily progress as the *bakufu* expected. Rather, toward the end of the Tokugawa period, Confucianism was directed toward criticizing the social reality of the *bakufu* and *han*, as not realizing the Confucian ethical ideal under that regime. This is why the advocates of anti-Tokugawa ideology in the last phase of the Tokugawa period were lower samurais who had been trained in Confucian thought. The thought that motivated these lower samurais was oriented to the emperor regime, not being modern thought as such. It had, therefore, to be overcome as the modernization process went on later. But it should be noted that the revolutionary thought that initiated the reform of the Tokugawa regime was derived from a distinctly Japanese version of Confucianism.

SUMMARY AND CONCLUSION

Max Weber's analysis of Chinese society was directed to comparing China with the Occident, to demonstrate that China lacked many of the sociocultural factors that pushed the West toward modernization. Weber's view of Asia was different from Hegel's "stagnation" thesis or Marx's "Asiatic mode of production" thesis, however, in that Weber recognized the diversity of structures of traditional societies and clarified the characteristics in which China differs from Japan, India, and other Oriental societies. My attempt in this chapter has been to compare China and Japan, making use of Weber's framework from the point of view of modernization theory. Such an attempt is possible because Weber's theory does not posit that Asian societies cannot be modernized.

Examining the items included in Weber's "only-in-the-Occident" proposition, I distinguished four aspects of modernization: scientific-technological modernization, economic modernization, political modernization, and sociocultural modernization. I started by admitting as historical fact that modern science-technology and modern capitalism were invented by Westerners. The modernization of non-Western societies

TABLE 5.1: Comparisons of China and Japan in Relation to Initial Conditions of Modernization

Five Structural Factors	China	Japan
1. Structure of domination	Patrimonial bureaucracy	Feudalism with some patrimonial elements
2. Patrilineal kinship group	*Zongzu*: firmly organized sib group that has a physical basis, such as common property and an ancestral hall	*Dozoku*: dependent relation of branch-families on the head-family without special physical basis such as common property
3. Guild	Spontaneous closed organization of trade and industry without government sanction, originating in the same province	Closed organization of trade and industry with governmental sanction of *bakufu* or *han*
4. Ruling class	The literati: orthodox intellectuals trained in Confucianism, becoming patrimonial bureaucrats after selection by a national examination system	Samurais: warriors, but in Tokugawa period with intellectual element trained in Confucianism, and also members of *bakufu* and *han* bureaucracy
5. Confucianism	Laymen's nonreligious religion and spiritual basis of patrimonial bureaucracy, ethical thought legitimizing inner-worldly order of the sib society	Spiritual basis in modus vivendi of samurais, ethical thought legitimizing hierarchical order of *bakufu-han* regime

such as China and Japan was based on accepting and digesting the science-technology and capitalism that the West had invented.

The problem of whether or not such an acceptance and digestion can be successfully done cannot be separated from the possibilities of political modernization and sociocultural modernization. As factors pertinent to the conditions of political and sociocultural modernization, I made use of Weber's conceptualization in his social-structural typology, of which patrimonialism and feudalism are the two extremes. In addition to that, I extracted the four elements of sib, guild, literati, and Confucianism—and, by adding the axis of patrimonialism-feudalism, we get a total of five—as the important sociological factors. Thus I attempted a comparative analysis of China and Japan for each of these five sociological factors.

The result of this comparative analysis is summarized in Table 5.1. From this summary table we can derive the following five conclusions regarding the social structure of the two traditional societies that constituted the initial conditions for modernization in China and Japan.

(1) In the stage of traditional society, both China and Japan had a different structure of domination from that of Europe. But Japan was situated much closer to Europe. From the reasons presented by Weber, we can see that feudalism had more advantageous characteristics to be a precursor to capitalist development than did patrimonialism. This worked favorably for the modernization of Japan after the Meiji era.

(2) In the stage of traditional society, both China and Japan developed the sib groups that in medieval Europe were already disorganized. But the sib groups of China, *zongzu*, were much more strongly institutionalized than those of Japan, *dozoku*. Cumulative kinship relations in the closed form tended to hinder the formation of role differentiation by the growth of functional groups. In contrast, *dozoku* in Japan was not sufficiently strong to hinder the modernization of the social structure.

(3) In the stage of traditional society, both China and Japan had developed trade and industry guild organizations in their cities. Chinese guilds were politically powerless because they were spontaneous organizations, but they were enduring because of their rural background that organized people of the same province. Japanese guilds were not politically powerless, but were subordinate to feudal political power. Neither made a contribution to modernization, but Japanese guilds hindered it less in the sense that they disappeared quickly after the turn to the modern era.

(4) The literati as patrimonial bureaucrats were the ruling class peculiar to China. While the literati acquired this status through success in national examinations, the literati were closely connected with the kinship group from which they came and to which they returned. They could not break the close relation with the *zongzu* groups that strongly characterized the traditional society of China. The ruling class in Japanese feudal society were samurais. Unlike the literati in China, they had limited economic opportunity, and they were separated from the land, so that it was not possible for them to become landowners in their communities of origin.

(5) In both China and Japan, Confucianism was the traditional thought. In both countries, the motivating force for modernization and industrialization could not arise directly from Confucianism. But Confucianism in Tokugawa Japan developed uniquely as the thought of samurais, and from this grew the thought of the lower samurais, who were oriented to the disorganization of the *bakufu-han* regime. Confucianism in Japan played a more innovative role in this respect than in China.

REFERENCES

Aruga, Kizaemon (Works 10). 1971. "Dozoku to Shinzoku" [Dozoku and Kinship]. Pp. 15-66 in *Aruga's Collective Works*. Vol. 10. Tokyo: Miraisha.

Hegel, Georg W.F. (Werke 12). 1970. *Vorlesungen über die Philosophie der Geschichte. Werke in zwanzig Bänden*, Bd. 12. Frankfurt am Main: Suhrkamp.

Huang, Yifeng et al. 1982. *Jiu Zhongguo de Maiben Jieji* [The old China's Comprador Class]. Shanghai: Shanghai Renmin Chubanshe.

Jacobs, Norman. 1958. *The Origin of Modern Capitalism and East Asia*. Hong Kong: Hong Kong University Press.

Kitano, Seiichi. 1976. *Ie to Dozoku no Kisoriron* [A Basic Theory of Ie and Dozoku]. Tokyo: Miraisha.

Lang, Olga. 1946. *Chinese Family and Society*. New Haven, CT: Yale University Press.

Makino, Tatsumi (Works 3). 1980. *Kinsei Chugoku Sozoku Kenkyu* [Studies on Sibs in Modern China]. Tokyo: Ochanomizushobo.

Marsh, Robert M. 1961. *The Mandarins: The Circulation of Elites in China, 1600-1900*. New York: Free Press.

Marx, Karl (in Marx-Engels, Werke 42). 1982. *Grundrisse der Kritik der politishen Ökonomie*. Berlin: Dietz.

Niida, Noboru. 1952. *Chugoku no Nosonkazoku* [Rural Families in China]. Tokyo: Tokyo University Press.

Okada, Yuzuru. 1959. "Nihon niokeru Dozoku Kenkyu no Igi" [Significance of the Study of Dozoku in Japan]. Pp. 25-38 in *Ie: Sono Kozobunseki* [Ie: Its Structural Analysis], edited by S. Kitano and Y. Okada. Tokyo: Sobunsha.

Shimizu, Morimitsu. 1939. *Shina Shakai no Kenkyu* [A Study on Chinese Society]. Tokyo: Iwanamishoten.

———. 1942. *Shina Kazoku no Kozo* [Structure of the Chinese Family]. Tokyo: Iwanamishoten.

———. 1949. *Chugoku Zokusan Seidoko* [A Study on the Sib Property in China]. Tokyo: Iwanamishoten.

Weber, Max. 1920. *Gesammelte Aufsätze zur Religionssoziologie (GAzRS)*. 3 Bde. Tübingen: J.C.B. Mohr.

———. 1972. *Wirtschaft und Gesellschaft (WuG*, 5. Aufl.), besorgt v. J. Winckelmann. Tübingen: J.C.B. Mohr.

Part III
Nation as Context:
Primary Analyses

6

Effects of Status-Inconsistency on the Intellective Process: The United States, Japan, and Poland

Kazimierz M. Slomczynski

In the late 1970s some scholars suggested abandoning the concept of status-inconsistency "after nearly 30 years of less than fruitless usage" (Crosbie 1979; see also Blocker and Riedesel, 1978a, 1978b). In the mid-1980s, the proceedings of a conference of the Research Committee on Social Stratification of ISA, *Status Inconsistency in Modern Societies* (Strasser and Hodge 1986) indicated a revival of interest in both the theory and the research on status-inconsistency. Reading the proceedings publication, one may infer that not all usage of status-inconsistency may be called "fruitless" and that a vivid theoretical debate on the functions of status-inconsistency (for both a society and an individual) continues. Moreover, recent methodological innovations (e.g., Sobel 1981), free of previously noted shortcomings (e.g., Blalock 1966), may inspire new research in this classic area of social stratification.

This chapter not only elaborates on a new method for analyzing the effects of status-inconsistency on psychological functioning but also provides substantive cross-national results. We show how status-inconsis-

AUTHOR'S NOTE: *This research was supported in part by the National Institute of Mental Health (Bethesda, Maryland, U.S.A.), the Japan Foundation (Tokyo), and the University of Warsaw (Poland). I am indebted to Melvin L. Kohn, Carmi Schooler, and Atsushi Naoi for providing me with the U.S. and Japanese data. Thanks are due to Duane Alwin, Melvin L. Kohn, Tadeusz K. Krauze, Bogdan W. Mach, Wlodzimierz Wesolowski, and Wojciech Zaborowski for their comments on earlier drafts of this manuscript. Some models in this chapter were estimated by MILS, developed by Ronald Schoenberg.*

tency can be measured so that it does not interact with status. By "status," we mean a construct located along a "vertical dimension" of social stratification, which "captures" most of the variance of the components of status: formal education, occupational rank, and job income. By "status-inconsistency," we mean a construct indexed by the same components but located orthogonally, that is, as a "nonvertical dimension" of social stratification. In presenting our method we utilize Hope's (1975) interpretation of Lenski's (1954) original definitions. Within this approach, "status-inconsistency effects" are conceived of as those over and above the effects of status. We examine these effects in a crucial area for psychological functioning: the intellective process, which is indicative of logical reasoning and open-mindedness. Two measures of intellective process are ideational flexibility and authoritarian-conservatism (Miller et al. 1985).

Our analysis uses data from the United States, Japan, and Poland. These data were collected to test the Kohn-Schooler hypothesis that job conditions are a mediating mechanism for the relationship between social stratification and psychological functioning (Kohn 1969; Kohn and Schooler 1969, 1983). For all three countries, it is well documented that people of higher social status are more intellectually flexible; they are also less authoritarian than people of lower status (Slomczynski et al. 1981; Naoi and Schooler 1985; Kohn et al. forthcoming). The Kohn-Schooler hypothesis, however, leaves open the following question: How does status-inconsistency affect psychological functioning? We consider status-inconsistency effects in the context of the relationships among social stratification, job conditions, and psychological functioning. Specifically, we ask: Does status-inconsistency explain ideational flexibility and authoritarian-conservatism over and above not only status but also job conditions?

THEORIZING ABOUT POSITIVE
ASPECTS OF STATUS-INCONSISTENCY

A decade ago, Slomczynski and Wesolowski (1977) developed the idea that social policies productive of status-inconsistency result in a *reduction of global social inequality*. In that paper, "general status" was defined as an additive function of an individual's positions in such dimensions of status as formal education, occupational rank, and job income. They argued that combining a high position in one dimension of status with a low position in other dimensions "regresses" general status to the middle of the social ladder and, therefore, produces some equality. Indeed, if a measure of inequality is applied to general status, a weak relationship between status components implies more equality than does a strong positive relationship. Taking this observation as a point of departure, Slomczynski and Wesolowski (1977; Wesolowski 1979; Slomczynski and Wesolowski forthcoming) posed two questions pertaining particularly to socialist societies that attempt to reduce social inequality:

(1) Are individuals with inconsistent status "deviant cases" or do they instead fit the usual patterns of distribution of status characteristics?

(2) If status-inconsistency is frequent among individuals, does it produce symptoms of stress and frustration or does it, instead, lead to innovative ways of thinking and acceptance of social diversity?

An answer to the first question can be considered in the context of the *ideology of meritocracy*, the most fundamental principle of the legitimation of social inequality not only in Western capitalist societies but also in European socialist societies. Recently, a German sociologist depicted the relationship between status-inconsistency and meritocracy in the following way:

According to the formalized version of the meritocratic ideology . . . the individual *ought* to acquire certified qualifications which *ought* to be fully convertible into an adequate occupational position; this occupational position *ought* to be remunerated by a suitable income. If interpreted in this way . . . there is *a direct correspondence between the ideological principle of meritocracy and the theoretical concept of objective status consistency*. Consequently, the empirical occurrence of status inconsistencies is to be interpreted as an empirical deviation from the institutionalized general norm of meritocracy. (Kreckel 1986, p. 194, emphasis in the original)

In contemporary societies, deviation from the norm of meritocracy is, however, considerable. Krauze and Slomczynski (1985) demonstrated that in the United States the allocation of persons according to formal education and occupational position is closer to random allocation than to meritocratic allocation. In this respect, neither Japan nor Poland diverges very much from the pattern established for the United States (Slomczynski and Naoi 1986; Slomczynski 1983). In view of recent findings, the claim that in socialist countries status-inconsistencies become much more pronounced than in capitalist countries (Slomczynski and Wesolowski 1977) seems to exaggerate the actual trends (Covello and Bollen 1980). Generally, status-inconsistency may be seen as "one of the normal by-products of social differentiation in modern society" (Bornschier 1986, p. 205; see also Müller 1986, p. 281). Therefore, the answer to the first question is that status-inconsistency is neither unusual nor deviant.

Until the mid-1970s a number of researchers were concerned with the impact of status-inconsistency upon various symptoms of stress and frustration (Jackson 1962; Jackson and Burke 1965; House and Harkins 1975; Hornung 1977). Slomczynski and Wesolowski (1977), however, argued that status-inconsistency can have a positive impact on psychological functioning, even in the situation in which an unbalanced position is in disagreement with social norms defining "who should get what" (Malewski 1966). The main argument is that coping with unmet expectations requires one to be innovative, open, and tolerant. This argument can be strengthened on the grounds of the theory of the psychological effects of a complex environment:

> According to the theory, the complexity of an individual's environment is defined by its stimulus and demand characteristics. The more diverse the stimuli, the greater the number of decisions required, the greater the number of considerations to be taken into account in making these decisions, and the more ill-defined and apparently contradictory the contingencies, the more complex the environment. To the degree that the pattern of reinforcement within such an environment rewards cognitive effort, individuals should be motivated to develop their intellectual capacities and to generalize the resulting cognitive process to other situations. (Schooler 1984, pp. 259-60)

Inconsistency of status is indicative of a complex environment, because it can be interpreted as a set of diverse stimuli. Thus one can expect that greater status-inconsistency should result in greater ideational flexibility and less authoritarian social orientations. We hypothesize that this would be the case if persons with relatively high levels of schooling and prestigious jobs received relatively small incomes. Such an expectation is consistent with the theoretical justification given by Geschwender (1967; see also Meyer and Hammond 1971) in terms of an unbalanced reward process. On the one hand, those persons who are "underrewarded"—that is, highly educated and working in prestigious jobs but for little money—must adjust to their lack of financial success and view it in relative terms. To be "underrewarded" may not require defensive action but does call for tolerance of an ambivalent or exceptional situation. On the other hand, those persons who are "overrewarded"—that is, least educated and working in nonprestigious jobs but obtaining high earnings—must defend their situation against well-established social expectations. In the defense of the status quo, repeating clichés and invoking tradition can be substitutes for a lack of an elaborated argument. Thus one can argue that the former situation requires more flexible reasoning and less conformity toward social norms than does the latter.[1] We test the hypothesis that particular forms of status-inconsistency result in different psychological outcomes.

ACCOUNTING FOR STATUS-INCONSISTENCY EFFECTS: THE STRATEGY OF ANALYSIS

In this chapter, we follow and further develop the conceptualization of the effects of status-inconsistency proposed by Hope (1975). His conceptualization is clearly stated for the situation in which y denotes a psychological variable, dependent on x_1 and x_2, two stratification variables:

> In the two-axis case for the investigation of status discrepancy effects, we first find weights b_i such that $(b_1x_1 + b_2x_2)$ is a measure of status and $(b_3x_1 - b_4x_2)$ is orthogonal to it. We then examine the coefficients c_i in the equation $y = c_1(b_1x_1 + b_2x_2) + c_2(b_3x_1 - b_4x_2)$ to see whether the difference term is contributing anything over and above the sum term, which represents the vertical axis of general status. (Hope 1975, p. 327)

Taking this statement as a point of departure, we use principal components analysis as a tool for extracting two constructs: status and status-inconsistency. We assume that status (S) and status-inconsistency (I) can be conceived of as a two-dimensional representation of the *social-stratification space* defined by a set of variables x_i, which are its original coordinates. Both constructs, S and I, can be regarded as newly introduced axes of this space: Status is identified with the "vertical" axis while status-inconsistency is identified with the axis orthogonal to it, that is, the "nonvertical" axis.

To avoid cumbersome complications, we take into account variables x_i in their standardized normal form $N(0, 1)$ without sampling error. We postulate a linear relation of x_i with S:

$$S = a_1x_1 + \ldots + a_nx_n \qquad [1]$$

[1.] "Underrewarding" and "overrewarding" are technical terms denoting two forms of a lack of equilibrium between "investments" (e.g., education) and "rewards" (e.g., income). As technical terms, they do not involve any moral judgment as to whether this lack of equilibrium is desirable or not. Social expectations about "who should get what", however, usually assume a strong relationship between "investments" and "rewards" (see Phillips 1983).

where a_i is a weight of x_i. *In our analysis we treat status as the weighted sum of formal education, occupational rank, and job income—three stratification variables expressed in a common metric.* We require that the linear combination (1) has a maximum variance normalized in such a way that the squared a_i's sum up to unity. Coefficients a_i can be obtained by solving an eigenvalue problem for the correlation matrix R of variables x_i. The first principal component is defined as an eigenvector associated with the largest eigenvalue, which after the normalization to its length gives the values of a_i. The stronger the correlation of variable x_i with all other variables, the greater the weight a_i. Thus, among all variables x_i, some are more important for general status S than are others. Because weights a_i are constant in the population, however, a person with a higher value of x_i obtains higher general status than a person with a lower value of the same variable, other things being equal. This property provides a *vertical interpretation of status.*

The relation between each x_i and S can be written as $x_i = a_i S + e_i$ where $\grave{a}_i$ is the first principal component loading and e_i is a residual of x_i. It follows that the status-specific part of x_i is $\hat{x}_i^{(s)} = a_i S$. Agreeing with Hope (1975) that status-inconsistency should be defined by those parts of variables that are not status-specific, we extract the expression $(x_i - a_i S)$ or, alternatively, $(x_i - \hat{x}_i^{(s)})$. Status-inconsistency is expressed by

$$I = \Sigma\, b_i\, (x_i - \hat{x}_i^{(s)}) \qquad [2]$$

subject to the constraints for the second principal component. *We treat status inconsistency as the weighted sum of those portions of formal education, occupational rank, and job income that are not related to status.* By definition, the second principal component is the normalized linear combination of x_i that is uncorrelated with the first principal component. Because the second principal component "catches" most of the variation of $(x_i - \hat{x}_i^{(s)})$, we do not consider further orthogonal components. In the considered space, the second principal component implicitly involves comparison of each stratification variable x_i with another status-specific variable $\hat{x}_{i+1}^{(s)}$. We notice that the difference term $(b_i x_i - b_{i+1} \hat{x}_{i+1}^{(s)})$ is a substitute for the term $(x_i - x_{i+1})$, crucial for the definition of status-inconsistency.

Conceptualization of status and status-consistency as orthogonal axes of the stratification space can be conveniently used for formulating the regression equation in which both constructs, S and I, are treated as independent variables vis-à-vis some other variables y_i. The resulting equation, in a standardized form, is

$$y = \beta_1 S + \beta_2 I \qquad [3]$$

where parameters β_1 and β_2 are normalized regression coefficients. Because S and I are orthogonal, the values of β_1 and β_2 are equal to the correlation coefficients of y_i with S, and y_i with I, respectively. Substituting $x_i^{(s)}$ for S and the set of $(x_i - \hat{x}_i^{(s)})$ for I does not lead to linear dependence in equation 3. To demonstrate a *net effect* of status and status-inconsistency on y_i, variables other than x_i should be included in the regression equation. In our analysis, we use a standard set of demographic and background variables, such as age, father's occupation, and the urbanness of the place where the respondent was raised.

SAMPLES AND METHODS OF
DATA COLLECTION

The original U.S. survey was based on interviews conducted in 1964 with a representative sample of 3,101 men employed in civilian occupations throughout the country; the sample, methods of data collection, and other pertinent information are given in detail in Kohn (1969, Appendix C). Ten years later, in 1974, a representative subsample of 687 of the men in the original survey was reinterviewed (Kohn and Schooler 1983, Appendix A). Both the baseline and the follow-up data are utilized in our analysis.

The Japanese survey, conducted in 1979, was based on a random probability sample of 629 employed men, 26-65 years old, in the Kanto plain of Japan. This area, one of the principal geographic regions into which Japan traditionally has been divided, includes Tokyo and six other prefectures in north-central Japan. Kanto is a mix of urban, suburban, and rural areas. The survey was based primarily on questions translated from the U.S. interview schedule. For details, see Naoi and Schooler (1985).

The Polish survey was conducted in 1978. The sample was designed to represent men aged 19 to 65, living in urban areas and employed full-time in civilian occupations. Although the rural peasantry is not fully represented, farmers living in proximity to urban centers are included. A sample of 1,557 men was obtained through a multistage probability sampling scheme. For further information about sampling procedure and quality control of the interview data, see Slomczynski et al. (1981).

Both the Japanese and the Polish surveys were designed to be exact replications of the main parts of the U.S. study. Questions pertaining to intellectual flexibility and authoritarian-conservatism were directly adopted from the Kohn-Schooler 1964 interview schedule. The initial translation of the U.S. interview schedule into Japanese and Polish involved a thorough assessment of the meaning of entire questions and of particular phrases. Some modification of the original questions appeared necessary to assure their relevance to a given country. For example, a measure of intellectual flexibility in the Kohn-Schooler study included the following question: "Suppose you wanted to open a hamburger stand and there were two locations available. What questions would you consider in deciding which of the two locations offers a better business opportunity?" Because people in Poland are not familiar with hamburger stands, the question was changed so that the word "kiosk" (or "newsstand") was used instead. Such modifications were introduced to assure a functional equivalence of indicators. In Poland the modified questions were pretested in an extensive pilot study.

MEASUREMENT OF INTELLECTIVE PROCESS: IDEATIONAL FLEXIBILITY AND AUTHORITARIAN-CONSERVATISM

We focus on ideational flexibility and authoritarian-conservatism as *two aspects of the intellective process* that allow one to assess the rigidity of an individual in his or her way of thinking and viewing the world. These aspects of the intellective process are measured on the basis of separate sets of indicators by models of confirmatory factor analysis. Details of these models can be examined in Kohn and Schooler (1983) for the United States, in Naoi and Schooler (1985) for Japan, and in Miller et al. (1985) for Poland (see also Slomczynski and Kohn 1988).

Ideational flexibility reflects an ability to think in relative terms and to provide balanced arguments. The measurement model of *ideational flexibility* includes various indicators: ratings of a respondent's answers to simple cognitive problems, the frequency with which a respondent agreed when asked to answer many agree-disagree questions, the summary score for his performance on the Embedded Figures Test, and the interviewer's appraisal of his intelligence. Although none of these indicators is assumed to be a completely valid measure of ideational flexibility, taken together they reflect the respondent's flexibility in attempting to cope with the intellectual demands of a complex interview situation. In the United States, Japan, and Poland the paths from the underlying concept, ideational flexibility, to all of its indicators are substantial; they do not differ much among countries.

The concept of *authoritarian-conservatism* is meant to represent orientations toward authority and tolerance for ambiguity. At one extreme, there is unreflexive conformity to the dictates of authority and rigid conventionality. At the other extreme, there is a worldview marked by open-mindedness and a sense of social reality as relative and evolving (Kohn 1977; Gabennesch 1972). To index this concept, we rely on re-

sponses to a set of attitudinal questions aimed at determining one's orientation to authority. For the United States, Japan, and Poland not all of the
indicators are the same; some indicators are nation-specific. In comparative perspective, authoritarian-conservatism in Poland is strongly
manifested in orientations toward hierarchically legitimized authority,
particularly an authority considered bureaucratically or legally justified.
The Polish construct is functionally equivalent to the one developed for
the United States, however (Miller et al., 1981). For the three countries,
our measure of authoritarian-conservatism is suited to cross-national
analysis (see Naoi and Schooler 1985; Slomczynski et al. 1981; Miller
et al. 1985).

THE PRINCIPAL-COMPONENTS MODEL OF
STATUS AND STATUS-INCONSISTENCY

The principal-components model of status and status-inconsistency is
based on three variables crucial in social-stratification analysis: formal
education, occupational rank, and job income. In the United States, *formal
education* is measured on a six-point scale of the level of educational
attainment. In Japan and Poland, years of schooling is used for the same
purpose. In all three countries, *occupational rank* is measured by national
prestige scales: Siegel's (1971) for the United States, Naoi's (1979) for
Japan, and Slomczynski and Kacprowicz's (1979) for Poland. These national scales are closely related to each other and to the Standard International Prestige Scale (Treiman 1977), with all correlations above .9. In all
three countries, *job income* refers to wages, salary, and other forms of
earnings from the main job.

The principal-components models of status and status-inconsistency
for the United States, Japan, and Poland are presented in Table 6.1. We
consider the model of status first. Occupational rank has the highest
loading (from .848 to .894), while job income has the lowest (from .644
to .726). The internal structure of the model is the same for all three
countries, not only in terms of the order of loadings but also in terms of
their explanatory power. The eigenvalues are similar across countries
(from 1.755 to 2.019) and the range of proportions of explained variance
in status components—formal education, occupational rank, and job income—is small (from .585 to .673). Thus we confirm previous findings
that the same operationalization of status fits data for Western and non-
Western capitalist societies and for a socialist society as well (Kohn et al.
1987).

In the models of status-inconsistency, both formal education and occupational rank load positively, from .355 to .457 for education and from

TABLE 6.1: Principal-Components Analysis of Formal Education, Occupational Rank, and Job Income for Men Employed in Civilian Occupations in the United States (1964 and 1974), Japan (1979), and Poland (1978)

| | Components Loadings | |
	Status	Status-Inconsistency
United States (1964):		
Formal education	.831	.399
Occupational rank	.876	.189
Job income	.687	−.720
Eigenvalue	1.930	.712
Proportion of variance	.643	.237
United States (1974):		
Formal education	.851	.355
Occupational rank	.877	.223
Job income	.726	−.685
Eigenvalue	2.019	.645
Proportion of variance	.673	.215
Japan (1979):		
Formal education	.784	.457
Occupational rank	.848	.147
Job income	.649	−.744
Eigenvalue	1.755	.784
Proportion of variance	.585	.261
Poland (1978):		
Formal education	.837	.413
Occupational rank	.894	.163
Job income	.644	−.740
Eigenvalue	1.940	.745
Proportion of variance	.646	.248

.147 to .223 for occupational rank. Both variables, however, are dominated by the very strong and negative impact of job income (from −.744 to −.685). The configuration of the signs of the loadings suggests that the nonvertical dimension of social stratification identifies the *unbalanced reward process*. The most educated persons, who work in prestigious occupations but earn little money, score highest; this is the situation of extreme "underrewarding." Persons who earn the most, but have little education and work in nonprestigious occupations, score lowest; this is the situation of extreme "overrewarding." In the United States, Japan, and Poland the internal structure of status-inconsistency is the same. Moreover, status-inconsistency explains a substantial proportion of the total variances of formal education, occupational rank, and job income (from

21% to 26%). The eigenvalue is far from zero, showing that the original stratification space is not reducible to one dimension—that of status.

We must also address the problem of whether the measure of status utilized here leaves more room for the effects of status-inconsistency than do alternative measures of status. In particular, our model of status should be compared with a factor-analytic model for which the impact of status on psychological functioning has already been well established (Kohn and Schooler 1983; Slomczynski et al. 1981; Kohn et al. 1987). In the framework of confirmatory factor analysis, status—called also stratification position—is conceptualized as a second-order construct, the first-order constructs corresponding to the same status components: formal education, occupational rank, and job income. In this approach, the first-order constructs directly reflect observed indicators such as various occupational scales, or different measures of income. The second-order construct explains observed indicators only by its relationship with the first-order constructs, that is, indirectly. Does this conceptualization lead to different results from those of the principal-components solution?

To answer this question, we have performed an analysis, using Polish data, in which there are two measures for education (years of schooling and the level of the educational certificate), three occupational scales (the Polish Prestige Scale, the Standard International Prestige Scale, and the Socio-Economic Index), and two indicators of income (earnings from the main job and total income derived from work). Using these raw variables we modeled status by a confirmatory factor analysis and by the two-stage principal-components analysis. In comparison with factor modeling, the principal components solution gives higher loadings for income and education and a lower loading for occupational prestige. The differences are not dramatic, however, because the ordering of loadings remains the same. Moreover, the correlation between scores of status computed according to the two methods is close to unity ($r = .963$). Very similar results have been obtained for Japan and the United States. Thus a measure of status based on the principal-components solution is not likely to exaggerate the effects of status-inconsistency in any of the three countries.

THE EFFECTS OF STATUS-INCONSISTENCY ON INTELLECTIVE PROCESS: SMALL BUT STATISTICALLY SIGNIFICANT

According to our operationalization of status and status-inconsistency, these constructs identify orthogonal dimensions of social-stratification space; they are uncorrelated. Thus if a psychological variable is regressed on only those two constructs, the regression coefficients must be equal to the correlations of these constructs with the dependent variable. Table 6.2 shows not only the total effects (A panels) but also "net effects," statistically controlling demographic and background characteristics (B panels). In both cases, the effects of status are substantial and in agreement with previous findings (Slomczynski et al. 1981; Kohn and Schooler 1983): People of higher status are ideationally more flexible and less conservative. The effects of status-inconsistency are much smaller but still substantial and their direction is the same as that for status: The greater the status-inconsistency, the more ideationally flexible people are; people of inconsistent status are also less conservative than people of consistent status.

With the exception of authoritarian-conservatism in Japan, the effects of status-inconsistency on intellective process remain statistically significant when controlled for such demographic and background characteristics as age, father's occupation, and the urbanness of the place where the respondent was raised. Moreover, even the statistically nonsignificant Japanese coefficient is substantial. Those persons who are well educated and work in prestigious occupations but earn little money are less conservative than those persons with substantial earnings, little education, and nonprestigious jobs. Thus we conclude that in the United States, Japan, and Poland the effects of status-inconsistency are essentially the same: persons who are "underrewarded" are more intellectually flexible and less conservative than those who are "overrewarded." These status-inconsistency effects occur over and above the effects of status.

As in all modeling of complex reality, our modeling also leads to a loss of some information contained in the raw data. It is well known that status and status-inconsistency cannot explain more variation of a given external variable than might a full set of variables from which these constructs have been derived; actually, they explain less (Hodge and Siegel 1970; Hope 1975). The question, however, is this: How much less? Comparing the proportion of variance explained by our two constructs (status and status-inconsistency) with the proportion of variance explained by three raw variables (formal education, occupational rank, and job income), one can evaluate the extent to which relying on the constructs diminishes the predictive power of the full set of variables. The difference between these proportions in no case exceeds .05 and for most cases ranges from .01 to .02 (see the last two columns of Table 6.2). Thus loss in predictive power would be a weak argument against using the constructs for explaining intellective process as measured in this chapter. The analysis utilizing status and status-inconsistency is parsimonious; this justifies a small loss in predictive power.

TABLE 6.2: Effects of Status and Status-Inconsistency on Ideational Flexibility and Authoritarian-Conservatism for Men Employed in Civilian Occupations in the United States (1964 and 1974), Japan (1979), and Poland (1978)

	Standardized Regression Coefficients		Proportion of Variance Explained by Status and Status-Inconsistency	Proporiton of Variance Explained by Education, Occupation, and Income
	Status	*Status-Inconsistency*		
United States (1964):				
A. without controlling other variables				
ideational flexibility	.730**	.184**	.567	.601
authoritarian-conservatism	−.543**	−.162**	.321	.339
B. controlling other variables[a]				
ideational flexibility	.703**	.168**	.474	.518
authoritarian-conservatism	−.530**	−.146**	.296	.297
United States (1974):				
A. without controlling other variables				
ideational flexibility	.776**	.165**	.629	.647
authoritarian-conservatism	−.588**	−.165**	.373	.397
B. controlling other variables[a]				
ideational flexibility	.718**	.063**	.586	.599
authoritarian-conservatism	−.522**	−.058*	.295	.313
Japan (1979):				
A. without controlling other variables				
ideational flexibility	.423**	.167**	.207	.228
authoritarian-conservatism	−.308**	−.077*	.101	.109
B. controlling other variables[a]				
ideational flexibility	.360**	.079*	.110	.119
authoritarian-conservatism	−.330**	−.052	.080	.084
Poland (1978):				
A. without controlling other variables				
ideational flexibility	.689**	.228**	.527	.546
authoritarian-conservatism	−.453**	−.265**	.275	.284
B. controlling other variables[a]				
ideational flexibility	.651**	.153**	.484	.493
authoritarian-conservatism	−.405**	.117**	.206	.207

a. Includes age, father's occupation, and the urbanness of the place in which the respondent was raised.
*p < .05; **p < .01.

STATUS, STATUS-INCONSISTENCY, AND
OCCUPATIONAL SELF-DIRECTION

Kohn (1969, p. 196) hypothesized that occupational self-direction would play a major part in explaining the relationship of social stratification to values and orientations in "all sizable industrial societies." Subsequent studies confirmed this hypothesis (for a review of the findings, see Kohn 1977; Kohn and Schooler 1983). Indeed, the relationship between social status and psychological functioning is, to a large extent, attributable to three job conditions that facilitate or deter the exercise of self-direction in one's work—namely, the substantive complexity of work, closeness of supervision, and the routinization of work. Expanding on earlier work, we rely on previously developed measurement models of occupational self-direction (see Slomczynski et al. 1981; Kohn and Schooler 1983; Kohn et al. forthcoming; Naoi and Schooler 1985).

In the United States, Japan, and Poland the correlation between social status and occupational self-direction is so strong that, in models containing these and other variables, the estimates of their impact on the intellective process become unreliable because of multicollinearity. Slomczynski et al. (1981) proposed a method of dealing with this problem and also demonstrated that in the United States and Poland the effect of social status on psychological functioning is substantially attributable to the effects of occupational self-direction (see also Kohn and Schooler, 1983). Because subsequent analysis for Japan leads to the same conclusion, we focus here on the parallel issue: Are the effects of *status-inconsistency* also attributable to occupational self-direction? If so, does status-inconsistency nevertheless have psychological effects independent of those of occupational self-direction?

Our rationale for asking these questions is that status-inconsistency is part of the stratification system and thus can be related to occupational self-direction in a similar way as status. Specifically, persons who are "underrewarded" occupy prestigious job positions demanding high qualifications; because of their location in the job system, they are likely to exercise self-direction in their work. Persons who are "overrewarded" may experience a low level of occupational self-direction, given that they tend to work in jobs requiring only low qualifications. Assuming such a relationship, it is plausible that the psychological effects of status-inconsistency would be entirely explained by occupational self-direction.

The effects of status-inconsistency are *partially* attributable to occupational self-direction (see Table 6.3) because these effects are smaller in this context than when considered alone. It is worthwhile to stress that these effects are not eliminated by the impact of occupational self-direction, indicating that the "nonvertical" combination of formal education,

TABLE 6.3: Effects of Occupational Self-Direction and Status-Inconsistency on Ideational Flexibility and Authoritarian-Conservatism for Men Employed in Civilian Occupations in the United States (1964 and 1974), Japan (1979), and Poland (1978)

	Standardized Regression Coefficients		Proportion of Variance Explained by
	Occupational Self-Direction	Status-Inconsistency	Occupational Self-Direction and Status-Inconsistency
United States (1964):			
A. without controlling other variables			
ideational flexibility	.639**	.092**	.433
authoritarian-conservatism	−.493**	−.091**	.264
B. controlling other variables[a]			
ideational flexibility	.573**	.060**	.334
authoritarian-conservatism	−.493**	−.066**	.260
United States (1974):			
A. without controlling other variables			
ideational flexibility	.545**	.032**	.320
authoritarian-conservatism	−.400**	−.118**	.185
B. controlling other variables[a]			
ideational flexibility	.486**	.111**	.319
authoritarian-conservatism	−.350**	−.102*	.124
Japan (1979):			
A. without controlling other variables			
ideational flexibility	.632**	.133**	.426
authoritarian-conservatism	−.390**	−.056*	.158
B. controlling other variables[a]			
ideational flexibility	.655**	.071**	.372
authoritarian-conservatism	−.442**	−.034	.149
Poland (1978):			
A. without controlling other variables			
ideational flexibility	.655**	.095**	.463
authoritarian-conservatism	−.537**	−.157**	.342
B. controlling other variables[a]			
ideational flexibility	.623**	.061**	.423
authoritarian-conservatism	−.563**	−.041*	.350

a. Includes age, father's occupation, and the urbanness of the place in which the respondent was raised.
*$p < .05$; **$p < .01$.

occupational rank, and job income form an important dimension of social stratification for explaining intellective process, quite apart from the relationship between status-inconsistency and occupational self-direction. As a result, the combined impact of occupational self-direction and status-inconsistency accounts for more than 30% of the variance of ideational flexibility and 12% or more of the variance of authoritarian-conservatism.

Controlling occupational self-direction, there are statistically significant effects of status-inconsistency on ideational flexibility in the United States, Japan, and Poland. In the United States and Poland there are statistically significant effects of status-inconsistency on authoritarian-conservatism. In Japan, the effect of status-inconsistency on authoritarian-conservatism becomes statistically insignificant if other variables are used for control purposes; still, however, the value of the coefficient is negative as it would be expected. Thus the conclusion of our analysis is, in general terms, straightforward: Status-inconsistency affects intellective process partially independently of occupational self-direction.

CONCLUSION AND DISCUSSION

We have conceptualized and indexed status and status-inconsistency on the basis of three stratification variables: formal education, occupational rank, and job income. We have modeled social status as a "vertical dimension," which "captures" most of the variance of the stratification variables. Status-inconsistency has been treated orthogonally, that is, as the "nonvertical dimension" of social stratification. We found that the internal structure of status and status-inconsistency, expressed in terms of loadings of both constructs, is remarkably similar in the United States, Japan, and Poland.

Status-inconsistency identifies an unbalanced reward process. The most educated persons who work in prestigious occupations but earn little money may be considered "underrewarded." Persons who earn the most but have little education and work in nonprestigious occupations may be considered "overrewarded." Thus the nonvertical dimension of social stratification is a continuum from "underrewarding" (high status-inconsistency) to "overrewarding" (low status-inconsistency). The main finding of this chapter is that persons who are "underrewarded" are more intellectually flexible and open-minded than are those who are "overrewarded." We interpret this finding as an indication that "underrewarded" persons adjust to their lack of financial success and view it in relative terms while "overrewarded" persons accept the status quo.

These status-inconsistency effects occur over and above the impact of status or the impact of occupational self-direction. With minor exceptions, the results of our analysis are consistent for the United States, Japan, and Poland. A minor exception involves authoritarian-conservatism in Japan, where the status-inconsistency effect proved to be statistically insignificant, although of the same direction as in the other countries. Thus we claim that the psychological effects of status-inconsistency are, in their essence, cross-nationally invariant, at least in a Western capitalist country (the United States), a non-Western capitalist country (Japan), and a socialist country (Poland).

In the tradition of status-inconsistency research, it has been assumed that "those individuals whose positions on the different dimensions are not crystallized—those whose status membership gives rise to conflicting values and expectations—are likely to experience more strain and tension than people whose status sets are crystallized" (Treiman 1966, p. 652). There are two possible reactions to strain and tension, however. First, experiencing strain and tension may be accompanied by stress and frustration leading to intellectual rigidity and a lack of tolerance. Second, some strain and tension can lead to more positive psychological functioning in the sense of broadening perception and enhancing ambivalence. Our analysis suggests that this second possibility—overlooked in previous research—is plausible. On the basis of what we know about the psychological effects of complex environments (Schooler 1984), one can expect status-inconsistency to result in ideational flexibility and a nonauthoritarian orientation. This expectation has been confirmed for three industrialized countries that nevertheless are diverse in their organization of economic, political, and cultural subsystems. Generalizing the results presented in this chapter, we advance the hypothesis that the effects of status-inconsistency on ideational flexibility and authoritarian conservatism would be the same in all countries sufficiently industrialized as to have produced pronounced status-inconsistency.

REFERENCES

Blalock, Hubert M., Jr. 1966. "The Identification Problem and Theory Building: The Case of Status Inconsistency." *American Sociological Review* 31:51-61.

Blocker, Jean T. and Paul L. Riedesel. 1978a. "Can Sociology Find True Happiness with Subjective Status Inconsistency?" *Pacific Sociological Review* 21:275-91.

———. 1978b. "The Nonconsequences of Objective and Subjective Status Inconsistency: Requiem for a Moribund Concept." *Sociological Quarterly* 19:332-39.

Bornschier, Volker. 1986. "Social Structure and Status Inconsistency: A Research Note." Pp. 204-20 in *Status Inconsistency in Modern Societies*, edited by Hermann Strasser and Robert W. Hodge. Duisburg: Verlag der Sozialwissenschaftlichen Kooperative.

Covello, Vincent T. and Kenneth A. Bollen. 1980. "Status Consistency in Comparative Perspective: An Examination of Educational, Occupational, and Income Data in Nine Societies." *Social Forces* 58:528-39.

Crosbie, Paul V. 1979. "Effects of Status Inconsistency: Negative Evidence from Small Groups." *Social Psychology Quarterly* 42:110-25.

Gabennesch, Howard. 1972. "Authoritarianism as a World View." *American Journal of Sociology* 77:857-75.

Geschwender, James A. 1967. "Continuities in Theories of Status Consistency and Cognitive Dissonance." *Social Forces* 46:160-71.

Hodge, Robert W. and Paul M. Siegel. 1970. "Nonvertical Dimensions of Social Stratification." Pp. 512-20 in *The Logic of Social Hierarchies,* edited by E. O. Laumann, P. M. Siegel, and R. W. Hodge. Chicago: Markham.

Hope, Keith. 1975. "Models of Status Inconsistency and Social Mobility Effects." *American Sociological Review* 40:322-43.

Hornung, Carlton A. 1977. "Social Status, Status Inconsistency and Psychological Stress." *American Sociological Review* 42:623-38.

House, J. S. and E. B. Harkins. 1975. "Why and When Is Status Inconsistency Stressful?" *American Journal of Sociology* 81:395-412.

Jackson, Elton F. 1962. "Status Consistency and Symptoms of Stress." *American Sociological Review* 27:469-80.

Jackson, Elton F. and Peter J. Burke. 1965. "Status and Symptoms of Stress: Additive and Interactive Effects." *American Sociological Review* 30:556-64.

Kohn, Melvin L. 1969. *Class and Conformity: A Study in Values.* Homewood, IL: Dorsey. (2nd ed., University of Chicago Press, 1977)

———. 1977. "Reassessment, 1977." Pp. xxv-lx in *Class and Conformity: A Study in Values.* 2nd ed. Chicago: University of Chicago Press.

Kohn, Melvin L., Atsushi Naoi, Carrie Schoenbach, Carmi Schooler, and Kazimierz M. Slomczynski. Forthcoming. "Position in the Class Structure and Psychological Functioning: A Comparative Analysis of the United States, Japan, and Poland." *American Journal of Sociology.*

Kohn, Melvin L. and Carmi Schooler. 1969. "Class, Occupation, and Orientation." *American Sociological Review* 34:659-78.

———. with the collaboration of Joanne Miller, Karen A. Miller, Carrie Schoenbach, and Ronald Schoenberg. 1983. *Work and Personality: An Inquiry into the Impact of Social Stratification.* Norwood, NJ: Ablex.

Krauze, Tadeusz and Kazimierz M. Slomczynski. 1985. "How Far to Meritocracy? Empirical Tests of a Controversial Thesis." *Social Forces* 63:623-42.

Kreckel, Reinhard. 1986. "Status Inconsistency and Status Deficiency in Meritocratic Society: Stepping Stones for a Macrostructural Theory." Pp. 188-203 in *Status Inconsistency in Modern Societies,* edited by Hermann Strasser and Robert W. Hodge. Duisburg: Verlag der Sozialwissenschaftlichen Kooperative.

Laumann, Edward O. and David R. Segal. 1971. "Status Inconsistency and Ethno-Religious Group Membership as Determinants of Social Participation and Political Attitudes." *American Journal of Sociology* 77:36-61.

Lenski, Gerhard E. 1954. "Status Crystallization: A Non-Vertical Dimension of Social Status." *American Sociological Review* 19:405-13.

Malewski, Andrzej. 1966. "The Degree of Status Incongruence and Its Effects." Pp. 303-8 in *Class, Status and Power,* edited by R. Bendix and S. M. Lipset. New York: Free Press.

Meyer, John W. and Phillip E. Hammond. 1971. "Forms of Status Inconsistency." *Social Forces* 50:91-101.

Miller, Joanne, Kazimierz M. Slomczynski, and Melvin L. Kohn. 1985. "Continuity of Learning-Generalization: The Effect of Job on Men's Intellective Process in the United States and Poland." *American Journal of Sociology* 91:593-615.

Miller, Joanne, Kazimierz M. Slomczynski, and Ronald J. Schoenberg. 1981. "Assessing Comparability of Measurement in Cross-National Research: Authoritarian-Conservatism in Different Sociocultural Settings." *Social Psychology Quarterly* 44:178-91.

Müller, Hans-Peter. 1986. "Life Chances and Life Styles: Towards a Reformulation of the Theory of Status Inconsistency?" Pp. 275-90 in *Status Inconsistency in Modern Societies*, edited by Hermann Strasser and Robert W. Hodge. Duisburg: Verlag der Sozialwissenschaftlichen Kooperative.

Naoi, Atsushi. 1979. "Shokugyo-Teki Chiishakudo no Kosei." [Construction of the Occupational Status Scale]. Chapter 14 in *Nihon no Kaisokozo* [Social Stratification Structure in Japan], edited by Ken'ichi Tominaga. Tokyo: Tokyo University Press.

Naoi, Atsushi and Carmi Schooler. 1985. "Occupational Conditions and Psychological Functioning in Japan." *American Journal of Sociology* 90:729-52.

Phillips, Derek. 1983. "The Normative Standing of Economic Inequalities." *Sociologische Gids* 30:318-50.

Pohoski, Michal, Kazimierz M. Slomczynski, and Wlodzimierz Wesolowski. 1976. "Occupational Prestige in Poland, 1958-1975." *Polish Sociological Bulletin* 4:86-94.

Schooler, Carmi. 1984. "Psychological Effects of Complex Environments During the Life Span: A Review and Theory." *Intelligence* 8:259-81.

Siegel, Paul M. 1971. "Prestige in the American Occupational Structure." Ph.D. dissertation, University of Chicago.

Slomczynski, Kazimierz M. 1983. *Pozycja zawodowa i jej zwiazki z wyksztalceniem* [Occupational Status and Its Relation to Education]. Warsaw: Polish Academy of Sciences, Institute of Philosophy and Sociology.

Slomczynski, Kazimierz M. and Grazyna Kacprowicz. 1979. *Skale Zawodow* [Occupational Scales]. Warsaw: Polish Academy of Sciences, Institute of Philosophy and Sociology.

Slomczynski, Kazimierz M. and Melvin L. Kohn. 1988. *Sytuacja Pracy i jej Psychologiczne Konsekwencje: Polsko-Amerykanskie Analizy Porownawcze* [Work Conditions and Psychological Functioning: Comparative Analyses of Poland and the United States]. Wroclaw: Ossolineum.

Slomczynski, Kazimierz M., Joanne Miller, and Melvin L. Kohn. 1981. "Stratification, Work, and Values: A Polish-United States Comparison." *American Sociological Review* 46:720-44.

Slomczynski, Kazimierz M. and Atsushi Naoi. 1986. *Educational Meritocracy in Japan in the Context of Labor Market Organization* (Mimeo). Osaka University, Department of Human Sciences.

Slomczynski, Kazimierz M. and Wlodzimierz Wesolowski. 1977. "Reduction of Social Inequalities and Status Inconsistency." *Polish Sociological Bulletin* [Special issue: The Structure of Polish Society].

―――. Forthcoming. "Nowe spojrzenie na badania nad struktura spoleczna, 1964-1980" [A new look at the research on social structure, 1964-1980]. In *Theoretyczne i metodologiczne problemy wspolczesnej socjologii*, edited by Edmund Mokrzycki and Anna Giza. Wroclaw: Ossolineum.

Sobel, Michael E. 1981. "Diagonal Mobility Models: A Substantively Motivated Class of Designs for the Analysis of Mobility Effects." *American Sociological Review* 46:893-906.

Strasser, Hermann and Robert W. Hodge, eds. 1986. *Status Inconsistency in Modern Societies* (Proceedings of a Working Conference of the ISA Research Committee on Social Stratification). Duisburg: Verlag der Sozialwissenschaftlichen Kooperative.

Treiman, Donald J. 1966. "Status Discrepancy and Prejudice." *American Journal of Sociology* 71:651-64.

―――. 1977. *Occupational Prestige in Comparative Perspective*. New York: Academic Press.

Wesolowski, Wlodzimierz. 1979. *Classes, Strata, and Power*. London: Routledge & Kegan Paul.

7

Universals and Particularities of Socialist Educational Systems: The Transition from School to Work in the German Democratic Republic and the Soviet Union

Artur Meier

In both the Soviet Union (USSR) and the German Democratic Republic (GDR), education has become highly important for occupational attainment. Thus in both countries the transition from school to work occupies a central place in analyses of the effects of educational systems. Current efforts to improve vocational and technical education are legitimated mainly by arguments pointing to the necessity of training a competent labor force. Current worldwide, rapid technological change is seen as a new challenge for the structure and content of education and its closer link to the sphere of work. In socialist society, much attention is given to mobilizing human resources as productive forces in the drive for greater economic efficiency.

Seen in this light, the emphasis on the assumed requirements of the scientific-technological revolution under socialist conditions serves to justify educational growth and, particularly, greater vocationalism. Without doubt, the technological-functional approach to issues of educational change has traditionally been part of the educational philosophy and policy of both countries. This approach still has—perhaps more now than ever before—a strong appeal to the very people who experience a direct connection between their own level of education, as certificated by qualification credentials, and their job entry and career. As a consequence, manpower concepts of educational growth remain nearly uncontested among sociologists and economists; and more than that, they are strongly advocated by prominent scholars who, especially in the USSR, offer scientific support for current educational reform policy (Titma 1985; Filippov 1986).

Despite some distinctions among the approaches of investigators who have investigated sociologically the structure, operations, and expansion of socialist educational systems, one can identify at least two overwhelming features of their concepts. First, they all try to present general explanations that pinpoint one or a set of particular variables that they see as universally responsible for the conditioning and effects of the educational system in socialist society, irrespective of the considerable cross-national variations in the origins and growth of the educational systems and despite all differences in the internal structures of the educational systems and in their interplay with external forces. Second, they—almost without exception—have treated socialist educational systems as if they were more or less uniform in their social nature and major purposes, in stark contrast to educational systems in capitalist societies.

UNIVERSALS OF SOCIALIST EDUCATIONAL SYSTEMS

Portraying the educational systems of socialist countries by pointing to their common features is doubtless correct insofar as it reflects the existence of universals in socialist patterning of education and training. Socialist educational systems can be regarded as uniform if we design a rough map on which to place analogous components that are characterized by the following features:

(1) They are highly centralized systems under the control of the state and the political hegemony of the Communist party ("ideological state apparatuses" is Althusser's [1971, p. 123] term). With the socialist revolution, which abolished the privileges of the former ruling classes, the school systems in socialist society became crucial agents of socialization, in particular for the younger generation, with the declared aim of educating the "new man" and of reshaping and strengthening a new socioeconomic formation. According to the main goal of the socialist transformation of society, namely, to overcome class contradictions, educational systems are to be tools for social equalization. This could be accomplished by a high degree of unification in basic education and training, single tracking on the primary and presecondary level, and smooth transition opportunities to upper and postsecondary education for all students, regardless of social background.

This does not mean, however, that the socialist educational system at any time supplies the services that it is expected to supply or that it always achieves its centrally approved goals. An analysis of the actual operations of the educational systems of the Soviet Union and the GDR tells a story of discrepancies between designed tasks and principles and deviant results or undesired consequences (Shubkin 1970; Meier 1980).

(2) In all the centralized socialist educational systems, a considerable degree of standardization can be observed. Educational legislation is directed from the political power center and quickly imposed throughout the entire country. Curricula for the general, compulsory school and for many colleges (and even for university courses) are standardized. Uniform, centrally licensed textbooks are used for instruction everywhere.

The logic of these forms of systematization, based on state planning and control, is closely linked to the state monopoly of all important educational degrees and certificates. As a consequence, the vast majority of all really attractive, "powerful" occupations are, in fact, accessible only through formalized educational training and an appropriate diploma. Centrally systematized curricula, standardized textbooks, and highly formalized outcomes are intended to achieve an optimal fit between schooling and societal needs.

But, of course, the educational systems of the Soviet Union and the GDR (and certainly of other socialist countries) experience a contradictory relationship between what is taught in schools and what is needed in social, particularly in working, life. The educational systems react with new curricula, new textbooks, altered criteria for examinations, and—foremost—the elaboration of polytechnical and vocational instruction to link the educational and productive spheres of socialist society more closely, sometimes with greater success than before, but certainly without any chance for perfect congruence (Ferge 1977; Meier 1980).

(3) The educational system in all socialist societies has to fulfill at least two universal functions: to provide as much social equality in educational opportunities as seems necessary for the stability and legitimation of the socialist order, and to produce an educated labor force, differentiated as seen to be needed in the state-planned economy, based on the belief that the scientific-technological revolution requires both a pool of highly trained and selected talents and a specialized, educated "normal" labor force.

Utilitarian and egalitarian functions, however, are not perfectly compatible. Educational systems in both the Soviet Union and the GDR have experienced situations in which the egalitarian principle of guaranteeing equal educational rights and chances to students from all classes and strata in practice came into conflict with the meritocratic principle by which recruitment for the different trades and professions is managed. The twofold universal use of education periodically creates tensions that hardly can be ignored. Educational planning from above tries to orchestrate the conflicting purposes in such situations by giving priority to one or the other goal and reversing the rank order of functions from time to time (Szczepanski 1974; Gaszo 1978; Adamski 1982).

(4) The pattern of educational change could be described as being very similar in all socialist countries. Educational reforms or other modes of educational change are usually initiated and politically directed by the state, under the supremacy of the party, which implies the participation of interested groups on more regional or local levels. Guided educational change is thought to make the best use of all social resources and is periodically legitimated by economic and social change originating outside the system. In general, no attention is given to internal systemic sources of change.

Although efforts, under the state and party's guidance, to adapt the socialist educational system to changing environments may bring success for a certain period and in certain directions, such efforts never completely satisfy all needs and interests. Nor are such efforts protected from unintended consequences and new demands.

Since the Socialist Revolution of 1917, the Soviet educational system has been changed four times, with a fifth reform now under way; and in the GDR we can distinguish at least two or three significant educational reforms since World War II. The interaction between schooling and work life has obviously been a main axis for policy change.

The existence of a set of universal characteristics of socialist education could lead one to conclude that there is one type of socialist educational system, with almost the same content, functioning in an analogous way at the base of nearly identical structures, pursuing one path of development. The uniform image of socialist educational systems, however, is too easily drawn; such a conception deemphasizes national "particularities," regarding them as only secondary. The official formula, "socialist in content, national in form," indeed allows one to view peculiarities as systemic epiphenomena, and consequently to see essential differences as irrelevant. Moreover, despite obvious practical tendencies, the theoretical expectation pervaded the literature (particularly as written by educational scientists) that, with the maturing of socialist society, convergence between educational systems will become greater and greater. There is still an ideological bias toward a future state of affairs when the particularities will fully disappear or at least become marginal.

Not long ago, it was strongly argued that the Soviet educational system, because of its "avant-garde" role, would represent the overall model for all socialist systems of education, including that of the GDR. "Les extremes se touchent": In Western literature particularly, the Sovietization thesis was pushed forward, especially with regard to certain trends in the GDR's educational policy.

I would like to present some counterarguments and to start with quite a different thesis, based on what I have learned from a cross-national comparative study of the transition from school to work in the USSR and the GDR, a study in which I had been involved for several years in the 1970s.

Having been immersed in that body of evidence, I became deeply impressed that the particularities of individual socialist educational systems may be anything but random or secondary, compared with the often-demonstrated universals. Cross-national research, pursued all too seldom by sociologists from socialist countries, seems to be a good method for perceiving the uniqueness of each national educational system.

PARTICULARITIES IN SOCIALIZATION

Empirical cross-national studies focusing on the socialization process in the school-to-work transition of young people have been carried out from 1971 to 1975 by collaborating research teams of educational sociologists in both countries.

The USSR sample was composed of 285 "apprentices" who had completed their general school education and were enrolled in vocational training units in factories, 369 students of technical colleges, and 600 young skilled workers aged 17-20 (N = 1,254). The GDR sample consisted of 478 students who, after ten years of high school, were apprentices, getting vocational education on the upper-secondary level (three days a week in special vocational schools and two days in enterprises); 115 with extended secondary education (i.e., who must pass the final "Maturity" examination); 210 college students; and 507 young skilled workers aged 20-24 (total N = 1,310). As is usual in comparative research, achieving full equivalence of groups and subgroups is nearly impossible because of problems in matching institutions in different nations. Thus the investigators tried to select the most representative and compatible samples that they could. The investigation of these samples formed the main, large-scale phase of the joint research program.

In preliminary and subsequent stages of the inquiry, we, in addition, interviewed educators, trainers, and masters—people who had been in direct contact with the respondents for a long time, and whom we saw as having pertinent information about both work requirements and students'/workers' behavior. The composition of the samples of these persons necessarily differed between the two countries. We interviewed more of these people in the USSR (N = 456) than in the GDR (N = 350).

During the three stages of investigation, several methods were used: in-depth interviews in the preliminary stage; paper-and-pencil questionnaires in the large-scale survey; and standardized interviews in the third stage.

Not much is known about the competence of students and former students in judging the values and aims of the educational system in which they studied. We asked them to compare those values and aims with the working standards that they had experienced during or after getting their vocational training. The collaborating research groups have had to be cautious in interpreting and generalizing the findings. The investigators thought it necessary to objectify the statements of the students and former students by contrasting them with those of other knowledgeable people, namely, the team leaders, masters, and trainers. (The European cross-national survey on the experiences and values of first-semester students, carried out in 1977-78 by investigators working under the sponsorship of the Vienna Centre [Bargel, Markiewicz, and Peisert 1982] used a similar research strategy.) Finally, it was possible to prepare internal research reports to which only limited access was given; only a few selected data have been published (Gurowa, Meier, and Steiner 1978; Meier 1982).

The results seem to be sufficiently noteworthy to be disseminated to a wider audience and to be discussed critically. The aggregate profiles of young people being trained by the two educational systems give evidence of striking differences instead of the similarities often assumed on the basis of a belief that socialist educational systems have identical features. Let us turn to some facts and problems identified by the inquiry.

The GDR apprentices and college students, as compared to corresponding groups in the Soviet Union, demonstrated significantly greater discipline, readiness for action, and critical thinking; the Soviet apprentices and students indicated greater self-reliance, sticking to principles, and studiousness. In both countries, the respondents indicated a great openness for innovation and collectivism.

Young skilled workers who had completed their vocational training gave nearly the same picture. The young workers' team leaders and masters, however, emphasized somewhat different qualities as necessary to job performance. In the GDR, the team leaders and masters insisted on innovative behavior, readiness for action, willingness to learn, and discipline. In the USSR, collectivism and self-reliance at work were required to a remarkably higher degree, and innovative and achievement-centered behavior to a decidedly lesser degree. Masters in the USSR pointed to a lack of discipline among the workers they had to lead.

As for the apprentices and students still enrolled in special forms of vocational training, the GDR apprentices and college students were more able to fulfill role expectations regarding disciplined work and readiness for action, while Soviet trainees and students were generally self-reliant and adherent to principles, again with a certain reluctance in the areas of discipline and achievement. Moreover, the young people in both countries were asked to evaluate the capacity of the compulsory general polytechnical secondary schools that they had attended to prepare them for work life. The GDR apprentices, students, and workers—despite making several critical comments about their school education—described a comparatively greater convergence between the qualities stressed at school and those needed for job performance.

In general, we found distinct structures of value orientations related to work and job aspirations in the two samples. The GDR respondents ranked high income and good chances for upward mobility significantly higher than did our Soviet respondents. The Soviet respondents were evidently more prepared "to help others," and were far less oriented to rapid promotion and high salary. Young people in both countries took job security for granted and hoped to find attractive work with creative potential and the chance to use one's special skills. The results also provided evidence, however, that the majority were not fully satisfied with their vocational choices and wanted to change their jobs some time after they finished their vocational training.

It has repeatedly been reported from the USSR that only 25%-30% of trained workers stay on the jobs for which they were trained. Research findings from the GDR indicate that almost 50% of the vocationally trained change their career within three years after completing their training. For young people in both countries, it is easy to start a new career, because there is no threat of unemployment. On the contrary, there are always a multitude of offers from many firms because of continuing deficits in qualified manpower in several branches of the economy.

In the upper-secondary level of the GDR educational system, there is both open and tacit competition for good school marks and appropriate educational credentials, which are tickets to attractive and well-paid jobs. In contrast, striving for personal material goods has long been stigmatized in Soviet education, reinforced by an official income policy with clear leveling objectives—now openly attacked, but in the past (Filippov 1977) often praised as bringing more equality or "homogeneity." The deemphasis in the Soviet Union, and the emphasis in the GDR, on meritocratic procedures and patterns resulted in obviously different outcomes of socialization and the transition from school to work.

Youth in the GDR, in fact, have to undergo a much longer (three years more on average) formal educational experience, in establishments that exert a remarkably high degree of social control on the students' activities, along with socialization by families that for many generations have esteemed discipline and have exerted considerable effort to instill disciplined habits. It is well known that a Puritan work ethic centered on abstinence and discipline is widespread among Germans. This work ethic is fully alive in the GDR, in all classes and strata of this society. In addition, we can quote Karl Marx, who described the disciplinary effects of industrial work when performed for a long time over generations. The contrast with the USSR, which has quite another tradition in industrialism, and a differently structured labor force, is too evident to need further elucidation. The young people start their job careers much earlier; they, therefore, become independent at an earlier age. An emphasis on autonomy and self-reliance, and a corresponding deemphasis of conformity, can be explained by these conditions of socialization, particularly in the transition phase from school to work.

It can be concluded, therefore, that different socialization aims and patterns, under different social conditions, exerted in two socialist countries, have resulted in different, even divergent, outcomes. These diversities in the socialization for work of the younger generation in the two countries lead us to examine the structural specificities of the two educational systems.

PECULIARITIES IN EDUCATIONAL STRUCTURES

There is a far-reaching difference in the structural conditions of the transitional stage from school to work in the GDR and the USSR. While the GDR educational system has an all-embracing subsystem for vocational training, the Soviet educational system does not.

In Germany, being a certified and fully skilled craftsman (*Facharbeiter*) has traditionally been regarded as a necessary prerequisite for a high standard of competence at work. A much larger percentage of youth in the GDR attend vocational schooling than in any other country of the world. All those who do not go on to an "extended" high school education (in preparation for the Maturity examination, which is required for admission to a university) are obliged under the constitution to undergo two years of vocational training up to the age of 18. That means that everyone who leaves the general, compulsory, ten-year high school, having received from the seventh grade on a general polytechnical education, has to undergo an obligatory apprenticeship of two years of vocational training until qualified as a *Facharbeiter*. By the beginning of the 1970s, when our research was conducted, 85% of the age cohort were completing the general high school curriculum and going on to extended high school or to vocational school. Of the remaining 15% who had left school earlier, usually after the eighth grade, the vast majority went on to train as skilled workers—in this special case—within a period of three years.

Vocational education and training in the GDR is designed as a combination of a state-controlled system of vocational schools, mainly located in large-scale factories, sometimes also in the more efficient cooperative farms, and on-the-job training, generally with half of the time in instruction in theory and half in practice. Training for the skilled-workers' certificate is offered in 316 trades, which are further divided into 639 specializations. Since 1970, all apprentices receive basic instruction in economics, civics, mathematics, data processing, and computer technology, and continue with their specialized training.

In the GDR, 75% of those who complete high school take the apprenticeship route from school to work; another 12% take a route through the Maturity examination to the university and then to work; and 13% enter an engineering or technical college (*Fachschule*). The standard of the German *Ingenieurfachschule* is relatively high and closer to the university level than to the post-high-school vocational training system. Therefore, admission to engineering or technical colleges requires the successful completion of the tenth grade, followed by two years of vocational training and a skilled-worker certificate, as well as, in general, one year of employment. Alternatively, a growing number of those who complete high school choose an apprenticeship, followed by the Maturity examination; this qualifies them to study at a university or at a technical or engineering college, both of which are respected types of higher education in the GDR. About 25% of the relevant age cohorts are enrolled in establishments of higher education.

The broad and compulsory vocational educational (sub)system in the GDR produces a highly qualified and flexible labor force of skilled blue- and white-collar workers, technicians, and engineers for industry, agriculture, and the service sector. From 1975 to 1985, the proportion of the labor force in the GDR who were qualified (certified) as skilled workers increased from 55% to 65%; the proportion with college-level training increased from 8.5% to 12.5%; and the proportion with university training increased from 5.5% to 7.5%. By contrast, the percentage of unskilled and semiskilled workers decreased from 31% to 15%.

The postschooling careers of young workers in the USSR are extremely different. In the beginning of the 1970s, when we started our research, we had difficulty even forming a Soviet sample of "apprentices," comparable to those in the GDR, because at the time the majority of youth in the USSR left school after completing the eighth grade and entered the work sphere immediately, there receiving only brief on-the-job training and nothing more. A small proportion of young workers enrolled in a "technical-vocational unit" of a factory, or in administration, acquiring training comparable to that of a semiskilled worker in the GDR. The technical colleges, which had long attracted Soviet youth, could be attended by only a small minority. These technical colleges seemed to have an intermediate status, between the fully developed *Berufsschule* of the GDR and its *Ingenieurschule*.

It is nearly impossible to reconstruct quantitatively the multiple tracking of the transition from school to work using Soviet statistics. From research done in the sociology of education, however, it appears that the situation has changed somewhat in the decade up to the beginning of the 1980s, when it was still the case that nearly 38.3% of the Soviet students left school after the eighth grade, 28% moving to technical-vocational facilities within firms and farms and 10.3% entering a technical college. It was reported that in 1982 only about one-third of those who left school after the eighth grade were enrolled in vocational or technical training institutions, and that even among those who finished ten years of schooling, only 37% went on to technical-vocational facilities and 14% to colleges (Filippov 1986), while the rest received no specifically vocational training. In the USSR, 15% of those who acquired high school certificates—for years, a stable percentage—were admitted to universities. Sociologists of education in the Soviet Union have criticized the lack of vocational-training opportunities, which severely conflicts with the job aspirations of young people, as well as with the needs of the national economy.

These facts about the channels of the school-to-work transition in the GDR and the USSR give evidence of just how divergent two socialist educational systems can be. The principal difference is the high degree of formalization of occupational training in the GDR, based on a fully elaborated subsystem of vocational education developed over the decades and the existence of state-controlled and universally recognized occupations. High degrees of formalization, regulation, and guidance; meritocratic principles; and, consequently, elaborated structural conditions for stringent selectivity in the transition from school to work in the GDR contrast with more equalized and level conditions, a much lower degree of formalization, and insufficient regulation and guidance from the educational to the occupational and employment systems in the Soviet Union. The German system, obviously, is more diversified and complex; the Soviet system more uniform and, though larger, comparatively less structured.

The explanation of the fully expanded vocational training system, intended to educate a highly qualified and flexible labor force, can be

partly derived from Karl Marx's writings. He had welcomed the establishment of technical and agricultural schools as necessary for the
functioning of modern industry, which

> compels society, under penalty of death, to replace the detail-worker of today,
> crippled by lifelong repetition of one and the same trivial operation, and thus
> reduced to the mere fragment of a man, by the fully developed individual, fit for
> a variety of labors, ready to face any change of production. (Marx 1889)

In "Capital," too, he correctly foresaw that technical instruction, both
theoretical and practical, will take its proper place in working-class
schools far beyond the level of merely combining elementary education
with some little instruction in technology and in the practical handling of
the various implements of labor (Marx 1889). Today, his predictions have
largely been realized.

The GDR has long been a highly industrialized country, with the
majority of its working people occupied in the modern industrial and
service branches of the economy. The work force is expected to react
flexibly to the fundamental changes in work induced by the present
scientific-technological revolution, which started earlier and has been
broader in scope in the GDR than in some other socialist countries. For
many years, the national economy—mediated by the state planning system—has pressed for an adequate supply of young workers, technicians,
and engineers, comprehensively as well as specially trained within an
educational system capable of contributing the needed quotas of personnel (and much more). In turn, by law, firms are obliged to employ the
young people who have the modern education and to sign contracts with
them one year before they finish vocational school, college, or the university. In this way, the GDR's educational system, in particular its highly
formalized vocational training subsystem, is very closely tied to the
employment system.

The German system of apprenticeship is unique in its format and has
been further developed under socialist conditions since World War II. The
national heritage creates a unique school-to-work transition in each
country. This leads us to consider the question of particular variations and
stages of educational development.

VARIATIONS AND PARTICULAR
STAGES OF EDUCATIONAL CHANGES

Remarkable differences between the educational systems of the GDR
and the USSR can be found, too, by examining the development of

educational systems of the two countries. The Soviet educational system continues to expand, while that of the GDR clearly experienced the "limits of growth." Soviet statistics and the reports of educational sociologists give impressive accounts of the extensive expansion of the Soviet educational system, particularly in the 1970s and now in the 1980s, while in the GDR only minor changes in number and structure can be registered.

Evidently, the systems are in crucially different phases of structural elaboration. Both educational systems have their specific roots in national history. In Prussian Germany, by 1888, the eight-year general school had become obligatory, and after the November revolution of 1918 attendance at vocational schools or equivalent educational establishments was regulated by law. The antifascist-democratic school reform following World War II and the succeeding socialist reforms at the end of the 1950s and during the 1960s were built on these fundamentals. Within a relatively short period, educational enrollment greatly increased, albeit with unintended discrepancies between an educational system that produced ever-increasing certified qualifications and an employment system that could not absorb this degree of "educational output."

In some countries, this stage of educational development is termed "overeducation" or "inflation" (Bourdieu et al. 1981; Archer 1982). In the GDR, such interpretations of educational excess were widely rejected, with the argument that there are still spheres in the national economy with a distinct deficit of qualified employees, and that the implementation of new technologies requires large-scale, high-level general and vocational education.

In any case, extensive educational growth has come to an end in the GDR and subsequent changes have been qualitative in nature, without any dramatic variation in the educational structure or any spectacular increase in numbers. Seen from a historical perspective, youth in the GDR today get much more schooling but no more social mobility, as compared, for example, with the first postwar generation. The time is past, when, after the abolition of the former ruling classes with their educational privileges, there was considerable upward mobility of working-class people and the peasantry—the main channel of which was the educational system.

Educational policy in the GDR has always officially aimed at greater equalization; but, in fact, the GDR established an educational system (1965) that provides general high school education for all, irrespective of social background, followed by very different paths, beginning at the upper-secondary level. The multiple-tracking system, following ten years of high-school attendance, now serves to recruit and reproduce the various strata of the consolidated new social structure of the "developed" socialist society. The matured educational system of the GDR has become a complex, structurally differentiated social organization, one that includes an effective working system of vocational guidance that allocates graduating students to the various sections of the labor force. Selectivity and regulation secure the qualification of skilled workers and employees, strata to which the majority of those who leave school are distributed, and provide the necessary share of professionals and midlevel technical personnel.

Compared to the educational system of the GDR, the Soviet educational system is very different in origin and in its course of historical development (Archer 1979). After the October Socialist Revolution in 1917, the Unified Labor School had been introduced, along with large-scale campaigns against illiteracy, with the goal of providing elementary education to the masses of peasants and workers. This definitely embodies egalitarian principles. The high degree of unification of the school system as a single institution covering all grades—except for the university and the technicum—was maintained even during the 1930s, when a meritocratic tendency seemed to lead to redifferentiation and to reformalization. The reform policy between 1931-1944 seemed primarily to aim at the recruitment and reproduction of a new Soviet intelligentsia, especially professionals and semiprofessionals needed for an expanding administration and for growing industry.

With the attacks against the character of the postrevolutionary Labor School, however, education and work were "divorced." The present Soviet educational system still rests very heavily on the forms of schooling that had been established in the 1930s, despite the subsequent reforms of the 1950s and 1960s. The educational system to a large extent lacks real polytechnical education. More than that, it lacks a comprehensive system of formal vocational training aimed at the large-scale education of a skilled working class. In fact, eight or ten years of general education is provided for all, followed by, at most, on-the-job training and facilities that provide semiskilled qualification for the masses without much selectivity. The exceptions, of course, are those who can attend a technical college or university but, at the most, no more than 15%-20% of any age cohort are able to attend these traditionally prestigious institutions of postsecondary education.

The current Soviet school reform is definitely devoted to the extension of general education, and to the promotion of links between schooling and work. Polytechnical and vocational education is to be given in general high schools, in cooperation with factories and farms, to students who are channeled into jobs of low occupational status, mainly in agriculture and the service sector. Training in vocational schools located in enterprises is designed to be the main avenue for better qualified, skilled workers (with increasing numbers of students striving for attractive jobs). Colleges serve, as before, to provide the national economy with engineers, technicians, and other medium-strata staff, but with an expected higher standard and probably with growing enrollments.

No doubt, the Soviet educational system, particularly with its links to the occupational and employment systems that are still expanding, with increasing numbers of students and schools, and with a decided turn to meritocratic principles, will be characterized by more formalization. Soviet economic planners and educational sociologists hope that educational reforms will bridge the gap between students' aspirations and the limited capacity of formal educational establishments to provide occupational training. In this way, too, they hope to reduce the mismatch between the educational system and the needs of the economy.

To sum up, compared with the GDR educational system, the educational system of the USSR (in the 1970s, when we did our research) was in a quite different stage of growth, a difference that has continued to the present. The end of expansion and a stop because of "overdevelopment" in the GDR can be contrasted with a still extensively expanding system in the Soviet Union. Although both educational systems experience contradictions with the economy, the educational system in the GDR is better able to supply a differentially educated and vocationally trained labor force, while the Soviet educational system is continually confronted with the criticism that it does not provide a well-trained labor force adapted to the needs of large-scale industry.

These clear variations in the development and functioning of the educational systems in the two countries can only be explained by their very different historical roots. The extent to which the systems themselves begin to function and develop on the basis of their own endogenous changes and their own elaborated internal structural conditions remains an open question (Archer 1982; Green, Ericson, and Seidman 1980). Conclusions derived from the recent history of the GDR educational system may support the hypothesis that, at least when a high degree of complexity is reached, the system develops a life of its own, with considerable strength to react to external social forces and demands (Meier 1974). Even though we cannot at this time be certain of the degree to which either the German or the Soviet educational system is acting as an independent factor, it is clear that without an account of their specific historical developments we could not explain their present particularities. There were different roots, as well as different "points of no return," in their educational histories, as well as in their national histories in general, that are responsible for peculiarities in the objectified systemic structures at this time and in these places.

CONCLUSIONS

On the basis of comparative investigation (partly done in the form of primary research, partly as desk research and secondary analyses) of the German Democratic Republic and the Soviet Union, we have found striking differences in the decisive transition phase from school to work. Why, then, should one continue to overestimate the universals and to treat socialist educational systems as if they were of one type, embodied in one and the same type of society, and following one path of convergence?

The findings of our comparative research suggest, rather, an alternative interpretation: that we accept the existence of distinctive particularities, growing in importance, and showing no sign of being only a temporary way station en route to a uniform, nondivergent socialist-bloc model. These peculiarities, deeply rooted in the histories of the national educational systems, as well as in the relationships of the educational system of each society with the particular economic, political, cultural, and social conditions of that society, and also the internal conditions of the particular educational system, are far more than simply functional alternatives leading to the same goal. The differences in the educational systems of the GDR and the USSR represent significant features of essentially different types of educational systems.

The time seems opportune for an analytic intervention that stresses the national particularities of socialist educational systems, just as we have long recognized the national specifics of Western countries. Although it is commonly understood that countries differ culturally, investigators have seldom noted the far-reaching differences in socialist educational systems and their causes. The national peculiarities of educational systems result not only from cultural specificity, but also from a wide range of differences in economic and political circumstances, associated with remarkable distinctions in social structures.

Thus if we really accept national and societal singularities as essential to socialist educational systems, not only with respect to variations in "form" but covering, indeed, their different contents, structures, functions, and histories, it follows that comparative analyses are fruitful only if they give national differences their proper, central place. Instead of designing oversimplified pictures of an assumed convergence, about which we know enough to have considerable doubts, our views of the future would be more accurate if we took into account a wide range of diversity.

To emphasize the specifics, and to envisage a multitude of distinct social systems and many courses from the past to the future, is not only an antidote to false generalizations, but is also perfectly compatible with sociological theories about general trends and patterns of development. Marx's historical-concrete analyses were in any case methodologically indispensable for avoiding a mechanistic view of rigid stages of development and a dogmatic scheme of infrastructures and suprastructures applicable to all societies at all times. The materialistic approach, which gives central importance to the progress of productive forces (which is quite different from technological or economic determinism), and which tries to explain variations and developments of suprastructural institutions, such as education, starting with analyzing the weight and influence of basic material factors, must always be a historical approach as well. Unlike some of his dogmatic followers, Marx never treated national particularities of the economic base, or of the suprastructural configurations, as secondary epiphenomena but, on the contrary, was careful to elaborate typical national distinctions. (A good example was his comparison of public education in the United States and the Prusso-German Empire [Marx 1875].) Within the boundaries of a particular socioeconomic formation, Marxist sociology explains the historical-materialist aspects of a wide range of national types of education, all of which enjoy relative institutional autonomy.

The other great founding father of our discipline, Max Weber, in contrast to Marx, would have explained the observed phenomena rather by pointing to an ongoing, inevitable general process of rationalization that produces a need for the kind of educational system with special examinations and trained expertise. But, again, despite the universal claim for the creation of educational certificates, Weber, the historian and sociologist, never denied the importance of national particularities. He regarded Germany, specifically, as the main breeding place for rational, specialized, and expert examinations depending on proper forms of education and training (Weber 1922).

National particularities of educational systems, especially of their vocational parts, are deeply rooted in history and thereby are individually structured, with a wide range of specificities that give them unique identity. Different types of socialist educational and training systems obviously operate under different internal and external conditions. It is not premature to hope that the awareness of different educational systems in socialist countries will lead to consideration of different types of socialist societies.

REFERENCES

Adamski, W. W. 1982. "Social Structure Versus Educational Policy: Polish and European Perspectives." In *The Sociology of Educational Expansion*, edited by M. S. Archer. Beverly Hills, CA: Sage.

Althusser, L. 1971. *Lenin and Philosophy and Other Essays*. New York: New Left.

Archer, M. S. 1979. *Social Origins of Educational Systems*. London: Sage.

————, ed. 1982. *Studies in International Sociology*. Vol. 27. *The Sociology of Educational Expansion*. Beverly Hills, CA: Sage.

Bargel, T., W. Markiewicz, and H. Peisert. 1982. "University Graduates: Study Experience and Social Role." In *Comparative Research on Education*, edited by M. Niessen and J. Peschar. Oxford-Budapest: Pergamon, Akademiai Kiado.

Bourdieu, P. et al. 1981. *Titel und Stelle: Über die Reproduktion sozialer Macht*. Frankfurt am: Europäische Verlagsanstalt.

Ferge, Z. 1977. "School Systems and School Reforms." Pp. 11-26 in *Studies in International Sociology*. Vol. 11. *Education in a Changing Society*, edited by A. Kloskowska and G. Martinotti. Beverly Hills, CA: Sage.

Filippov, F. R. 1977. "School Structure and Systems of Education." Pp. 59-72 in *Studies in International Sociology*. Vol. 11. *Education in a Changing Society*, edited by A. Kloskowska and G. Martinotti. Beverly Hills, CA: Sage.

————. 1986. "Lebenspläne der Jugend und die Bildungsreform in der UdSSR." In *Staatliche Steuerung im Bildungs- und Erziehungswesens osteuropäischer Staaten und der DDR*, edited by O. Anweiler. Berlin (West): Arno Spitz Verlag.

Gaszo, F. 1978. "Social Mobility and the School." In *Hungarian Society and Marxist Sociology in the Nineteen-Seventies*, edited by T. Huszar, K. Kulcsar, and S. Szalai. Budapest: Corvina.

Green, T. F., D. P. Ericson, and R. H. Seidman. 1980. *Predicting the Behavior of the Educational System*. Syracuse: Syracuse University Press.

Gurowa, R. G., A. Meier, and I. Steiner. 1978. *Auf das Leben vorbereitet—Untersuchungen an Schulabsolventen in der UdSSR und DDR. Fortschrittsberichte und Studien* (Internal Research Report). Berlin: Akademie der Pädagogischen Wissenschaften der DDR.

Heinz, W. R. 1986. "The Transition from School to Work in Crisis: Coping with Threatening Unemployment." Paper presented at the AERA Annual Meeting, Chicago, April.

Karabel, J. and A. Halsey, eds. 1977. *Power and Ideology in Education*. New York: Oxford University Press.

Marx, K. [1875] 1972. "Critique of the Gotha Programme." Pp. 171-72 in *Education: Structure and Society*, edited by B. R. Cosin. Harmondsworth: Penguin, Open University Press.

————. [1889] 1972. "Capital." Pp. 150-70 in *Education: Structure and Society*, edited by B. R. Cosin. Harmondsworth: Penguin, Open University Press.

Meier, A. 1974. *Soziologie des Bildungswesens*. Berlin: Volk und Wissen Verlag und Köln: Pahl Rugenstein Verlag.

————. 1980. "The Dialectical Relationship Between Education and Employment. Rethinking the Economic and Non-Economic Factors in Educational Change and Re-Assessing Some Theoretical Approaches." Paper presented at the Paris Conference of ISA-Research Committee on the Sociology of Education, August.

————. 1982. "Socialization and Preparation for Working Life in the German Democratic
    Republic and the Soviet Union." Pp. 123-34 in *Comparative Research on Education*,
    edited by M. Niessen and J. Peschar. Oxford-Budapest: Pergamon, Akademiai Kiado.
Niessen, M. and J. Peschar. 1982. "Comparative Research on Education 1975-1980: Review
    and Appraisal." Pp. 3-36 in *Comparative Research on Education*, edited by M. Niessen
    and J. Peschar. Oxford-Budapest: Pergamon, Akademiai Kiado.
Shubkin, W. 1970. *Sociologicheskie Opyty* [Sociological Knowledge]. Moscow: Mysl.
Slomcyzynski, K. M., J. Miller, and M. Kohn. 1981. "Stratification, Work and Values: A
    Polish-United States Comparison." *American Sociological Review* 46:720-44.
Szczepanski, J. 1974. "Higher Education in Eastern Europe" (Occasional Paper no. 12). New
    York: ICED.
Titma, M. C. 1985. *Zisneny put' pokolenya: ego vybor i utverzdenie* [Generation's Career:
    Its Choice and Realization]. Tallin: Esti Raamat.
UdSSR in Zahlen für. 1985. *Statistisches Handbuch.* Moskau: Verlag Financy i Statistika.
Weber, M. 1922. *Wirtschaft und Gesellschaft.* Reprinted in *From Max Weber: Essays in
    Sociology*, edited and translated by H. Gerth and C. W. Mills. Excerpt pp. 225-29 in
    Education: Structure and Society, edited by B. R. Cosin. 1972. Harmondsworth: Penguin,
    Open University Press.

8

Class Structure and Class Formation: A Comparative Analysis of the United States and Sweden

Erik Olin Wright
Carolyn Howe
Donmoon Cho

At the very core of the Marxian tradition of class analysis is the problem of the relationship between class structure and class struggle. While in one way or another, most Marxists believe that class structures help to explain class struggles, there is no consensus at all over how the causal linkage between the two should be understood. At one extreme there are Marxist analyses in which it is claimed that one can basically read off patterns of class struggle directly from the class structure; in the long run, at least, class structures are thought to determine class struggle. At the other extreme, the class structure is viewed as at most providing us with the vocabulary of identifying potential actors in class struggles; it does not, however, necessarily have a more powerful role in determining actual patterns of class struggle than many other mechanisms (ideology, the state, ethnicity, and so on).

We wish to propose a general model of the relationship between class structure and class struggle that captures both of these intuitions, that is,

AUTHORS' NOTE: *We would like to thank Michael Burawoy for his insightful criticisms of earlier drafts of this chapter. This research was funded in part by grants from the National Science Foundation and the Wisconsin Alumni Research Foundation.*

which simultaneously treats class structures as in some sense the fundamental determinant of class struggles but nevertheless potentially allows other causal factors greater weight in explaining the concrete variations in patterns of class struggle. In the next section we will lay out the general contours of this model. This will be followed by a finer-grained elaboration of one linkage in this model, the linkage between class structure and class formation. Finally, this aspect of the model will be examined empirically in a comparison of class structure and class formation in Sweden and the United States.

A GENERAL MODEL OF CLASS STRUCTURE, CLASS FORMATION, CLASS STRUGGLE

A number of concepts, all of which are deeply contested within Marxist social theory, need to be defined before we can elaborate the theoretical model that guides this research: class structure, class interests, class formation, class practices, and class struggle.[1]

Class structure. A "class structure," as we will use the term, is a structure of relationally defined positions filled by individuals (or families) that determines the objective class interests of those individuals. There are three things to note in this rather cumbersome initial definition. First, the concept of class structure designates a set of positions distinct from the human individuals who occupy those positions. This does not mean, of course, that the positions exist independently of people per se, but simply that they exist independently of the specific incumbents of positions. Second, class positions are relational positions. This means that specific classes are definable only in terms of the relations that bind them to other classes. Finally, the concept of class structure is intimately tied to the concept of (objective) class interests. A *social* structure can be understood as consisting of many different kinds of relationally defined positions—positions within gender relations, power relations, class relations, and so on. One central basis for differentiating among these different sorts of relations is the kind of interests that are generated by the relations. Class structures are those structures that distribute class interests across individuals and families.

Class interests. The concept of class interests plays a pivotal role in the general analysis of classes. If one wants to know whether a given concrete

---

[1.] For a more extended discussion of these concepts, see Wright (1978, chap. 3, 1985, chap. 2). The concept of exploitation used in the discussion of class interests is derived from the work of John Roemer (1982).

social relation, for example, racial relations between Blacks and Whites, is a class relation, the answer depends crucially upon the linkage of this relation to class interests. If racial mechanisms directly determine class interests, then they would be an instance of a class relation; if they are linked to class interests via the way they distribute people into class positions, but do not, in and of themselves, determine class interests, then they would not constitute a class relation.

What then are *class* interests? As we will use the term, "objective class interests" are interests defined with respect to mechanisms of material exploitation. The concept of exploitation is a complex one. As a first approximation, we can say that *exploitation exists when one group of people satisfy their interests at the expense of the satisfaction of the interests of another group*. This is a very general definition and it encompasses a wide variety of exploitations: It can be used to identify sexual exploitation, cultural exploitation, and, most important for our present purposes, material exploitation. Material exploitation, accordingly, is a situation in which one group of agents systematically satisfies their material interests at the expense of the satisfaction of the material interests of another group. When such material exploitation is linked to relationally defined positions, then we can speak of class exploitation and class interests.

Class formation. The expression "class formation" is used either to designate a process (the process of class formation) or an outcome (*a* class formation). In both cases the expression refers to the formation of classes as collectively organized social forces rather than simply as structures of relationally defined positions. If class structures are defined by the social relations *between* classes, class formations are defined by the social relations *within* classes.

Class capacities. Class capacities refer to the ability of individuals and collectivities to realize their class interests. In these terms, class *formations* are important above all because of the ways in which they determine class capacities.

Class practices. Class practices are activities engaged in by members of a class using class capacities in order to realize at least some of their class interests. "Practice" in these terms implies that the activity is *intentional* (i.e., it has a conscious goal); "class" practice implies that the goal is the realization of class-based interests.

Class struggle. When class practices are directed *against* the interests of other classes, these practices can be referred to as "class struggle." Given the antagonistic nature of the interests determined by class structures, within a Marxist class analysis class practices will in general take

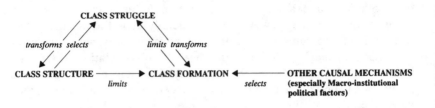

Figure 8.1: Model of Determination of Class Structure, Class Formation, and Class Struggle

the form of struggle—that is, the realization of the interests of one class implies a confrontation with other classes.

Within this conceptual terrain, there is a logical sense in which the concept of class structure is conceptually prior to class formation and class struggle: It is necessary to understand the nature of the social relations that generate opposing class interests before we can identify the class content of the collective formations that engage in struggle. This does not mean, however, that in any given empirical problem class structure has causal primacy in explaining class struggles. It may well be in a given historical context, for example, that variations in class formations matter more for explaining variations in class struggles than do variations in class structures.

Class structure, class formation, and class struggle can be causally linked together in what can be called a model of determination (Wright 1978, 1985). The basic model that underpins our analysis is presented in Figure 8.1. In this model, class struggles are not a simple, direct effect of class structures. Rather, class struggles occur within limits set by class formations, and class formations occur within limits set by class structures. Class struggles, in turn, have transformative effects on both class structures and class formations.

The concept of "limits" is crucial to understanding this model. To say that class structure imposes limits on class formation means that class structures generate a set of opportunities and obstacles, incentives and sanctions, that make some class formations more likely and stable than others, some class formations extremely difficult to create and precarious to maintain, and some even impossible. Class structures, in short, determine a terrain of probabilities for possible class formations, but which actual class formation occurs on that terrain depends upon the effects of a range of other causal processes. The same limiting relation occurs between class formation and class struggle. One of the central tasks of class analysis, then, is to try to understand the nature of these limits and the process by which concrete outcomes within such limits are produced.

CLASS STRUCTURE AND CLASS FORMATION

In this chapter we will focus on only one aspect of this general model of determination, the linkage between class structure and class formation. We will proceed in three steps. First, we will briefly elaborate the concept of class structure that we will use in the analysis. Second, we will discuss the essential logic by which class structure conceptualized in this way imposes limits on possible class formations. Once these conceptual tasks are completed, we will then use this model to explore the relationship between class structure and class formation in Sweden and the United States.

Class Structure

We will conceptualize class structure in terms of social relations built up around mechanisms of exploitation (Wright 1985, chap. 3). To call a society "capitalist" implies that the most fundamental mechanism of exploitation in the society is based on the ownership of capital and the exploitation of wage labor.[2] This does not imply that other forms of exploitation are absent from the economic structure, but simply that in various ways they are subordinated to the distinctively capitalist mechanisms.

In capitalist societies, three mechanisms of exploitation are particularly important: exploitation centered on the ownership of means of production, on control of organizational assets, and on ownership of scarce skills (especially when socially validated in the form of credentials).[3] The first of these defines the central class relation between capital and labor, the second between managers and workers, and the third between experts and nonexperts. Some people, of course, may be exploited in terms of one of these dimensions of class relations while, simultaneously, being an exploiter in terms of another. Such positions constitute what in common

[2.] By "most fundamental" we mean that capitalist mechanisms of exploitation define the basic constraints of the class system as a whole. Other mechanisms of exploitation operate within limits established by the logic of capitalist exploitation.

[3.] Two of the authors of this chapter—Carolyn Howe and Donmoon Cho—are fairly skeptical that the control of organizational assets and skills should be treated as mechanisms of exploitation underlying distinct dimensions of class relations in capitalist society. Nevertheless, as Howe (1987) argues in her dissertation, even if it is problematic to treat relations of organizational control and skill as bases for class divisions, they can be considered important sources of structural variation *within* classes. The class structural "matrix" used in this chapter can, therefore, be accepted as a structural foundation for the analysis of class formations even if the specific conceptualization of this matrix in terms of exploitation relations is rejected.

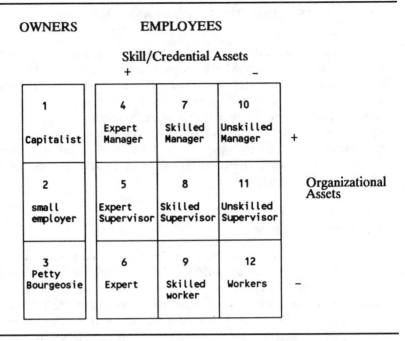

Figure 8.2: Matrix of Class Locations Within the Class Structure of Contemporary Capitalism

language is referred to as the "middle class," or what we will call "contradictory locations within class relations."

Understood in this way, class structures can be pictured as a relationally defined matrix of locations within exploitation relations. A relatively simple picture of such a class structural matrix is presented in Figure 8.2. Twelve locations are defined within this particular matrix. These should not be regarded as twelve distinct *classes*—they are twelve locations within class relations. Some of them are contradictory locations; others are proper class locations. Together they define the relationally constituted terrain upon which class formations are created.[4]

Class Formation

Class formations should be understood as constituting specific patterns of solidaristic social relations that are constructed within the structural

---

[4] The concept of a class structural "terrain" is similar to Bourdieu's (1985) concept of "social space" that shapes the probabilities of stable group formation.

map of classes illustrated in Figure 8.2. Typically, class formations involve creating formal organizations (especially parties and unions) that bind together the people within and across different cells of this typology, but class formation is by no means limited to formal organization. Any form of collectively constituted social relation that facilitates solidaristic action in pursuit of class interests would be included as instances of class formation.

Class formations should not be thought of as simply the forming of social relations *within* the individual locations of a structure such as the one illustrated in Figure 8.2. The forging of solidaristic relations across the boundaries of the locations within the matrix is equally important. Class formation thus includes the formation of class alliances as well as the internal organization of classes as such.

To say that class structures impose limits on class formations is to say that, within any given class structure, certain class formations are relatively easy to create, others are more difficult, and certain class formations may be virtually impossible. The class structure imposes obstacles and opportunities that make some projects of class formation quite precarious and unstable, and others relatively easy to accomplish and sustain.[5]

Two kinds of mechanisms are generally viewed by class theorists as being central to this limiting process: the nature of the *material interests* embedded in class structures and the patterns of *identities* that emerge from the lived experiences of people in different locations in the class structure.[6]

The argument about material interests is the simpler of the two. "Material interests," as we will use the term, are interests with respect to toil, leisure, and consumption.[7] The central thesis of the Marxist theory of class structure is that the underlying mechanisms of exploitation in an economic structure determine the fundamental material interests of people in that structure. The matrix of class locations in Figure 8.2 can

[5] To claim that a particular kind of class formation is virtually impossible is not to claim that the *attempt* to forge such a class formation will never occur, but simply that such attempts have a low probability of success, and if they were to succeed because of highly contingent conditions, they would have a very low probability of surviving over time.

[6] For a general theoretical discussion of the relationship between these two mechanisms, see Wright and Shin (1988) and Wright (1988).

[7] To say that a person objectively has particular material interests is not to say that they have an objective interest in *maximizing* their consumption (or income) per se. Material interests are defined by the package of toil-leisure-consumption available to a person. What is objectively imposed on people, therefore, is the terms of the trade-off between these elements of material interests. While people have an "objective interest" in having more favorable trade-offs between toil, leisure, and consumption, they do not inherently have an objective interest in increasing consumption itself.

thus be viewed as a map of the degree of inherent antagonism of material interests of people located in different places in the structure. All things being equal, class formations that link locations with relatively similar material interests are easier to create than class formations that link locations with quite disparate interests. From the vantage point of working-class locations in the class structure (the lower right-hand corner of the matrix, cell 12), as you move toward the upper left-hand corner of the matrix (cell 4, expert managers, and cell 1, capitalists), class interests become progressively more antagonistic, and thus class formations joining workers with such locations are more and more difficult to forge. This does not mean, it must be emphasized, that material interests alone determine class formations; but they do define a set of obstacles with which parties, unions, and other agencies of class formation have to contend in their efforts to consolidate and reproduce particular patterns of class formation.

The second mechanism through which class structures shape the possibilities of class formations centers on the ways class affects the daily lived experiences of people, particularly within work, but also potentially in families, communities, and other arenas of social life.[8] The essential idea is that the ways in which people are linked to the basic productive resources of the society determines a wide range of micro events in daily life: the necessity to go to work, interactions with bosses and coworkers, dilemmas faced in making choices, conflicts of various sorts. Such daily lived experiences constitute, to use Bourdieu's expression, a set of common conditions that generate common conditionings.[9] These, in turn, shape the class identities of people, whom they see as similar and different to themselves, as their potential friends and enemies within the economic system.

[8.] The linkage between location in a class structure and daily lived experiences is much more direct and determinate for workplace experiences than for experiences in families, communities, churches, and so on. It is for this reason that if we want to understand the ways in which lived experience constitutes a mechanism linking class structures to class formations, workplace experiences are likely to be at the very center of the analysis. For an example of a class analysis of lived experience and class formation that emphasizes micro interactions within work, see Michael Burawoy (1985). For a contrasting approach that gives much more weight to lived experiences in community and family, see Bourdieu (1985, 1987).

9. Bourdieu's (1985) concept of *class habitus* is meant to encompass the full range of nonconscious subjective effects on actors that result from such common conditionings/experiences. A "class habitus" is defined as a common set of dispositions to act in particular ways that are shaped by a common set of conditionings (subject-forming experiences) rooted in a class structure. "Identity," in these terms, is a specific aspect of "habitus": it is that aspect of a person's subjective dispositions that defines who they see as basically similar to themselves and who they see as different.

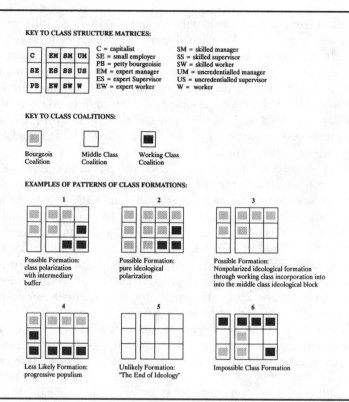

KEY TO CLASS STRUCTURE MATRICES:

C	EM	SM	UM
SE	ES	SS	US
PB	EW	SW	W

C = capitalist
SE = small employer
PB = petty bourgeoisie
EM = expert manager
ES = expert Supervisor
EW = expert worker

SM = skilled manager
SS = skilled supervisor
SW = skilled worker
UM = uncredentialled manager
US = uncredentialled supervisor
W = worker

KEY TO CLASS COALITIONS:

Bourgeois Coalition   Middle Class Coalition   Working Class Coalition

EXAMPLES OF PATTERNS OF CLASS FORMATIONS:

1 — Possible Formation: class polarization with intermediary buffer

2 — Possible Formation: pure ideological polarization

3 — Possible Formation: Nonpolarized ideological formation through working class incorporation into into the middle class ideological block

4 — Less Likely Formation: progressive populism

5 — Unlikely Formation: "The End of Ideology"

6 — Impossible Class Formation

Figure 8.3: Formable and Unformable Class Formations in Contemporary Capitalism

As in the case of material interests, it would be expected that class formations that attempt to bind people together with similar identities are likely to be easier to accomplish and more stable than class formations that combine highly disparate and potentially conflicting identities. Unlike the analysis of material interests, however, it is much harder to construct a general *deductive* account of precisely how identities will be distributed across the class map in Figure 8.2. The theory of identity formation is not nearly as systematically developed as the theory of exploitation. Thus, while it is plausible to argue that there should be some rough association between the objectively given material interests of actors and the kinds of identities they develop, there is no reason for these two aspects of class to be isomorphic.

The combination of these two class-based mechanisms—(exploitation → material interests) and (lived experiences in a class structure → class

identities)—determines the underlying probabilities that different potential class formations will occur. Figure 8.3 illustrates a range of class
formations that might be constructed on the basic class structure in
Figure 8.2. The first two of these follow the contours of the central
tendencies generated by the class structure itself: Class formations directly mirror the exploitation-generated interest configuration. In the first
model, a middle-class formation is a buffer between working-class and
bourgeois-class formations; in the second model, a pure polarization
exists between two "camps." In the third model, the structural division
between workers and contradictory locations has been severely muted in
the process of class formation: Workers have been incorporated into a
middle-class ideological block. The fourth and fifth models are perhaps
less likely, but still consistent with the underlying class structure: In
model 4 one class formation of capitalists and managers confronts a
"populist coalition" of workers, intellectuals (nonmanagerial experts and
semiexperts), and petty bourgeois, with a weak intermediary formation; in
model 5 a broad cross-class ideological consensus has been forged in
which no clear ideological class coalitions appear. Finally, model 6 represents a structurally very improbable class formation: Workers, managers,
and capitalists collectively organized into a working-class coalition while
experts and petty bourgeois are organized into a bourgeois coalition.

A fully developed theory of the relationship between class structure
and class formation would attempt to construct deductive models of the
formability of different patterns of class formation within different kinds
of class structures. Such models would help to give greater precision to
the effectivity of processes other than class structure in explaining actual
formations. For example, a question that has often been raised in discussions of class formation concerns the importance of the strategic choices
by political parties over which social groups to mobilize. Models of the
relationship between class structure and class formation would help us to
understand the parameters within which such choices are made. They
would make it possible to distinguish the "easy" from the "difficult"
strategies, the strategies that followed the inherent pressures of the class
structure from the strategies that tried to overcome those pressures.[10]

We will not attempt to build such formal deductive models in this
chapter. Rather, our objective will be to explore the empirical contours of
the problem by comparing the actual patterns of class formation in two
countries, Sweden and the United States.

[10.] For an exceptionally interesting attempt at forging such formal models of class
structural constraints on class formation, see Adam Przeworski and John Sprague (1986). As
Michael Burawoy (1988) has stressed, Przeworski's analyses of these constraints lack
adequate micro foundations in the lived experiences of actors. The constraints come entirely
from the nature of the material interests generated by class relations.

THE EMPIRICAL FOCUS OF THE RESEARCH

There are a variety of ways that one could propose to measure patterns of class formation. We could, for example, study organizational membership or affiliation in various kinds of collective organizations—parties and unions, in particular—that represent class interests. Or we could study the patterns of social networks and friendship ties across class boundaries that could be interpreted as tapping an interpersonal dimension of class formation. Or, if we are willing to assume that class formations are closely tied to configurations of ideologies, we could study the patterns of ideological orientations toward class interests across the class structure.

In this chapter we will focus on the class patterning of class consciousness as an indicator of class formation. By doing so we are not implying that class formations can be reduced to the attitudes people hold in their heads about class interests. Our claim is simply that the formation of ideological configurations reflects and contributes to solidaristic collectivities and is, therefore, an appropriate empirical indicator for studying the relationship between class structure and class formation.

More specifically, we will treat the distribution of class-relevant attitudes held by individuals across the class structure as an indicator of the patterns of ideological coalitions within class formations. We will examine these patterns in the United States and Sweden with two general objectives in mind: First, the general pattern of association between class location and ideology can serve as partial test of the underlying logic of class structure analysis that we have adopted in this chapter. If the class map presented in Figure 8.2 does define a matrix of opposing class interests, then it would be expected that there would be a basically monotonic relationship between location in this matrix and ideological orientation. That is, as you move from the working-class "cell" (cell 12 in Figure 8.2) to the expert manager cell (cell 4) along each of the dimensions of the matrix, and as you move from the petty bourgeois cell to the capitalist cell, ideological orientation should become increasingly procapitalist. Because this is a consequence of the essentially capitalist character of the class structure, this essentially monotonic relationship should occur in both the United States and Sweden in spite of the important political and ideological differences between these two societies.

Second, we will use the patterns of association between ideology and class location as a way of specifying the boundaries between class formations rather than simply between structurally defined class locations. The basic theoretical model represented in Figure 8.1 argues that, while class structure imposes limits of possibility on class formation, within those limits concrete class formations will be shaped by a range of historical and institutional factors that vary independently of class structures. In order to study class formation, therefore, it is useful to compare societies with roughly comparable class structures, but with quite different historical trajectories and political characteristics. Sweden and the United States constitute appropriate cases for such a comparative analysis: They are both capitalist class structures with roughly equivalent levels of technological development, they have roughly the same distributions of their labor forces across the class structure matrix, but have sharply different political institutions and political histories.[11] It would, therefore, be expected that the patterns of class formation should significantly differ between these two countries even though the underlying association between ideology and class location will be rather similar.

Because we do not have a strong, deductive theory of variations in class formations, we will not propose any systematic a priori hypotheses about how such class formations will vary between the United States and Sweden. While we will offer some post hoc interpretations of the differences we observe and will present data in support of these interpretations, our basic objective is to specify empirically the descriptive variations in class formations between these two countries. This, we hope, will help to demonstrate the utility of the overall framework we have adopted and give greater precision to what needs explaining in future research.

DATA AND MEASURES

Data

The data for this analysis come from the Comparative Project on Class Structure and Class Consciousness (see Wright 1982 for details). These are both national random samples of adults in the labor force conducted in 1980. The total U.S. employed labor force sample consists of 1,498 cases, and the Swedish sample, 1,145. Details of the samples are given in Wright (1985, pp. 159-61). The analysis in this chapter will exclude all nonemployed respondents (i.e., unemployed people in the labor force and housewives).

[11.] In popular discourse, Sweden is often thought of as a kind of "socialist" country. In fact, while the state sector is quite large in Sweden, there are virtually no nationalized industries in Sweden. The economy in Sweden continues to be organized in a highly capitalistic manner. It should, therefore, be seen as an example of a capitalist society with a highly developed welfare state rather than as a socialist society.

TABLE 8.1: Operationalization of Class Structure

Category	Self-Employed	Number of Employees	Occupation[a]	Authority[b]
1. Capitalists	yes	10+	any	NA
2. Small Employers	yes	2-9	any	NA
3. Petty Bourgeois	yes	0-1	any	NA
4. Expert Managers	no	NA	expert	manager
4. Expert Supervisors	no	NA	expert	supervisor
5. Expert Nonmanagement	no	NA	expert	nonmanagement
6. Skilled Managers	no	NA	skilled	manager
7. Skilled Supervisors	no	NA	skilled	supervisor
8. Skilled Workers	no	NA	skilled	nonmanagement
9. Unskilled Managers	no	NA	unskilled	manager
10. Unskilled Supervisors	no	NA	unskilled	supervisor
11. Workers	no	NA	unskilled	nonmanagement

a. Occupational definitions: experts = professional occupations; skilled = technicians, teachers, managers, crafts occupations.
b. Authority: manager = job is formally classified as "management" (not just "supervisor") in the authority hierarchy *and* respondent has real decision-making responsibilities over organizational decisions *and* respondent has subordinates; supervisor = respondent satisfies at least one of the following criteria, but not all three—(1.) respondent has subordinates (2.) respondent has decision-making responsibility in the organization (3.) respondent's job is classified as managerial or supervisory in the formal authority hierarchy

Weights

For reasons that are not entirely clear, the overall U.S. survey contains a disproportionate number of respondents with high levels of education and high occupational status. To correct for this overrepresentation we have applied a set of post hoc weights to the U.S. sample that have the effect of reproducing the 1980 census occupation-by-education distributions in the sample. The weights are designed in such a way that they do not alter the number of cases in the analyses. These weights will be used throughout this analysis. In no instance do they change the results in ways that would substantively alter the interpretation of the findings. No weights were needed for the Swedish sample.

Class Structure

Class structures are measured by using a range of questions on the individual's relation to the means of production, authority, and occupations. The details are given in Table 8.1. It should be noted that the criteria adopted are designed to be fairly restrictive at the corners of the class structure matrix. Thus, for example, we have selected the criteria for the organization assets dimension in such a way that people in managerial locations are unambiguously "managers"—they must make decisions,

UNITED STATES

	OWNERS	EMPLOYEES			
		experts	skilled	unskilled	
Capitalists	30	31	49	12	managers
Small Employers	86	60	164	125	supervisors
Petty Bourgeoisie	103	36	197	581	workers

N = 1474

SWEDEN

	OWNERS	EMPLOYEES			
		experts	skilled	unskilled	
Capitalists	9	28	16	9	managers
Small Employers	53	34	95	54	supervisors
Petty Bourgeoisie	58	51	226	484	workers

N = 1116

Figure 8.4: Distribution of Respondents in the Class Structure: United States and Sweden

have subordinates, and be formally in the managerial hierarchy. Most of the problems of measurements, therefore, are packed into the intermediate locations within each dimension. The distribution of respondents in each country into the locations in the class structure is given in Figure 8.4.

Ideology

Six questions will be used to assess ideological coalitions. These questions are drawn from a larger inventory of attitude questions in the Comparative Survey on Class Structure and Class Consciousness. They were chosen because they most transparently reflect class dimensions of ideological beliefs.

Five of the items we will use are Likert-type questions in which respondents were asked whether they strongly agreed, agreed, disagreed, or strongly disagreed with each of the following statements:

(1) Corporations benefit owners at the expense of workers and consumers.
(2) During a strike, management should be prohibited by law from hiring workers to take the place of strikers.
(3) Many people in this country receive much less income than they deserve.
(4) Large corporations have too much power in American/Swedish society today.
(5) The nonmanagement employees in your place of work could run things effectively without bosses.

Responses were coded on an integer scale from −2 to +2, with "don't know" being given the value of 0, and thus considered a "class-neutral" response.[12]

In the sixth item, respondents were asked the following question:

(6) In a protracted strike over wages and working conditions, which outcome would you like to see happen:
  (a) workers win most of their demands;
  (b) workers win some of their demands and make some significant concessions;
  (c) workers win only a few of their demands; or
  (d) workers go back to work without winning any of their demands.

This item was also coded from −2 to +2. Response category b in this item was considered the "class-neutral" response (equivalent to "don't know" in the Likert items above) and was thus given a value of 0. Response category a was given a value of +2; response c, a value of −1; and response d a value of −2. In this way the item goes from an unequivocally pro-working-class value (+2) to an unequivocally anti-working-class response (−2) in a way parallel to the Likert items.

We will use these six items to construct two different kinds of indices:

(1) Additive working-class ideology scale. Each of the items in the scale was recoded +1 if the respondent expressed the pro-working-class ideological position (a value of 1 or 2 on the original items) and −1 if he or she took a procapitalist class ideological position (a value of −1 or −2 on the items). A value of 0 was given for the response "don't know" or for a "class compromise position" on item 6 above (response b). These values were then summed to form the additive working-class ideology scale. A positive value indicates that overall the respondent agreed with the

---

[12] "Don't know" was not an explicit response category in the interview, but interviewers indicated this response if the respondent gave it.

proworking-class pole of the questions more often than the procapitalist pole; a negative value indicates the opposite.[13]

(2) Confirmatory factor analytic scales. In addition to the simple additive scale, these six items were used to construct variables within a confirmatory factor analytic model (using LISREL IV). We first tested a model in which we assumed unidimensionality among all six of these items in each country. This model was clearly inferior to a range of two-factor models, suggesting that the simple additive scale discussed above in fact merges two cognitively distinct dimensions of ideology. We experimented with a wide range of two-factor models using these six items.[14] The best fitting model in both countries indicated two latent variables, which we shall call "anticorporate ideology" and a "prounion ideology." In the best fitting model for the United States, the income equity item above (item 3) appeared on the first of these scales, whereas in Sweden it appeared only on the second, the prounion scale. In other respects the two scales were quite similar in the two countries. To simplify the analysis, therefore, we decided to drop the item that behaved differently in the two countries and redo the models. The final result, then, is a model using five indicators to measure two latent variables.[15] The paths from concepts to indicators for each country are given in Table 8.2.

There are analytical and interpretative advantages and disadvantages to each of these measurement strategies. The advantage of this simple scale is that the values on the scale have the same direct, prima facie interpretation across countries. If the mean value for workers in the United States is much lower than in Sweden, for example, we can conclude that on average they take the pro-working-class ideological position on fewer of these items than do their Swedish counterparts. The metric is the same in both countries and the interpretation of magnitudes in the results straightforward. The disadvantage is that the simple scale obliterates the multidimensionality of the ideologies we are studying and is insensitive

---

[13.] In this scale, all items are weighted equally in both the United States and Sweden. We also constructed a scale based on the factor loadings of a conventional principal-components factor analysis of the six items (computed separately for each country). None of the results for the simple additive scale was substantively different using the one-dimensional factor scale.

[14.] Given the limited number of items with which we were working, it was not appropriate to test three-factor models.

[15.] The chi-square statistic in the final model was 5.18 in the United States and 6.00 in Sweden (with four degrees of freedom). In the corresponding one-dimensional model using the same five indicators, the chi-square statistic was 22.27 for the United States and 18.22 for Sweden (with 5 degrees of freedom). The one-dimensional model using all six indicators had a chi-square of 30.77 in the United States and 34.55 in Sweden (9 degrees of freedom). The two-dimensional model is thus clearly superior.

TABLE 8.2: Confirmatory Factor-Analytic Models for Ideology Measures

| | United States | | Sweden | |
Items	Anticorporation	Prounion	Anticorporation	Prounion
1. Corporations benefit owners	.521	0	.773	0
2. Managers should be prohibited from hiring scabs	0	.640	0	.578
3. Large corporations have too much power	.284	0	.382	0
4. Nonmanagement employees could run things	.547	0	.729	0
5. Desired outcome of protracted strike	0	.268	0	.645
	chi-squared = 5.18		chi-squared = 6.00	
	d.f. = 4		d.f. = 4	
Correlation coefficient between the factor scores	.272		.548	
Correlation coefficient between two latent variables	.600		.878	

201

to the different measurement properties in the two countries of the relationship between item responses and underlying conceptual variables that are captured in the LISREL scales.

If we were primarily interested in predicting ideological orientations of individuals as such, then it would clearly be the case that the two-dimensional LISREL variables would be unequivocally superior to the simple additive scale. The central empirical objective of this chapter, however, is to use attitude data tied to individuals as a way of mapping patterns of collectively formed ideological coalitions. Ideological coalitions as socially constituted *collectivities* have to somehow transcend the cognitive multidimensionality of the ideological orientations of the *individuals* within such coalitions. In this sense, it might be argued, even though the confirmatory factor analysis demonstrates that our indicators of ideology tap two conceptually distinct dimensions, it is nevertheless appropriate to map out the coalitions using all of the indicators in a one-dimensional scale. The working-class coalition, in these terms, is precisely the coalition of *positions* that are basically similar in overall ideological orientations across these dimensions.[16] This kind of ideological coalition may be better measured by the simple additive scale than by the more technically sophisticated LISREL variables.[17] In any case, because some readers may be skeptical of this rationale for including the simple additive scale, we will present results for both types of variables throughout the analysis.

METHOD

Our basic goal is to produce a set of class-formation maps for Sweden and the United States similar to those illustrated in Figure 8.3. The methodological problem is to generate a nonarbitrary criterion for defining a "class coalition." The strategy we have adopted involves conducting a series of statistical tests on the differences in means for the various measures of ideology across the cells of the class structure matrix and then defining "coalitions" as sets of cells that (a) do not differ among them-

[16.] An alternative would have been to define the working-class coalition as the coalition of all *individuals*—rather than of positions—who hold a pro-working-class ideological orientation. If that had been our methodological strategy, than there would be little defense of using the one-dimensional scale.

[17.] The reason why we are using the simple additive scale for this purpose rather than a one-dimensional LISREL model is to facilitate direct comparisons of magnitudes on these scales across countries.

selves on these dependent variables, but (b) do differ from other coalitions. More formally, the strategy we will adopt involves the following steps:

(1) The means and standard deviations for each dependent variable are calculated for each of the cells in the class structure matrix.

(2) The capitalist cell is then compared to the expert manager cell (cell 1 compared to cell 4 in Figure 8.2). If the means on the dependent variables for these two cells do not differ significantly, they are combined for subsequent analyses as the *"provisional* core bourgeois coalition." The reason for this step is strictly pragmatic: Because the sample size of the capitalist cell is so small—30 in the United States and 9 in Sweden—it was impossible to build the ideology coalition models strictly around this category. Because, in fact, the values on the ideology variables are so similar for the capitalist cell and expert managers in every case, we decided to combine these categories for purposes of subsequent analysis.[18]

(3) We then calculated t-tests of the differences between each cell and the "pure" working-class cell of the matrix and between each cell and the provisional core bourgeois coalition.

(4) Any cell that does *not* differ from the provisional core bourgeois coalition and that *does* differ significantly from the working-class cell (by a .05 significance-level criterion) is a member of the *core bourgeois coalition*; any cell that does not differ significantly from the working-class cell but does differ from the provisional core bourgeois coalition is a member of the *core working-class coalition*. These two coalitions are designated "– – –" (core bourgeois coalition) and "+++" (core working-class coalition). Means and standard deviations are then calculated for these coalitions.

(5) All cells in the matrix that are not already in these coalitions are then tested against these two core coalitions. A cell that does not differ from the core bourgeois coalition but does differ from the core working-class coalition is called a member of the *broad* bourgeois coalition, and is designated "– –." Members of the broad working-class coalition are defined in a complementary manner and designated "++."

(6) Cells that differ significantly from *both* core coalitions are called a "middle-class coalition" and are designated "0." A cell that differs from *neither* core coalitions is called "ambiguous" and is designated "?."

[18.] Alternatively, we could have combined the capitalist and small employer cells into an extended employer category. Because, however, in a number of the tables, capitalists and expert managers are ideologically more like each other than are capitalists and small employers, it made more empirical sense to combine capitalists and expert managers in these analyses.

(7) One final step in the coalition-testing is needed. Because the means, standard deviations, and sample sizes of the coalitions change as cells are added, it is possible that a member of a core coalition or broad coalition as defined in steps 4 and 5 above might not significantly differ from the complementary broad coalition.[19] It is also possible that a cell within a broad coalition might not differ from the "middle-class coalition" defined in step 6. We, therefore, carried out the following two additional tests:

(7.1) If a middle-class coalition exists in a matrix, every cell in the broad or core bourgeois and broad or core working-class coalitions is compared to the middle-class coalition. If they do not differ significantly from the middle-class coalition, they are designated "+" (marginal member of the working-class coalition), or "-" (marginal member of the bourgeois coalition).

(7.2) If there is no middle-class coalition in the matrix, then every cell in the broad or core bourgeois coalition is compared to the broad working-class coalition (and vice versa). If they do not significantly differ from the opposing coalition, they are designated "+/-" or "-/+" (in each of these expressions, the first symbol indicates the classification according to steps 4 and 5, while the second symbol indicates the classification according to step 7.2). It turns out that no cases of this sort occurred in the results we will examine.

These steps yield the categories of class-formation coalitions illustrated in Table 8.3.

RESULTS

The General Association of
Class Structure and Ideology

Figures 8.5 and 8.6 present the distribution across cells of means and standard deviations for the three ideology variables (the simple additive scale, the anticorporate factor scale, and the prounion factor scale) in the class structure matrices for the United States and Sweden. In both the United States and Sweden, for all three of these measures of ideology, there is a close monotonic relationship between class location and ideology. The results are particularly striking in the Swedish case, where with almost no exception ideological orientation becomes systematically more procapitalist as you move from the working-class corner of the matrix

[19.] This is because the core coalitions are constructed through tests of differences between individual cells and the poles of the class matrix, and the broad coalitions are constructed through tests between cells and the core coalitions. No tests of differences of cells with broad coalitions had been conducted up to this point.

TABLE 8.3: Criteria for Class Coalitions

	Different from Worker Cell (cell 12)	Different from Provisional Core Bourgeois Category[a] (cells 1+4)	Different from Core Working-Class Coalition (+ + +)	Different from Core Bourgeois Coalition (- - -)	Different from Middle-Class Coalition (0)
I. Core coalitions:					
- - -	YES	NO			YES
+ + +	NO	YES			YES
II. Broad coalitions:					
- -	YES	YES	YES	NO	YES
- -	NO	NO	YES	NO	YES
+ +	YES	YES	NO	YES	YES
+ +	NO	NO	NO	YES	YES
0	YES	YES	YES	YES	
0	NO	NO	YES	YES	
III. Marginal members of coalitions					
-	YES	NO			NO
+	NO	YES			NO
-	YES	YES	YES	NO	NO
-	NO	NO	YES	NO	NO
+	YES	YES	NO	YES	NO
+	NO	NO	NO	YES	NO
?	NO	NO	NO	NO	

NOTE: Definitions of coalitions: + + + = core working-class coalition; + + = broad working-class coalition; + = marginal member of the working-class coalition: 0 = middle-class coalition; - - - = core bourgeois coalition; - - = broad bourgeois coalition; - = marginal member of the bourgeois coalition; ? = ambiguous status with respect to possible coalition.

a. This category is formed by combining the capitalist cell with the expert manager cell of the class structure matrix.

along the rows, columns, or diagonals to the expert manager corner of the matrix, and from the petty bourgeoisie to the capitalist class. The only significant deviation from strict monotonicity that runs counter to the general expectations of the class structure model occurs in the U.S. results for the anticorporate ideology variable. On this variable, *unskilled* managers (upper right-hand corner of the matrix) are more procapitalist than are *skilled* managers (the difference is statistically significant at the .05 level, one-tailed test), whereas the logic of the class structure concept suggests that they should be less procapitalist.[20] We do not have an explanation for this deviation. Nevertheless, overall, the patterns in both countries are strongly consistent with the expectations embedded in the concept of class structure we have adopted.

Ideological Patterns of Class Formation

Figures 8.7 and 8.8 presents the results of the formal statistical tests for the coalition patterns using the method described in Table 8.3. In both Sweden and the United States, skilled and unskilled workers are at the core of the working-class ideological coalition and, in both, capitalists and expert managers are at the core of the bourgeois ideological coalition. Where the two countries differ is in which other class locations are also part of these coalitions: In Sweden, unskilled supervisors are also consistently part of the working-class coalition, whereas they are not in the United States, while in the United States, expert supervisors, expert workers and skilled managers are consistently part of the bourgeois coalition, whereas in Sweden they are not. The bourgeois coalition in the United States thus penetrates more deeply into employee class locations than in Sweden, whereas the working-class coalition has a broader class base in Sweden than in the United States.

As a result of the greater scope of the bourgeois coalition in the United States, it appears at first glance that the *middle-class* coalition in the United States is considerably more truncated than in Sweden. In Sweden, for the additive pro-working-class ideology scale, the middle-class coalition encompasses a broad band of class locations (seven out of the twelve) along the off-diagonal of the class structure matrix. In contrast, in the United States, only skilled supervisors among wage earners and the petty bourgeoisie and small employers among owners are unambiguously part of a middle-class ideological coalition. When we disaggregate the items in this additive scale into the two variables from the confirmatory factor analysis, we find a similar contrast for each variable. For the anticorporate variable only small employers in the United States are unambiguously

[20.] There is one other limited deviation from strict monotonicity: In both the Swedish and United States results, skilled workers have virtually identical values to unskilled workers (in no table for either country do the values for these two categories significantly differ statistically). Because unskilled workers are not actually significantly more procapitalist than skilled workers, this does not really violate the general logic of the class structure concept.

Note on the entries:
The number not in parentheses is the mean value for ideology scale for the location;
The number within the parentheses is its standard deviation.

A. Additive Pro-working class Ideology Scale

	owner		expert	skilled	unskilled	
Cap	-1.775 (2.408)		-2.126 (3.251)	-1.183 (3.006)	-1.721 (2.523)	mgr
small emp	-.424 (2.835)		-1.157 (3.319)	.103 (2.732)	.855 (2.612)	sup
p.b.	-.116 (2.693)		-.610 (3.028)	.958 (2.955)	1.121 (2.711)	wkr

Extended Bourgeois Category (*capitalists* and *expert managers* combined): -1.953 (2.847)

B. Anti-corporation ideology factor scale

	owner		expert	skilled	unskilled	
Cap	-.372 (1.199)		-.519 (1.367)	.035 (1.512)	-.770 (1.270)	mgr
small emp	.312 (1.337)		.003 (1.537)	.545 (1.279)	.821 (1.234)	sup
p.b.	.503 (1.281)		.192 (1.476)	.835 (1.254)	.750 (1.193)	wkr

Extended Bourgeois Category (*capitalists* and *expert managers* combined): -.446 (1.278)

C. Pro-Union ideology factor scale

	owner		expert	skilled	unskilled	
Cap	-.518 (1.078)		-.603 (.979)	-.451 (1.055)	-.061 (1.069)	mgr
small emp	-.453 (.976)		-.289 (1.029)	-.029 (1.079)	.048 (1.147)	sup
p.b.	-.155 (1.130)		-.205 (.959)	.290 (1.167)	.309 (1.110)	wkr

Extended Bourgeois Category (*capitalists* and *expert managers* combined): -.5610 (1.021)

Figure 8.5: Distribution of Ideology Scales Across Class Locations: United States

Note on the entries:
The number not in parentheses is the mean value for ideology scale for the location;
The number within the parentheses is its standard deviation.

A. Additive Pro-working class Ideology Scale

	owner		expert	skilled	unskilled	
Cap	-2.822 (4.172)		-1.862 (2.801)	.282 (4.220)	.843 (3.583)	mgr
small emp	-.587 (3.287)		-.049 (3.143)	1.069 (3.167)	2.194 (3.104)	sup
p.b.	.294 (3.261)		.876 (3.482)	3.007 (3.356)	2.987 (3.074)	wkr

Extended Bourgeois Category (*capitalists* and *expert managers* combined): -2.090 (3.068)

B. Anti-corporation ideology factor scale

	owner		expert	skilled	unskilled	
Cap	-1.442 (1.547)		-1.417 (2.264)	-.178 (2.632)	-.010 (2.221)	mgr
small emp	-.655 (2.096)		-.498 (2.253)	.440 (2.084)	.962 (1.796)	sup
p.b.	.014 (1.938)		.266 (2.063)	1.516 (1.900)	1.441 (1.859)	wkr

Extended Bourgeois Category (*capitalists* and *expert managers* combined): -1.423 (2.096)

C. Pro-Union ideology factor scale

	owner		expert	skilled	unskilled	
Cap	-.336 (1.427)		-.076 (1.299)	.883 (1.376)	.779 (1.445)	mgr
small emp	.047 (1.391)		.603 (1.029)	1.029 (1.085)	1.238 (1.111)	sup
p.b.	.644 (1.180)		.754 (1.025)	1.520 (1.132)	1.522 (1.131)	wkr

Extended Bourgeois Category (*capitalists* and *expert managers* combined): -.138 (1.314)

Figure 8.6: Distribution of Ideology Scales Across Class Locations: Sweden

A. Additive Pro-working class Ideology Scale

	owner		expert	skilled	unskilled	
cap	---		---	---	---	mgr
small emp	0		---	0	+++	sup
p.b.	0		-	+++	+++	wkr

B. Anti-corporation ideology factor scale

	owner		expert	skilled	unskilled	
cap	---		---	-	---	mgr
small emp	0		-	+	+++	sup
p.b.	+		-	+++	+++	wkr

C. Pro-Union ideology factor scale

	owner		expert	skilled	unskilled	
cap	---		---	---	?	mgr
small emp	---		-	0	0	sup
p.b.	0		-	+++	+++	wkr

Patterns are based on results in Figure 8.5

See Table 8.3 for definitions of entries in cells

Figure 8.7: Patterns of Ideological Coalitions: United States

A. Additive Pro-working class Ideology Scale

	owner		expert	skilled	unskilled	
cap	- - -		- - -	0	0	mgr
small emp	0		0	0	+++	sup
p.b.	0		0	+++	+++	wkr

B. Anti-corporation ideology factor scale

	owner		expert	skilled	unskilled	
cap	- - -		- - -	-	-	mgr
small emp	- - -		- - -	0	+++	sup
p.b.	0		0	+++	+++	wkr

C. Pro-Union ideology factor scale

	owner		expert	skilled	unskilled	
cap	- - -		- - -	0	?	mgr
small emp	- - -		0	0	+++	sup
p.b.	0		0	+++	+++	wkr

Patterns are based on results in Figure 8.6

See Table 8.3 for explanations of entries in cells

Figure 8.8: Patterns of Ideological Coalitions: Sweden

part of the middle-class coalition, whereas in Sweden this coalition includes expert workers, skilled supervisors, and the petty bourgeoisie. For the prounion variable the middle-class coalition in the United States is limited to skilled and unskilled supervisors and the petty bourgeoisie, whereas in Sweden it extends to expert workers and supervisors and skilled managers.

Taken literally, these results, therefore, suggest that in the United States class formations more closely approximate a polarized pattern than in Sweden: In Sweden there is a fairly broad ideological "buffer" between the working-class coalition and the bourgeois coalition; in the United States this buffer occupies a much narrower space within class formations. This image, of course, runs completely counter to the usual contrast between the two countries: The United States is the paradigmatic "middle-class society" where class formations are diffuse and antagonisms muted; Sweden, on the other hand, has a solidaristic and relatively class conscious working-class formation capable of sustaining a social democratic compromise over a long period of time.

If we look more closely at the actual ideological content of these coalitions, however, we get a different picture. This can be done most directly for the results in the simple additive ideology scale, given that the metric in this scale is identical for the two countries. The locations in the working-class coalition in the United States for this scale have values of .855 to 1.121, whereas in Sweden the values within the working-class coalition range from 2.194 to 3.007. The heart of the *middle-class* coalition in Sweden—the off-diagonal among wage earners—has values between .843 and 1.069. What this means is that, as measured by this scale, the United States working-class formation shares the same overall ideological orientation as the Swedish middle-class formation. In contrast, the bourgeois coalitions in the two countries have quite similar ideological orientations.

These results suggest the following alternative description of class formations in the two countries: In Sweden there is an ideologically well-constituted working-class formation, middle-class formation, and bourgeois-class formation; in the United States, the working class is ideologically incorporated into what is essentially a middle-class formation while much of the structurally defined middle class is ideologically incorporated into the bourgeois-class formation.[21] Or, to say it slightly differently, the patterns of class formation in Sweden are characterized by two differentiations that are much sharper than in the United States: The

[21.] For alternative interpretations of these patterns using somewhat different measures of class and ideology, see Howe (1987, chap. 9).

Swedish working-class formation is more sharply differentiated from the middle class and the Swedish middle-class formation is more sharply differentiated from the bourgeoisie.[22]

Why should the pattern of class formation differ in this way between Sweden and the United States? It is beyond the scope of the present research to present a systematic historical and institutional explanation for these differing patterns. Nevertheless, we will venture as a general hypothesis that two factors are likely to be particularly important in explaining the differences in patterns of class formation between the United States and Sweden: first, the centrality of the state for the Swedish middle class, and, second, the importance of the social democratic party and union movement for constituting the Swedish working-class formation.

In order for a middle class to be sharply differentiated ideologically from the bourgeoisie, there needs to be an institutional basis for it to articulate its own interests. Within the capitalist corporation, the material interests of managers and experts are closely tied to the profitability of the corporation itself, and thus the general class interests of the middle class tend to be closely tied to those of the bourgeoisie. Within the state, however, this link between middle-class interests and bourgeois interests is much less direct. State employment, therefore, could potentially constitute a basis for the middle class to develop a sense of its own class interests relatively differentiated from those of the capitalist class. All things being equal, in a society with a large state sector, therefore, it would be expected that the middle class would be more autonomous ideologically from the bourgeoisie than in a society with a relatively small state sector.

In the United States, the material fate of the middle class is much more directly tied to the fortunes of corporate capitalism than in Sweden. Only 18% of the labor force as a whole is employed by the state, and while the figures are generally higher for principal middle-class locations—about 23% (for cells 4-8 and 10 in Figure 8.4 taken together)—it is the still case that most middle-class jobs are in the private sector. In Sweden, in con-

---

[22.] A potential methodological problem with this characterization of the patterns should be noted. In the formal procedure we have adopted for defining the boundaries of coalitions, it will in general be the case that, all things being equal, the more ideologically polarized is the overall class structure, the more likely it is that there will be a residual "middle class" or buffer coalition. This is so simply because there is more ideological distance possible between the middle and the poles when the poles are more polarized. It could, therefore, be the case that, instead of there being a genuine intermediate coalition in Sweden, what we simply have is a more ideologically polarized overall class structure that generates as a statistical artifact a residual middle-class "coalition." There is no way within the constraints of the present data to distinguish this interpretation of the data from the one that we have elaborated.

trast, over 40% of the entire labor force, and 50% of the middle-class contradictory locations in cells 4-8 and 10, are directly employed by the state. This makes middle-class interests less immediately tied to those of the capitalist class, and thus creates greater possibilities for the formation of a distinctive middle-class ideological coalition.

Some limited evidence in support of this interpretation is presented in Table 8.5. If we examine those "middle-class" wage earners that are outside of the broad working-class formation, then, as indicated in Table 8.5, in the United States, middle-class wage earners in the state sector have, on average, a significantly less procapitalist ideological orientation than middle-class wage earners in the private sector for both the simple additive ideology scale and the anticorporation factor scale.[23] Furthermore, U.S. middle-class employees in the state sector do not differ on the simple additive scale (the scale in which we can directly compare values across countries) from Swedish middle-class state employees.[24] The significantly more conservative profile of the U.S. middle class, therefore, is largely concentrated in the private sector of the U.S. economy.

The sharper Swedish differentiation in class formation of the working class and middle class may be at least partially the result of the effects of the particular organized labor movement in Sweden. While it is certainly true in Sweden that most middle-class wage earners are union members, and thus unions may contribute to the class formation of the middle class itself, there is a fairly sharp organizational division in the Swedish labor movement between traditional working-class unions and unions for white-collar, technical, and managerial employees. What is particularly important in the present context is that unions representing working-class wage earners in Sweden are organized into a large, centralized national organization that bargains in a corporatist manner with the formal association of employers, not simply with individual firms. This means that collective bargaining serves to unify the working class as a whole in opposition to the bourgeoisie, rather than to fragment it along sectional and particularistic lines. This form of collective organization of labor also clearly differentiates the working class from the bulk of the middle class, which is organized into its own union confederation that bargains separately with

[23] We have excluded from this analysis those middle-class wage earners—unskilled supervisors and skilled workers—who are part of the working-class formation. The result holds whether expert managers are considered part of the middle-class coalition or the bourgeois coalition.

[24] In Sweden, the difference between state and private sector middle-class employees is in the same direction as in the United States, but is not statistically significant. This suggests, perhaps, that, under conditions of a large state sector, the middle class as a whole has greater ideological autonomy from the bourgeoisie, not simply those middle class who are actually employed in the state.

TABLE 8.4: Ideological differences Between State and Private Sector Employees and Between Unionized and Nonunionized Employees: Frequencies

Class[a]	State	Private	Union	Nonunion	Total
United States:					
Middle class	80	272	36	316	352
Working class	179	725	223	681	904
Sweden:					
Middle class	119	113	193	39	232
Working class	343	422	609	156	765

a. Middle class = all wage earners who are not unskilled supervisors, skilled workers or unskilled workers; Working class = unskilled workers, skilled workers and unskilled supervisors

TABLE 8.5: Ideological Differences Between State and Private Sector Employees

	United States			Sweden		
	State	Private	t-test[b]	State	Private	t-test
1. Additive scale						
middle class[a]	.229	–.875	2.90**	.656	.231	.95
working class	1.156	1.022	.59	2.773	3.070	1.29
2. Anticorporation factor scale						
middle class	.662	.071	3.30***	.129	–.172	1.03
working class	.966	.732	2.33*	1.326	1.513	1.38
3. Prounion factor scale						
middle class	–.047	–.247	1.50	.854	.649	1.34
working class	.154	.297	1.52	1.485	1.514	.36

NOTE: Entries = means on the various ideology scales.
a. Middle class = all wage earners who are not unskilled supervisors, skilled workers or unskilled workers; Working class = unskilled workers, skilled workers and unskilled supervisors.
b. Statistical tests: *p < .05; **p < .01; ***p < .001 (two-tailed test).

capital. While it is certainly the case that this kind of corporatist unionism has lead to a highly stable form of class compromise in Sweden, it may also act to institutionalize and reproduce a pattern of class formation that is both relatively polarized ideologically from the capitalist class and differentiated from the middle class.

The micro-level data of ideological differences between union members and nonunion members is not entirely appropriate for testing this explanation for the different patterns of working-class formation, because the key part of the argument centers not so much on the fact of being a union member as such but on the institutional form of unionization (cor-

TABLE 8.6: Ideological Differences Between Unionized and Nonunionized Employees

	United States			Sweden		
	Union	Nonunion	t-test[b]	Union	Nonunion	t-test
1. Additive scale						
middle class[a]	1.475	−.862	4.51***	.827	−1.401	3.87***
working class	1.759	.815	4.50***	3.283	1.584	6.13***
2. Anticorporation factor scale						
middle class	1.043	.111	3.77***	.254	−1.347	4.24***
working class	.999	.705	3.16***	1.660	.531	6.93***
3. Prounion factor scale						
middle class	.684	−.302	5.51***	.877	.153	3.63***
working class	.779	.101	8.04***	1.620	1.036	5.89***

NOTE: Entries = means on the various ideology scales.
a. Middle class = all wage earners who are not unskilled supervisors, skilled workers or unskilled workers;
Working class = unskilled workers, skilled workers and unskilled supervisors.
b. Statistical tests: *p < .05; **p < .01; ***p < .001 (two-tailed test).

poratist in Sweden versus industrial and craft unions in the United States). Nevertheless, the interpretation would predict significant differences between unionized and nonunionized wage earners in each country. This is, in fact, what occurs (see Table 8.6): Unionized employees in the broad working-class formation are, in general, more polarized ideologically from the bourgeois coalition than nonunionized employees in both countries. What is more, in Sweden, but not in the United States, unionized workers are much more anticapitalist than unionized middle class on all three ideological scales. While there are many possible interpretations of this result, it is consistent with the view that the character of the Swedish labor movement has served to more sharply differentiate the Swedish working class from the middle class.

CONCLUSION

The central thesis of this chapter is that, while class structure may impose limits on possible class formations, political and ideological factors play a central role in explaining the actual pattern of class formation that empirically occurs on a given structural foundation. By shaping the material interests and daily lived experiences of individuals, class structures constitute a terrain of obstacles and opportunities upon which individual and collective actors attempt to build organizations and pursue their class interests. These obstacles and opportunities make certain class formations relatively easy and others relatively difficult to forge and maintain, but by themselves they do not uniquely determine the actual patterns of class formation that occur. To understand the actual patterns that emerge within these "limits of possibility," the analysis must shift to an investigation of political and ideological determinants and the historically contingent process by which these affect the victories and defeats of actors engaged in collective projects of class formation.

The empirical investigations of the chapter provide a range of empirical support for this general thesis. In particular, we would like to stress three basic conclusions.

First, the basic pattern of correspondence between ideological orientation and class structure is consistent with the underlying concept of class structure deployed in the analysis. In both Sweden and the United States, there is essentially an isomorphic relationship between ideological orientation and location within the class structure matrix.

Second, by examining patterns of ideological coalition formation in Sweden and the United States, we have tried to demonstrate the variability of class formations within basically similar class structures. In many respects, the two countries have rather similar kinds of class structures: both have working classes around 40%-45% of the labor force; both have large segments of the labor force in contradictory middle-class locations; both have relatively small property-owning classes. In spite of this rather similar underlying class structure, the patterns of ideological class coalitions are distinctively different in the two countries. In Sweden there are three clearly differentiated coalitions: a bourgeois coalition, a working-class coalition, and an intermediate, middle-class coalition. In the United States, the bourgeois coalition extends much deeper into the contradictory class locations of the middle class, and the working class can be seen as ideologically much less differentiated from the middle-class coalition. The result is that in the United States it is appropriate to characterize the pattern of class formation as consisting of a bourgeois/middle-class formation and a working-class/middle-class formation.

Third, we have offered a preliminary explanation of these different concrete patterns of class formation in terms of state employment and unionization. State employment can be viewed as providing the middle class with a material basis for ideological autonomy from the bourgeoisie, and centralized working-class unionism can provide a basis for generating more ideological autonomy of workers from the middle class. The result of much higher levels of state employment and unionization in Sweden, therefore, is that the middle class is more differentiated ideologically from the bourgeoisie and the working class is more ideologically differentiated from the middle class.

REFERENCES

Bourdieu, Pierre. 1985. "The Social Space and the Genesis of Groups." *Theory and Society* 14(6):723-44.
———. 1987. "What Makes a Social Class? On the Theoretical and Practical Existence of Groups." *Berkeley Journal of Sociology* 32:1-17.
Burawoy, Michael. 1985. *The Politics of Production*. London: Verso.
———. 1988. "Marxism Without Microfoundations." Unpublished manuscript.
Howe, Carolyn. 1987. *Class Structure and Class Formation in Contemporary Capitalism: The Problem of Knowledge Controllers*. Ph.D. dissertation, University of Wisconsin, Madison, Department of Sociology.
Przeworski, Adam and John Sprague. 1986. *Paper Stones*. Chicago: University of Chicago Press.
Roemer, John. 1982. *A General Theory of Exploitation and Class*. Cambridge, MA: Harvard University Press.
Wright, Erik Olin. 1978. *Class, Crisis and the State*. London: Verso.
———. 1982. "The Comparative Project on Class Structure and Class Consciousness: An Overview" (Technical paper no. 1, The Comparative Project on Class Structure and Class Consciousness). Madison: University of Wisconsin, Department of Sociology.
———. 1985. *Classes*. London: NLB/Verso.
———. 1988. "Exploitation, Identity and Class Structure: A Reply to Critics of *Classes.*" *Critical Sociology* (Summer).
Wright, Erik Olin and Kwang-Yeong Shin. 1988. "Temporality and Class Analysis: A Comparative Analysis of Class Structure, Class Trajectory and Class Consciousness in Sweden and the United States." *Sociological Theory* (Spring).

9

Class Mobility During the
Working Life:
A Comparison of Germany and Norway

Karl Ulrich Mayer
David L. Featherman
L. Kevin Selbee
Tom Colbjørnsen

The topic of this chapter is the trajectories within the class structure along which men move individually or collectively during their working lives. The setting is the Federal Republic of Germany from the end of World War II up to 1982, mirrored in the employment histories of the men born in 1929-31, 1939-41, and 1949-51, and Norway from the middle of the 1930s to 1971 as mirrored in the employment histories of the men born in 1921, 1931, and 1941. The social and economic development of these countries was very different in both character and timing. The focus of our research is whether or not these countries exhibit similar patterns of class formation, particularly as this is seen in the potential for developing demographic identities.

AUTHORS' NOTE: *We gratefully acknowledge the research support received from the Deutsche Forschungsgemeinschaft (Sonderforschungsbereich 3 "Mikroanalytische Grundlagen der Gesellschaftspolitik," Teilprojekt A 4 'Lebensverläufe und Wohlfahrtsentwicklung'); the Max-Planck-Institute for Human Development and Education, Berlin; the National Institute on Aging (PO1 AGO4877); the National Science Foundation (SES 852008); and the John Guggenheim Foundation. Sigrid Wehner and Joachim Wackerow provided skillful research assistance. The work invested by Mel Kohn far exceeded his editorial duties.*

The selection of the two countries was in part motivated by the availability of two very similar data sets: the Norwegian Life History Study (NLHS) conducted by Natalie Rogoff Ramsøy in 1971 and the German Life History Study (GLHS) conducted by Karl Ulrich Mayer in 1981-82. The similarity between the two studies arose by construction. The German study was designed as a three-cohort study with ten-year intervals after the model of the Norwegian study. Their comparability is a consequence of the cross-national scientific community, provided and fostered by the Research Committee on Social Stratification and Mobility of the International Sociological Association.

The purpose of this chapter is to explore patterns of work life mobility among men and to describe the similarities and disparities in such patterns between the two countries. We shall present straightforward outflow transition matrices between first class and last class observed and matrices on all transitions during the work life.

We believe that multicohort life history data are particularly suited for cross-national comparisons because they make it possible to discover the impact of historical conditions, socioeconomic development, and institutional and political factors in a much more fine-graded manner than the gross aggregations of conventional cross-sectional studies.[1]

SOCIETY AND CLASS STRUCTURE IN THE GERMAN REICH AND THE FEDERAL REPUBLIC OF GERMANY

The contemporary class structure of West Germany is the product, on one hand, of a historical configuration reaching back to the end of the Thirty Years War (1618-48) and, on the other hand, of structural transformations resulting from modernization, the changes in political regimes (Empire 1871-1918, Weimar Republic 1918-33, Third Reich 1922-45, Bonn Republic 1948), and two world wars lost.

The historical legacies of the times before the foundation of the German Empire in 1871 are the following. First, the regional and religious scattering of a multiplicity of states within Germany was one of the conditions for the development of an educated civil service and profes-

[1.] This chapter is a sequel to studies on class mobility during the work life for each of the two countries (Featherman and Selbee 1988—on Norway; Carroll and Mayer 1986; Mayer and Carroll 1987; Mayer 1987; Blossfeld forthcoming; Blossfeld and Mayer 1988—on Germany). In regard to cross-national comparisons between Norway and Germany on the basis of life history data, it adds to work on intergenerational mobility by Sørensen, Allmendinger, and Sørensen (1986) and on intragenerational mobility by Featherman, Mayer, and Selbee (1987/forthcoming) on the basis of the same data sets.

sional class as an estate of its own (Bildungsbürgertum)—tied to office and authority rather than land or capital (Sagarra 1977). Second, in the time period between 1732 and 1834, a tripartite system of schools was established—Volksschule, Real- or Mittelschule, and Gymnasium—sorting out persons into the class structure at a very early age (around 10 years). For more than 100 years, this educational system has regulated entry into the class and status system on almost all levels—despite institutional modifications and radically changed levels of relative participation (Leschinsky and Roeder 1976; Lundgreen 1980-81). Third, conflicts between the traditional crafts and a free trade system in the middle of the nineteenth century resulted in highly regulated forms of vocational training. From the end of the nineteenth century until today, vocational training is shared between the firms and state vocational schools—hence the name "dual system" (Arbeitsgruppe am Max-Planck-Institut 1984).

Between 1848 and 1914 Germany underwent a drastic transformation—delayed and rapid nation building, delayed and rapid state building, late and state-regulated industrialization, population growth, and modernization of life-styles. One of the consequences of this muted capitalism from above was the early introduction of welfare state insurance systems as a paternalistic means to combat the labor movement (Flora 1976; Alber 1982). Within the insurance system, manual workers and white-collar employees were tied to different public insurance companies (until 1973 white-collar employees also had separate legal provisions for period of payment, sick leave, vacation, and firing). White-collar employees thus became a specific social category, which even within the private sector increasingly modeled itself according to the prototype of the civil servant in regard to age-graded payment, levels, and careers (Kocka and Prinz 1983).

Up to World War I the class system was structured and differentiated more in terms of status than in terms of class; thereafter dedifferentiating tendencies prevailed, including the virtual abolition of nobility and great estate ownership as a social estate, the disappearance of the Imperial court and the military as status-determining institutions, the undermining and collapse of local status systems brought about by the huge migrations during and after World War II, and the effects of massive income transfers within the welfare system.

Finally—and this will be more visible in our data—both wars and the postwar periods delayed the shrinking of the agricultural sector especially in regard to self-employed farmers (Lutz 1984). This process has been speeding up since the 1960s. In the occupational and sectoral employment structure, changes have been gradual but persistent: the proportion of white-collar employees has surpassed that of manual workers (Mooser 1983). About one out of five manual workers are foreigners from the

Mediterranean countries. Although this inflow of foreign workers has increased the opportunities of the native population as had the earlier inflow of German refugees from the East, a stable underclass has—contrary to expectation—not been formed (Baker, Ezmer, Lenhardt, and Meyer 1985).

SOCIETY AND CLASS
STRUCTURE IN NORWAY

Norway, unlike the Federal Republic of Germany, has a rather recent history of industrially based social classes and a much longer history of rather egalitarian class relations. The origin of egalitarianism predates industrialism and the rise of the labor movement. Because Norway was under foreign rule for five centuries until 1905, and because the topography is unfavorable for large estates, a strong aristocracy and landowner class did not emerge. The preindustrial economy was based extensively on small independent peasants who combined agriculture with fishing (in the north) or with forestry (in the south). There were some exceptions to this pattern, especially in the southern regions, where a landowner class exists. In comparative perspective, however, the facets of early social and economic history engendered egalitarianism, although, as has been pointed out by several observers, it was an "equality of poverty."

Like Germany, but unlike other Western European nations, Norway industrialized rather late in the nineteenth century. Several specific features characterized Norway's industrialization. First, industrial growth occurred mainly in rural rather than urban places, tied to capital intensive enterprises in timber, iron ore extraction, and use of hydroelectric power. The capital intensity kept the industrial working class smaller than in many other countries, and rural locations prohibited the emergence of a large urban working class. Second, foreign capital, and later also the state, played an important part as financiers of industrialization. This meant that a strong national industrial bourgeoisie never developed. In this way the industrially based class structure became more egalitarian in Norway compared to several other countries. After World War I Norway underwent a process of deindustrialization that lasted well into the 1930s. This had a large impact on the cohorts entering the labor market at that time. For lack of anything better to do, they simply stayed home on the family farm (Rogoff Ramsøy 1987).[2] A large group of independent small farmers and fishermen survived the pre-World War II industrialization, and an

[2] We are indebted to Natalie Rogoff Ramsøy for commenting on the chapter and making us aware of the reversals in the socioeconomic development during the economic crisis of the 1920s and 1930s.

alliance between them and the working class gave the labor movement sufficient political power to take control of the government in 1935. This supported even further the egalitarian character of Norway's class structure.

Immediately following World War II, the rate of economic growth shot to 9.2% per year (1946-48) and leveled at 3.0% through the 1960s, a rate below postwar recovery in West Germany (Visher 1982). During this period a "third wave" of industrialization took place. This time it took place more in urban areas, for example, through expansion of the shipbuilding industry. In a comparative context, industrialization resulted in rather small firms, being less craft oriented than, for example, Swedish firms (Esping-Andersen 1985, p. 55). Hence, even if the educational system in Norway has a structure that appears to be similar to that in Germany, containing among other things an apprenticeship system, there might nevertheless be fewer craft demarcations within Norway's industrial working class.

The postwar period was also characterized by a strong growth in the service industries. During this period, the primary sector of the economy shrank from 29.5% in 1950 to 11.6% in 1970. The outflow of small farmers filled vacancies in both the new secondary and the tertiary economies that were located in the expanding urban areas.

The expansion in the tertiary sector also reflects the growth of the state and the impact of state planning in the postwar economy. Led by social democratic governments, this development was made possible by the widespread consensus that developed among several elite groups in Norway during World War II, and by a class compromise and economic growth, rather than redistribution of income, the primary political goal.

Therefore, we expect countervailing tendencies. On one hand, rising opportunities resulting from structural shifts in the labor force, together with fewer barriers according to craft in the labor market, might have promoted more mobility. In addition, the amount and distance in mobility processes were exacerbated as a consequence of the Depression. On the other hand, the egalitarian character of the Norwegian class structure may have made mobility less attractive and rewarding, as class differentials probably have been smaller and less subjectively felt.

COMPARING CLASS TRAJECTORIES
ACROSS NATIONS

The pattern of mobility propensities of different classes should be directly deducible from the resources and conditions that form the basis of class competition, super- and subordination and exploitation: labor, capital, landed property, skill, and authority. We should, therefore, expect a high degree of similarity and consistency in such mobility propensities across societies with similar economic systems and at similar stages of socioeconomic development. And, in fact, this outcome has been seen repeatedly in cross-national analyses of intergenerational mobility (Erikson and Goldthorpe 1987; Kurz and Müller 1987).[3]

What then is the rationale for comparing class mobility across nations and, specifically, between Norway and Germany? Both countries were latecomers in the industrialization process and in both this contributed to the weakness of the indigenous capitalist bourgeoisie. In Germany the formation of a strong centralized state preceded industrialization and allowed traditional status groups to be preserved. In Norway an egalitarian agrarian social structure maintained its imprint.

The effects of such "deviant" capitalist class formation may have been opposite in the two countries. In Germany we might expect that traditional status demarcations (such as the academic bourgeoisie or the layers of the craft system) and new state-induced barriers (such as the distinction between *Arbeiter* and *Angestellte*) should have superimposed and exacerbated class barriers. Status distinctions and status aspirations should have intensified and channeled the mobility process. In contrast, in Norway transitions between classes should have been easier, because classes were in a more nascent state and small communities played an integrative social role. Mobility incentives, however, were probably of a more economic than symbolic kind and thus were probably weaker.

Alternatively, it is possible that career mobility is a much more direct function of the distribution of the labor force between class categories and their compositional changes over time. Differences in the mobility regimes between countries should then simply reflect differences in this transformation. If this is the case, the countries should be similar to the extent that the class distributions are similar. Any or most of the differences that exist in mobility patterns result from differences in the supply of class positions.

Even under such assumptions, however, countries might vary as to how they "process" exogenous structural changes. Structural changes may be brought about almost exclusively via the entrance of new cohorts into the labor market and thereafter class positions might be highly fixed during the working life—despite ongoing structural change. Or changes may be brought about by a constant, age-independent reshuffling of persons during their careers. Here we would expect cross-national differences in

[3.] The research on intergenerational mobility, however, also demonstrates cross-national differences related to political-institutional features rather than economic ones and shows remarkable similarities between capitalist and state-socialist countries (see Erikson and Goldthorpe 1987).

the process of allocation of persons to class positions. In Germany the educational and vocational system is highly determinative of class entry and ensuing careers (König and Müller 1986; Blossfeld forthcoming; Mayer and Carroll 1987). Therefore, in Germany we would expect distributional differences between cohorts relative to the differences within cohorts larger than in Norway.

From the country portraits above one might get the impression of widely differing sectoral shifts out of agriculture in the two countries. In fact, the shift from agriculture appears to have been fairly similar in magnitude, but located somewhat differently in historical time (Flora et al. 1983, pp. 512-71).[4]

The main differences in the development of the sectoral structure in the two countries lie rather in the relative shares and development of the industrial and service sectors. For the period under consideration the industrial labor share was steadily 10% higher in Germany than in Norway. In addition, while in Norway from the turn of the century until the present the service sector was always larger than the industrial sector, the opposite held true in Germany until only very recently.

On the basis of information on sectoral shifts (Flora et al. 1983, pp. 512-71), one would assume a rather similar degree of transformation of the occupational structure, although different in kind. Moreover, the historical decline in self-employment and increases in dependent work exhibit similar patterns, although the levels of self-employment were always higher in Norway. Both countries—but in a more pronounced manner in Norway—experienced a delay in the shrinking of the agricultural sector during and following the Depression and World War II.

DATA AND CLASS CLASSIFICATION

The German Life History Study (GLHS)

We use retrospective data from the German Life History Study (GLHS), the fieldwork of which was conducted in the years 1981 to 1983. Three cohorts of men and women born in the years 1929-31, 1939-41, and 1949-51 were sampled and interviewed by GETAS, a professional survey research firm. The sample of 2,172 persons is representative of the

---

4. Around the turn of century in both countries about 40% of the labor force worked in agriculture. By the 1920s the proportion in Germany had dropped to about 30%, while Norway still had a share of about 37%. After the war the proportion in Norway had dropped to 25%, almost identical to the German figure. Since 1950 the decline was somewhat faster in Germany as compared to Norway.

German populace living in private households in the Federal Republic and West Berlin. It should be noted here that foreign workers are excluded.[5]

The comparative analysis relies primarily on the job history component of the German Life History Study. For each respondent, data were collected on the dates of the beginning and ending of each job held. Respondents were also asked to identify the occupation, wage rate, industry, and size of firm for each job. Changes in jobs were flagged when they occurred within the same firm.

These basic data were used to code the structural variables of interest on social class. For the Goldthorpe (1980) class schema, we used adaptation rules developed by Walter Müller and his associates at the University of Mannheim for the German occupational structure.

The Norwegian Life History Study

The Norwegian data are retrospective life histories of three single-year cohorts of Norwegian men born in 1921, 1931, and 1941. The Norwegian Life History Study was conceived and initiated by Natalie Rogoff-Ramsøy and directed by her and Kari Skrede at the Institute of Applied Social Research in Oslo, Norway.

Interviewing was done between March 1971 and March 1972, when the youngest men had reached their thirtieth birthday and men from the oldest cohort, their fiftieth. Interviews were completed with 1,322 men from the 1921 cohort, 1,094 from the 1931 cohort, and 1,054 from the 1941 cohort, representing response rates varying between 83% and 87% (INAS 1978). For each respondent, event histories beginning at age 14 and ending at the time of the interview were recorded.

The NLHS data cover many aspects of the men's lives: residence, education and training, main and secondary occupation, marital status, children, household composition, health, and pensions and benefits. In addition, data were collected on the respondent's social background, on his wife's education, occupation and labor force experience, and on various aspects of the current work situation. The retrospective data are a continuous record of each activity or state that lasted at least one month. Beginning and ending dates for each event are recorded in addition to information characterizing it.

Each job event was assigned a class category according to the classification by Goldthorpe. For each respondent, successive job events with the same class code were collapsed to form a single class event. Successive job events with different class codes were treated as different class

---

[5.] Details of the sampling plan, field procedures, and data coding can be found in Mayer and Brückner (1988).

events. Each class event, therefore, contains one or more job events. In the Norwegian data all respondents were omitted who had more than ten jobs.

Conceptualization and
Classification of Social Class

We take the view that the formation of the class structure as a system of relations within the spheres of production and intraorganizational authority is largely independent of the movements of individuals between class categories. But such mobility might be highly deterministic of the degree of homogeneity, maturity, and demographic identity of a given class and, in consequence, its potential as a collective actor (Featherman and Selbee 1988; Mayer and Carroll 1987).

In the conceptualization of social class, we thus follow the position developed by Goldthorpe (1980, p. 39), where classes and their boundaries are defined independently of the mobility process on the basis of homogeneous market and working conditions. Mobility propensities derive from the "location" of a class in the total structure of the class system, and depend specifically on the attributes of the position that influence the likelihood of movement into and out of the class. These, in turn, underlie the potential for the emergence of demographic identities because they reflect the tendency of a class to "hold" its members over time, forming the stable and permanent class core that gives content to a unique demographic identity.

The corresponding *class schema* that Goldthorpe has developed shows two advantages in addition to the theoretical rationale outlined above. It has precisely specified measurement rules to map occupations and jobs into classes and make use of the information on both occupational activity and employment status. Further, it has come to be widely used in cross-national research (Erikson and Goldthorpe 1985, 1987; König and Müller 1986; Kurz and Müller 1987) and thus allows our findings to be related to a growing body of literature.

Goldthorpe's classes and a brief description of their underlying occupational and employment units are as follows (from Goldthorpe, 1980, pp. 39-41):

CLASS I: All higher grade professionals, self-employed or salaried;
    higher-grade administrators and officials in central and local government
    and in public and private enterprises (including company directors);
    managers in large industrial establishments; and large proprietors.
CLASS II: Lower-grade professionals and higher-grade technicians;
    lower-grade administrators and officials; managers in small business and

industrial establishments and in services; supervisors of non-manual employees.

CLASS III: Routine non-manual—largely clerical—employees in administration and commerce; sales personnel; and other rank-and-file employees in services.

CLASS IV: Small proprietors including farmers and small-holders; all other 'own account' workers apart from professionals: a) with employees, b) without employees, c) in agriculture.

CLASS V: Lower-grade technicians whose work is to some extent of a manual character, and supervisors of manual workers.

CLASS VI: Skilled manual wage-workers in all branches of industry, including all who have served apprenticeships and also those who have acquired a relatively high degree of skill through other forms of training.

CLASS VII: a) All manual wage-workers in industry in semi- and unskilled grades; and b) agricultural workers.

DESIGN OF THE INVESTIGATIONS
AND POTENTIAL FOR COMPARISONS

Table 9.1 shows the design of the two studies.

TABLE 9.1: Design of the Investigations and Potential for Comparisons

Country	Birth Cohorts				Year of Interview
Norway	1921	1931	1941		1971
Germany		1929-31	1939-41	1949-51	1981-82

Accordingly, we may compare the Norwegian "1921" cohort and the German "1931" cohort up to age 50, if the length and maturity of a career trajectory would be the sole criterion. We may compare the "1931" cohorts of both countries up to age of about 40 and the "1941" cohorts up to age of about 30, if year of birth, that is, age and historical period, are to be made most similar. There are two arguments to support the latter selection for comparison. First, we might expect a high age dependency in class trajectories in the manner well known from job trajectories (Carroll and Mayer 1986). Accordingly, there might be many and major class shifts early in the career and increasing stability in later age. If this is the case, it is, as above, of utmost importance to compare national class trajectories pertaining to the same age or career span. Second, at first glance one might also want to compare countries at about the same historical period. Because mobility regimes are not expected to change rapidly, a ten-year difference in time of survey would usually not be considered too serious a fault. In the case of these two particular countries and historical times, one has to reckon with the impacts of World War II on employment structures and career lines. Identity of historical times via identity of birth cohorts seems, therefore, mandatory.

In regard to the effects of World War II, it seems at first glance obvious that one should compare birth cohorts that were at similar ages during and after the war. We know, for instance, that losses of lives were considerable for the cohorts of men born around 1920 both in Germany (Mayer 1987) and in Norway (Rogoff Ramsøy, 1975). These deaths not only led to a selective group of survivors, but most likely also enhanced the career opportunities of the men born around 1930 who must have found more open positions to move into more rapidly than they would have if the excess mortality of the preceding cohorts had not occurred.

We also know, however, from the sources cited above that the impact of World War II on occupational and educational opportunities most probably did not affect the same birth cohorts in the two countries. In Germany those most affected in these respects were definitely the 1929-31 cohort and in Norway, the 1921 cohort. On this basis the three cohorts in the two countries could legitimately be treated in a strictly parallel manner.

This discussion shows that we cannot make a priori decisions in selecting the birth cohorts and ages for comparison. Rather, we will have to rely on the empirical analysis to inform us about the degree of comparability between cohorts in the two countries.

DIFFERENCES IN CLASS STRUCTURES

In this section we lay out the basic marginal distributions in order to assess the extent of dissimilarity in class structure. As a first step we map all distinct job episodes into the class schema. As a second step we give the distribution of all observed class episodes. These two types of employment episodes are aggregated across the work trajectories up to the respective ages at interview and, therefore, do not sum up to the number of respondents. These data are primarily given to document how both the observed number of job episodes and the number of class episodes varies between countries.[6]

[6.] Although we have no specific reasons to assume so, we cannot rule out that differences in the number of jobs observed per person are partly due to differences in the degrees of precision in the data collection. Such artifacts of measurement are, however, much less likely for the number of observed class episodes, because shifts between class boundaries are well defined and intersubjectively recognized.

TABLE 9.2: Class Distributions of Men in Germany

Class	All Jobs	All Classes[a]	Classes by Cohort[a]			First Class by Cohort		
			1929-31	1939-41	1949-51	1929-31	1939-41	1949-51
I	6.1	7.2	6.7	7.2	7.8	2.1	2.9	6.7
II	12.2	12.7	9.5	11.5	18.8	5.5	7.8	15.0
III	4.9	6.3	5.3	5.7	8.3	5.2	5.5	7.7
IVa, IVb	3.1	4.9	5.1	5.5	3.9	.3	.3	.3
IVc	2.1	2.8	4.0	2.5	1.4	6.4	4.6	1.6
V	9.9	11.9	10.1	13.8	11.5	2.1	5.2	7.0
VI	36.1	31.6	27.7	33.6	34.3	42.1	56.4	51.8
VIIa	22.5	18.8	23.8	17.8	13.3	21.5	14.2	8.6
VIIb	3.0	3.9	7.9	2.4	.7	14.8	3.2	1.3
n[b]	3610	2067	751	751	565	330	346	313

a. All observed class episodes.
b. Without cases, namely, job spells that could not be coded into the class scheme.

The class distributions for the three cohorts at time of career entry and at time of interview provide information about the structural changes between cohorts, the net class shifts within cohort, and—for a given criterion—about structural differences between countries.

Table 9.2 provides descriptive information on the distribution of social classes in the GLHS data. The work histories of these three cohorts of 1,077 West German men comprise 3,846 jobs or employment episodes. Following strict coding procedures, 3,610 jobs could be mapped into class categories. Of these, a majority of more than 60% are in skilled and unskilled manual work. About a fifth of all jobs are in the two "service" classes I and II, that is, the higher professional, administrative, and managerial classes. About 5% constitute spells of self-employment.

Aggregating these job episodes to class episodes (changes in jobs are ignored unless they occur across two distinct classes) results in 2,067 distinct and codable spells. The mean class episode consists of 1.75 jobs, although for the skilled manual class it goes as high as 1.99.

One way to examine these data is to look at the distribution of class of first employment across the different cohorts. From Table 9.2 it appears as though from the period 1945 to 1970 (the time of entry of these cohorts), the class structure has shifted "upward" in its distribution. The professional and upper service classes I and II—and, for the most recent cohort, the routine white-collar class III also—have increased, while the un- and semiskilled manual workers and farm workers in class VII have declined greatly as starting positions. Skilled manual work has sharply increased up to the middle cohort and has thereafter diminished in size.

TABLE 9.3: Class Distributions of Men in Norway

Class	All Jobs	All Classes[a]	Classes by Cohort[a]			First Class by Cohort		
			1921	1931	1941	1921	1931	1941
I	4.6	4.6	4.0	5.3	4.8	2.0	4.8	4.7
II	5.7	8.0	6.9	8.2	9.2	4.3	4.9	9.5
III	11.0	11.3	7.0	11.7	13.8	8.6	10.7	14.9
IVa, IVb	2.6	4.9	9.6	4.0	4.0	.6	1.3	1.6
IVc	3.1	4.2	6.0	3.8	2.2	1.7	1.2	1.0
V	8.9	7.0	5.6	8.3	6.7	3.9	6.9	5.1
VI	15.3	15.7	15.1	15.8	16.6	9.5	13.8	13.5
VIIa	32.3	28.5	27.5	28.5	30.0	28.8	32.3	32.3
VIIb	16.3	15.9	18.9	14.3	12.8	40.7	24.0	17.4
n^b	26813	11390	4845	3536	3009	1165	999	996

a. All observed class episodes.
b. Without cases, namely, job spells that could not be coded into the class scheme.

The class distributions for Norway are shown in Table 9.3. What is most striking about the Norwegian data is the higher number of jobs per person (8.7 versus 3.6), the higher number of jobs per class (2.4 versus 1.8), and the higher number of classes per person (4.6 versus 2.1). In Norway, almost 50% of all job episodes fall into the unskilled workers' classes and only slightly less for the class episodes. The relative proportion of the skilled workers is less than half of those in Germany. Also noteworthy are the shares in classes II and III. While in Norway class III comprises about as many jobs or class episodes as classes I and II together, in Germany class II is by far the largest class in terms of both criteria.

The historical changes.follow the same upward direction as in Germany. There is strong growth in the white-collar classes, but—as we just noted in the aggregate—in Norway mostly in class III while in Germany in class II.

CAREER MOBILITY BETWEEN
FIRST AND LAST CLASS

According to Table 9.4 the German men of the 1929-31 cohort experienced class mobility to a remarkable extent up to about age 50. Except for the group of farmers, there are few moves downward. The upper service class stays at the top. More than 40% of the lower service class moves up to the upper managerial and professional class, and of those who started in routine white-collar jobs, nearly two-thirds leave that class to attain more advantageous positions. Half of all those men who started as skilled

TABLE 9.4: Career Mobility Between First and Last Class: Germany, 50-Year-Old Men Born 1929-31 (outflow proportions)

Class	I	II	III	IVa, IVb	IVc	V	VI	VIIa	VIIb	
I	100	–	–	–	–	–	–	–	–	2.2
II	44	39	6	6	–	–	6	–	–	5.6
III	19	44	19	13	–	–	6	–	–	5.0
IVa, IVb	–	–	–	100	–	–	–	–	–	0.3
IVc	–	5	–	–	29	10	5	52	–	6.5
V	14	29	–	–	–	43	14	–	–	2.2
VI	6	10	4	9	–	22	35	13	–	41.8
VIIa	7	9	9	8	–	11	14	42	–	22.0
VIIb	2	6	4	4	11	11	13	45	4	14.6
Total	10.2	12.4	5.6	7.8	3.4	14.6	20.7	24.8	0.6	323

workers—42% of the total sample of men—leave the working class and move to a higher level; about a fifth becomes deskilled. Similarly, more than 50% of the un- and semiskilled men move upward, in some cases considerably.

In a manner well known from studies of intergenerational mobility, there exist broad collective pathways operating in a chainlike fashion and transcending class boundaries. Working-class origins have the nature of a recruitment pool from which moves to other classes take place. Nonetheless, each of the three working classes VII, VI, and V (unskilled, skilled, and supervisory) retain about two-thirds of those men who started their careers in manual work. Initial lack of qualifications (in unskilled manual or routine white-collar as the first class) does not seem to be a hindrance in further mobility. Qualifications, then, must have been acquired during the career.

We now turn to the 50-year-old Norwegian men of the 1921 cohort for comparison (Table 9.5). In the white-collar classes the career patterns are remarkably similar, if we allow some margin of error due to both sampling variation and coding. At best we find support for somewhat superior career opportunities in Germany. In Germany men of the upper service class are less likely to move out and down and the men of the lower service class and in routine white-collar positions move up more frequently than in Norway.

One must be cautious in interpreting trajectories out of self-employment in a first-class/last-class transition table, because the origin groups are very small and, at least for Germany, we know that farmers often

TABLE 9.5: Career Mobility Between First and Last Class: Norwegian 50-Year-Old Men Born 1921 (outflow proportions)

	I	II	III	IVa, IVb	IVc	V	VI	VIIa	VIIb	
I	87	9	4	–	–	–	–	–	–	2.0
II	34	50	10	–	2	2	–	2	–	4.3
III	20	29	24	13	–	3	3	8	–	8.6
IVa, IVb	–	–	17	50	–	–	17	17	–	1.5
IVc	5	10	–	–	60	5	–	10	10	1.7
V	11	17	4	11	2	30	15	9	–	3.9
VI	6	7	6	18	4	12	30	17	–	9.5
VIIa	5	9	13	9	3	14	13	34	1	28.8
VIIb	6	6	5	7	22	6	17	26	5	40.7
Total	9.7	11.2	9.1	9.1	11.2	9.2	14.2	23.8	2.4	1165

allocate themselves in the group of self-employment for the beginning of their career if they have been working on the family farm (Mayer 1979). Nonetheless, in Norway there seems to be much less stability for the self-employed outside agriculture and much more stability (60% versus 29%) in farming as compared to Germany, where moves out of farming for a great majority mean unskilled manual work.

The career trajectories of the skilled workers—as the first class, four times larger in Germany than Norway—are again remarkably similar— with two exceptions. The chance of becoming self-employed is more than twice as good in Norway. And in Germany about a fifth of the skilled workers end up as foremen or *Meister*, whereas only about a tenth do so in Norway. Semi- and unskilled workers are more immobile in Germany, but, once they leave, they follow a similar pattern in the two countries. The major differences in class trajectories are displayed by unskilled labor in agriculture. In Norway more than 40% start in this class; in Germany, 15%. Immobility is almost double in Germany (45% versus 26%). This difference is partially the result of a fifth of the farmhands in Norway becoming self-employed farmers, whereas half do so in Germany.

Thus, although the starting positions were quite dissimilar in the two countries, a remarkably similar mobility regime transformed these initial class distributions into a converging class structure at age 50. Again the exception is the higher proportion of self-employed in the destination states and here mainly in agriculture in Norway. But also the classes of routine white-collar, manual supervisors, and skilled workers are larger in Germany.

TABLE 9.6: Career Mobility Between First and Last Class: German Men Born 1929-31 at Age 40 (outflow proportions)

Class	I	II	III	IVa, IVb	IVc	V	VI	VIIa	VIIb	Total
I	100	–	–	–	–	–	–	–	–	2.2
II	33	50	6	6	–	–	6	–	–	5.6
III	19	38	25	6	–	–	13	–	–	5.0
IVa, IVb	–	–	–	100	–	–	–	–	–	0.3
IVc	–	–	–	–	35	5	10	50	–	6.2
V	14	29	–	–	–	43	14	–	–	2.2
VI	5	6	6	10	–	20	38	15	–	42.2
VIIa	6	6	9	6	–	10	7	57	–	21.5
VIIb	2	6	4	4	11	6	19	45	2	14.6
Total	9.0	10.0	6.5	7.2	3.7	12.8	22.4	28.0	0.3	321

TABLE 9.7: Career Mobility Between First and Last Class: Norwegian Men Born 1931 at Age 40 (outflow proportions)

Class	I	II	III	IVa, IVb	IVc	V	VI	VIIa	VIIb	Total
I	80	17	3	–	–	–	–	–	2	4.8
II	33	57	6	–	–	4	–	–	–	4.9
III	20	18	36	7	2	3	4	11	–	10.7
IVa, IVb	39	8	8	31	15	–	–	–	–	1.3
IVc	–	17	–	17	50	–	17	–	–	1.2
V	9	13	9	7	1	42	9	10	–	6.9
VI	9	17	10	8	4	11	25	13	2	13.8
VIIa	6	11	11	7	3	15	12	35	–	32.3
VIIb	2	5	6	7	22	9	15	30	6	24.0
Total	12.4	13.8	11.4	6.7	8.0	11.7	12.2	22.0	1.7	999

If we now turn to the age-constant and period-constant comparisons of the birth cohorts 1929-31 in Germany and 1931 in Norway at age 40 (Tables 9.6 and 9.7), there is very little to be changed in the comparative story told above in regard to the mobility matrix. The major difference to be noted is that skilled workers in Norway more often move to routine white-collar positions and the lower service class instead of self-employment—both in comparison to their age peers in Germany and the 50-year-old Norwegian men of the 1921 cohort.

CAREER MOBILITY: ALL CLASS
TRANSITIONS IN THE
CUMULATIVE MOBILITY TABLE

The analysis up to this point shares the assumption of all conventional career mobility or status attainment studies, which is that the static two-time-point comparisons sufficiently capture the dynamics of class during the work life. We shall now examine this assumption by including in our outflow tables all class states ever held.

What can we learn for the comparison between the two countries by using the two modes of representing career mobility: as transition from first to last class as against all transitions (and nontransitions) from a given class? In the latter case the units of analysis differ. We shift from number of persons to number of class transitions plus the number of stayers. Prior juxtapositions of the representation of class career mobility in a first-class/last-class transition table and a cumulative table (Featherman and Selbee 1988; Mayer 1987) have demonstrated that first-last tables tend to overestimate the proportion of stayers and underestimate the extent of moves to less advantaged classes, and also, partially, the opportunities for upward mobility. They also tend to create an overly stable impression of self-employment. Thus first-class/last-class tables provide at best partial insights into career dynamics.

The first observation to be made on the basis of the cumulative mobility tables (Tables 9.8 and 9.9) for the 50-year-old men of the 1921 cohort in Norway and the 1929-31 cohort in Germany is that there were many more class shifts in Norway than in Germany. The proportion of the number of all class transitions up to age 50 plus the number of stayers in comparison with the number of men in the birth cohort is 1.3 in Germany and 3.2 in Norway, although for Norway cases with ten and more classes have been omitted.[7]

Thus in Norway these men changed much more frequently between classes and across large distances. As a consequence, the class structure appears to be much more open and permeable. In particular, there seems to be much more interchange between the manual class and both self-employed farming and farm labor. This comparison also reveals the very different career ladders in the two countries.

In Germany more than a quarter of the skilled workers move up to become foremen or *Meister* and more than two-thirds of the latter class then become white-collar or self-employed. Class VI is, therefore, a

---

[7.] About 10% of the cases with ten or more class shifts have been omitted from the analysis in order not to introduce an undue bias. Apart from misreporting, these cases mostly represent seasonal labor. We checked whether these omissions affect the mobility patterns and found no differences.

TABLE 9.8: Career Mobility: All Class Transitions of German Men Born 1929-31 up to Age 50 (outflow proportions)

Class	I	II	III	IVa, IVb	IVc	V	VI	VIIa	VIIb	
I	47	13	–	33	7	–	–	–	–	3.0
II	58	21	9	3	–	3	6	–	–	6.7
III	8	63	17	–	4	4	4	–	–	4.8
IVa, IVb	22	11	11	11	–	–	11	33	–	1.8
IVc	4	8	–	–	21	–	21	38	8	4.8
V	6	37	13	9	–	9	22	3	–	6.5
VI	3	5	2	9	1	27	23	31	–	35.8
VIIa	2	8	9	6	–	12	36	21	7	24.6
VIIb	–	–	–	–	10	5	15	63	7	11.9
Total	8.3	11.5	5.3	6.1	2.8	14.3	22.0	26.3	2.8	495

TABLE 9.9: Career Mobility: All Class Transitions of Norwegian Men Born 1931 up to Age 50 (outflow proportions)

Class	I	II	III	IVa, IVb	IVc	V	VI	VIIa	VIIb	
I	16	36	20	3	3	5	2	10	4	2.5
II	27	8	20	9	1	6	13	12	5	5.8
III	15	23	3	7	1	3	11	28	9	9.7
IVa, IVb	3	10	7	1	8	6	35	28	3	4.9
IVc	1	1	3	13	5	2	19	35	21	4.0
V	4	12	10	11	2	4	24	28	5	5.2
VI	1	6	9	13	4	11	2	41	12	15.2
VIIa	2	6	14	8	5	11	25	4	26	28.7
VIIb	2	3	7	4	17	3	16	49	1	24.0
Total	5.0	8.1	9.9	7.6	6.9	6.9	16.7	27.0	11.9	3730

definite career channel for skilled workers in Germany. In Norway there is no similar pattern. It seems just as easy or difficult to move from skilled worker to foremen or white collar as from unskilled labor. Likewise, in falling from white collar, the destination is often manual work, with no effective boundaries between skilled and unskilled labor.

Thus the analysis of first-class/last-class outflow patterns and marginal distributions shows Germany and Norway to be remarkably similar, despite their respective histories, which suggest that there should be notable differences. Yet, the apparent similarity in these patterns masked real differences in the structure and volume of the career transitions.

CONCLUSIONS

In sum, our results allow us to make a strong case for considerable cross-national differences in the regimes governing career mobility. From a methodological standpoint, this analysis has significant implications for comparative analysis. While the hypothesis of similar regimes of in-tragenerational mobility in Norway and Germany would be supported if the analysis were based on comparable first-last tables of career mobility, our analysis shows that it would clearly not be supported when the intragenerational transition takes into account all class moves that occur between first and last class. Because mobility during the work life is more accurately portrayed in the cumulative table, cross-national comparisons should rely on truly longitudinal data rather than aggregated first-class and class at time of interview matrices.

From a substantive point of view, our analysis bears on the overriding question of class formation in both countries. The class structure of Germany is distinctly less open and permeable than that of Norway. Because the formation of class-specific demographic identities is a central component of class formation, and is enhanced to the degree that there exists a stable group of individuals within a class position, mobility patterns reflect the potential for such identities to develop. The greater class rigidities in Germany thus suggest that this country is more likely than Norway to exhibit a more highly developed stage of class formation.

This suggestion is not consistently supported by data, however. For example, using degree of unionization and percentage of electoral votes for socialist parties as indicators of working-class formation, Korpi (1983, pp. 39-41) found that in Norway there is a higher level of working-class mobilization than in West Germany. This represents a puzzle, because the higher number of jobs per class, as well as the higher number of classes per person, would suggest lower working-class mobilization in Norway. How can we account for this?

Space does not allow a detailed discussion of this topic here, but let us suggest some possible answers. First, the importance of demographic identities for class formation may have been exaggerated in the literature. Although not conclusive, evidence from Norway supports this. Within the working class, there is no difference in class identification according to how long a worker has held the same job (Colbjørnsen 1987, pp. 64-65). Second, demographic identities may still have an effect, but they are dominated by other determinants of class formation. In particular, class formation is not determined uniquely by class structure; it is also a result of the "continual effects of struggles enclosed within the structure of economic, ideological, and political relations upon the organization and consciousness of the carriers of the relations of production" (Przeworski

1985, p. 79). Instead of being viewed as decisive, structural properties of class relations, such as their demographic identities, should be viewed as the raw material that is transformed into class formation through class struggle.

When comparing Norway and West Germany, the historical differences in strength and unity between the labor movements in the two countries are especially noteworthy. By following a more consistent social democratic policy, the Norwegian labor movement has been able to promote the conditions for stronger working-class organization. For example, the welfare state reduces working-class members' dependence upon individualistic market strategies (Esping-Andersen 1985).

Interpreted this way, our results are consistent with other comparative research on class structure and class mobility: To explain differences between highly industrialized nations, it is insufficient to consider their socioeconomic structure alone; one must focus in addition upon differences in political regimes, that is, on the result of those strategies that actors use when they respond to and change, among other things, the socioeconomic structure (e.g., Ahrne and Wright 1983; Erikson and Goldthorpe 1987).

REFERENCES

Ahrne, Göran and Erik Olin Wright. 1983. "Classes in the United States and Sweden: A Comparison." *Acta Sociologica* 26:211-35.

Alber, Jens. 1982. *Vom Armenhaus zum Wohlfahrtsstaat. Analysen zur Entwicklung der Sozialversicherung in Westeuropa*. Frankfurt/New York: Campus.

Arbeitsgruppe am Max-Plank-Institut für Bildungswesen. 1984. *Das Bildungswesen in der Bundesrepublik Deutschland*. Reinbek b. Hamburg: Rowohlt.

Baker, David, Ylmaz Ezmer, Gero Lenhardt, and John Meyer. 1985. "Effects of Immigrant Workers on Educational Stratification in Germany." *Sociology of Education* 58:213-27.

Blossfeld, Hans-Peter. Forthcoming. "Labor Market Entry and the Sexual Segregation of Careers in the Federal Republic of Germany." *American Journal of Sociology*.

Blossfeld, Hans-Peter and Karl Ulrich Mayer. 1988. "Labor Market Segmentation in the Federal Republic of Germany: An Empirical Study of Segmentation Theories from a Life Course Perspective. *European Sociological Review 4*, 2: 123-140.

Carroll, Glenn and Karl Ulrich Mayer. 1986. "Job-Shift Patterns in the Federal Republic of Germany: The Effects of Social Class, Industrial Sector, and Organizational Size." *American Sociological Review* 51(3):323-41.

Colbjørnsen, Tom. 1987. "Klasseinteresser og klasseidentitet." In *Klassesamfunnet paa hell*, edited by Tom Colbjørnsen et al. Oslo: Universitetsforlaget.

Erikson, Robert and John H. Goldthorpe. 1985. "Are American Rates of Social Mobility Exceptionally High? New Evidence on an Old Issue." *European Sociological Review* 1(1):1-22.

———. 1987. "Commonality and Variation in Social Fluidity in Industrial Nations." Part I: "A Model for Evaluating the 'FJH Hypothesis.' " Part II: "The Model of Core Social Fluidity Applied." *European Sociological Review* 3(1):54-77, 3(2):145-66.

Erikson, Robert, John H. Goldthorpe, and Lucienne Portocarero. 1982. "Social Fluidity in Industrial Nations." *British Journal of Sociology* 33:1-34.

Esping-Andersen, Gøsta. 1985. *Politics Against Market: The Social Democratic Road to Power.* Princeton, NJ: Princeton University Press.

Featherman, David L., F. Lancaster Jones, and Robert M. Hauser. 1975. "Assumptions of Social Mobility Research in the U.S.: A Case of Occupational Status." *Social Science Research* 4:329-60.

Featherman, David L., Karl Ulrich Mayer, and Kevin Selbee. 1987. "Social Class and the Structuring of the Life Course in Norway and West Germany." Paper presented to the Conference on Comparative Perspective on Age Structuring in Modern Societies, October 19-20, 1987, University Park, Pennsylvania. Forthcoming in *Social Structure and Aging: Comparative Perspectives on Age Structuring in Modern Societies,* edited by David Kertzer, John Meyer, and K. Warner Schaie. Hillsdale, NJ: Lawrence Erlbaum.

Featherman, David L. and Kevin Selbee. 1988. "Class Formation and Class Mobility: A New Approach with Counts from Life History Data." Pp. 247-266 in *Social Change and the Life Course.* Vol. 1. *Social Structure and Human Lives,* edited by Matilda White Riley. Newbury Park, CA: Sage.

Featherman, David L. and Annemette Sørensen. 1983. "Societal Transformation in Norway and Change in the Life-Course Transition into Adulthood." *Acta Sociologica* 26:105-26.

Flora, Peter. 1976. *Modernisierung und die Entwicklung der westeuropäischen Wohlfahrtsstaaten.* Habilitationsschrift. Mannheim: Universität Mannheim.

Flora, Peter, Jens Alber, Richard Eichenberg, Jürgen Kohl, Franz Kraus, Winfried Pfenning, and Kurt Seebohm. 1983. *State, Economy, and Society in Western Europe 1815-1975: A Data Handbook.* Frankfurt am Main: Campus.

Goldthorpe, John. 1980. *Social Mobility and Class Structure in Modern Britain.* Oxford: Clarendon.

Grusky, David B. and Robert M. Hauser. 1984. "Social Mobility Revisited: Models of Convergence and Divergence in Sixteen Countries." *American Sociological Review* 49:19-38.

INAS. 1978. *Datadocumentasjon for Yrkes Historie Undersokelsen.* Notat m 16. Oslo: Institute for Applied Social Research.

Kocka, Jürgen and Michael Prinz. 1983. "Vom 'neuen Mittelstand' zum angestellten Arbeitnehmer: Kontinuität und Wandel der deutschen Angestellten seit der Weimarer Republik." Pp. 210-55 in *Sozialgeschichte der Bundesrepublik Deutschland,* edited by Werner Conze and Mario Rainer Lepsius. Stuttgart: Klett-Cotta.

König, Wolfgang and Walter Müller. 1986. "Educational Systems and Labour Markets as Determinants of Worklife Mobility in France and West Germany: A Comparison of Men's Career Mobility 1965-1970." *European Sociological Review* 2(2):73-96.

Korpi, Walter. 1983. *The Democratic Class Struggle.* London: Routledge & Kegan Paul.

Kurz, Karin and Walter Müller. 1987. "Class Mobility in the Industrial World." *Annual Review of Sociology* 13:417-42.

Leschinsky, Achim and Peter M. Roeder. 1976. *Schule im historischen Prozeβ.* Stuttgart: Klett.

Lorentzen, B. 1969. *Norsk Neringsliv Gjennom Tidene.* Oslo: Univeritetsforlaget.

Lundgreen, Peter. 1980-81. *Sozialgeschichte der deutschen Schule im Überblick.* Teil I: 1770-1918. Teil II: 1918-1980. Vandenhoek und Ruprecht: Göttingen.

Lutz, Burkhardt. 1984. *Der kurze Traum der immerwährenden Prosperität.* Frankfurt: Campus.

Mayer, Karl Ulrich. 1979. "Strukturwandel in Beschäftigungssystem und berufliche Mobilität zwischen generationen." *Zeitschrift für Bevölkerungswissenschaft* 3: 267-298.

Mayer, Karl Ulrich. 1987. "Gender and Class in Worklife Mobility—Results from the German Life History Study." Working paper prepared for the meetings of the Research Committee on Stratification and Mobility of the International Sociological Association, Nürnberg, April 22-24.

————. 1988. "German Survivors of World War II: The Impact on the Life Course of the Collective Experience of Birth Cohorts." Pp. 229-264 in *Social Change and the Life Course*. Vol. 1. *Social Structure and Human Lives*, edited by Matilda White Riley. Newbury Park, CA: Sage.

Mayer, Karl Ulrich and Erika Brückner, eds. 1988. *Lebensverläufe und gesellschaftlicher Wandel. Methodendokumentation zur Haupterhebung der Geburtskohorten 1920-31, 1939-41 und 1949-51. Materialien aus der Bildungsforschung*. Berlin: Max-Planck-Institut für Bildungsforschung.

Mayer, Karl Ulrich and Glenn R. Carroll. 1987. "Jobs and Classes: Structural Constraints on Career Mobility." *European Sociological Review* 3(1):14-38.

McRoberts, Hugh A. and Kevin Selbee. 1981. "Trends in Occupational Mobility in Canada and the United States: A Comparison." *American Sociological Review* 46:406-21.

Mooser, Josef. 1983. "Abschied von der 'Proletarität.' Sozialstruktur und Lage der Arbeiterschaft in der Bundesrepublik in historischer Perspektive." Pp. 143-86 in *Sozialgeschichte der Bundesrepublik Deutschland*, edited by Werner Conze and Rainer Mario Lepsius. Stuttgart: Klett-Cotta.

Przeworski, Adam. 1985. *Capitalism and Social Democracy*. Cambridge: Cambridge University Press.

Rogoff Ramsøy, Natalie. 1972. *The Norwegian Occupational Life History Study: Design, Purpose, and a Few Preliminary Results*. P. 8. Oslo: INAS.

————. 1975. "On Social Stratification in a Temporal Framework." Manuscript, Institute for Applied Social Research, Oslo.

————. 1987. "From Necessity to Choice: Social Change in Norway 1930-1980." In *The Scandinavian Model: Welfare States and Welfare Research*, edited by Robert Erikson, Erik Jorgen Hansen, Stein Ringen, and Hannu Uusitalo. Armonk/London: Sharpe.

Sagarra, Elisabeth. 1977. *A Social History of Germany, 1648-1914*. London: Methuen.

Sørensen, Annemette, Jutta Allmendinger, and Aage B. Sørensen. 1986. "Intergenerational Mobility as a Life Course Process." Paper presented at the meeting of the American Sociological Association, New York, August.

Visher, Mary. 1982. "Notes on Industrialization in Norway: Some Facts and Figures" (Mimeo). Madison: University of Wisconsin.

Part IV
Nation as Context:
Secondary Analyses

10

Cross-National Research and the Analysis of Educational Systems

Margaret S. Archer

Why should we study educational systems in cross-national perspective? After all, the overwhelming majority of sociologists of education have never seen the necessity. Perhaps we should start with a second question and ask why this has been the case. The answer to that is startlingly straightforward—it is because they have never accepted the need to study educational systems at all. As I have bemoaned elsewhere (Archer 1982a), the single most neglected question in the vast literature on education concerns the "educational system" itself. The very concept is ill defined, used with negligence, and applied to anything "educational" from tribal initiation onward.

To be clear about what has been neglected, a state "educational system" is defined as "a nationwide and differentiated collection of institutions devoted to formal education, whose overall control and supervision is at least partly governmental, and whose component parts and processes are related to one another" (Archer 1979, p. 54). Two main issues are raised by viewing the emergence of state systems as a crucial break in the educational history of any nation. The first concerns their *origins*—where do educational systems come from and why do they have different internal structures and external relations to other parts of society? The second is about their *operations*—what difference do their particular structural properties make to processes of interaction within them and to subsequent patterns of educational change? These are theoretical concerns that have simply not been addressed by the majority of sociologists of education, and their methodological corollary is that they only can be tackled from a cross-national perspective.

Instead, explanations of educational development have, until very recently, rested upon a particularly facile epiphenomenalism—either structural or ideational. Thus the best-known theories of educational growth—Human Capital Theory, Consumption Theory, Modernization Theory, Political Integration Theory, Social Control Theory, and Ideological Diffusion Theory—all represent *general* explanations that pinpoint some *particular variable or process* as universally responsible for it. Fundamentally, the types of theories listed embody an unwarranted epiphenomenalism that denies that "an educational system is at least partly an autonomous element in the total society, not just an adjunct of more decisive processes or institutions" (Ringer 1979, p. 2). Significantly, the social constitution of educational systems as opposed to the existence of schools or colleges is accorded no theoretical importance by them. Their attention is riveted on the quantitative—mass education—never the qualitative—structural elaboration. The reason for this neglect is intrinsic to these approaches: If some process or property is indeed universally responsible for educational development, then systemic differences are truly insignificant.

Such theories, however, are not merely of a deceptive simplicity, they are simply deceptive. They can provide no explanatory purchase upon the interactional mechanisms structuring education in different ways and the conditioning influence exerted by such differences in structure upon subsequent educational interaction and change. Many of these strictures might simply be laid at the door of latter-day empiricism (Karabel and Halsey 1977), with a mea culpa for our past collective misdeeds and a clear conscience about our present doings. This I believe would be misplaced, for though some of the crudities of "methodological empiricism" may have been abandoned as part of the growing repudiation of positivism, the epiphenomenal approach to the educational system remains very alive if not at all well in more recent qualitative approaches. And because epiphenomenalism continues to gain endorsement, theoretical deficiencies are perpetuated and cross-national study is persistently neglected. The most serious consequence of this is creeping ethnocentrism—the illicit assumption that because the causes of all things educational are transnational in character then this licenses inductions from the national system familiar to the investigator and their generalization to all others. Because such a sweeping critique is highly contentious, I want to demonstrate its pervasiveness among the majority of contemporary sociologists of education.

EPIPHENOMENALISM AND THE
FALLACY OF STRUCTURAL PERMEATION

In most current approaches, properties pertaining to the structure of educational systems are *never* considered vital to theorizing about patterns of interaction within them, processes available for changing them, or the structural elaboration undergone by them. Dismissal of the system is a common denominator of neo-Durkheimian theorists of cultural transmission and reproduction (led by Bernstein and Bourdieu); the neo-Marxist cohort (spearheaded by Bowles and Gintis); the neo-Weberian "credentialists" (Collins), adaptors of the Wallersteinian "world-system" perspective, and critical theorists of Frankfurt school inspiration.

It will be argued that, in all these theories, neglect of the structure of the educational system (i.e., the articulation of the system with society and the interrelationship of its component parts) derives from three shared and mutually supporting assumptions:

(1) the assumption of *penetrability*
(2) the assumption of *complementarity*
(3) the assumption of *homogeneity*

Taken together, the combined effect of these assumptions is to deprive the structure of educational systems of any theoretical significance because these are nothing more than the administrative framework, the "passive mediator," through which power relationships in society are given educational expression. This I have termed the "fallacy of structural permeation" and Figure 10.1 summarizes its constitutive assumptions together with their mutually supportive implications—every one of which makes its own contribution to reducing our capacity for explaining educational phenomena.

Penetrability

The educational system is neglected because it is assumed to be ever open to and reflective of external social relations whose influence penetrates educational practice directly. Direct penetration is given axiomatic status because it is presumed that power relations between groups or classes are the universal basis of instruction: Educational knowledge is presented as nothing but a saturate of class-culture, and sociocultural reproduction is automatically taken to be the prime function of education. Consequently, questions about *what* genetic processes enable power relations to be translated into symbolic hegemony never arise. Similarly, questions about *whether* they are converted without com-

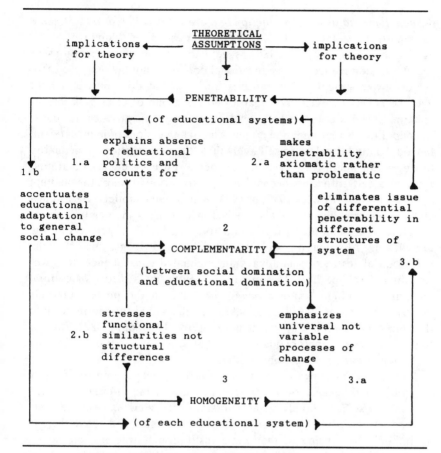

Figure 10.1: Assumptions of Penetrability, Complementarity, and
Homogeneity as the Basis of Epiphenomenalism

NOTE: In the following discussion, which amplifies on this figure, the implicative relationships will be highlighted by use of the numerical notations (1.a, 1.b, and so on) in the text.

promise, or *if* they are the exclusive social pressures to penetrate education are never considered to be really problematic (implication 1.a from Figure 10.1). By corollary, this axiom dispenses with any need to examine the structure of educational systems, for if penetration is universal and universally unproblematic then systemic differences are irrelevant (implication 1.b). Theories that are predicated upon the perfect alignment of social domination and educational control, however, have further defects in common that derive from this unjustified presumption.

The assumption of penetrability plays the same role in any theory that embraces it. *Permeability makes the relationship between power in society and control of education axiomatic but it leaves them mute about the actual mechanisms of interaction that are responsible for it* (1.a). Here the significant point to note is that however much the "dominant ideology" (Abercrombie et al. 1980) is held to rest on power relations in society, its dominance in the educational domain is not the outcome of an actual power struggle. The transmission of social principles to school practice never involves investigating how a group or class gets into or remains in a position of educational hegemony. This absence of educational politics is glaring in the cruder American versions of neo-Marxism. Indeed, Samuel Bowles himself avers that "the perpetuation of inequality through the schooling system has been represented as an almost automatic, self-enforcing mechanism, operating only through the medium of class culture" (Bowles 1977, p. 147). With greater subtlety, Bernstein's cultural transmission thesis also insists that changes in society's power structure pass unproblematically into formal education, penetrating the organization, distribution, and evaluation of knowledge, such that the definition of instruction is always an attenuated consequence of power relations (1971, p. 200). In similar vein, Bourdieu's theory of cultural reproduction hinges upon a *pédagogie*, "which the power relations between the groups and classes making up the social formation put into the dominant position" (Bourdieu and Passeron 1970, pp. 21-22). Thus he too substitutes the unproblematic act of "putting" for the problematic act of "winning out" in educational politics.

It appears to me, however, that the notion of direct penetration can only be entertained because of a misrepresentation of the interface between system and society, involving an oversimplified view of both elements and the interplay between them. In the theories mentioned above there is an implicit condensing of the whole institutional structure into social stratification, or at least into a hierarchy universally dominated by it. Thus no institutional operations—economic, political, bureaucratic, religious—are ever admitted to have different relationships of contradiction or complementarity to education. Instead it is presumed that their highest common denominator is the shared desire of their respective elites (or one solitary elite for that matter) for reproduction of their social position. Yet not only is it perfectly valid to ask which parts of the social structure exert most influence upon educational activities (when, where, and under what conditions), but this seems to be one of the most important questions to ask—given the magnitude of cross-national variations.

In turn, this reemphasizes the indispensability of a politics of education: for if the differential responsiveness of education to different parts of the social structure is to be explained, then we must deal with the decision-making processes involved. In doing so, it becomes indispensable to introduce the structures of the educational system itself, in order to account for what these are, where they are located, and who has access to them—particularly as these facets of decision making vary cross-nationally, alter over time, and, in consequence, change the specific parts of the institutional order to which education is most responsive. Fundamentally, the same group (e.g., the entrepreneurial elite or religious leadership) enjoys neither the same amount of educational influence in different national systems nor a constant amount over time in any one system. On the contrary, *educational systems are differentially penetrable to different social groups, they are never equally permeable to all, and at any given time they are usually impenetrable to some.* Only an analysis of these systemic properties, in conjunction with a politics of educational interaction, can explain these variations: Theories based upon a simple analogy with the process of osmosis must always remain baffled by them.

The very notion of education as a completely permeable institution, however, militates against any importance being attached to systemic structure (1.b). Because external power relations are mirrored by internal educational practices, then the system by definition has no gatekeepers, does not mediate between society and the schools, and does not filter the demands to which instruction proves responsive. In short, the complete permeability of education makes its structure completely uninteresting. At most, systemic properties are viewed as dependent variables that represent institutional adaptation to general socioeconomic change, usually the development of advanced industrial society, rather than constituting durable differences in the structuring of particular state systems.

Complementarity

A proper study of educational interaction would allow for the fact that the balance of power in education at any time is not necessarily in complete alignment with the balance of power in society, because of compromises or concessions and degrees of success or failure on the part of the groups involved. Here, however, though it is rarely asserted that the socially dominant group personally dominates education, it is assumed that educational activities always complement the interests of the dominant group or class. It is precisely because the maintenance of complementarity is held to be a guaranteed rather than a problematic state of affairs, as it always must remain in educational politics, that we are dealing with another central axiomatic premise.

Once again the assumption of complementarity plays an identical role for the theorists who adopt it. Ultimately it enables them to evade specification of the actual social processes that *assure* educational eufunctionality to the dominant group or what *ensures* that dysfunctions are avoided or corrected. Instead of concrete mechanisms we are presented with unexplained homologies. Bowles's "rules of the game,"

Bernstein's "knowledge codes," and Bourdieu's "cultural arbitraries" are all held to work through a vast series of individual acts, which, although politically unorganized and frequently exercised in ignorance of their consequences, are nevertheless perfectly functionally orchestrated in their effects. Despite the deceptive use of Marxist terminology in such theories, they ultimately rely upon functional adaptation.

Consequently, to adopt the assumption of complementarity is to dispense with any examination of the *conditions* under which different social groups can influence the prevailing definition of instruction (implication 2.a) and also with a detailed specification of the systemically *structured processes* through which educational change or stasis can actually be produced (implication 2.b).

Deficient explanations result from the adoption of this axiom because the proffered accounts rest upon the machinations of "hidden actors" and the mechanics of "latent functions" (Johansson 1982) rather than upon the interplay between agency and structure. Thus if one questions what ensures the lasting complementarity between social and educational domination, "hidden actors" are wheeled into play, as is particularly evident in the treatment of teachers as collective secret agents of class interests—usually "operating blind," of course, but necessarily reproducing the symbolic conditions of their own production, or reflecting the socialization they received in the course of training. In turn, professional formation is assumed to be impregnated with the values, code, or ideology of the dominant group or class. This then begs a series of questions—how does such a group attain control over training and why is its universal hegemony over professional formation taken as a foregone conclusion? Why is it assumed that the uses to which hard-won professional freedoms are put always reinforce and never threaten power relations? Instead of presuming any eternal and universal complementarity between these two groups, I would suggest that in each particular instance the machinations of educational politics have to be assessed in order to understand the goodness of fit or the lack of complementarity between the professional educators and the dominant group or class *and* the directions in which the two are trying to push the definition of instruction *through* educational politics.

In other words, it appears crucial to reject the premise of complementarity and implication 2.a—namely, that one group or class alone, anywhere and everywhere, possesses the conditions for imposing its definition of instruction. Instead, specification of the circumstances under which any group will influence educational stability or change would be expressed in *interrelational terms* (i.e., what gives one group more negotiating strength than the parties with which it interacts) rather than *positional terms* (e.g., the political elite or dominant class) that supposedly guarantee unqualified success in educational interaction.

Similarly, the assumption of universal complementarity does not seem to square with the observation that the socially dominant themselves are often found clamoring for a more technical, vocational, scientific, or "progressive" instruction and for the limitation of useless and dangerous disciplines like the social sciences. In short, if we believe what they say, the dominant groups are not getting what they want out of education. This manifest discontent can only be squared with the postulate of complementarity by invoking a hidden hand that ensures, in Bourdieu's words, that educational activities "always objectively serve the dominant classes since they never sacrifice the technical interests of those classes except to the advantage of their social interests" (1970, pp. 47 ff.). In other words, whatever education does and whatever manifest discontent this evokes, its latent function of social reproduction is sufficient to offset the frustration of other demands and thus to represent a state of complementarity. Only in this way can universal functional similarities (assumption 2.b) be assigned to varied educational provisions where the degree of manifest satisfaction with them also shows independent variations. Such functional similarities are, of course, emphasized at the expense of structural differences, which leads directly to the last member of the trio of assumptions.

Homogeneity

Only by homogenizing all educational systems is it possible to deprive their structural organization of any theoretical importance. Thus while the consequence of the permeability assumption (1) was to deny significance to real political struggles, and that of the complementary assumption (2) was to dismiss the significance of avowed educational objectives, the implication of the homogeneity assumption (3) is to downgrade concrete structural differences, which then become irrelevant to explanation. Educational systems are artificially homogenized by the accentuation of their shared features and the corresponding neglect of their nonuniversal properties. Consequently, educational systems are characterized by their most general features, the best evidence of this being that the very term "system" is stripped of its normal connotations and denotations and is used with complete negligence to refer to anything from tribal initiation rites onward. In its place, and effecting the homogenization of structures, are substituted terms like "institutionalized education," or "mass education"—the preferred designation because it refers only to numbers and is thus totally astructural.

The first implication of this repression of systemic variations is that it does indeed enable universal rather than variable processes of change to be emphasized (3.a). In contradistinction, if systemic organization is taken seriously, then any analysis of change involves examining the particular processes of negotiation, varying with the structure of systems, which determine *how* educational demands can be influential; it also entails investigating the variable relations between educational outputs and institutional operations, for these determine *which* parts of society will seek to change or defend the educational status quo. Instead, the homogenized system, it is imputed, behaves in a fully homogeneous fashion vis-à-vis power, bourgeois society, the dominant ideology, the diploma society, credentialism, or capitalism. At its worst, the absence of any consideration of how education is internally coordinated and externally articulated with society encourages the descent into the abyss of correspondence "theory"—among whose grosser defects is a constant inability to explain fluctuations in "complementarity."

Nevertheless, for a great many theorists, this homogenization *artificially* serves to confirm the unimportance attached to the *system level* and to the structuring of education in general. If systems are so alike in all significant respects and their differences are so insignificant in their implications, we come full circle back to the unimportance of this boundary, and by implication (3.b) have eliminated the issue of whether different systems are differentially penetrable. Consequently, the three assumptions—the *penetrability* of education, its *complementarity* with the dominant group or class, and the *homogeneity* of educational systems— are mutually supportive: together they strike systemic considerations off the agenda of the sociology of education.

ETHNOCENTRISM: THE NATIONAL
SYSTEM AS NORMAL AND THE
NORMALIZATION OF THE NATIONAL SYSTEM

If the structures of educational systems are considered to be of no account, because the same cultural processes are held to permeate them all, then detailed cross-national analysis of structural differences can be bypassed. The result, however, is an unholy alliance between epiphenomenalism and ethnocentrism that mars the best contributions to the sociology of education. Thus, for example, Bernstein and Bourdieu advance general theories that purport to be universally applicable, yet both of them draw freely upon illustrations from their own systems of education without prior examination of these in their own right. Three consequences follow from this, each of which appears to damage the *universality* claimed for these theories of cultural transmission and reproduction.

The first is that the price of overtly neglecting the systemic level is the covert incorporation of national features as the norm: to a considerable extent, Bernstein presents an English theory and Bourdieu a French one. The second is that this unsystematic culling from their own national experience leads both authors to neglect certain structural features *distinctive* of each system. Third, the joint effect of treating some *variable* structural features as *universal* (the national system as normal), while minimizing other structural features more *particular* to it (the normalization of the national system) is *artificially to homogenize* educational systems. This in turn serves, of course, to justify the neglect of systemic structure.

Yet both Bernstein and Bourdieu are themselves persuaded that they have distanced their own theories from any particular educational system, including their own. Despite Bernstein's acknowledged induction of concepts on the basis of his personal (English) experience, he believes that his references to England play nothing more than a simple illustrative role (Bernstein 1975, p. 94). Similarly, Bourdieu admits to induction from French practice (Bourdieu and Passeron 1970, p. 9) but maintains that he has separated the universal from the ethnocentric. Thus *Reproduction* is divided into two parts; the first is an abstract presentation of universal propositions and the second an analysis of contemporary French education, relating it to the theoretical principles of Book I, which were themselves "logically required" by the empirical findings of Book II. Neither Bernstein's distinction between theory and illustration nor Bourdieu's between the general and the particular succeed in protecting their theories from entanglement with the educational system in question and their own perceptions of it.

The National System as Normal

Precisely because educational systems are not examined as such, certain characteristics of the English and French systems are treated as *normal* and are incorporated, respectively, into the two theories. It will clarify the following discussion if I make use of certain concepts, developed in full elsewhere (Archer 1979), to characterize different structures of educational systems. State systems of education universally display four characteristics: *unification* (development of a national framework of educational administration), *systematization* (transition from the summativity of parts to a coordinated whole), *differentiation* (separation from other parts of society), and *specialization* (diversification of education inputs, processes, and outputs). The configuration in which *differentiation* and *specialization* predominate represents the *decentralized* system (as in England, the United States, or Denmark); the predominance of *unification* and *systematization* signifies a *centralized* system of education (as in France, the Soviet Union, or Japan).

The specific contention concerning Bernstein's theory is that he assumes *weak unification* and *systematization* to be normal and thus, unaware, incorporates two features *distinctive* of English decentralization into his *general* theory of cultural transmission. Bourdieu, on the other hand, makes exactly the opposite assumption and interprets *strong unification* and *systematization*, which are characteristics *only* of centralized systems like the French one, as universal features that are then built into his *general* theory of cultural reproduction.

Thus, for example, when discussing "open schooling," Bernstein states: "I am not concerned whether all the relationships I refer to are factually present in all schools. *Clearly*, some schools will have shifted not at all, others more; the shift may be more pronounced in the education of special groups of pupils or within different subjects. *I am interested only in the general movement*" (Bernstein 1975, p. 69; emphasis added). There is no "clearly" about all this, except as properties of the weakly unified and systematized nature of decentralization. Yet it was these very properties of the English system that allowed the partial and discontinuous *manifestations* of those changes, *the recognition* of which Bernstein uses to designate a "general movement." This is why the ethnocentric assumptions are *fundamental* to the theory, rather than being confined to exemplifications of it. But they do not hold for the centralized structures of most European systems, which require leverage from the center to produce change rather than allowing any movement, like that toward open schooling, to get off the ground locally.

The fact that the French and the English systems are so different in structure helps to signal the points at which both authors, without warning or awareness, start incorporating nationalist assumptions—for these tend to be the exact opposite of one another. Thus while Bernstein took weak unification and systematization to be normal, Bourdieu takes it that normally these two characteristics are strong.

Thus *intense unification* and *strong systematization* are attributed to the "logic of pedagogic action" and are, therefore, assumed to be universal rather than merely reflecting the detailed imposition of central administrative controls. Hence, for example, Bourdieu categorically asserts that every educational system necessarily monopolizes teacher training and imposes standardized methods, texts, and syllabi to safeguard orthodoxy (Bourdieu and Passeron 1970, p. 74). These are the familiar weapons elaborated by the polity in a centralized system (Vaughan and Archer 1971), but they are alien in decentralized systems, where the state possesses no monopoly over teacher training, where textbook, timetable, and curricular anarchy can prevail and modes of assessment and examination boards proliferate.

Bourdieu's attempts at distancing his theory from the particularities of all educational systems merely shackles it more closely to the French system. Indeed, a constellation of features drawn descriptively from France's history are built into the very foundations of his concept of educational institutionalization, which is meant to be applicable both comparatively and historically. These include, among others, the standardization of educational organization over a wide area, national examinations, and civil servant status for teachers (Bourdieu and Passeron 1970, p. 72). By these criteria, however, countries like England and the United States have not yet reached (and appear unlikely to reach) those "thresholds in the process of institutionalization," which work much better for centralized systems because of their structural affinities with the French system. Yet it would be entirely unwarranted to represent these (decentralized) systems as being "less" institutionalized: educational development is not a unilinear process and different historical patterns of structuring defy compression into a single continuum.

The Normalization of the National System

In direct parallel to the above, Bernstein and Bourdieu also minimize features that pertain *only* to decentralized or centralized systems and this irons out the differences between them—it "normalizes" each national system by underemphasizing its distinctive aspects, thus *making* it more like others. More specifically, and using the same concepts as in the last section, it seems that while Bernstein fails to recognize or to explore the *strength* of *differentiation* and *specialization* that is distinctive of decentralized systems like the English one, Bourdieu minimizes the especial weakness of *differentiation* and *specialization* that is typical of centralized systems like the French one (Archer 1979, pp. 173-82 ff.). This normalization of the two systems has serious theoretical implications. A great diversity of educational activities is part and parcel of strong differentiation and specialization in decentralized systems. This leads one to query if national education does display one dominant "knowledge code" in a country like England with its plethora of parallel, competing, independent, and uncoordinated provisions. Bernstein did not confront this patchwork when formulating his concepts, for we have his own avowal that these were developed by condensing his own experience (Bernstein 1975, p. 2), which necessarily must have been time-bound and limited in scope. This raises the serious question of whether his formulation of a dominant "knowledge code" did not depend upon accentuating only those parts of the English educational array that had ready cross-national equivalents, despite the fact that one of the most important comparative differences is precisely that some systems (the decentralized) contain a range of specialized institutions, courses, and qualifications, in addition to mainstream and prestige secondary schooling, which others (the centralized) simply do not possess at all.

The greater ease with which a dominant "cultural arbitrary" could be delineated in France created a different problem in Bourdieu's theorizing, namely, was it particular features of the French system that allowed him to speak *so readily* about a dominant "cultural arbitrary"? If this were possible only *because* differentiation had been kept low historically (for fear that educational autonomy would decrease its political responsiveness) and specialization had been restricted over time (in case it jeopardized essential educational services to state), then it would be dependent upon this organizational streamlining and internal standardization of the French system. In other words, if the existence of a dominant "cultural arbitrary" were contingent upon the low level of educational diversity in a centralized system then the possibility of theorizing in this way varies with the structure of the educational system and could only be generalized to other systems of the same type.

Bernstein and Bourdieu have been criticized for separating the discussion of culture from any consideration of structure in the educational field. The most unfortunate consequence of their neglect of the educational system qua system is that their theories of cultural transmission and cultural reproduction are severed from the historical and comparative sociology of education.

Thus, as it stands, the reproduction thesis gives an excellent account of certain sociocultural processes that take place *if* a system has been structured in a particular way, but provides no explanation of this structuring. To get full value from Bourdieu's theory, one needs to know *when* (historically) and *where* (comparatively) it works most and least well. Otherwise it remains a kind of "extreme" type whose approximation to empirical reality varies greatly for different countries or different times and can only be generalized at the price of ethnocentrism.

Equally, both authors cut their theories off from comparative sociology because their homogenization of educational systems precludes the cross-national examination of systemic structuring. In turn this means that the only dimension of international variation is the cultural one itself and this alone cannot account for all the variance in educational practice and provision. What this points to is the need to reopen discussion on the *relation* between structure and culture in the sociology of education as in social theory generally. For example, Bernstein's key concepts, "classification" and "framing," upon which the typology of "knowledge codes" is built, appear to vary directly in their strength or weakness with central-ized and decentralized structures of systems, respectively. In other words, different kinds of educational systems could be seen to furnish the condi-tions and controls necessary to introduce and sustain different types of curricular, pedagogical, and evaluative practices, but this could only be established by cross-national investigation, which resolutely repudiated ethnocentric generalizations.

THE STRUCTURING OF
STATE EDUCATIONAL SYSTEMS

At rock bottom, the reason for attaching considerable importance to the structural characteristics of national educational systems is that without this the really big questions about educational matters simply cannot be adequately answered. Fundamental problems, like what is the definition of instruction—who benefits and who has a say—how can change be introduced—what pattern of changes ensues—all of these can only be solved by addressing the structure of the system. State educational sys-tems differ in terms of the internal articulation of their parts and their external relations to other parts of society. Reference to these cross-na-tional differences is crucial to answering the big question posed above and to explaining why the answers are not the same everywhere. Thus the first task in the attempt to develop a more complete sociology of education is to explain the social origins of educational systems; to account, in short, for why historically different nations generated varying structures of system.

The attempt to account for the characteristics and contours of national educational systems is a sociological enterprise that runs counter to the two main strands in the literature on educational development. On the one hand, educational historians have usually opted for a narrative account of historical specificity that defies generalization except in those cases where accounts are dubiously wedded to an implicit belief in evolutionary mechanisms, spontaneous adjustments to social change, or a Whiggish commitment to "progress," all of which tend to be conceived in unilinear and ethnocentric terms. Thus, insofar as there is a general theory, it is one of catching up with "us" (whoever "we" happen to be), and insofar as this ethnocentrism is avoided, we are left with brute historical uniqueness, which frustrates any sociological enterprise in this area.

On the other hand, sociological forays into the problem of educational development have settled for a straightforward epiphenomenalism of which the best-known versions are secularization theory and industrial-ization theory, along with their many variants. Given such blunt instruments, the *explicandum* ceases to be the characteristics and contours of national educational systems. Instead, we are given a verbal statement of a correlation coefficient between the purported *explicans* and some now universal characteristics of education like "compulsory schooling," which skirts the problem of systemic structure altogether.

In these cases, sociological ingenuity is devoted to explaining away manifest cross-national discrepancies. For example, if we compare England and France, the former as the first industrialized nation nevertheless developed its state system of education a century after the latter. How is it possible to explain the continued educational hegemony of the Anglican church in nineteenth-century England and the educational powerlessness of a largely unenfranchised but economically dominant middle class during most of this period? Only by postulating Anglican socialization in schools and universities as having latent functions for the middle classes, despite their manifest discontent with these practices, or by falling back on the unsatisfactory notion of "cultural lag." How is it possible to account for the emplacement of a secularized and instrumental system in rural France 100 years earlier? Only by construing the French revolution as a bourgeois one that preadapted the new educational provisions not to its current professional interests but with extraordinary prescience to industrial developments yet to take place. Such theorizing hands over the explanatory burden to disembodied social forces and in true epiphenomenal fashion reduces actors to *träger*, thus riding roughshod over their declared promotive interests and the intricacies of their interaction.

As far as the structuring of state educational systems is concerned, the problem is how to steer a course between historical specificity, which denies sociological generalization, and gross epiphenominal generalizations, which withhold purchase on variations in structure and processes of interaction producing them. The method of proceeding seems to be to identify the point at which state educational systems, as defined above, emerged in various countries (where this was not due to external imposition) and then to backtrack historically, inspecting the interaction chains giving rise to them to see whether it is possible to theorize about regularities in processes and outcomes despite considerable socioeconomic variations accompanying their emergence. Indeed, at the beginning of my own study, *Social Origins of Educational Systems* (Archer 1979), the aim was specifically to maximize these variations by selecting countries as historically diverse as England, France, Russia, and Denmark (as well as Japan and the United States, which did not appear in the final text), because a theory worth having could only be one that was not defeated by such diversity.

Ironically, one of the criticisms occasionally voiced against this enterprise, which seeks to incorporate rather than deny relevant national variations, is that the task is wrongly conceived because it does not compare like with like in either social or educational terms. For instance, it has been pointed out that some of the factors that are known to be important in educational change (e.g., mode or level of economic production, nature of social stratification, or type of political organization) differ greatly in the countries examined. Because such factors are not controlled (they are not present or absent or the same for all), the social contexts themselves are very different. It has then been objected that any educational changes observed later on simply reflect these initial variations; an objection that appears to rely upon the very epiphenomenalism that this approach seeks to avoid with its constant respect for the independent, varied, and indispensable contributions of collective human action in determining outcomes. Certainly, such an argument would be unanswerable were the problem in hand the examination, for example, of economic influences upon educational development. It is not; on the contrary, the aim is precisely to see whether general propositions about educational change can be advanced in the presence of such variations. The existence of broad socioeconomic differences cannot, therefore, be used as a basis from which to prejudge the outcome of this theoretical undertaking. If it is possible to develop general theories about education, then they must be ones that embrace cross-national differences.

The outcome of this analysis (with its respect for the intricacies of interplay between structure and agency as opposed to the endorsement of epiphenomenalism) allowed the disengagement of cross-national generality—the emergence from a prior context of private ownership in education, through intricate chains of purposive interaction, of state educational systems universally sharing the four properties of Unification, Systematization, Differentiation, and Specialization. Simultaneously, however, and dependent on the interaction process employed to demolish private ownership, it was also possible to explain the emergence of two very different structures of state system in different nations—the centralized system where Unification and Systematization predominated, and the decentralized system, where Differentiation and Specialization predominated in the emergent system. Thus both common and variable properties of the new state educational systems, emerging at different times in different countries, could be explained (Archer 1982c). Needless to say, this would have been impossible were one simply to have extrapolated from the chain of structural conditioning → social interaction → structural elaboration taking place in one country alone and shaping its particular educational system.

Although space prevents a summary of either the arguments or the evidence, perhaps it is useful to indicate a few of the payoffs from having derived this crucial break in educational development, the emergence of state systems, from anterior social interaction. First, as far as social groups and classes are concerned, this type of analysis tells us what part each played in bringing their respective system about and where they stood in relation to its control at the time of emergence. Such a specification stands in stark contrast to simplistic theories of correspondence or complementarity with the educational aims of some putative dominant group: on the contrary, the precise forms that education takes are held never to be precisely what *anyone* wanted. Being the political products of power struggles, they bear the marks of concession to allies and compromise with opponents. Thus to understand the nature of emergent educational systems we need to know not only who won the struggle for control but also how: not merely who lost, but also how badly they lost out.

Second, as far as the form and content of the new systems are concerned, we are now in a position to understand why some are organizationally streamlined, have a high degree of coordination between their component parts, a standardized definition of instruction, a national uniformity of curricula and credentials, and a high degree of responsiveness to the political center, while others differ in each of these respects. Moreover, these differences between the centralized system, deriving from the displacement of private ownership in education by a process akin to "nationalization," and the decentralized system, stemming from market competition, cease to be theoretical embarrassments (to be treated by artificial homogenization) and become explanatory assets. As will be seen next, the particular structural properties make a great deal of difference to subsequent processes and patterns of change within them.

At this point, however, and quite validly, it might be objected that if we are really concerned with cross-national developments, then the majority of countries have not had the freedom to generate their own educational systems, whereas the theory being summarized here is predicated upon the autonomous emergence of the state system. All of this is perfectly true— most countries did indeed acquire an educational system through military conquest or colonial imposition. Yet *what* they acquired coercively requires explanation, for the structure imposed was not forged on the spot but replicated that of the conquering power. The problems surrounding the retention, rejection, or adaptation of externally imposed educational systems warrant considerable study in their own right, but a major element in such investigations must always be the structure of what is being retained, rejected, or adapted because of, inter alia, the vested interests it distributes to different indigenous groups.

Once state educational systems are in place, their differences in structure make the greatest difference to processes of change available, to who
has access to these, and to their outcomes. As the products of educational
politics, neither kind of system is assumed to be better adapted to society
or to generate less grievance and desire for change among its component
members. Let us look briefly at three major types of educational interest
groups and what they can do to bring about change in decentralized and
centralized systems, respectively.

First, professional interest groups in the decentralized system have
much greater autonomy as teachers (they are not civil servants), in the
classroom (where curricula, texts, and assessment are not centrally controlled), and as professional associations (which develop early with strong
unionist rights). Thus they are in a powerful position for the "internal
initiation" of changes in line with professional values—hence, for example, the quiet movement toward progressive child-centered teaching in
schools or that the introduction of Black Studies or Women's Studies in
colleges and universities could be accomplished by English teachers and
academics without the sanction of the central authorities. In contrast, their
counterparts in the centralized system are much more constrained: fewer
changes can be attributed to them because internal initiation is confined
to matters of academic concern that attract no central opprobrium. Consequently, they can serve themselves to some degree but cannot respond to
pupil requirements or community demands. Such change as can be introduced represents an intensified academicism (as Bourdieu once put it,
every student is treated as an apprentice professor rather than a professional apprentice), beyond which professional action is negative and
reduces to blocking and resisting central policy.

Second, external interest groups of all kinds in wider society stand in a
different position vis-à-vis the two kinds of system. Given greater institutional autonomy in decentralized systems, they can engage in "external
transactions" with various institutions, directly negotiating their training
and research requirements with private and public sectors alike, provided
only that the terms are right. Many institutional elites gain educational
satisfaction from this process and whole strings of colleges, courses, and
qualifications are attributable to such transactions. In centralized systems,
the lesser autonomy of public education, and the greater control and lesser
prestige of private provisions, reduce the scope of external negotiations.
Even rich and powerful groups cannot buy the changes they seek but are
forced to resort to pressurizing the central authority for change rather than
introducing it locally.

Finally, in the decentralized system, all educational demands do not
crowd into the political arena: many are satisfied institutionally or locally
thus reinforcing systemic diversity, creating new vested interests in the

defense of the new provisions, and ultimately making the system still less amenable to central control. In the centralized system, even professional and elite demands have to be politically aggregated, transmitted upward to the decision-making center and ultimately passed down to education as polity-directed changes—usually diluted to such a degree that the resulting Educational Acts typically have tepid supporters and vitriolic critics. Yet unless the center can be successfully manipulated to respond to these aggregated pressures, no change ensues and the reservoir of discontent continues to build up, threatening to break its banks, as in the French *événements* of 1968.

This contrast between the relative importance of the three processes of change in the different structures of system finds a perfect exemplification in the movements for comprehensivization in England and France. In the English case the movement could get off the ground autonomously in the 1920s by internal initiation in rural areas; it snowballed by local imitation and experimentation in the next three decades, until the Labour party politically endorsed and extended this change that was taking place beneath its feet. In the French case, the movement for an *école unique* started at about the same time and with similar aims, but was constrained to draft plans and recruit unionist allies and party supporters in the hope of changing central policy. What followed were forty years of failed "political manipulation" (given the inability of the left to gain office or hold together in it the divided interests of primary and secondary teachers, and the opposition of the church). And in a centralized system, failed "political manipulation" means no change: Throughout this battle of paper projects, the bifurcated and discriminatory structure remained unaltered because change comes from the top down, never from the bottom up, in centralized educational systems.

Last, it is worth pursuing this example to illustrate the difference in outcomes in the two types of system. Were a foreigner to ask what the English comprehensive school is like, there is no concise reply for we do not have *a* comprehensive school but a variety of local organizational forms, age ranges, and streaming and setting practices, which constitute local interpretations of comprehensivization and deny standardization. When France finally introduced the *Collège Unique* in the late 1970s, it was a polity-directed and polity-defined innovation, applied nationwide according to a standardized format.

In conclusion then, centralized and decentralized systems work in different ways: Different groups have differential control over them; different processes of negotiation are of differential importance in changing them; and the different patterns of interaction thus conditioned generate equally distinctive patterns of change within them. None of this is bound to last for ever: None of this logically precludes convergence because all depends on future configurations of changing structural factors in conjunction with shifting promotive interest groups. Until or unless this occurs, however, the lasting structural differences between the two kinds of system, which still allow them to be characterized as centralized or decentralized, continue to exert their different influences.

In other words, structural conditioning continues to shape interaction in different ways in the two systems; interaction itself still follows two distinctive patterns, and the structural elaboration that results reconfirms the differences that caused one to distinguish between centralization and decentralization in the first place. The force of this argument rests on the endurance of differences in the structural conditioning of interaction and change between the centralized and the decentralized system.

Any temptation to assume that the incidence of some international phenomenon, such as world economic recession, will automatically standardize systemic structuring is not only an overly hasty reading of the "signs of the times" but threatens to reimmerse educational analysis in the very epiphenomenalism from which it is still being extricated. It is an explicit repudiation of lasting cross-national differences in structuring, which always mediate the impact of international events.

Here instead, to pay attention to variations in institutional structure carries the supreme advantage of being able to specify the *mechanisms* by which such effects are mediated nationally: the epiphenomenalists are eternally short on mechanism. Equally, any temptation to generalize educational policy transnationally (however desirable the goals of such policies) threatens to replunge educational planning into the pit of ethnocentrism. What policies are desirable and how such policies could be introduced depends on the closest respect for enduring differences in state educational systems: The policies and the politics of the possible depend in short upon continued cross-national research in the sociology of education conducted from a theoretical perspective that provides explanatory purchase on it.

REFERENCES

Abercrombie, Nicholas, Stephen Hill, and Bryan Turner. 1980. *The Dominant Ideology Thesis*. London: Allen & Unwin.

Archer, Margaret S. 1979. *Social Origins of Educational Systems*. London: Sage.

———. 1982a. "The Sociology of Educational Systems." In *Sociology: The State of the Art*, edited by T. Bottomore, S. Nowak, and M. Sokolowska. London: Sage.

———., ed. 1982b. *The Sociology of Educational Expansion*. London: Sage.

———. 1982c. "Morphogenesis Versus Structuration." *British Journal of Sociology* 33:4.

Bernstein, Basil. 1971. *Class, Codes and Control*. Vol. 1. *Theoretical Studies Towards a Sociology of Language*. London: Routledge & Kegan Paul.

———. 1975. *Class, Codes and Control*. Vol. 3. *Towards a Theory of Educational Transmissions*. London: Routledge & Kegan Paul.

Bourdieu, Pierre and Jean-Claude Passeron. 1970. *La Reproduction*. Paris: Ed. de Minuit.

Bowles, Samuel. 1977. "Unequal Education and the Reproduction of the Social Division of Labor." In *Power and Ideology in Education*, edited by Jerome Karabel and A. H. Halsey. New York: Oxford University Press.

Buckley, Walter. 1967. *Sociology and Modern Systems Theory*. Englewood Cliffs, NJ: Prentice-Hall.

Johansson, Lena. 1982. "On Latent Functions and Hidden Actors: Some Notes on Functionalist Analysis and Functionalist Explanations, with Special Reference to Educational Systems." In *The Sociology of Educational Expansion*, edited by Margaret S. Archer. London: Sage.

Karabel, Jerome and A. H. Halsey. 1977. *Power and Ideology in Education*. New York: Oxford University Press.

Ringer, Fritz K. 1979. *Education and Society in Modern Europe*. Bloomington: Indiana University Press.

Vaughan, Michalina and Margaret Archer. 1971. *Social Conflict and Educational Change in England and France: 1789-1848*. Cambridge: Cambridge University Press.

11

Alternatives in the Health Area:
Poland in Comparative Perspective

Magdalena Sokolowska
Andrzej Rychard

The purpose of this chapter is to examine the sphere of health needs in Polish society and ways of satisfying these needs. The starting point is the *thesis of the declining role of formal ways of satisfying these needs and the increasing role of alternative ways.* We shall look at the sources of the process, its forms, and also at certain consequences for the social structure.

There is a rich literature regarding alternative ways of satisfying social needs, or the institution of "alternativeness" in general, in various Western countries. This type of analysis is particularly strong in the sociology of medicine and in studies of life-styles and economic systems. Our particular interest is alternative mechanisms operating in a system of centralized political power. The system is one of "officially limited alternativeness"—limited by reason of political doctrine. Yet, these limitations are to a certain degree only formal. For *pragmatic* reasons the system permits and tolerates various kinds of alternativeness in social, economic, and even, to some extent, political life.

We concentrate, in this chapter, on alternative mechanisms operating in the health field. This is a first attempt to shed some light on this phenomenon, to link alternative mechanisms in health care to the broader societal context. We present a general model of "alternativeness" in the health area, a model that is relevant for international comparisons.

263

Although we think that our general model of alternativeness is fairly well developed, in our present formulation we have not developed the framework for comparative analysis very fully. Unfortunately, there are virtually no empirical data enabling international comparisons of alternativeness in the health area. Students of health care in Europe have been rather slow to develop systematic studies of the alternatives, even in Western European countries. In Poland and other Eastern European countries, systematic sociological investigations in the health field are only just beginning to be undertaken; moreover, alternatives to the formal system of health care are only just emerging in Eastern Europe. "East-East" comparative analyses hardly exist and there are no "East-West" comparisons. Scholars from the East and West have recently engaged in a pioneer work to compare their welfare systems, but the health element of welfare systems has not thus far been the object of these studies.[1] Even in those Western European countries where such alternatives as self-help groups are far advanced, there has been a general lack of theory and explanation (World Health Organization [WHO] 1987).

TWO SOURCES OF ALTERNATIVENESS: INEFFECTIVENESS OF THE HEALTH SYSTEM AND GENERAL CONDITIONS

Medical institutions do not fully accomplish their professed goals. Generally speaking, such a goal as "good societal health" is formulated in a too general and all-encompassing way. It is obvious that expecting these goals to be realized exclusively, or even mainly, in the operations of the official health system is a misunderstanding. As is well known, health does not result mainly from medical practice. Nonetheless, the expansion of the definition of health has generated excessive expectations with respect to the medical system. The medical system has been unable to meet such expectations. This is, of course, part of the more general process of the "crisis" of the welfare state. During a meeting of European experts on social development programs, the participants "saw the growth of [new social] initiatives [in the area of welfare] as some kind of response to alleged failures in the operation of welfare states, both in socialist countries and welfare capitalist societies in Western Europe" (*Eurosocial Reports,* 1985, p. 7).

[1.] We have in mind the activities of the International Social Policy Research Unit, Leeds Polytechnic, and the Institute of Sociology, Hungarian Academy of Sciences. Comparative studies of the health element of welfare systems have been presented for the first time at the international conference "Social Policy and Socialism," Leeds, U.K., April 11-14, 1988.

This universal process is reflected in Poland. It seems, though, that there are also some other factors at play in Poland, perhaps specific to this country. Empirical data cited below support this thesis. These are findings from international studies on health care utilization carried out in 12 regions of the world, including the Lodz area[2] (Kohn and White 1976; Rychard 1984). The need for health care, as measured by infant mortality rates, number of ill persons, chronicity, severity of illness, and other measures, is greater in Lodz than in many other areas studied. On the other hand, the volume of health care resources is at the median level, and the organization of health care resources makes utilization difficult. A large problem is the shortage of general practitioners. The result is an overloading of the hospital system with its modest resources (and so, in Lodz, we observed the longest average hospitalization time, which was 23.6 days).

The health system is a part of the larger social, political, and economic system. The ineffectiveness of the state health system is not the only factor necessitating the appearance of alternative solutions. For alternative solutions to arise, certain general conditions must exist.

Among these general conditions, the most prominent feature of the sociopolitical system, its nominal absence of alternatives, becomes— paradoxically—an additional stimulus to the appearance of alternativeness. This thesis is only a paradox on the surface. It is firmly rooted in the theory of organization, mainly the theory of bureaucracy, which posits that the spontaneous appearance of informal arrangements as an unintended effect of pressure for complete formalization is unavoidable. Here one can also cite analyses by Polish sociologists showing, mainly with respect to the economy, how the tendency toward total control gives rise to effects that lead to the loss of real control (e.g., Staniszkis 1980).

There is still another reason specific to Poland for the occurrence of alternative solutions in health care. Socialist ideology has created rather high expectations connected with the protective functions of the state. For example, a new health service was one of the most attractive elements of the socialist system introduced in Poland after 1945. A universal, easily accessible, and free health care system was an enticing slogan that immediately found response in a nation exhausted by the recent war, still remembering the pre-1939 conditions when economic barriers made it difficult for most people to avail themselves of health care. The new model was also favored by many physicians, because, in the Polish historical and cultural traditions, the physician's profession was much less a free profession than in many other countries. It was always strongly

[2] The study covered certain districts of Lodz, the second largest city in Poland, a large center of light industry, and certain suburban regions. Although the data concern the years 1968 to 1969, one can be confident that this picture is relatively stable.

marked by elements of vocation, or even mission, and of public service. The new system provided freedom to the physicians in treating their patients, and to the patients, freedom in availing themselves of medical assistance. All this was immensely attractive.

In the early 1950s, Poland entered a period of accelerated industrialization. This led to an expansion of the industrial health service that was to put into effect the principles of a class-based policy, offering to the workers privileges in the sphere of health care. The then minister of health wrote:

> Without refusing to any social group the [medical] assistance necessary for the preservation of life and avoidance of disabilities, we shall pursue a class-based policy. We have to bear in mind the fact that the large masses of those covered by social insurance are quite heterogeneous. We shall concentrate our means and efforts primarily on health care for the working class and its leading groups, namely miners and large-industry workers. . . . The health service, which formerly used to serve mostly the propertied classes, now has the task of shifting the principal focus of its activity and of providing medical assistance to the working masses who are building the better, socialist future of our country, and above all to the leading working class. (Sztachelski 1950, 1951)

The new form of health care elicited needs and demands that industrial workers had never before experienced. The bringing of medical assistance close to the workers taught them to avail themselves of the health service, but also made them feel all of its defects and shortcomings more and more acutely. Where, several years before, people clamored for a nurse, they now wanted to have a physician; where, not long before, access to a physician seemed to be a final demand, they now felt the need of having several specialists at their disposal. From that point of view, the industrial health service really did carry out its tasks (Sokolowska 1983, pp. 91-92).

The gap between slogans and facts was being more and more clearly felt on a national scale. In sum, "the socialism which people see is compared with the socialism which they would like to see and of whose rightness they are convinced: the clash between reality and the standard gives rise to highly negative opinions here" (Nowak 1979, p. 163).

The final reason for searching for alternative solutions is not universal, to be sure, but neither is it entirely specific to Poland. It is the economic and social crisis that has been going on for several years. It is obvious that this situation has a bearing on the functioning of the health system. We see here a double influence. On the one hand, the crisis means continued underinvestment in the health system and hence its overloading—which, in and of itself, is conducive to the development of alternative solutions. And, on the other hand, alternatives to the formal health system can be welcomed and even encouraged by the state, because this results in a saving of government expenditures.

We mentioned earlier the universal reasons and those specific to Poland for the appearance and development of alternative solutions in the health field. We wish to end this brief description by recapitulating our thesis. We believe that *Poland is subject to the influence of several, multidimensional factors contributing to the appearance and development of alternatives.*

First, one should mention the universal, medical reason. Poland belongs to the Western disease and aging pattern. Polish society has expectations about health care that are similar to those of developed countries. Second, there are economic reasons. Although these are rather universal, nevertheless the extent of these economic limitations differs from one country to another. Third is something that we are inclined to call specific to the Polish scene: This is the very nature of the Polish sociopolitical system. We devote the next part of this chapter to its brief description.

NATURE OF THE SOCIOPOLITICAL
SYSTEM IN POLAND: CRUCIAL POINTS

Never, at any time, did a system completely without alternatives function in Poland. The government that introduced a new political system after World War II refrained from liquidating such institutions as private ownership of land in agriculture and the Roman Catholic church. In the field of politics as well, even though one political party began to play the dominant role, the government nevertheless decided to retain, at least in form, certain institutions of parliamentary democracy. The first group of deviations from the centralized model, then, are those that make allowances for *national historical* traditions.

In addition, we must recognize alternative mechanisms that result from the dynamics and transformations of the new system. Some of them are unintended effects of the effort to achieve total control; others, in turn, result from various counterpressures by the society. The informal sphere that has been described as the "second economy," and also as the "second system of health care," belongs to this group of phenomena.

The subject of "alternativeness" in the socioinstitutional life of socialist societies has attracted the interest of researchers for several years. For example, Besancon (1984) has applied such a concept to the Soviet economy and Sharlet (1984) has used the notion of the "contra-system" in analyzing several spheres of life. Noteworthy among numerous

Polish analyses of this phenomenon is Wnuk-Lipinski's (forthcoming) distinguishing of three kinds of "dualities"—in the political, economic, and sociocultural spheres.[3]

The common feature of these conceptions is the thesis that there is a certain variety of ways of satisfying various needs. This diversity comes from the ineffectiveness of official mechanisms in satisfying those needs (Sharlet 1984; Koralewicz-Zebik and Wnuk-Lipinski 1986; Rychard 1986; Adamski 1985).

One of the most promising *concepts* is Hankiss's idea of the "second society." His theory concerns Hungary—which is why it can be useful for analyzing the situation not only of Poland but also of socialist countries more generally. According to Hankiss (1986) there are in Hungary now four forms of social organization: a first society (in both its formal and its informal sphere), a second society, and an alternative society. The main difference between the second society and the alternative society is that the second society is transitory: it retains none of the features of the first society, but it does not *yet* contain some of the distinctive features of the alternative society.

The problem of alternatives is to some extent universal, not only for Western countries but also for socialist countries, which seem at first glance to have very centralized and hierarchical structures. The difference between Western and Eastern alternativeness is that Western alternative mechanisms can be more readily adapted to the official, established institutions than can Eastern mechanisms. The source of this difference seems to be ideological: it lies in a greater tolerance for pluralism in the official ideology of Western countries.

The attitude of state or official systems to these alternatives varies considerably. Focusing again on Poland, we can say that the official attitude is one of ambivalence. There are conflicting reasons for this: doctrinal and pragmatic. For doctrinal reasons, the state cannot relinquish its aim to attain a monopoly of control over various spheres of life. Hence, it should have a rather negative attitude toward alternative solutions. On the other hand, for pragmatic reasons it is necessary to increase the effectiveness of centralized official mechanisms. This gives rise to a

[3.] Various kinds of alternatives have been analyzed by scholars of life-styles (e.g., Sicinski 1983, 1985) and also by sociologists dealing with ways of reacting to the economic crisis (Nowak 1984), to processes of accommodation (e.g., individual and collective strategies for survival distinguished by Marody 1985), the concept of innovative accommodation (Turski 1983), and the typology of reactions to external compulsion (Koralewicz-Zebik 1983). We are here mainly interested in mechanisms of *organizational* alternativeness. Following Mrela (1984), we assume that this is a problem of the "suitability of the repertoire of organizations vis-a-vis the repertoire of interests appearing in the society" (Mrela 1984, p. 6).

tolerant attitude toward some deviations from inflexible rules—toward informality. As scholars note (e.g., Staniszkis 1984; Marody 1985), the informalities of, for example, the second economy, perform stabilizing functions for the system. Hence, official tolerance is a rational reaction. Some of the deviations from inflexible rules are even consciously built into the system by the state. Staniszkis calls this a peculiarly "authoritative system" (see also Iwanowska, Federowicz, and Zukowski 1986).

The 1980s are witness to a rapidly changing situation in such socialist countries as Poland, Hungary, China, and the Soviet Union. These ongoing changes produce a new type of alternativeness, understood as attempts at democratization and decentralization. This means that the notion of alternativeness may refer not only to informal social forces but also to officially undertaken (but still not really implemented) reforms.

Hence, in sum, reactions of the state to alternative solutions are distributed along a continuum from certain doctrinal obligations to certain necessities of a pragmatic nature. We believe that this duality or ambivalence is one of the characteristic features of the institutional system, not only in Poland but also in other countries.[4]

The argument presented in the first two parts of this chapter makes it possible for us to formulate a general model that describes the conditions under which alternative mechanisms for the satisfaction of health needs arise. We present this model in a diagram that attempts to recapitulate our argument thus far (see Figure 11.1).

The essence of our argument is the thesis that only the combined influence of all of the factors in the diagram can cause the appearance and the development of alternatives in the system of health care. The relative importance of these factors differs from one socialist society to another. For example, in Poland there is a kind of "institutional tradition" in the area of alternativeness. We mean here the role of private agriculture and the position of the Roman Catholic church. These are independent institutions—quite unique in socialist countries. This tradition certainly contributed to the emergence of mass organization (*Solidarnosc*). Because there was no such tradition in any other socialist country, the emergence of alternativeness in these countries had to rely on initiatives stemming from the system itself. We can mention here the economic reform policy in Hungary, which was implemented by the Communist party. The only

[4.] In *Eurosocial Reports* (1985, no. 25), "European Experts Meeting on Established Social Services Versus New Social Initiatives," it is reported that one of the researchers called attention to ambivalence on the part of the established services: "sometimes seeing them [new initiatives] as positive in terms of community competence and self-reliance; but sometimes viewing them with suspicion because the initiatives do not always fit very well within the framework of official regulations and arrangement for social welfare."

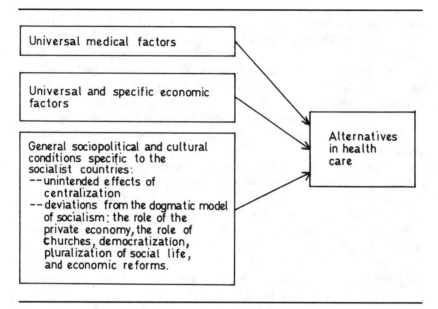

Figure 11.1: Factors Influencing the Development of Alternatives in Health Care in the Socialist Countries

extrasystemic alternativeness in most of the socialist countries was small-scale initiatives in the areas of human rights, ecology, and welfare. Poland is the only socialist country in which all the factors of alternativeness are at play: "the reforms from above," mass movements "from below," and the importance of historical and cultural heritage. Nevertheless, whatever the local specificities, the main processes occurring in the Eastern European countries are similar. All of them point to the opening up of the system.

A PRELIMINARY TYPOLOGY OF THE ALTERNATIVES IN POLAND

According to our analyses thus far, the mechanisms of alternativeness are not specific to Poland. Thus we must develop a theoretical rationale for *studying* this phenomenon cross-nationally. According to Swinnen (1986, p. 13), it is possible to analyze alternativeness in the *economic* area from three perspectives: segmentation theories (dual labor market theories), dual economy theories (distinguishing the formal and informal parts of the economy), and "the democratic socialist alternative" (with the idea of "useful work" as a central concept). Other theoretical typologies are also possibly useful for specific types of alternatives, for example, the concept of the "patron-client relationship" in the area of political life or the theories of alternative life-styles in the area of "everyday life." There are two important features of all these theories:

(1) They are limited to specific social spheres (the economy, politics, and so on).
(2) These theories are at the same time universal in the sense that they can be adapted for interpreting *alternativeness* both in socialist and in capitalist societies.

Among many typologies of the "new social initiatives," that is, alternative ways of coping with social problems, the most interesting seem to be those in which the authors explicitly define the theoretical criteria for their typologies. For example, Swinnen (1986) asserts that one of the most important dimensions of the new Dutch initiatives in local economic development is their horizontal versus vertical policy. The main difference between these two forms seems to be the emphasis on self-help ideology in the first versus the emphasis on defense against "bureaucracy" in the second. In this typology, internal structures and modes of activity are the main factors. In our schema, other factors are more important: these are the relations of the alternative mechanisms with the official, state-owned health system.

It does seem, though, that Swinnen's approach is relevant to our purposes, albeit from a slightly different point of view. In Poland we have to approach the issues more broadly than he does, because we must deal with the general question of highly centralized and bureaucratic power, as against local, democratic power. The issues here have been addressed systematically for the first time by *Solidarnosc*. Of course, these issues relate to health. Otherwise, slogans like "community health," "community participation," and the like make no sense.[5]

Our analysis here is not addressed to the detailed description, or to the characteristics of the specific forms, of alternatives in health in Poland. Our intention instead is to formulate some more general questions. We should first define the types of alternatives that we are discussing. We

---

[5.] These slogans are nevertheless frequently used by representatives of the socialist countries, for example, in their contacts with the World Health Organization.

have in mind here mechanisms alternative to the official health system, which predominates in Poland.[6]

The typology of alternative ways of satisfying health needs that we suggest here is based on two criteria. First, the criterion of formality versus informality of a given solution: By "formal" we mean such solutions, which although different from state health care, are nevertheless recognized and legitimized by the state. Second, the criterion distinguishing alternative solutions within the system from those outside the system: The first type consists of officially recognized private medical cooperatives; the second type consists of self-help groups, healers, or activities under the auspices of the Roman Catholic church. Such activity is specific to Poland. Unfortunately, we do not know how the Polish situation compares to that of the other socialist countries. Empirical comparative studies are badly needed.

We present our typology in Figure 11.2.

We have provided typical examples for each category. Our typology is a simplification of the phenomena in the sense that, in principle, mixed types of solutions are the most frequent. More important than including certain phenomena of particular types is to consider the relationships among the four types and between all four types and the official health system. We can assume that all four types are required by each other and by the society. We have no empirical data, but it is safe to assume that there are certain links between all four types of alternative institutions, as well as between each of them and the official system. This four-part whole is dynamic: in certain periods some solutions are informal and beyond the system; at other times, they are incorporated within the system.

It is safe to say that each of the four types has its own relationship with the official health system. There is a continuum of the "involvement" of each of them with the official system. Some of them penetrate the system almost completely (private medical practice). Others have far-reaching independence.

[6.] According to data obtained by Sokolowska and Moskalewicz, the official health system of Poland includes 95% of the country's health personnel, resources, and services. This 95% "contains" within it, however, many alternatives and informalities. There are alternatives that are accessible to citizens in general. In addition, there are alternatives of another kind. There is an official system of health care for persons in certain positions on the so-called nomenclature list. There are also separate health care systems for employees of particular branches of the economy. These are the counterparts of special sectors of the economy (e.g., Besancon 1984; Wnuk-Lipinski forthcoming). We omit them from our analysis because of their elitist character. They are extremely important as a feature of the *system*, but they are not alternatives available to *society* as a whole, which is the subject of our analysis. Nor do we deal with the family, which in all societies is a major source of care for the chronically ill, the aged, and disabled family members.

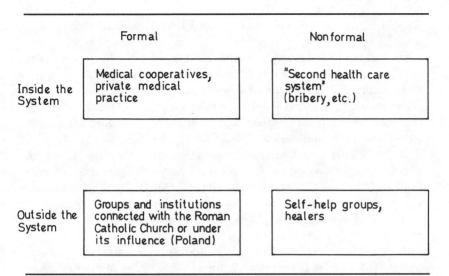

Figure 11.2: A Typology of Alternative Ways of Satisfying Health Needs: The Case of the Socialist Countries

When analyzing the relations between alternative mechanisms and official systems, we face the problem of delineating the main structural differences between these entities. According to some Western authors, the main differences between formal services and the new informal initiatives should be analyzed in the following terms: explicitness of definition of functions; universality (formal services are more universal); limits of period of activity (formal services are unlimited); hierarchical organization; and based on taxation versus other sources of financing (*Eurosocial Reports,* 1985, p. 17).[7]

The usefulness of our typology is that it enables us to define more precisely the attitude of the state toward alternative solutions. This depends on which of the four alternatives we are dealing with, and on the political and economic situation. We can hypothesize that in periods of economic crisis combined with relative political stability, the state tends to tolerate external solutions—both formal and informal. During a period of political tensions combined with economic crisis, however, tolerance of alternativeness declines. Under these circumstances, the authorities do not believe that the economic gains from acceptance of alternativeness provide adequate compensation for the political costs—a certain loss of monopoly of control. It seems that in Poland we still have the former

[7.] These distinctions are based on an international discussion in which new social initiatives in Western and some socialist countries were presented.

situation: The state has to tolerate various kinds of alternatives, although it uses a specific strategy regarding them, namely, attempting to exercise control without bearing any financial responsibility. Sometimes, promises of financial help can be a way of making these alternatives dependent on state structures. This is a well-known phenomenon, not only in Poland.[8]

We should initially distinguish the following types of relations between the state-owned health system and alternative solutions: antagonism, coexistence, cooperation, and containment (partly based on Sharlet 1984, p. 145).[9] We believe that the relations between the state system and alternative solutions within the system are part of the process of cooperation or of "sponging," but relations with external solutions are more often antagonistic. The antagonism of these relations is influenced, in an important way, by conflicts of this type being more probable, the greater the extent to which alternative solutions become a *substitute* for "old" solutions. Conflict is avoided when alternative solutions are *complementary* to the existing ones (*Eurosocial Reports,* 1985, p. 28). We believe, however, that this postulate can be fulfilled only in the case of "controlled alternatives," that is, alternatives that are in a certain sense created by the state. The alternatives that seem to be dominant in Poland are often of a substitute character.

From this point of view, it is useful to compare some Polish and Hungarian institutions. There is a new type of nonprofit cooperative in Hungary, created to cope with some everyday problems of the elderly, children, and families "which cannot be dealt with either by the families themselves or by the established services" (*Eurosocial Reports,* 1985, p. 25). These cooperatives (called "LARES") do work that is essentially nonprofessional. As the authors of the report stress: "Enterprises like LARES cannot and should not be seen as potential substitutes for state services provided by paid, professional staff" (*Eurosocial Reports,* 1985, p. 26). We do not know how widespread the use of this complementary and nonsubstituting mechanism of activity is in Hungary. Nor do we have systematic knowledge about such mechanisms in Poland. Nevertheless, it is possible to hypothesize that, in Poland, alternative institutions are more often a kind of substitute for the "official" institutions than is the case in Hungary. Differences in the effectiveness of economic and social welfare systems between Poland and Hungary seem to be one of the explanatory factors.

[8.] *Eurosocial Reports* (1985, no. 15, Vienna): "Financial support for a new initiative from public funds is often seen as constraining."

[9.] Generally speaking, antagonism in the health sphere is much milder than in the political sphere.

The situation in Poland with respect to the "opening up" of the formal system, however, is far from stable. Especially in recent years (if not months), we are witnessing rapid changes in all areas. These changes involve politics, the economy, culture, education, and also health.

Most analyses of these issues have been addressed to the economy (Rychard 1987a). We think, though, that there are types of alternatives in health care that are similar to those in the economy. It can be observed generally that our political system more readily tolerates those alternative solutions that are located in the peripheries of the system, while the nature of the system itself remains intact. Staniszkis (1987) asserts that these "peripheric" changes stabilize the "core" of the system and that privatization outside the state system is easier than privatization inside the system. In our opinion, all types of changes at the peripheries or outside of the system are more tolerable for the power elite than are changes of the system itself. For example, it is much easier to establish small private firms than to reform the state-owned economic sector in any basic way. We cannot rule out, however, the possibility that in the future the growing number, diversity, and quality of the "peripheral" institutions will change the nature of the core of the system. The influence of extrasystemic changes on the core of the system is not exclusively a Polish phenomenon. Such processes are present also in the other socialist countries. The most important process is that many innovative firms are located outside the state-owned economic sector but have an impact on that sector (Iwanowska 1988). The "innovation" consists not only in the location of these industries but also in the type of industry—which is often electronics.

There have recently been interesting events occurring in the Polish economy, which signify the growing importance of an individualistic, market orientation resembling—we would say—early capitalistic values. At the same time, there has been some decrease in a "socialized" orientation, such as workers' councils, cooperatives, and self-governments. It is striking that these changes stem from such disparate sources as the government and independent oppositional circles (Rychard 1987a).

In the area of welfare and health, new slogans have emerged, slogans such as "reprivatization." These slogans correspond precisely to those used in Western European countries. For example, there are more and more advertisements in the daily press offering private (paid for out-of-pocket) home visits of medical specialists, home nursing care, and even special examinations, such as EKG. There are also, however, powerful hindrances to getting approval for foundations that could alleviate the health burden of the society. This is a good illustration of the thesis that our political system tolerates changes on the peripheries more readily than at the "core" and—paradoxically—changes that are more conservative (privatization) than those that are "socially oriented."

Changes in the socialist countries are occurring very rapidly. Our typology (Figure 11.2) distinguishes four elements and emphasizes the borderlines between them; but the borderlines are becoming less accentuated and the interconnections among all four elements are increasing rapidly. These changes, of course, are not only occurring in Poland. The dominant role of the state sector is decreasing in the socialist countries, while the role of nonstate institutions is increasing. According to Szalai (1988), who describes the situation in Hungary, one can say that we are witnessing the "dead end" of the postwar period in real socialism. Szalai also stresses the role of emerging civic initiatives around health services.

CONCLUSION

Do alternative solutions in health care have an elitist or egalitarian influence on the society? Bednarski (1984) addressed this problem with respect to the "second economy" in Poland. He tends to believe that the second economy has an elitist function, because not everyone can take advantage of it. We believe that, in the case of alternative ways of satisfying health needs, the matter is somewhat different. Most alternatives result from the inefficiency of the state health system. Can we assume that these largely social reactions will have exclusively elitist effects on the society? The diversity of these forms is so great that it would be hard to find a family in Poland that does not have recourse to at least one of these alternatives.[10] To be sure, not all of the alternatives are equally accessible to everyone, but let us not forget that the official health system itself often intensifies social inequalities (e.g., the previously mentioned branch enclaves). Hence, one can hardly speak of alternative ways of satisfying health needs as unequivocally and uniquely elitist. This, of course, does not mean that alternative solutions are always free from limitations and weaknesses of several types.

They are not universally available, in terms either of every disease or of every country or local area. Not everyone, in any case, finds them to be an appropriate solution to his or her particular needs for care. They should be viewed as an important complement of existing systems of health and social care and in no way a substitute for them. (WHO 1987)

[10.] We refer not only to health but to welfare in general.

Although the quoted opinion was written specifically with respect to self-help groups, we think that it is pertinent to all alternatives in the health area. Above all, alternative mechanisms concentrate mainly on individual health and do not cover group health at various levels, from micro to macro. The development of these mechanisms, both unavoidable and appreciated, cannot reduce the responsibility of national governments in the West and in the East for the health of their societies.

REFERENCES

Adamski, Wladyslaw. 1985. "Aspiracje—interesy—konflikt" [Aspirations—Interests—Conflict]. *Studia Socjologiczne* 2.

Bednarski, M. 1984. "Drugi obieg" [Second Economy]. *Zycie Gospodarcze* 35.

Besancon, Alain. 1984. *Anatomia widma* [Anatomy of Specter]. Warszawa: Krag.

Eurosocial Reports. 1985. "European Experts Meeting on Established Social Services Versus New Social Initiatives." No. 25.

Hankiss, Elmer. 1986. *Pulapki spoleczne* [Social Traps]. Warsaw.

Iwanowska, Anna. 1988. "Prywatni modernizatorzy panstwowego sektora gospodarki" [Private Modernizers of the State Economy]. Paper presented at the Polish Sociological Association Conference "Reform and Alternatives," Warsaw, June 9-10.

Iwanowska, Anna, M. Federowicz, and T. Zukowski. 1986. "Rynek—demokracja—swiadczenia wzajemne" [Market—Democracy—Reciprocal Services]. (Mimeo).

Kohn, Robert and Kerr L. White. 1976. *Health Care—An International Study.* Oxford: Pergamon.

Koralewicz-Zebik, Jadwiga. 1983. "Postawy wobec zewnetrznego przymusu" [Attitudes Toward External Compulsion]. In *Styl zycia, obyczaje, ethos w Polsce lat 70-tych,* edited by Andrzej Sicinski. Instytut Filozofii i Socjologii PAN.

Koralewicz-Zebik, Jadwiga and Edmund Wnuk-Lipinski. 1986. "Wizje spoleczenstwa, zroznicowan i nierownosci w swiadomosci spolecznej" [Visions of Society, Social Differences and Inequalities in Social Consciousness]. (Mimeo).

Marody, Miroslawa. 1985. "Sens zbiorowy a stabilnosc ladu spolecznego" [Collective Sense and Stability of Social Order]. (Mimeo).

Mrela, Kazimierz. 1984. "Lad spoleczny i tozsamosc organizacji: rzeczywistosc organizacyjna socjalizmu realnego" [Social Order and the Identity of Organizations: Organizational Reality of the Real Socialism]. (Mimeo).

Munday, Brian. 1984. "European Expert Meeting on Established Social Services Versus New Social Initiatives—Conflict, Change and Cooperation." *Eurosocial Reports* (Vienna) no. 25.

Nowak, Stefan. 1979. "System wartosci spoleczenstwa polskiego" [Value System of the Polish Society]. *Studia Socjologiczne* 4.

———. 1984. "Poslawy wartosci i aspiracje spoleczenslwa polskiego" [Attitudes, Values, and Aspirations of the Polish Society]. In *Spoleczenslwo polskie czasu kryzysu.* University of Warsaw, Instytut Socjologii.

Rychard, Andrzej. 1984. "The Health Care System in Poland: The Case of Lodz as Compared with Foreign Regions: A Secondary Analysis." *Social Science and Medicine* 19(8).

——— 1986. "Poza legitymizacja systemu: Procesy przystosowawcze w Polsce lat 80" [Beyond the System's Legitimacy: Adaptation Process in Poland of the 80's]. (Mimeo).

————. 1987a. "Wladza i interesy w gospodarce polskiej u progu lat 80" [Power and Interests in Polish Economy in the Beginning of the 80's]. Warszawa: Uniwersytet Warszawski.

————. 1987b. "Granice reform gospodarki" [Limits to Economic Reforms]. (Mimeo).

Sharlet, R. 1984. "Dissent and the 'Contra-System' in the Soviet Union." In *The Soviet Union in the 80's,* Vol. 35, no. 3, edited by E. P. Hoffman. New York: Academy of Political Sciences.

Sicinski, Andrzej. 1983. *Styl zycia, obyczaje, ethos w Polsce lat 70 z perspektywy roku 1981* [Life Styles, Customs, Ethos in Poland in the 70's from the Perspective of 1981]. Instytut Filozofii i Socjologii, Polska Akademia Nauk.

————. 1985. "Style zycia miejskiego w Polsce" [Urban Life Styles in Poland]. (Mimeo).

Sokolowska, Magdalena. 1983. "Health as an Issue in the Workers' Campaign." *Sisyphus* 3.

Sokolowska, Magdalena and Bozena Moskalewicz. 1987. "Health Sector Structures: The Case of Poland." *Social Science and Medicine* 14(9).

Staniszkis, Jadwiga. 1980. "Systemowe uwarunkowania funkcjonowania przedsiebiorstwa przemyslowego" [The System Determinants of the Functioning of the Industrial Enterprise]. *Przeglad Socjologiczny* 32.

————. 1984. "Racjonalnosc—wlasnosc—dynamika" [Rationality—Property—Dynamic]. In *Przyjaciel Nauk* 1-2.

————. 1987. "Dynamika uzaleznienia" [Dynamics of Dependency]. *Kontakt* 65(September).

Swinnen, Hugo. 1986. "Dutch situation of LEIs: Theoretical Background for Local Economic Development." *Eurosocial Reports* nos. 43-44.

Szalai, Julia. 1988. "Social Crisis and Reform Alternatives." Paper prepared for the international conference "Social Policy and Socialism," Leeds, U.K., April 11-14.

Sztachelski, Jerzy. 1950. "Plan 6-letni w sluzbie zdrowia" [The 6-Year Plan in the Service of Public Health]. *Zdrowie Publiczne* 9/12.

————. 1951. "Wytyczne pracy sluzby zdrowia na 1951 rok" [Guidelines for the Functioning of the Health Service in 1951]. *Sluzba Zdrowia* 11/12.

Turski, Ryszard. 1983. "Kryzys struktury spolecznej" [Crisis of the Social Structure]. In *Polityka spoleczna a struktury spoleczenstwa polskiego.* Polskie Towarzystwo Ekonomiczne.

Wnuk-Lipinski, Edmund. Forthcoming. "Inequalities and Social Crisis." *Sisyphus* 5.

World Health Organization. 1987. *Self-Help and Chronic Disease* (Report on a Workshop). Leuven: WHO.

12

Ethnicity, Immigration, and Cultural Pluralism: India and the United States of America

T. K. Oommen

> . . . social facts vary with the social system of which they form a part; they cannot be understood when detached from it. This is why two facts which come from two different societies cannot be profitably compared merely because they seem to resemble each other; it is necessary that these societies themselves resemble each other, that is to say, that they be only varieties of the same species. The comparative method would be impossible if social types did not exist, and it cannot be usefully applied except within a single type. What errors have not been committed for having neglected this percept! (Durkheim [1912] 1965, pp. 113-14)

India and the United States of America, the two biggest democracies of the world, together account for nearly one-fourth of humanity. The diversities of their populations—physical, economic, cultural—too are staggering. Pundits of academia would hesitate to attempt a comparative analysis of these two mega societies within the limited space permissible in a research paper. And yet, I propose to do precisely that in spite of the obvious risks involved in the effort. My justification is that it could be perhaps more gratifying to limp on the main road rather than to run on the side lane. But I should hasten to add that my purpose is not simply to provide a "thick description" of the two societies.

AUTHOR'S NOTE: *I thank Professors Melvin Kohn, Martin Albrow, B. K. Srivastava, and Narindar Singh for their comments on earlier versions of this chapter. The conventional disclaimer holds.*

Notwithstanding the persisting proliferation of conceptual clarifications on the theme under discussion (for two recent examples, see Riggs
1986, pp. 111-23; Richmond 1987, pp. 3-18), it is necessary to begin by
identifying the relevant conceptual kit to understand the specific situations of the two countries. Once again, I will not indulge in an elaborate
conceptual entourage but only attempt to unfold the historicity of the
concerned concepts. Finally, an effort will be made to specify the conditions that facilitate the emergence and continuance of cultural pluralism
under differing historical and socioeconomic situations. In so doing, the
possibility of differing conceptualizations and practices of cultural
pluralism will be hinted at. In sum, my exercise is neither empirical nor
theoretical as such but an effort to establish *contact* between concepts and
data from different contexts, so as to chisel the former with the aid of the
latter.

NATION, STATE, AND ETHNICITY:
HISTORICITY OF CONCEPTS

The concept of ethnicity is in wide currency in social science writings.
In spite of this, I suggest that it is not entirely suited or apt enough to
capture the situation obtaining in most of the old societies that became
new nations recently, of which India is a prime example. But the concept
seems to be particularly appropriate to comprehend the empirical reality
prevalent in the new nations emerging out of new societies, the United
States being a significant example. In fact, ethnicity is a new concept and
an American coinage at that. Therefore, it is not surprising that the
concept is most widely accepted and used in the United States. As Yancey
et al. (1976, p. 401) correctly observe: "Ethnicity may have relatively
little to do with Europe, Asia or Africa, but much more to do with the
requirements of survival and the structure of opportunity in this country."
But its spread to and currency in other parts of the world as a conceptual
tool is more an indication of the influence of American social science
rather than its appropriateness to comprehend the nature of reality in those
regions and countries.

Let me begin by specifying the *contexts* out of which the three concepts—nation, state, and ethnicity—crucial for the present discussion
have emanated. I must hasten to add that I do not intend to define these
concepts but only to unfold their historicity. In the hoary past there were
no "states" in the modern sense of the term; indeed, stateless societies
continue to exist even today. Closed societies and immobile populations
of the past could not have produced ethnicity precisely because it is a
product of interaction with and awareness of "other cultures." Human

societies were then constituted into "nations" in the European sense of the term. A "nation" is "a people, a folk, held together by some or all of such more or less immutable characteristics as common descent, territory, history, language, religion, way of life, or other attributes that members of a group have from birth onward" (Petersen 1975, p. 181).

It is clear that the concept of the nation was essentially cultural in content and it encapsulated a variety of attributes; nationhood was a product of the conjoint existence and interaction of these attributes. But as nations started to constitute themselves as states, as political entities, in Western Europe—following the maxim, one nation, one state—a new sociopolitical formation emerged and the hyphenated term "nation-state" came into vogue. It is often forgotten that the nation-state implies a process, however, and it is possible and historically true that the process can even be reversed. Not only that a nation can be constituted into a state, but a state can dismantle and destroy nations. Further, a state can *create* a new nation. It seems, the eclipse of the nation as a cultural entity is almost complete and it has invariably come to mean a political entity. Yet, it is necessary to place the notion in its historical context so as to understand the difference between nation and ethnicity.

While a nation may constitute itself into a state, the state covers an immense variety of political structures—kingdoms, empires, city states, principalities, republics, federations. And state only implies establishing successful claim within a territory, which gives it the monopoly of legitimized use of physical force (Weber 1947). Keeping these considerations in mind, it would be helpful to list the varieties of situations represented by nation-states (or state-nations?) in the world today.

(1) One-nation, one-state: Although this is an ideal and even a possibility, there is hardly any case of such a pure type. Japan, however, could be cited as an example.

(2) Parts of different nations come to constitute a state for geopolitical reasons (e.g., Switzerland).

(3) One nation is divided into two (it could be more) states for ideological reasons (e.g., Germany, Korea).

(4) Part of a nation is constituted into one sovereign state and the remaining part is attached or affiliated to another sovereign state (e.g., Bangladesh and West Bengal in India).

(5) A nation may be divided between two sovereign states and constitute parts of them along with other nations (e.g., Indian Punjab and Pakistan Punjab).

(6) A number of nations come to constitute a state (e.g., India, the Soviet Union).

(7) A set of migrants drawn from a multiplicity of nations constitute a state (e.g., the United States).

It is clear, then, that state and nation need not be coterminous. And the term "nation" connotes society in the sense in which sociologists use the term. But the difficulty arises (in a multination state) when one of the constituent units is designated as a nation by the people concerned with the intention of establishing a state. For example, in India, if one were to speak of Tamil, Kashmiri, Sikh, or Naga society, there is, and perhaps there can be, no objection. But the moment the term "nation" is invoked to refer to these societies, considerable alarm is expressed because it is believed to be a threat to the territorial integrity of the Indian state and change of citizenship status to a section of its population. And those who assign the label "nation" to their "society" invariably imply precisely this.

I would like to suggest, however, that once a multinational or polyethnic state emerges and consolidates, it becomes a reality-in-itself. The coexistence and interaction between the different nations or ethnic groups produce certain emergent properties, which gives a new meaning and a collective self-definition to the constituent units. That is, just as state can dismantle or divide nations, as I have noted above, it can also weld and fuse together different nations as in India or different ethnic groups as in the United States. Mega societies such as India and the United States are products of such historical processes; they are societies-in-the-making.

Ethnicity emerged through interaction between different peoples; it is a product of conquest, colonization, and immigration. That is, ethnicity implies dislocation from one's *original* country, region, or nation, that is, homeland. In contrast, the nation inevitably alludes to a people belonging to a specific territory whose claim to political authority over it is perceived as legitimate. Ideally, the nation fuses three dimensions: territory, culture, and citizenship. That a whole nation can be uprooted from its territory and rendered into an *ethnie* (a people without a common territory and citizenship) only points to the historical process and possibility of one category being transformed into another. When this happens in the immediate temporal vicinity we are horrified and perturbed. But when it is a matter of the hoary past we are reconciled and undisturbed.

It is my contention that it is the rupture between territory and other primordial attributes that creates ethnicity. What deserves our attention is the process through which a nation dissolves into an ethnic group and an ethnie crystallizes into a nation. This is so because an ethnie endowed with legitimate political authority over a territory leads to the formation of a nation-state. Thus the link between nation, ethnicity, and state is clear. A few instances will clarify the position.

The *native* Fijians are not an ethnic category but a nation, even as they are a demographic and political minority. The immigrants into Fiji are an ethnic category, notwithstanding their dominant position in some contexts. If the natives are asserting their national status and resisting *eth-*

nification, the immigrants are struggling to transform their ethnic status into a national one. In contrast, both Singhala Buddhists and Tamil Hindus of Sri Lanka claim that they are the initial immigrants into the island. The fact that both are of Indian origin does not in any way lessen the intensity of conflicts and claims; they are competing nations in an alien territory. Through diaspora the Jews have been transformed into an ethnic category all over the world. But the Zionist movement was nationalist, in that it was an attempt to affirm and create an accredited homeland for Jews so that ethnic Jews are transformed into a nation. To argue that there are ethnic divisions among the Jews of the reconstituted Israel is to ignore the historical process to which they are subjected. Jewish ethnicity is a function of diaspora; it emerged in different parts of the world under differing existential conditions.

Most discussions of ethnicity focus on a wide variety of attributes of ethnic groups—religion, sect, language, region, caste, race, color, culture, and so on. These attributes singly or in different combinations are used to define ethnic groups. While it is widely acknowledged that the saliency of these attributes varies under different circumstances, rarely does one come across any discussion and specification of the crucial or independent variable. Methodologically it is not even possible to specify the crucial attribute because what is crucial is determined by the context. Therefore, it is not so much the attributes of ethnicity that are important, but the *property of the situation* in which they obtain and operate. No particular attribute of ethnicity can assume stable importance, which varies with historical circumstances and existential conditions. In contrast, the concepts of homeland and territory are crucial in the case of a nation. Even if all other attributes are present together, a nation does not come into being unless it establishes legitimate claim over a territory, which in turn provides it with the potential of state formation. The *ethnification* of a nation takes place precisely when it does not have the resources for state formation, namely, a homeland and legitimate political authority over it. What I am suggesting is that ethnie, nation, and state should be viewed in a processual relationship. When an ethnie acquires legitimate claim over a territory, it becomes a nation, and when a nation secures political jurisdiction, it becomes a state. Pursuant to this, to be an ethnic group is to operate *within* a nation-state or to be dispersed into several of them. By the same token, to be an ethnie is to be in the periphery, and to be a nation is to be in the center of the polity. If a state has different nations in it, that state will and should have multiple cultural centers.

In the 1950s and 1960s only minorities and the economically deprived and politically powerless groups were labeled as "ethnics." But once these groups started perceiving this label as a stigma or at best a pejorative and giving expression to their feelings, analysts readily expanded the connotation of the term so as to include "all the groups of a society characterized by a distinct sense of differences owing to culture and descent" (Glazer and Moynihan 1975, p. 4). This clever device has extended semantic equality to all but has also caused severe social inequality to be concealed insofar as it has obliterated the distinction between the majority and the minority, the dominant and the dominated. To distinguish groups based on culture and descent is simply to acknowledge differences among them. But if groups use these differences so as to bolster their perceptions of superiority and to exercise power and authority over other groups, they create contentious issues. Similarly, if ethnicity imparts deprivation and invests a collectivity with stigma, it becomes a liability. Therefore, it is useful to distinguish between minorities and ethnics as Vincent (1974, pp. 375-79) does. An ethnic group is a collectivity that shares common culture, identities, and behaviors. In contrast, a minority group is one whose members are subjected to discrimination and are victims of prejudice by others in society, particularly by a dominant group.

The terms "ethnic" and "ethnicity" are most favored and popular in the United States, as they should be, because they aptly capture and convey the social situation there; the United States is a conglomeration of varieties of people "uprooted" from different nations. But the equivalent concepts that are suited to describe the overall situation in Europe are nation and nationality, given the strong attachment people have to their homelands. This is equally true of Asia, although, of course, these terms are scarcely used. And this reluctance should be understood in terms of the prevailing situation in Asian countries. Most Asian states encapsulate within them several nations and the process of state formation is not yet complete and stable largely because of their multinational composition. Therefore, to assert one's identity in national terms is to spell danger to the state. These identities are delegitimized to uphold the integrity of the state (Oommen 1986a, pp. 107-28). Thus, identity assertions based on religion, language, region, tribe, and the like are viewed as "communal," "parochial," even "antinational."

The point I want to make is that all concepts that are intended to describe and explain social reality have emerged out of specific contexts. To assume that they have universal validity is to ignore their historicity; to decontextualize them is to drain them of their meaning and content. Further, social science concepts often entwine collective conscience and they need to articulate group sentiments. Concepts such as ethnicity, nationality, communalism, and so on are expressions of the collective conscience of particular people in specific historical contexts. The moment we recognize the historicity of social science concepts, we can steer clear of a lot of muddle and confusion.

THE UNITED STATES AND INDIA:
PROFILES OF TWO MEGA SOCIETIES

The society of the United States, the oldest of the new states, has only a short history of 500 years counting from the initial European intrusion in the late fifteenth century; it is a new society. In contrast, India, one of the oldest societies of the world with a history of 5000 years, is a fledgling state as it emerged just forty years ago. If the United States is one of the most developed countries of the First World, India threatens to slide back into the Fourth World from its present precarious position on the edge of the Third World. Admittedly, the problems of the two countries vary on numerous counts. And yet they are amenable to comparative analysis for two reasons. First, both countries belong to the same type of political system—parliamentary democracy—variations in their content and style of operations notwithstanding. Second, both the societies are multicultural and are characterized by stupendous cultural variety. The present task is to attempt a general profile of the two countries so as to highlight the nature of cultural pluralisms that obtain in them and to understand how they are perceived and managed. As a prelude to this, it is necessary to recall, albeit briefly, the process through which the two societies came to be constituted.

The society in the United States is formed through the twin processes of *extermination* of the native population (see Porter 1979) and *accretion* by successive waves of immigrants (Handlin 1951). In the contemporary United States, literally numerous collectivities are labeled as ethnics. But yet, consensus seems to be emerging that there are a few major ethnic clusters, viewed in terms of the structure of deprivation and patterns of interaction (see, for example, Yancey et al. 1985, pp. 94-116). These ethnic clusters are Native Americans, Blacks, Hispanics, Asian Americans, Jews, and Whites.

Three points may be noted about this categorization. First, it has no common basis; several factors—physical type, religion, national origin, region—are invoked to arrive at different clusters. Second, several categories are merged together, ignoring specific identities. For example, some 500 tribes are lumped together in the category of Native American; three different major national groups—Mexicans, Puerto Ricans, Cubans—constitute Hispanics. Asian Americans can be easily disaggregated into two major categories—the Browns from South Asia and the Yellows from East Asia. Third, the categorization does not reveal the distinction between the privileged ethnics and the deprived ethnics—the minorities. While Native Americans, Blacks, and Hispanics are clearly minorities, the Jews have already become ethnics and Asian Americans seem to be well on the road to achieving ethnic status. In portraying the ethnic profile of the United States, I shall concentrate mainly on the "minorities" precisely because the label "ethnic" does not adequately capture their existential conditions.

The earliest settlers, the Red Indians, latterly referred to as American Indians and currently labeled as Native Americans, have been gradually displaced from most of their original territory. Currently they constitute less than 1% of the total American population. Of these, nearly 50% live in reservations meant for them, the remaining being either "integrated" with others living in mixed localities or persisting as "cultural islands" in agency towns. The 260 reservations with a mere 750,000 persons are self-governed entities as they are outside the purview of the U.S. Constitution. The "isolationist" policy of the U.S. state coupled with the "retreatist" mentality persisting among a minority of the natives have left them behind with the lowest average income. As Jarvenpa observes (1985, p. 29): "Reservations and reserves [have] perpetuated racial segregation, administrative paternalism and lower-class status for Indian people." But yet in the ethnic stratification of the United States, the Native Americans constitute the last but one layer.

The estimates of Native Americans at the time of European contact vary between 2 to 5 million (see Snipp 1987). In the four centuries following contact, their population dwindled to about 250,000 by the early twentieth century. The factors contributing to this dramatic decline were disease, war, forced migration, and slavery (Nagel and Snipp 1987, pp. 1-41). From 1920 onward, however, the population of Native Americans started increasing and by 1980 they were counted as 1,423,000. The leading factors contributing to this stupendous increase are (1) federal policy that helps stabilize the Native American land base and provides specific services to reservations, (2) urbanization of the Native Americans, and (3) change in the Census Bureau's definition of "Indian," which relied on respondents' self-definition of race in enumeration (see Nagel and Snipp 1987).

The nature and content of self-definition by a collectivity is crucial in determining its identity. Invoking the two perspectives on ethnic identity—fixed and fluid—Nagel and Snipp (1987, p. 7) conclude: "Some portion of the 1.4 million American Indians no doubt conforms to the fixed identity model—continuously biographically and culturally American Indians. Another portion of the 1.4 million American Indians conforms to the fluid identity model—discontinuously, situationally and volitionally American Indians." As for the content of self-definition, there are two possible referents in the present case: specific tribes or the broad category of Native Americans. The 1980 Census data reveal that Native Americans tend to be affiliated with tribes and these are federally recognized ones, because "federal recognition endows tribes with legal, material, and cultural resources that greatly enhance their survival" (Nagel and Snipp 1987, p. 18).

In terms of our conceptualization the Native Americans who live in reservations and agency towns are national groups; they are in their homeland and maintain a style of life distinct to them. Only those Native Americans who are dislocated from their original habitats and not fully assimilated constitute an ethnic group. But ignoring the distinction between nation and ethnie, all Native Americans are put in the same category by most analysts. On the other hand, given the federal policy of according official recognition to specific tribes, the Native Americans tend to underplay their "pan-Indian" national identity. "Pan-Indianism is still a segmented, decentralized political movement, and some tribes have remained relatively autonomous ethnic enclaves removed from the mainstream of pan-Indian political ideology" (Jarvenpa 1985, p. 43).

Brought to the United States as slaves, the Negroes have had a checkered history of struggle, protest, and gradual emancipation (see Franklin 1967; Meier and Rudwick 1975); and yet, the lowest societal layer is constituted by them. But the American Negroes have been latterly labeled as Black Americans, the semantic change being indicative of the increasing dignity with which others perceive them and they define themselves. The most recent label preferred by them, however, seems to be Afro-Americans, suggestive of their attachment to homeland. They now constitute about 12% of the American population. The policy of affirmative action initiated by the state did facilitate the upward mobility of a large number, if a small proportion, of Blacks. The vast majority of Blacks, however, still predominate in the lower income groups and income disparity between them and Whites still persists (see Farley 1984). Concentrated in specific urban settlements, the Blacks could capture political power in several city governments, leading to the phenomenon of the "Blackening of Urban America," a phrase with racialist motif but that captures the mobility pattern of the U.S. Blacks. This in turn, however, has reinforced the segregationist syndrome in the U.S. metropolitan schools catering mainly to Black children (see Farley 1985, pp. 18-20).

While the American dilemma, the gap between constitutionally guaranteed rights and privileges to all citizens and their translation into practice, to which Myrdal (1944) called attention four decades ago, still persists, the gap between profession and practice has certainly been reduced by the 1980s. There is no consensus in this regard, however, and there exist at least three distinct views. First, there is the optimistic view, which holds that the practice of racial discrimination has declined considerably, if not disappeared entirely, and that a person's skin color has little to do with his or her achievements in education and occupation. Second, there is the pessimistic perspective, which portrays the changes that have occurred as superficial and minimal. Third, there is the cautionary opinion, which holds that mobility among Blacks has led to sharp differentiation among them—between a successful elite group and an impoverished underclass.

After a careful examination of the available data, Farley (1985, pp. 4-28) suggests that none of these views can be sustained. While in sectors such as education, occupation, and earnings of employed workers, there is considerable reduction of disparity between Whites and Blacks, there is no improvement in regard to employment. Further, "there is a great deal of convincing evidence showing that blacks and whites seldom share the same urban neighborhoods . . . and that economic factors account for little of the observed residential segregation of blacks from whites" (Farley 1985, p. 17). This racial segregation is not a consequence of the desire of Blacks to live in all-Black areas; in fact, they prefer to live in racially mixed areas (see Pettigrew 1973, pp. 21-84). In regard to schooling the picture is mixed in that in most rural areas of the South, in small- and medium-sized cities in all regions and in southern metropolises where schools are organized on a countywide basis, Black and White children attend the same schools. Similarly, the majority of Black college students now do not go to traditionally Black colleges but attend predominantly White colleges and universities. Thus the dual educational system is disappearing at a rapid speed (see Bullock and Lamb 1984). On the other hand, the changing demographic profile of the largest metropolises of the United States renders the educational institutions in them predominantly Black. Admittedly, race and color, not ethnicity as such, continue to be critical in rendering Blacks a minority.

Hispanics, whose presence in the United States predates the emergence of the American nation-state, do not fit into the melting pot metaphor of the White European ethnic immigrants. Racially the Hispanics are mixed; they include brown, black, and white. Linguistically they have the same origin, being Spanish speakers, and the use of Spanish has not disappeared even among second- and third-generation Hispanics reared in the United States. Although they constitute a nation, the Hispanic immigrants to the United States are drawn mainly from three states—Mexico, Puerto Rico, and Cuba—and their incorporation experiences are drastically different (Nelson and Tienda 1985, p. 50).

The Mexicans came as immigrant workers to meet the rapidly expanding needs of the capitalist economy and yet they were politically and socially vulnerable in that they could be deported to their neighboring homeland. The hegemony of the United States over Puerto Rico imparted to the immigrant workers from the island a visibly colonized position. In contrast, the Cubans came as political refugees; they were fleeing to the United States to breathe freedom. Understandably, they were drawn from heterogeneous occupational backgrounds—professionals and white- and

blue-collar workers. Invoking the distinction between minorities and ethnics, Nelson and Tienda (1985, pp. 49-74) show that Mexicans and Puerto
Ricans fit into the category of minorities, as there is convergence of ethnic
origin and economic disadvantage in their case. In contrast, given their
more favorable class position, the Cubans, particularly the upwardly
mobile section, tend to assimilate more quickly with the cultural
mainstream. Even when ethnicity is retained and invoked by them, it is
symbolic in content (see Gans 1979, pp. 1-19). Thus, notwithstanding
their common national origin, the Hispanics should be differentiated into
minorities and ethnics.

The status of White immigrants seems to be determined by the point of
their entry. This was reflected in what awaited and was available to the
new immigrants: "The members of each new wave of immigration were
assigned the lowliest tasks, the longest hours of work, the poorest and
dirtiest living quarters" (Lerner 1957, p. 503). The relatively late entrants
of the yellow race and brown people are appropriately perched in the
ethnic stratification system, between the Whites and the Blacks.

From all available accounts it is clear that the crucial factors that
determined the position of a collectivity in the status ladder were color
and race, the visibility of which make social interaction utterly oppressive
for those with the wrong color and excessively advantageous to those with
the right color. Given similarity in color and race, the congruence between
point of entry and social status of a collectivity could be maintained only
when one of three conditions was met. First, the immigrants should be
peasants and/or in unskilled/low-skilled occupations. Second, they should
have more or less similar class background at the point of departure. Third,
immigration resulted from economic and/or political crises in home
countries at the time of departure as in the case of the potato famine in
Ireland or pogroms in the case of Jews from Eastern European countries.
Generally speaking, the migrants came in at the bottom of the economic
and social structure but their precise slot was determined at least partly by
the levels of development—economic and technological—of the United
States at the time of their arrival. This meant that the United States could
and did accommodate peasants and unskilled workers at the initial phase.
These conditions seem to have facilitated the initial large-scale migration
of successive waves of White migrants.

But once industrialization and technological development reach a high
pitch, both at the point of departure and at the point of destination, the
immigrants get sharply differentiated in terms of status, right at the point
of entry. Immigrants into the United States today are admitted for their
brains as well as for muscles. In such a situation, if a recent immigrant
group has a large proportion of professionals and scientists in its ranks, it
would quickly acquire the image and status of the middle class even as an

earlier group with a large proportion of unskilled workers remains at its lower-class status. That is, the significance of the point of entry as a determinant of status would be on the decline. This seems to have happened in the case of recent migrants from Asia.

The migrants drawn from a variety of places and backgrounds occupying a common territory can emerge as a well-knit society only if they acquire political authority over the territory. The American War of Independence provided this much needed cementing force. But it is important to remember that there was no basic difference between the colonial master and the subjects (at least between the most significant of them) in terms of religion, language, race, color, or perhaps even culture. The colonizer was territorially alien and politically inimical but culturally affined. That is, the American freedom movement was essentially instrumental in orientation and not expressive in content. It was an effort on the part of the immigrants to assert their territorial, political, and economic independence and not cultural autonomy. To recall the pregnant phrase of Max Lerner, it was an exercise in "the slaying of the European father."

Not only did the social formation of American society occur through waves of immigration but the ethos of contemporary American society is also maintained through constant movement of people from one location to another. Americans are a people in motion, not simply as tourists but for jobs and residences. As Max Lerner (1957, p. 99) puts it: "The internal migrations are opportunity-and-advancement migrations. They are made not out of land hunger or the quest for freedom, as was true of the original migrations from abroad, but of the pursuit of better chances of business and profits, for work and wages, for climate, schools, living conditions."

Americans remain incessantly in search of prosperity through spatial mobility and they dread getting "stuck." Apparently there is no anxiety to put down roots in a town or village that itself has few roots in American history. The goal is a runaway success wherever one is: On the other hand, there is the usual nostalgia for home. This produces the Home is Heaven—the Home is Hell syndrome. And yet, the overall ethos of the American society is one in which people are restlessly on the move to climb up the social ladder.

It is clear then that the factors that conjointly determine the position of an ethnic category in the stratification system of the United States are race and color, point of entry, proportion of educated and occupationally skilled persons in the category, and willingness to shift jobs and residences. This would logically produce a continuum of the most privileged—the highly educated and spatially mobile among the early White settlers—and the most deprived—the unskilled, spatially immobile late entrant Blacks. Between these polar points a large number of permutations and combinations are possible and as and when certain structural conditions are met, these collectivities articulate their interests through voluntary associations, press, and lobbying. This seems to be the process of the birth of ethnicity in the United States. Given the multiplicity of collectivities and factors involved and the legitimacy accorded to political bargaining to pursue interests of ascriptive groups, it is logical to expect a continuous multiplication of ethnic groups and a vociferous articulation of their interests. The point I want to stress at the present juncture is that there is an organic link between immigration and ethnicity in the United States, be it the original act of entering the country or the subsequent acts of moving from one part to another within the country.

It is necessary to familiarize ourselves with the distinctive processes involved in the formation of Indian society, before we proceed any further. While one can identify five such processes in the case of India, the essential parallels between the two societies are striking, variations in details apart.

The Indian society was formed through the processes of the *accretion* of immigrants and the *dislocation* of the original inhabitants. The first recorded large-scale immigration of a culturally distinct people into India occurred some 3500 years ago with the Aryan invasion, which pushed the native Dravidians into the Southern as well as to the relatively less hospitable geographical regions—the hilly tracts. Notwithstanding this dislocation, at least 40% of the total population of India today is constituted by those who claim to be the original inhabitants—the Dravidians, the Scheduled Castes, and the Scheduled Tribes. The Aryans evolved not only a distinct religion (Hinduism) and language (Sanskrit) but also a whole new scheme of social life (the *varna* or color-based stratification), which were at variance with those of the original inhabitants. But, in contemporary India, that which is hailed as truly national is essentially Aryan. Today, 83% of Indians are Hindu and 72% of Indians speak one or another language of Aryan origin. This provides eloquent proof of an ethnie transforming itself into a nation, in its newfound home. We do not often comprehend this possibility precisely because of the long time span involved. After all, in the hoary past we were all unborn: If the WASPs of the United States (the equivalent of the upper caste, Hindi-speaking Hindus of India) are still viewed as an ethnie and not a nation, it is because (1) their entry is only a few hundred years old, (2) the time that separated their entry and that of others is rather short, and (3) those of British descent constitute a tiny fraction of the U.S. population. English is, however, the only national language of the United States and the U.S. culture and political institutions are essentially British. This illustrates the possibility of cultural hegemony by a demographic minority. But its political domination, that is, transforming itself from a cultural to political community, is a limited possibility in a democratic polity.

The second major cultural accretion occurred in India with the waves of Muslim conquests spanning eleven centuries beginning with the conquest of Sind in the eighth century. Although only a small section of the conquering group had settled down, due to the policy of vigorous proselytization, a substantial number of the local people embraced Islam. Consequently, India has the third largest Muslim population (75 million) in the world, even after two Muslim states (Pakistan and Bangladesh) have been carved out of its erstwhile territory. Similarly, Persian became the official language and a new hybrid language, Urdu, emerged through its interaction with local north-Indian languages; and it is strongly identified (in popular conception) with the Muslim population of India, even to this day.

The third major cultural influence on India was the Western intrusion, particularly the British colonial rule for a period of two centuries. The British did not pursue a policy of proselytization, although, of course, Western Christian missionaries did involve themselves in large-scale conversion movements, particularly among the traditionally deprived sections. And yet, the Indian Christian population now accounts for barely 2.5% of the total. But the English language has a powerful presence and it is virtually the only language of learning and administration particularly at the higher levels, although it does not enjoy any constitutional status.

The fourth major factor that contributed to the social formation that is India is the freedom movement. It is no exaggeration to suggest that the "Indian consciousness," as we understand it today, crystallized for the first time during the national liberation movement. By the same token, "national" is a political and not a cultural referent in India. And yet, the Indian freedom movement was totalistic in its orientation. The domination by the colonizer was not simply economic and political but also cultural, racial, and even psychological. Admittedly, the unity provided by the movement was all-embracing. This was in spite of the fact that all the major religions of the world were professed and as many as 1650 languages and dialects were spoken in India as mother tongues. There was nothing like an all-India dress, cuisine, painting, dance, music, or style of life. Perhaps the only institution that had near-universal presence in India was the caste system. The importance of Indian unity in the freedom movement ought to be weighed against this background.

The emergence of the Indian state was possible only through the partition of British India into India and Pakistan on the basis of religion, which was the fifth major factor in the formation of India, leading to large-scale, and, in fact, one of the biggest, population transfers in human history. Between 1946 and 1951 nearly 9 million Hindus and Sikhs came to India and about 6 million Muslims left India for Pakistan. Of the former, 5 million came from West Pakistan (that is, today's Pakistan) and

4 million came from East Pakistan (that is, Bangladesh). The majority of the Muslims who left India were from North India, however, and only a small number left East India. Thus the influx from East Pakistan to India was not balanced by a corresponding efflux from India. Further, while the migrations from West Pakistan stopped by 1951, they continued for over three decades from East Pakistan. This has resulted in the colonization of relatively underpopulated tracts (e.g., certain districts of Assam and Tripura) by the Bengali refugees, leading to situations of ethnic conflict between them and the locals. In the case of the refugees from West Pakistan, the Sikhs constituted a high proportion and they are also socially more visible because of the religious symbols (long hair, turban, and so on) with which they are associated. While a substantial number of them did settle down in Punjab itself, they also colonized parts of other states, particularly those that are contiguous with Punjab, as peasants. The enterprising Sikh refugees, however, went far and wide to distant towns and cities. Their mood then was "home was where we earned our living." But gradually emotional attachment to and psychological need for a separate homeland for Sikhs also crystallized. Given that religion was not an acceptable basis for the creation of an administrative unit in "secular" India, language was used as the basis of creating the Punjabi Suba, a state inhabited predominantly by Sikhs, whose mother tongue, Punjabi written in Gurumukhi, is closely associated with their religion. At least a small section of the Sikhs are not satisfied with this limited notion of homeland and they are currently leading a movement for an independent sovereign Sikh nation-state, Khalistan.

It is interesting to note certain striking parallels between the "ethnic" stratification system of India and the United States. Like the native Americans, the *Girijans* (the dwellers of hilly tracts) of India were also dislocated from their habitats by the Aryan intrusion, as noted earlier. But there are some 400 of such groups labeled as Scheduled Tribes by the government, numbering over 50 million and constituting 7% of the population. Today they prefer to be called *Adivasis*, the earliest settlers. The Adivasis may be grouped into two categories in terms of the political-administrative arrangements under which they are organized. Those in Northeast India, the tribes inhabiting international borders, are organized into separate states and the encysted tribes are usually administratively linked to one or another state, constituted on the basis of one of the major languages of India.

According to the traditional system of stratification, the Hindu population was divided into five categories based on *varna* (color) system, the Brahmins believed to be the purest of the Aryan strain constituting the apex and the *panchamas*, those of the fifth order, stigmatized as untouchables positioned at the bottom. If the primary disability of the American

Black is color, that of the Indian "untouchable" is attributed ritual impurity. But they do not belong to any distinct physical type and, therefore, untouchability can be practiced only in those situations wherein persons and groups recognize one another's social background. The practice of untouchability has been legally abolished and in official parlance the erstwhile untouchables are called Scheduled Castes. While Mohandas Karamchand Gandhi christened them as *Harijans* (children of God), the articulate among them prefer to be called *Dalits* (the oppressed). The Scheduled Castes count 100 million and constitute 14% of India's population. They also claim to be the settlers of India before the Aryan intrusion.

The *Dalits* occupy the lowest step in the social ladder of India and the *Adivasis* may be viewed as a bridge group between them and the ritually clean castes, who constitute the third block in the Indian stratification system. But this is an amorphous category inclusive of a wide variety of religious, caste, and linguistic groups. The salient identity of the groups in this block varies depending upon the context and the situation. Their placement in the system is more horizontal than hierarchical.

When we compare the patterns of the internal migration in India with those of the United States, we get a completely different picture. If Americans are a people-in-motion, Indians are a people-stay-put. If Americans perceive spatial mobility as a source of social mobility, Indians prefer to climb up the social ladder while continuing to live and work at the same place. If Americans dread getting stuck, Indians are congenitally inclined to stick. I am acutely aware of the exaggerations involved in these contrasts. But it is fairly certain that these "images" are by and large factual and sustainable.

Internal migration in independent India is around 30%, a migrant being a person who lives away from his or her birthplace. But according to the 1981 Census of India statistics (the latest available), 62% of these migrations are within the same district and 26% are within the same state. That is, an overwhelming majority of migrants move within the same culture area as the states in India are organized on the basis of language. Only 12% of migrants move across state boundaries and only a small proportion among them actually leave their cultural zone, because about 40% of the total population live in the five Hindi-speaking north Indian states. That is, discrimination based on ethnic considerations occurs only when the religious, caste, tribal, or regional background of the migrants is known and distinct. But the most widespread discrimination is practiced against "outsiders."

It is instructive to note here that in all Indian languages the distinction between *desh* (homeland) and *videsh* (foreign land), and consequently that between natives and foreigners, is clearly made. In fact, fellow Indians

belonging to cultural zones other than one's own are often referred to as
"foreigners" (see Oommen 1982, pp. 41-64). *Desh* implies not merely a
territory but also a people, language, style of life, and pattern of culture;
in fact, a "nation" in the European sense of the term. A particular state may
have several such "nations" or parts thereof within it. That is, political-administrative units and folk regions are not coterminous and the concept of
desh is essentially anchored to the notion of the cultural homeland. Insofar
as a person is within his or her own *desh* and state, he or she is an insider,
his or hers is a "national" identity. But should he or she cross the boundaries of this region, he or she becomes an outsider and assumes the label
of an ethnic.

One may identify several situations wherein "ethnicity" becomes
salient in the Indian context: (1) the demand for a distinct homeland,
either a sovereign state (e.g., the demand for Khalistan by a section of the
Sikhs) or a political-administrative unit within the Indian state (e.g.,
Gorkhaland for Nepalis, Jharkhand state for the tribes of Central India);
(2) the demand for expulsion of "outsiders" when the entire state is
engulfed by migrants from other states or neighboring countries (e.g.,
Assam and Tripura); (3) the demand for the expulsion of *videshis* ("foreigners") belonging to other folk regions within the state (e.g., the
Chotanagpur tribal demand to expel fellow Biharis of the plains) or from
other states (Bengalis or Marwaris); (4) the demand to expel those who do
not belong to the same cultural region although they are from the same
state (e.g., the demand for the expulsion of Andhras from Telangana
region); and (5) the demand to expel migrants from other linguistic states
who come to work and reside in metropolitan centers (e.g., mobilization
against Tamils in Bombay and Bangalore).

What is common to all these situations is the strong identification of
the collectivities with specific territories and the notion of homeland.
Those who belong to the homeland are insiders, they constitute "a nation,"
and the outsiders are "ethnics." But the ethnics of India also have
homeland normally elsewhere *within* India. This makes the effort by
nations to expel ethnics easier and often appear even legitimate. This is
quite a contrast to the American situation, wherein the notion of homeland
or nation for specific ethnic collectivities is absent. Not that the ethnic
collectivities in the United States do not have an attachment to homelands;
their homelands, except that of Native Americans, are *outside* their
country. Europe, it is said, is always full of White Americans searching for
their homelands. And Blacks consider Africa as their homeland; the expression "Afro-American" points clearly to this. Admittedly, the notion of
homeland is qualitatively different in the United States and in India; in the
former it is largely a matter of symbolic identification, in the case of the
latter it provides not only symbolic attachment but also meets instrumen-

tal needs. This I suggest is the key to understanding the differences in the contexts and contents of ethnicity in India and the United States.

CONDITIONS FOR THE EMERGENCE AND MAINTENANCE OF CULTURAL PLURALISM: INDIA AND THE UNITED STATES

That India is "multinational" and the United States is "multiethnic" and both are multicultural is evident from the social profiles of these countries. What follows is an effort to identify the conditions that facilitate the emergence and maintenance of cultural pluralism. But before I take up this discussion, a few clarifications are in order.

First, modernization, it is argued by many, leads to a great deal of standardization of cultures and life-styles; modern technology and market are great solvents of traditional cultures and diversity. Be that as it may, modernization also creates new cultures and life-styles. If we often get the impression that these are not easily and quickly crystallizing, it is only because we are too close to the ongoing process and/or we are impatient. Given the nature of the change involved, when we refer to cultural pluralism, the concern is with the distinctive and persistent elements in the group life of different collectivities. People may change their dress pattern more easily than their worship styles.

Second, it is necessary to differentiate between the instrumental and symbolic dimensions involved in ethnicity/nationality. When it is employed as a resource for instrumental benefits (political representation, recruitment to occupation, admission to educational institutions) of the collectivity, in the final analysis, the beneficiaries are specific individuals, although they may provide role models to those who belong to the same collectivity. Further, instrumental benefits can be obtained through bargaining done by collectivities, constituted on other bases (e.g., political parties and trade unions). Finally, instrumental benefits can be availed of by an individual through ethnic mobilization only if he or she is competent, motivated, and hardworking. In contrast, symbolic rewards accrue to collectivities and this assumes their cooperation. For instance, congregational worship and the speaking of language assume the presence of coreligionists and members of one's speech community. That is, the structural properties of the situation rather than the psychological attributes of the individual are more crucial to utilize symbolic rewards. Therefore, the contention that the content of ethnicity has latterly shifted from expressive to instrumental orientation and that people would rather forgo symbolic rewards in favor of instrumental ones cannot be sustained (see Patterson 1975, pp. 305-49). These are qualitatively different rewards and one cannot be a substitute or compensation for the other.

Third, the frequent tendency exhibited by the *statists* (those who perceive and define everything from the perspective of the state) and *ethnicists* (those who define and cognize everything from the perspective of ethnic categories) does not help foster cultural pluralism or even the interests of nation-states (see Smith 1973, pp. 16-18). The statists advocate cultural assimilation of all varieties of minorities, which in effect would lead to the cultural hegemony of the mainline culture and what I have called elsewhere the *culturocide* of the minorities (see Oommen 1986b, pp. 53-74). In contrast, the ethnicists obstinately persist in the maintenance of all the cultural practices irrespective of the contexts. This may sometimes endanger the interests of the wider collectivity if distinctiveness and even superiority are claimed, which often is the case, by some groups. If the statist cannot be always defended from a *humanist* perspective, the ethnicist cannot be completely accommodated from a *political* perspective. What is required is a value orientation buttressed by accommodation and reconciliation.

Fourth, it is helpful to recognize that all societies and traditions may have both negative and positive dimensions. Further, what is positive or negative is not given forever; they change contextually, in terms of space and time. The explicit recognition of this fact is necessary insurance against the trappings of cultural relativism, which holds that all ethnic cultures have a permanent value and must be conserved in their "pure" forms. Thus the American Anthropological Association in its memorandum on human rights contended that there could be no general human rights for all peoples (see "Memorandum on Human Rights," 1947, pp. 539-43). Robert Redfield correctly criticized this memorandum suggesting that its relativism could be used to justify racism, slavery, and Nazism (Redfield 1957, p. 148). The point I want to make is this: In the process of maintaining cultural pluralism and promoting cultural diversity, it may be necessary and possible for societies to retain the assets in their traditions and add new and desirable elements from alien societies. Similarly, it may be necessary to discard the liabilities in their traditions. A judicious strategy of maintaining cultural pluralism would entail selective retention of the assets and rejection of the liabilities in the tradition.

Armed with these clarifications, let us identify the prerequisites for the maintenance of cultural pluralism or, if you so prefer, ethnic specificities. I prefer to view the problem from below, that is, from the perspective of the weak and the marginalized cultural collectivities. The properties of the social situation that are crucial in maintaining cultural pluralism may be grouped under four broad heads: physical, psychological, political, and societal. I shall discuss each of these in turn.

The set of properties designated as physical may be seen as *resources* the collectivity possesses to maintain its cultural identity. As I have indicated earlier the *size* of the population and its *concentration* in a specific locale are important. If the size of an ethnic group is small and it is dispersed over a wide territory, the usual option open to it is assimilation. The Native Americans living in the reservations are in a position to maintain their cultural specificity in spite of their small size precisely because they are identified with and live in a specific territory. This is even more true of several tribes of India. Such demographic enclaves of tribes have also facilitated the formation of appropriate political-administrative units—states, districts, *panchayats*—under the federal system set up in India. This in turn has facilitated the maintenance of the life-styles specific to them. That is, instead of culturally liquidating the group or even ethnicizing it, they are encouraged to develop as a "nation," as an integrated cultural entity.

The properties of the situation under which different immigrant groups exist would drastically vary. A relatively less developed colonizing agrarian community is likely to be territorially concentrated or even insulated. In contrast, a collectivity that is displaced from its ancestral home and involved mainly in urban occupations in the host society is likely to be dispersed and thinly distributed over a wide territory. It is unlikely that such a group can or will ever develop a claim to a homeland within the host society. It usually does not have the potential to develop into a nation and is destined to remain as an ethnic group. But that need not and should not lead to its cultural liquidation. To maintain its culture, religion, and language, however, it should develop a deep psychological disposition toward its collective identity, which in turn seems to be the function of its collective experience and memory. The Jews and Blacks in the United States, and the Sindhis, Bahais, Jews, and Parsees in India, seem to fit this description. These people were uprooted from their ancestral homes and persecuted for religious, racial, or political reasons. Understandably, they develop a collective memory and a deep psychological disposition, both of which help maintain their ethnic identity.

The third important property of the situation that fosters cultural pluralism in a country is the nature of state policy. The constitution of the country should not only explicitly disapprove cultural hegemony of particular collectivities but it also should have provisions to ward off the tyranny of the majority. Constitutional provisions, however, are necessary but not sufficient conditions to foster cultural pluralism. Happily, the situation in the United States and India is favorable in this respect. The stable two-party system, the long tradition of voluntary associations operating as countervailing powers, and the ubiquitous club that acts as a vehicle of articulating all types of interests necessarily create a societal ethos that makes survival of cultural pluralism possible in the United States. But the thrusts of the U.S. motto "from many to one," and the U.S. policy of affirmative action, which recognizes only the individual as the unit, are assimilation and integration.

India is characterized by one-party dominance, and the tradition of voluntary associations is not very strong. But a multiplicity of regional, caste, religious, tribal, and linguistic political parties does foster and represent a wide variety of "ethnic" and nationality interests in the political context. Further, freedom of association of all varieties of groups is guaranteed by the Indian Constitution. The policy of protective discrimination recognizes Scheduled Castes and Tribes as the beneficiaries of state action. The states in India are organized based on cultural and linguistic factors. The Indian motto "unity in diversity" is explicitly geared to facilitate the promotion of cultural pluralism.

Whatever may be the constitutional guarantees and legal provisions, the creation of an appropriate climate for cultural pluralism would not be possible unless the attitudes and value orientations of the cultural mainstream foster the same. The most important value in this context is the striving for composite culture, a process in which each ethnic/national group adds a new dimension to the whole and the old. The realization of this goal is possible only if the different groups cherish and foster their traditions while refusing to isolate themselves from the larger culture. The development of such an orientation is possible if the existential conditions are favorable. This I suggest is to be viewed as the fourth element in the property of the situation.

The cultural mainstream of the United States, drawn predominantly from the Protestants, has a long tradition of religious tolerance. English, which has come to be perceived as a global language, is firmly accepted as the lingua franca in the United States. This in spite of the rumblings created by the Spanish speech community, which constitutes about 6% of the total population. The acceptance of English, in spite of, and perhaps largely because of, the fact that the single largest ethnic category in the American mainstream is constituted by Germans, is noteworthy. Economically and occupationally, several smaller groups have a disproportionately large representation (Jews, with 3% of the total population, for example) in the entrepreneurial and intellectual categories. The social support base of the two political parties is multiethnic.

Hinduism, the religion of the majority in India is known for its doctrinal catholicity and metaphysical tolerance. Although Hindi is the official language of the Indian Union, there are 15 other languages to which legal status has been accorded that are equally developed. A disproportionately large proportion of Indian entrepreneurs are drawn from tiny ethnic groups such as Marwaris, Parsees, Sindhis, and Sikhs, who are dispersed all over the country. The support base of the leading political party, the Indian National Congress, is provided by a wide variety of groups. The intellectuals and professionals are drawn from all "national" groups, notwithstanding the continuing dominance of the Brahmins, who have the widest all-India spread as a caste category. The point I am hammering here is that the conditions in both the countries permit only *dispersed dominance*. The fact that no single ethnie or nation has *decisive dominance* in all the contexts—cultural, economic, political, and intellectual—makes *cumulative dominance* by a particular group and, consequently, majoritarian tyranny an impossibility. This situation is conducive to the flowering of cultural pluralism.

Dispersed dominance coupled with social mobility unsettles identity-sets and traditional images (see Horowitz 1975, pp. 111-40). State-initiated policy measures coupled with other forces of social change leading to both upward and downward mobility provide the most eloquent testimony to this phenomenon. The emergence of the Black bourgeoisie in the United States and the Harijan elite in India point to the unsettling of identity-sets and the shattering of the traditional stereotypes. Conversely, the pauperization of the WASP and the proletarianization of the twice-born Hindu have the same impact. These processes at least partly loosen the grip of the dominant collectivities on the cultural contours of society, which in turn fosters cultural pluralism. The attempt to create and the plea to recognize Black and Dalit intellectual traditions in the United States and India, respectively, are indicators of this development.

As a finale to this analysis, let us recognize three possible responses, from "ethnic" groups with differing backgrounds, that have implications for cultural pluralism. First, from those who are socially disadvantaged or even stigmatized, which qualifies them to avail of instrumental advantages through state policy: The Scheduled Castes and Tribes in India and the Blacks and Native Americans in the United States are cases in point. Their situation would prompt a tendency to emphasize one's identity selectively depending upon the context. With the public authority one would claim and even insist on the disadvantaged identity, but with the public-at-large, one would try to ignore and underplay this identity. But this strategy of *duality* in the presentation of the self in everyday life is possible, and would succeed, only when the category involved is not distinct in terms of race and color. The phenomenon of "passing off" points to the practice of this strategy.

Second, from those who are socially stigmatized (although to a lesser extent as compared with the first category) but are not entitled to have much material reward because of the nonapplicability, or limited applicability, of state policy toward them: The "Other Backward Classes," Muslims, Anglo-Indians, neo-Christians, and neo-Buddhists in India, and the Asians (i.e., the Brown and Yellow people) in the United States, fall into this category. This group gets no instrumental payoff even if it accepts its disadvantaged social identity. Consequently, it would put pressure on the public agencies either to extend the policy to include it in its purview or to scrap the policy itself. If it does not succeed in this effort, it may attempt to create a new identity rejecting the socially stigmatized status assigned to it.

Third, from those who do not suffer from any social disadvantages, the traditionally privileged, but who perceive and may actually suffer some material deprivations because of state policy: The Whites and the upper castes whose merit may be overlooked or underplayed to accommodate others may respond in three different ways: (1) protest against state policy and mobilize public opinion so as to discontinue or change the basis of the policy; (2) shift to those areas of activities wherein the policy is inapplicable; and (3) claim or acquire the identity of the disadvantaged—through adoption, marriage, or simple "passing off," if feasible.

Viewed in a short-term perspective, these responses are antithetical to the interest of nurturing cultural pluralism. But if pluralism is viewed as a situation that recognizes differences and assumes complementarity between different groups, then equality of opportunity is a precondition for sustaining it. The policies of affirmative action and protective discrimination can contribute to this process provided they are so devised as to progressively exclude from their purview those who become materially well off. This would facilitate the percolation of the benefits down to the poorest among the socially disadvantaged. Equality of opportunity should lead to the dispersion of benefits not only across but within the groups.

CONCEPTUAL TOOLS AND
COMPARATIVE METHOD

Émile Durkheim warned us, some 75 years ago, about the danger involved in comparing social types that do not belong to the same social species (see Durkheim [1912] 1965, pp. 113-14). There is another danger the master ignored—or at any rate did not articulate adequately—the danger of applying inappropriate concepts across societies while undertaking comparative analyses. I have started this chapter by noting the importance of three concepts—state, nation, and ethnie—and their empirical referents for our analysis.

State is an institution that has a monopoly on legitimate political authority over a territory; nation is a people having legitimate moral claim to a territory as their homeland; ethnie is a people with a common culture and style of life not confined to a specific territory. A nation may or may not aspire to become a state. If it does and realizes its aspiration, then state, nation, and ethnie come to coexist. If a nation does not aspire to have its exclusive political roof or it fails to realize its aspiration, it has to coexist along with other nations under a common political roof, thereby constituting a multinational state. This does not mean, however, that the nations involved would, or need to, surrender completely their political autonomy to a central state authority. A decentralized polity can meet the political aspirations of nations within a multinational state in varying degrees. Such a political arrangement would, however, in all probability throw up tensions between the central and regional/local governments and between governments of different nations within the multinational state particularly in regard to allocation of economic resources, sharing of political authority, and preservation of national cultures and boundaries.

Ethnicity, I have argued, is a product of disjunction between territory and culture; it results from territorial dislocation of people from their homeland. Historically, the factors that contributed to the rupture between territory and culture varied over time. Prior to the eighteenth century, if geographical explorations and political conquests were the prime movers in this context, during the eighteenth and nineteenth centuries, colonialism and immigration assumed greater importance. Consequently, by the twentieth century, a majority of the human population became citizens of multinational and/or polyethnic states. India and the United States afford two leading examples of this contemporary world scenario; the former, a multinational, and the latter, a polyethnic state.

The fact that India is a multinational state does not mean that ethnics do not exist in India. Given the vast size, cultural diversity, disparity in development between regions, and freedom of migration ensured through single citizenship, ethnics do emerge and exist. But most ethnics in India do have and are identified with a nation (their homeland) *within* the country except in the case of such small groups as Zorastrians, Jews, and Bahais, who sought asylum in the country from religious and/or political persecution in their homelands. Thus there are two types of ethnics in India: those who do not lay any claim on India as their homeland and those who do but live outside their specific homeland. Pursuant to this, it is possible and necessary to distinguish between those who are nationals and ethnics simultaneously and those who are ethnics exclusively.

In the United States, according to the conceptual distinction made in this chapter, everybody except the Native Americans, who constitute a nation, qualifies to be an ethnic. The indications are, however, that a collectivity—the unhyphenated Americans—that would identify the United States as its homeland is slowly but surely emerging; that is, a nation is crystallizing. But given the policy of immigration pursued, particularly since 1965, ethnics and ethnicity will continue to be an inevitable dimension of the U.S. social situation in the foreseeable future.

Ethnicity is not merely a popular but also an overburdened concept in contemporary social science. I have already indicated the need and advantage in distinguishing between nation and ethnie. Similarly, it is necessary and useful to insist on the distinction between "races" and "ethnics," the latter term reserved to denote only those culturally different collectivities *within* the same race or physical type. (In those situations wherein the differences in both—race and culture—coexist, the crucial variable that determines interaction—it is known from all available evidence—is race.) Unless this is done, the fluid model of ethnicity that assumes voluntary ethnicity and admits self-definition of identity will be rendered redundant. True, Europeans can and do shift their ethnic identity (say from Italian to German or from Catholic to Jew) through voluntary choice but this happens within the same physical type. It is not possible, however, to exercise voluntary choice of ethnicity across physical types. Given this constraint, I think it is necessary to distinguish between *attributional ethnicity* and *interactional ethnicity*, the former being fixed and the latter, fluid.

Earlier in this chapter I referred to the notion of ethnic clusters. Examples of these are Native Americans and Hispanics in the United States and Scheduled Tribes and Scheduled Castes in India. This *encompassing* ethnic labeling is a function of one or more of the following factors operating singly or in combination—administrative convenience and state policy, simplification invented for the convenience of the majority, or resultant of political alliance among the disadvantaged ethnics. But irrespective of the reasons and motives behind the labeling, the constituent units usually insist on their specific identities in their day-to-day lives and interactions. That is, self-defined identities of those who are lumped into an ethnic cluster can only be discerned through *disaggregative* ethnicity. Keeping these considerations in mind, I suggest that it is useful to maintain the distinction between encompassing ethnicity and disaggregative ethnicity. But self-definitions of identity are motivated by drastically different considerations in the case of the disadvantaged and the privileged, which brings me to my last comment.

The disadvantaged ethnics are of two types: the deprived and the stigmatized. The deprived often accept the definition imposed on them by the state or the dominant group not because of its sociological authenticity but because it has instrumental payoff. The self-definition of the stigmatized is often geared to concealing the actual identity and projecting a socially approbated identity. If deprivation and stigmatization are conjointly present in the case of a category (e.g., Scheduled Castes of India), the acceptance of imposed definition or the invention of a self-definition will be dictated by material conditions; the poor would accept the imposed definition and the well-off would reject it and try to "pass off" with the help of a self-definition.

In contrast to the disadvantaged, the self-definition of privileged ethnics is motivated by symbolic identification with one's own or with another prestigious collectivity. That is, the structure of motivation in self-definition is qualitatively different in the case of the disadvantaged and the privileged. To ignore this difference is to sacrifice the sociological authenticity of self-definition. Therefore, it is necessary to distinguish between *symbolic ethnicity* and *instrumental ethnicity*. In turn, pursuing instrumental ethnicity transforms the deprived ethnics into minorities; ethnicity becomes a political resource for them. That is, the conceptual distinction between *ethnics* and *minorities* should be insisted upon. To ignore the distinction between the ethnicity of the deprived and the ethnicity of the privileged is to perpetuate analytical anomie and block unambiguous policy choices in regard to cultural pluralism.

REFERENCES

Bullock, Charles S. and Charles M. Lamb, eds. 1984. *Implementation of Civil Rights Policy.* Monterey, CA: Brooks/Cole.

Durkheim, É. [1912] 1965. *The Elementary Forms of Religious Life*, trans. by J. W. Swain. New York: Free Press.

Farley, Reynolds. 1984. *Blacks and Whites: Narrowing the Gap?* Cambridge, MA: Harvard University Press.

———. 1985. "Three Steps Forward and Two Back? Recent Changes in the Social and Economic Status of Blacks." Pp. 4-28 in *Ethnicity and Race in the U.S.A.: Toward the Twenty-First Century*, edited by Richard D. Alba. London: Routledge & Kegan Paul.

Franklin, John Hope. 1967. *From Slavery to Freedom: A History of Negro Americans.* New Delhi: Amerind.

Gans, Herbert J. 1979. "Symbolic Ethnicity: The Future of Ethnic Groups and Cultures in America." *Ethnic and Racial Studies* 2(1):1-19.

Glazer, Nathan and Daniel P. Moynihan. 1975. "Introduction." Pp. 1-26 in *Ethnicity: Theory and Experience*, edited by Nathan Glazer and Daniel P. Moynihan. Cambridge, MA: Harvard University Press.

Handlin, Oscar. 1951. *The Uprooted: The Epic Story of the Great Migration That Made American People.* Boston: Little, Brown.

Horowitz, Donald L. 1975. "Ethnic Identity." Pp. 111-40 in *Ethnicity: Theory and Experience*, edited by Nathan Glazer and Daniel P. Moynihan. Cambridge, MA: Harvard University Press.

Jarvenpa, Robert. 1985. "The Political Economy and Political Ethnicity of American Indian Adaptations and Identities." Pp. 29-48 in *Ethnicity and Race in the U.S.A.: Toward the Twenty-First Century*, edited by Richard D. Alba. London: Routledge & Kegan Paul.

Lerner, Max. 1957. *America as a Civilization.* 2 vols. New Delhi: Allied.

Meier, August and Elliott Rudwick. 1975. *CORE: A study on the Civil Rights Movement, 1942-1968.* Urbana: University of Illinois Press.

"Memorandum on Human Rights." 1947. *American Anthropologist* 49(3):539-43.

Myrdal, Gunnar. 1944. *An American Dilemma: The Negro Problem and Modern Democracy.* New York: Harper & Row.

Nagel, Joane and C. Matthew Snipp. 1987. "American Indian Tribal Identification and Federal Indian Policy: The Reflection of History in 1980 Census." Paper submitted to the annual meeting of the American Sociological Association, Chicago, August 17-21.

Nelson, Candace and Marta Tienda. 1985. "The Structuring of Hispanic Ethnicity: Historical and Contemporary Perspectives." Pp. 49-74 in *Ethnicity and Race in the U.S.A.: Toward the Twenty-First Century*, edited by Richard D. Alba. London: Routledge & Kegan Paul.

Oommen, T. K. 1982. "Foreigners, Refugees and Outsiders in the Indian Context." *Sociological Bulletin* 31(1):41-64.

―――. 1986a. "Social Movements and Nation-State in India: Towards Re-Legitimisation of Cultural Nationalisms." *Journal of Social and Economic Studies* 3(2, New Series): 107-29.

―――. 1986b. "Insiders and Outsiders in India: Primordial Collectivism and Cultural Pluralism in Nation-Building." *International Sociology* 1(1):53-74.

Patterson, Orlando. 1975. "Context and Choice in Ethnic Allegiance: A Theoretical Framework and a Caribbean Case Study." Pp. 305-49 in *Ethnicity: Theory and Experience*, edited by Nathan Glazer and Daniel P. Moynihan. Cambridge, MA: Harvard University Press.

Petersen, William. 1975. "On the Subnations of Western Europe." Pp. 177-208 in *Ethnicity: Theory and Experience*, edited by Nathan Glazer and Daniel P. Moynihan. Cambridge, MA: Harvard University Press.

Pettigrew, Thomas F. 1973. "Attitudes on Race and Housing: A Social-Psychological View." Pp. 21-84 in *Segregation in Residential Areas*, edited by Amos H. Hawley and Vincent P. Rock. Washington: National Academy of Science.

Porter, H. C. 1979. *The Inconstant Savage: England and the North American Indian: 1500-1600.* London: Duckworth.

Redfield, Robert. 1957. *The Primitive World and Its Transformation.* New York: Cornell University Press.

Richmond, Anthony H. 1987. "Ethnic Nationalism: Social Science paradigms." *International Social Science Journal* 39(1):3-18.

Riggs, Fred W. 1986. "What Is Ethnic? What Is National? Let's Turn the Tables." *Canadian Review of Studies in Nationalism* 13(1):111-23.

Smith, Anthony D. 1973. "Nationalism." *Current Sociology* 21(3):5-185.

Snipp, C. Matthew. 1987. *The First of this Land.* New York: Basic Books.

Vincent, Joan. 1974. "The Structuring of Ethnicity." *Human Organization* 33(4):375-79.

Weber, Max. 1947. *From Max Weber: Essays in Sociology.* London: Routledge & Kegan Paul.

Yancey, William L., Eugene Ericksen, and Richard Juliani. 1976. "Emergent Ethnicity: A Review and Reformulation." *American Sociological Review* 41(3):391-403.

Yancey L. William, Eugene P. Ericksen, and George H. Leon. 1985. "The Structure of Pluralism: 'We're all Italian Around Here, Aren't We, Mrs. O'Brien?' " Pp. 94-116 in *Ethnicity and Race in the U.S.A.: Toward the Twenty-First Century*, edited by Richard D. Alba. London: Routledge & Kegan Paul.

Part V
Nation as Context:
Multinational Analyses

13

The Professional-Proletarian Bind: Doctors' Strikes in Western Societies

Aaron Antonovsky

I began to come of age in a poor Jewish neighborhood of New York in the late 1930s. Given this background, it is almost axiomatic to say that I grew up knowing that strikers were right, and that one of the cardinal sins in life is to cross a picket line. I sang with zest the refrain from one of the Talking Union songs, "You either are a union man or a thug for J.H. Blair." Such deeply rooted orientations are not easily shaken (though it takes some longer than others), and it was not until the spring of 1983 that I came to confront this one with full force. At that time, the Israeli Medical Association, representing the 11,895 physicians in the country, conducted a strike that lasted 118 days—the longest doctors' strike on record—and ended only after an 11-day hunger strike in which some 2,000 doctors took part.

For a decade, I had been a senior professor in one of the four Israeli medical schools, and hence in daily contact with colleagues who were now on strike. What had brought me to join my particular faculty at Beersheba was a deep concern about unmet health care needs, and the hope that I, as a medical sociologist, could contribute to building a faculty committed to significant improvement of the health care system. The bind I found myself in was disturbing. I "knew" automatically that strikers were right, and I was aware of my colleagues' just grievances. Yet I also knew that millions of Israelis were being deprived of routine health care. It is against this background that I gladly agreed to participate in this symposium, and chose the topic of physician strikes in a cross-cultural context.

The average medical sociologist in the United States, in his or her insular way, will have heard of the Saskatchewan strike in 1962, the dramatic 1964 Belgian strike, and, if he or she has some interest in Israel, the 1983 strike. But once we begin to go into the matter, we find that we have to go back to Cork County, Ireland, in 1894, and then to Leipzig and the strikes under the leadership of Dr. Hartmann's Leipziger Verband in the first decade of the century, as well as to other places and times, if we are to understand not only the phenomenon of doctors' strikes, but also their broader implications.

The scholarly data on doctors' strikes (in contrast to the broader issue of professional dominance) are sparse. To the best of my knowledge, there is but one book on the subject (Badgley and Wolfe 1967), and one issue of a journal (*International Journal of Health Services*, Vol. 5, no. 1) devoted to scholarly analysis of the subject. Few of the papers I cite are scholarly. Not a single one of the indices of the dozen or so medical sociology texts I looked at sandwiches "strikes" between "stress" and "stroke." In preparation of this chapter, I was not able to conduct a major research effort in digging up primary sources. Moreover, one would have to know the history, culture, and political systems, as well as the health care systems, of at least a dozen societies before one could begin to write a definitive paper. So all I can do here is to offer some impressions—not even hypotheses—that have emerged in the course of a fascinating initial exploration. As I hope will be seen, the question of doctors' strikes raises some fundamental issues relating to professions, professional autonomy, and social change. Let me note that I will here avoid all reference to the ethical issues that provided my initial motivation for the inquiry.

THE "DATA"

As a contribution to the scholar who will some day give the subject its due attention, I have prepared Table 13.1, which lists all the "strikes" of which I have learned, as well as at least one source, to which the reader can refer, in each case. Please note that the sources range from a passing reference to a very partial account, in most cases, and reasonable documentation in only a few.

Two things will be noted about Table 13.1. I have placed the word "strikes" in quotes. The actions referenced in the table include full-fledged strikes in the usual sense of the word, that is, doctors leaving their regular medical activities en masse, though invariably with arrangements for emergency treatment. But they also include a wide gamut of other protest actions: work-to-rule, limited hours, resignation from employment, nonrenewal of malpractice insurance, and so on. Populations

TABLE 13.1: Physicians' "Strikes" Recorded in the Literature[a]

Location	Date	Source
Cork, Ireland	1894	Badgley and Wolfe (1967, p. 137[b])
Germany	1898; 1900-1911 "about two hundred conflicts per year"	Stone (1980, pp. 45-48)
Leipzig	1904	von Moschke (1975)
Russia	1905	Kuzmina (1973)
Soviet Union	1917-18	Nesterenko (1966)
Germany	1923, 1977	Arnold (1984[b])
Israel	1950[c]	Arnold (1984[b])
Austria	1955-1962	Arnold (1984[b])
Sweden	1957	Arnold (1984[b])
Europe (7 countries)	1960-68 ("16 doctors' strikes")	Badgley (1975[b])
Italy	1960s, 1974	Arnold (1984[b]), Badgley (1975[b])
France	1960, 1982-83	Arnold (1984[b])
Saskatchewan	July 1962	Badgley and Wolfe (1967)
Belgium	April 1964	Editorial (1964), International Comments (1964)
Quebec	1970	Arnold (1984[b])
Chile	Oct. 1972-Mar, 1973 (sporadic); Aug. 1973	Belmar and Sidel (1975)
Israel	1973; Sept.-Dec. 1976	Yishai (1986, p. 45[b]), Modan 1986, p. 20[b]), Penchas (1987[b])
Nigeria	Jan. 2-19 1975; May-July 1978; Feb.-Mar. 1981; Sept. 10-18 1984	Alubo (1986)
New York City	March 1975	Applebaum (1975), McNamara and Green (1976)
California	1975-76	Phillips (1975), Gamble (1976), James (1979)
Great Britain	Dec. 1975	Editorial (1975), Anonymous (1975)
Great Britain	1975-76	Arnold (1984[b])
Los Angeles	Jan. 1976	Roemer (1979, 1981)
Chicago	"recent"	McKinlay (1978, p. 180[b])
Canada (B.C., Manitoba, Ontario, Quebec)	"recent"	Coburn, Torrance, and Kaufert (1983, p. 422[b]), Penchas (1987[b])
Ontario	Nov. 1980	Desky et al. (1986)
Denmark	1981	Heidenheimer and Johansen (1985)
Israel	Mar.-June 1983	Yishai (1986), Modan (1986), Ellencweig (1983), Greenberg (1983)
France	1983	Penchas (1987[b])
Australia	Mar.-July 1984	Green and Castaldi (1985), Arnold (1984[b])
Peru	1984	Arnold[b] (1984)

a. I would ask the reader to keep in mind that I make no claim that my list is exhaustive. My attention has been called to two major strikes in Belgium other than the 1964 strike; to "a long history of strikes in Italian hospitals"; to an important strike in Ontario in 1985-86; and to a strike in Greece in 1986. I also happen to know of a three-day "relay hunger strike" in Bombay in 1986. I am sure there have been many others. The actions listed in the table are those that are referred to in print in the material that came to my attention after a computer search. Because I had no intention of writing a definitive history of doctors' strikes, I trust the reader will accept this limitation, and remember that, throughout the chapter, "as far as I know" is always meant.
b. Indicates a passing reference to a "strike" without any details or original source; nor could I locate any other reference to the "strike".
c. Although I am an Israeli and fairly familiar with the history of the Israeli health care system, I have never heard of a 1950 "strike," nor have I encountered any reference to it elsewhere.

involved range from all physicians to surgeons or radiologists or anesthesiologists; from local to regional to national "strikers"; from interns to residents to attending; from salaried to entrepreneurial to contract fee-for-service doctors. There is no "classic" doctors' strike in participation, form, or content.

Second, it will be noted that strikes in the interbellum period were well-nigh nonexistent. I cannot begin to explain this, particularly in view of the vast scope of strikes in other industries during the Depression years.

THE SEARCH FOR PATTERNS

A "strike" is a social phenomenon of enormous complexity which, in its totality, is never susceptible to complete description, let alone complete explanation. (Ross and Hartman 1960, p. 24)

Every strike has its own particular context and content. Our search—perhaps a vain one—is for underlying similarities and identification of fundamental patterns cutting across time and place. Can extant theories of strikes be of help? In relating to this question, I shall refer to two most useful works (Eldridge 1972; Cronin 1978).

Of the five schools of thought proposed by Smelser, as summarized by Eldridge (1972, pp. 53-54; see Smelser 1963), the "class warfare" approach, emphasizing systematic capitalist exploitation, is patently irrelevant. There is no strike on record, as far as I know, that can even partially be characterized in this way. Conceivably, when interns were regarded as students and paid room and board and pocket money at best, in return for very hard labor, one might speak of exploitation. But they simply did not strike. (See Roemer's 1986 justly sarcastic remarks about "inherently exploitative proletarianization" of doctors.) Yet there is one element that might be related to this approach and that is involved in doctors' strikes. In discussing what he calls the "structural" theory of strikes, Cronin (1978, p. 202) refers to the workers' collective consciousness, to an "us/them view of the world" (as exemplified by miners in an isolated community). It may well be that the widespread self-image of doctors as being a community apart—one finds nothing like the God-doctor jokes in any other professional group—may be a relevant prerequisite for striking. But part of this self-image includes a no-strike ethos. Hence the special collective identity would be as pertinent to explaining why doctors do not strike as to why they do.

Second, what Smelser calls the "political" approach, emphasizing union recognition as the goal of a strike, cannot, at least until now, be used to explain any doctor strike. The one possible exception in which this

issue was indirectly involved was the New York City Committee of
Interns and Residents strike in 1975 (Applebaum 1975; McNamara and
Green 1976). I know of no case in which "management" (which very often
means the state) refused to recognize and negotiate with a group that
claimed to represent doctors. Once again, Cronin's discussion of Shorter
and Tilly's political-organizational model (1978, pp. 206-10) relevantly
enriches the approach. Strikes, they emphasize, invariably require organization, the ability to act collectively, an ability that is, in their view,
primarily determined by the technology of the work situation. One of the
patterns that seems to emerge from the review of doctors' strikes is that
the internal heterogeneity of physician specialization is often an *inhibit-
ing* factor in calling or maintaining a strike. Thus, for example, the
Australian radiologists and pathologists, far more than other doctors, were
vehement in refusing to sign new contracts required by the change introduced by the Labour government in the health insurance law (Arnold
1984). Similarly, over and over again we find that the organizational
differentiation between hospital and ambulatory physicians, characteristic
of most European countries, or house staff, salaried teaching hospital
physicians, and attending doctors characteristic of the United States,
strongly affect the character and duration of a strike.

We might note in passing one strike that must be included under the
rubric "political," though Smelser surely did not have this in mind. In
1905 some physicians took an active part in agitation for a Constitutional
Assembly in Russia. When the activists in the city of Balashov were fired
in July, 18 physicians and 30 nurses went on strike in protest (Kuzmina
1973). Individuals and small groups of doctors have been active politically in leftist movements—Allende in Chile is, of course, the most well
known. But when strike theorists talk of "political" explanations, this is
not what they have in mind. We shall, subsequently, return to the "political" explanation in a different, but most relevant sense.

The New York City strike is an example of a strike in which Smelser's
third and fourth approaches, which he calls "economic advantage"—
focusing on wage gains—and "job security"—focusing on long-term
work conditions—do seemingly help us to understand. This is particularly
true if the approach is expanded by the crucial element in Cronin's version
of the economic approach (1978, p. 204), which emphasizes the gap
between expectations and achievements. The major demands of the Committee of Interns and Residents centered on a reasonable limitation of
work hours and adequate personnel to handle the work load pressure, as
well as being free from the demand to do the work of nurses and technicians. The two California strikes (Gamble 1976) in which physicians
refused to renew their malpractice insurance were aimed at net income

maintenance. But, in both cases, one gets a sense of the problem being one of unfairness rather than a question of the absolute level of compensation.

This is particularly seen in the case of the Israeli strikes of 1973, 1976, and 1983 (Modan 1986; Yishai 1986). A very great majority of Israeli physicians have, for many decades, been salaried employees of institutions belonging to Kupat Holim, the sick fund of the Histadrut, the national trade union federation, or to the government. Until the 1960s, Israel was a strongly egalitarian society. Doctors' incomes were similar to those of other white-collar employees. In the 1970s income differentials grew rapidly, but doctors were not major beneficiaries of this development. It is in this context that the strike of 1976 took place, resulting in very significant increases for overtime work. These gains were largely wiped out by soaring inflation. As Greenberg (1983, p. 683) noted, a senior hospital physician took home a total monthly salary of some $1500 (the cost of living being similar to that in the United States), far less than many other professionals and executives. The unprecedented four-month strike in 1983 took place at a time when a national wage policy limited to a 22% increase was in force, while doctors demanded a far greater increase. The economic explanation, then, does have merit; but, as we shall see, it is at best partial.

Smelser's fifth explanation, the analysis that emphasizes "human relations," begins to bring us closer to understanding doctors' strikes, but hardly in the sense that Elton Mayo meant. This rubric includes two components, as Mayo saw it. The first, the breakdown of primary groups among workers as a source of unrest leading to strikes, is, if anything, precisely the opposite of what happens when doctors go on strike (and, in all likelihood, not only doctors). Over and over again, one sees the emergence of primary group relations among striking doctors whose previous relations had been formal and structured at most. During the 11 days of the hunger strike that led to the ending of the 1983 Israeli strike, I witnessed a sense of solidarity among my medical colleagues that I had not seen in a decade of working with these men and women.

Mayo's second component, the lack of communication and understanding between management and workers, begins to take us closer to the heart of the matter. At a recent top-level meeting of Israeli physicians, after the word "alienation" had been used over and over again, the single most powerful person in the Israeli health care system, a man of considerable intelligence and sophistication, rose and said something to the effect of "I simply don't know what you're talking about." Now this man, whom I know personally, knows reasonably well what "alienation" means. But because of the role he and his colleagues play as architects of the Israeli health care system, he cannot afford to acknowledge that this structure is alienating. Doing so would have too many implications for his power.

As sociologists know well, real conflicts are not resolved simply by listening courteously and talking honestly. But the focus of the human relations school on the hearts and minds of people does provide a thread, which, I believe, can begin to lead to an understanding of doctors' strikes. As Cronin puts it in criticizing the Shorter-Tilly model of strikes (1978, p. 210): "By leaving out the subjective dimension, they telescope and oversimplify the complicated process by which the structural features of industrial society come to inform collective action." To follow this thread, I turn to a powerful though neglected sociological concept.

DOCTORS AND *RESSENTIMENT*

Merton (1957, p. 156) points to the three interlocking elements in Scheler's concept of *ressentiment*: "First, diffuse feelings of hate, envy and hostility; second, a sense of being powerless to express these feelings actively against the person or social stratum evoking them; and third, a continual re-experiencing of this impotent hostility."

In 1983, as I lived through the lengthy strike of Israeli doctors, the words "bitterness" and "frustration" kept coming to mind. Over and over again, as I went through the accounts of doctors' strikes, *ressentiment* seemed to be a key clue to understanding. For a start, I would propose that the reader turn to an easily available paper (Marcus 1975) in a journal issue devoted to health workers' strikes. Marcus, a physician active in union organization, has written an impassioned speech, not particularly useful as analysis, but outstanding as an expression of a sense of frustration and beleaguerment. "Within the next very few years," he writes (p. 40),

> the inevitable phasing out of private practice by direct government subsidy to other forms of practice will render all physicians totally dependent on government policy and whim. . . . In this "Brave New World of Medicine", with the forces that are arrayed against him . . . the physician must certainly be reduced to the level of a public functionary . . . physicians . . . are no longer able to play a dominant role in the determination of their own professional lives or livelihoods.

Alubo (1986, p. 470), analyzing the four doctors' strikes in Nigeria, uses words like "downgrading (perceived and real) . . . the status of their profession [has been] 'prostituted.' " He quotes (p. 472) the late president of the Nigerian Medical Association as saying: "The Time of the humanitarian doctor is past." Badgley and Wolfe (1967, p. 47), in characterizing the atmosphere leading up to the 1962 Saskatchewan strike against the introduction of provincial health insurance, quote a leading spokesman as saying "never since the days of Charles II has there been such legislation reversing the civil rights and liberties of citizens," and (p. 168) compare the doctors to the machine-wrecking Luddites. Another doctor is quoted (p. 166) describing the striking doctors as "torn by one of the great tortures of the soul, the agony of those who face exile."

Belmar and Sidel (1975), tracing the developments leading up to the 1973 strike against the transformation of the health care system under the regime of Allende, himself a physician, note the bitterness with which Allende and those physicians who enthusiastically cooperated with him were attacked as traitors, which reminds us of Merton's comment, in his discussion of *ressentiment* (1957, p. 157), that it is "the renegade who . . . renounces the prevailing values that becomes the target of greatest hostility."

The *British Medical Journal* (*BMJ*; Editorial 1975) directly expresses the mood of doctors in a period of "industrial action" by doctors in terms of "frustration . . . cheated . . . deceived . . . skepticism . . . threatening ultimatum . . . anger . . . gulf of confidence . . . an obstinate opponent who refuses to modify political dogma." (The reference is to Mrs. Barbara Castle, then Labour Secretary of State for Social Services. I cannot refrain from wondering whether not only her political views and actions but also the fact that she was a woman might not have fueled the hostility of the British doctors.) *BMJ*'s colleague, *The Lancet* (Anonymous 1975) expressed the atmosphere of the time by quoting a leading surgeon as saying that "there will be no hope at all for patients or ourselves if we are squeezed into becoming acquiescent pawns of the Department of Health and Social Services."

In the following year, Gamble (1976, p. 61), commenting on the California strikes, writes: "If there had not been a malpractice problem, in time some other issue would have brought the mounting undercurrent of discontent to the surface . . . a climate for fostering similar frustrations." He goes on to warn his hospital administration colleagues that "California's recent mass withdrawals of medical services by physicians in private practice is a phenomenon that will be repeated in other parts of the United States," linking the mood to the student demonstrations of the 1960s and the Watts riots. (No matter that his predictions have not been confirmed; it is his sense of the ambience with which we are here concerned.)

Greenberg (1983, p. 682), an American observer of the 1983 Israeli strike, comments: "But in terms of duration, intensity, and bitterness, the Israeli experience is a landmark." The bitterness is directly expressed throughout the book recounting the strike by its leader, the chair of the Israeli Medical Association (Yishai 1986; see, e.g., pp. 37-38). Yishai quotes one of Israeli's leading physicians and the dean of one of its four medical schools (p. 49; my translation from the Hebrew):

> For more than 40 years there have been attempts to place the physicians in the same furrow as workers in other occupations. The doctors and their organizations have been robbed of the sense of uniqueness. Let them, then, not be reproached with complaints that it is not appropriate that their organization behave like every other trade union.

The bitterness, anxiety, and hostility of the "junior doctors" in Denmark are well described by Heidenheimer and Johansen (1985). These emotions constitute a major factor, in their view, which explains the Danish strikes in 1981, in contrast to their nonstriking Swedish colleagues who faced the same issues at the same time but continued negotiations without striking. The Swedes, they contend, in contrast to the Danes, are far less resentful, far more integrated within both the medical profession and the political structure (see Twaddle and Hessler 1986 on Sweden).

Finally, and perhaps most poignant, I would quote (International Comments 1964) from the Flemish slogan of the second mass protest meeting in Brussels on January 25, 1964, which preceded the dramatic April strike of Belgian physicians, when almost all the doctors left the country for four days. Some 6,500 of Belgium's 10,000 doctors attended the electrifying meeting, held in the spirit of "Not *geneesknechten*—menial serfs of the healing art—but *geneesheeren*, the word in Flemish for physicians, *heeren* signifying lords or masters."

But, surely, my sociological colleagues who have encountered Scheler directly, or through Merton, or through Coser's editing (Scheler 1961), will say that *ressentiment* is not the appropriate concept to apply to doctors. True, there may be hate and hostility, but there is not envy. There may be "free-floating ill-temper . . . intensely repressed" (Friedenberg 1962, p. 410), but there hardly is a sense of powerlessness or of impotence. Doctors by and large cannot be said to have made a deal with the system in which they forgo genuine goal-achievement and the overt expression of anger at the system in return for legitimation of taking one's anger out on the less powerful, such as Friedenberg proposes teachers have done. (My Israeli reader, however, may well be tempted to point out that at least some ambulatory care physicians are indeed in this situation.)

If we put the question in these terms, then only conceivably in communist societies can we expect to find *ressentiment* as a characteristic of doctors. There is no evidence that this is the case elsewhere. *But there is, nonetheless, a powerful sentiment that characterizes, nay, that seems to be an essential ingredient, in the eruption of doctors' strikes, a sentiment sufficiently powerful and pervasive to overcome a very deeply rooted antistrike norm.* If *ressentiment* is not the appropriate concept, what is?

After considerable thought, and with some uncertainty, I have come to the tentative conclusion that what Sorokin calls *Spannung* perhaps best conveys the sense of bitterness, frustration, free-floating ill temper, and repressed hostility that is in the air in almost every doctors' strike reviewed. As Sorokin ([1937-41] 1961, p. 1317) puts it:

> Finally, *between these types stand the intermediate systems, which are neither congeries nor perfectly integrated systems.* Such are the social systems where only the causal interdependence is found but where relationships of the elements of the system are somewhat eclectic, not quite consistent, and actually or latently conflicting between and in each of its components. In such systems there is always found what Max Weber, M. Scheler and E. Barthel style, *Spannung*, a kind of tension or latent antagonism; a hidden split or crack, which flares into an open split of the system as soon as the respective adverse interference of the external conditions takes place.

Doctors make up a social group that is like Sorokin's intermediate type, as are teachers. But if Friedenberg is correct in seeing teachers (at least at the time he wrote, over 25 years ago) as characterized by *ressentiment*, then why is this not true of doctors? Why do I see *Spannung* as a more appropriate concept? The core of the distinction, I suggest, lies in the fact that teachers have made a deal with the system that involves relinquishing the goal of being the dominant actor in the system and the acceptance of powerlessness. The distinction between doctors and teachers leads me to suggest that the sentiment that underlies doctors' strikes is a distinction that is related to a very significant historical-structural fact: *Doctors have made it, while teachers never have!*

But if doctors have made it, then why *Spannung*? What are the historical and structural contexts in which this sentiment comes to the fore and comes to be expressed in a strike?

THE HISTORICAL-STRUCTURAL
CONTEXTS OF *SPANNUNG*

I should note that I do not wish to imply that the sentiments I have discussed are inherent in the nature of the two respective professions of teaching and medicine. (See Stone 1980, pp. 5 ff., for a fine discussion of whether professional power is shaped by the nature of medical care or by the political context in which it operates.) While I know little about the teaching profession, my sense is that, with widespread unionization in many countries, *ressentiment* may no longer characterize teachers. And it may well be, as I have implied in my earlier remark about doctors in Communist societies, that *Spannung*, as a sentiment found to presage doctors' strikes, may, under given historical conditions, be transformed into *ressentiment*. But in reviewing doctors' strikes, the generalization that seems to me to be most powerful can be formulated as follows:

Doctors, constituting the profession par excellence that has achieved professional autonomy and dominance in the fullest sense of the word, both at the individual and societal levels, come to be confronted, in certain historical situations, with serious challenges to their dominance. Such challenges give rise to the sentiment of Spannung. When, as Sorokin puts it ([1937-41] 1961, p. 1317), "the respective adverse interference of the external conditions takes place," a strike becomes a serious possibility.

The transformation of this possibility into a concrete strike action depends upon a constellation of trigger events, personalities, and relations within doctors' organizations and between doctors and employers or public bodies. But it is a widespread sense of *Spannung*, I believe, that is the underlying motive force, without which doctors are most unlikely to strike (or at least not to go beyond sporadic, limited actions that are not "real" strikes). We would require far more careful data than exist, to the best of my knowledge, before we could even begin to formulate generalizations about the constellations that facilitate the expression of *Spannung* in a strike.

Of the various theories of strikes, Kerr's theory of modernization (Cronin 1978, pp. 200-2) seems to me to be most applicable to understanding doctors' strikes. At its core, this theory proposes that strikes are a response to the "stresses and strains" (what I have called *Spannung*) that occur as changes in technology, organization, and values *undermine or threaten to undermine the way in which a given social group has been previously integrated into the institutional structure*. It is in this sense that I earlier referred to doctors' strikes as political, that is, as struggles for power over the health care system, and distinguished between the manifest functions of strikes, which sometimes relate to financial rewards and work conditions, and the latent function, which is one of the struggle for professional dominance and autonomy.

Let us now remove from the level of abstraction and briefly consider some of the major strikes whose elements have led me to this generalization. Obviously, I can here do little more than hint, in each case, at the historical situations that provided challenges to physician dominance. It is not accidental that the six examples I have chosen are each taken from a different continent.

The story of the struggle of German physicians to maintain dominance in an era of social transformation that challenged their relatively secure position as family physicians is fascinatingly told by Stone (1980, chap. 3; see also Light et al. 1986). The story must be understood in the context of a society in which sickness funds, health insurance, and a powerful Social Democratic party were becoming an increasingly important part of the scene. Though the Deutsche Aertzvereinsbund (DAV) had been formed as a national union of medical associations in 1873, it was not until the first decade of the twentieth century that the head-on struggle for power erupted into scores of strikes. These were directed at the sickness funds and conducted by the Leipziger Verband (LV; the "Union of German Physicians for the Defense of their Economic Interests"), founded by Dr. Hartmann. (For a detailed though ideologically partisan account of one such strike in 1904, see von Moschke 1975.) In 1903 the LV became the "economic department" of the DAV. By 1913, 75% of all German physicians were members of the LV. In parallel fashion, the many sickness funds began to associate. "At this point," Stone writes (1980, p. 51), "the government stepped in to mediate between the funds and the physicians, and the result was the historic Berlin Treaty of 1913." Conflict was not to disappear, but the basic institutional structure of relations had been established for many decades to come, as we can see by referring to Pflanz (1978). As Stone puts it (1980, p. 18): "Instead of fragmenting the medical profession to keep it weak, the government deliberately *consolidated* it, but confronted it with strong countervailing organizations."

Though they make no reference to the German experience, Badgley and Wolfe's (1967) account of the Saskatchewan strike (the only book-length sociological account of a doctors' strike) a half century later provides a striking parallel. In 1944 the Canadian Commonwealth Federation (CCF) had gained control of the provincial government and began the introduction of a variety of social measures. Health care, in the hands of small entrepreneurs, with a number of doctor-controlled or owned insurance companies, remained untouched until the election of 1960. Compulsory health insurance then became a major CCF plank and dominated the campaign. Though the bill was passed in November 1961 and scheduled to go into effect in July 1962, it was not really until May that physicians embarked on a campaign that, at least as described by Badgley and Wolfe, who are self-described partisans, reminded me of the hysteria of antifluoridation campaigns. Physician confidence that the threat to their dominance would be overcome was enhanced by the Conservative victory in the federal election on June 18. But the provincial government held fast, played it cool, and made detailed plans for replacing doctors when the strike started on July 1. By July 10 it had begun to falter; it collapsed on July 23. The subsequent agreement hardly proved to be the debacle that the physicians had anticipated, though the institutional structure of health care had been radically changed.

The Chilean story, a decade later, told by Belmar and Sidel (1975), had a different denouement. Since 1952, the SNS, Chile's national health service, provided curative care for 70% of the population and preventive and environmental care for all. White-collar workers, making up 20% of the population, were registered with an insurance plan. But only 5% of the doctors worked full-time for the SNS, while another 80% averaged four hours a day. In September 1970, Allende, a self-proclaimed socialist physician, at the head of the Unidad Popular, a leftist coalition, was elected president of Chile. A broad radical program of economic and social reform was put forward, including a substantial restructuring of the health services, at the heart of which was decentralization of services, an emphasis on prevention and community programs, and "democratization." Physician opposition remained on the policy debate level for the first two years. But as the process of social transformation proceeded, most physicians took their place in the opposition movement, with occasional sporadic strikes. Following the elections in March 1973, in which Allende's support rose from 36% to 45%, open political opposition was marked, culminating in the doctors' strike in August, as part of a broad strike movement. With Allende's assassination and the coup on September 11, the physicians averted what in their view would have been a catastrophic social transformation (though not in the view of those doctors who supported Allende and who were "appropriately" dealt with, by torture, exile, and murder, by the new regime).

As a footnote to history, I cannot refrain in passing from referring to the strike of Moscow physicians from December 1917 to March 1918 (Nesterenko 1966). Here, too, the doctors' strike was part and parcel of a broader political struggle against the Bolshevik Revolution, but with a different outcome. The account of this strike, incidentally, quotes a demand by workers' councils to have the striking physicians, seen as saboteurs of Soviet medicine, executed.

Since 1975 there have been four doctors' strikes in Nigeria. As Alubo (1986) puts it, doctors were, as employees of the Nigerian Health Service, civil servants. But prior to independence in 1960, they were not only the highest-salaried civil servants; "doctors as a collectivity have always distinguished themselves from *other* civil servants" (p. 469). They were at home, in colonial Nigeria, in the corridors of power. With the emergence of a native bourgeois elite and other political developments, doctors felt an increasing sense of "relegation." Nor could their salaries, unless augmented by private practice, allow them to be a part of the elite. It is in this context that the strikes are to be understood. In 1975 a government review of salaries, which threatened the special differentials of doctors, led to a move to cut down to normal "civil service hours." In 1978, a decree prohibiting private practice until a doctor had served for five years led to another strike in working hours, and the decree was rescinded. But in the 1981 overtime wage strike, the doctors' demands were largely unmet. Finally, the 1984 strike, ostensibly dealing with inadequate teaching hospital staff and supplies, brought about the replacement of the minister of health by a physician, government promises, and the setting up of a task force. Again and again, Alubo stresses that while material interests are manifest, the underlying issue is really that of control of the health care system (with national health insurance taken for granted) and the position of the medical profession in the society's power elite.

National health insurance may be taken for granted in Nigeria, but this was not the case in Australia.[1] As in Canada, the crisis emerged in the context of the coming to power of a Labour government. The new Medicare Plan involved replacement of previous insurance fund reimbursement as of February 1, 1984. A 1% universal tax, covering all of Australia, would fund coverage of 85% of expenses. In effect, this would drastically limit the number of private patients. But far more fundamental, as Arnold (1984, p. 177) put it, writing two months after the March strike, "The new legislation would give the minister the power to control their [consultants'] fees." Heretofore, consultants had had the right to see private patients in public hospitals in return for unpaid work with charity patients. Henceforth all patients would be covered by national insurance. From mid-March 1984 there were "rolling work stoppages one day each week" by New South Wales consultants (Green and Castaldi 1985, p. 62), followed by a variety of actions. Doctors began submitting resignations from government hospital staff. Of the 800 members of the Australian Association of Surgeons, 700 voted in June to resign. By July 2, resignations had been received from 1559 doctors. The government had included a provision in the law that a doctor who resigned would be banned from public hospital affiliation for seven years. On June 20 a one-day strike by attending physicians was called; on June 27, 5000 of the 8020 public hospital staff doctors struck. The government backed down on the seven-year ban, and by July 23 a compromise was reached. But the government persisted in its basic position: Medicare as such was not negotiable. Flare-ups continued sporadically, but the crisis had been surmounted. Henceforth government was to be deeply involved in payment mechanisms and levels.

[1.] In passing, we may note the mystery of the complete absence of strikes with the inauguration of the much more meaningful national health insurance in Britain. Not until the 1970s do we find reference to "industrial action" by British doctors. To discuss this issue would take us too far afield; the interested reader would do well to refer to Gill (1980), even though he does not deal explicitly with the question of strikes, and to Taylor (1984).

In contrast to all the above strike confrontations, the Israeli strike of 1983 was, as it were, strictly about compensation levels, not involving structural changes. But a close reading of the two major published accounts of the strike—written by the chair of the Israel Medical Association (Yishai 1986) and the then director-general of the Ministry of Health (Modan 1986)—suggests that more underlying issues were at stake. (Unfortunately, these accounts are in Hebrew. The English reader will have to be content with Ellencweig 1983; Greenberg 1983; Warner 1984.)

I always find it amusing to ask visitors to Israel what stands they expect leftists and rightists, respectively, to take on national health insurance, for Israel is the one country in which leftists oppose and rightists favor it. The reason is simple. Kupat Holim, providing near-total health insurance coverage for some 85% of the population, is part of the Histadrut, the national trade union federation. One pays one's union dues and gets insurance benefits. Kupat Holim also owns the neighborhood health centers in which ambulatory care is provided, as well as hospitals with 31% of all general hospital beds in the country (18.5% of all hospital beds). Kupat Holim is financed by union dues, employers' contributions, and government subsidies. Thus most physicians are Kupat Holim employees, the majority of the remainder, government employees. National health insurance would strike a major blow against the power of the Histadrut.

Physician dissatisfaction with salaries and work conditions, then, is inextricably intertwined with resentment of perceived trade union bureaucratic control, with the severe limitations on private practice imposed as a condition of employment, and with the government perception that the Israeli Medical Association (IMA) is simply another trade union. (It should be noted that the IMA had formerly been part of the Histadrut, much as other professional organizations are.) A central element in the 11 months of acrimonious wage negotiations that preceded the 1983 strike was the position of the Treasury: flush with having successfully broken the power of the hitherto impregnable union of El Al Airlines employees, the Treasury was perceived as arrogantly assuming it could do the same with doctors. They, like all other workers covered by the collective wage agreement signed at the end of 1982, would be held to a 22% salary increase.

It would take us too far afield to discuss a component in the sense of *Spannung* among Israeli doctors that relates to Jewish culture and is relevant to doctors' strikes in Israel. The physician, as all even vaguely familiar with Jewish culture know, is a culture hero. Though I cannot provide scientific evidence, it is nonetheless my observation, after having been part of the Israeli medical world for 25 years, that many Israeli doctors feel a profound depreciation of the esteem in which the physician is held. As Warner (1984, p. 459), a resident writing about the 1983 strike, put it, "What amazed doctors and government alike was the apathy of the public. . . . The vast majority [of Israelis], however, were silent." The culture hero, it was clear, was no longer on a pedestal. In a society in which monetary reward has increasingly come to symbolize status, a strike for increased wages has far more meaning than might on the surface seem to be the case.

On June 27, 1983, the 118th day of the strike, arbitration terms were signed and the strike ended. In September, the binding arbitration decision provided for terms about which Yishai, chair of the IMA (Warner 1984, p. 463), said: "We could have achieved basically the same thing without the agony of the strike." We would do well to end this account of the Israeli strike by quoting from Yishai's concluding remarks (1986, p. 277; my translation):

> Since the strike, I have observed great indifference among many doctors who were very active in the struggle. "It's a wasted effort" they say—and they open a private clinic. The strike taught them too that there is another way. Among patients too there is despair about the existing framework of medical services. And thus every day we see private clinics and practices opening. Serious economic companies are taking an interest in investments in alternative medical care or in private hospitals.

It is clear, then, that the struggle over the Israeli public health care system is far from over.

CONCLUDING REMARKS

The picture that emerges from these accounts is one that sees strikes as a response to the confrontation by doctors with a "developmental transition." (I intentionally use the Eriksonian term, to be explained below.) The medical profession, in the era of scientific medicine, had become accustomed to a structured pattern of relations that allowed unchallenged professional dominance, that allowed doctors as individuals and as collectives to shape care, organization, and policy at all levels. They lived as God in the Garden of Eden, in control of the Trees of Knowledge and of Life. And behold—God Himself is to be banished from the Garden of Eden.

But does this mean that the future of the medical profession is one of proletarianization, and, as a presumed concomitant, unionization and the struggle for better conditions through strikes? McKinlay (1978; see McKinlay 1984), in an important and challenging paper, has forcefully presented this thesis. True, his paper refers to American physicians; but it is published in a volume with an international perspective. Moreover, he speaks of "medical care production under advanced capitalism," and hence implicitly is discussing a thesis as appropriate to Britain, Italy, and Sweden as it is to the United States. True, he is referring to a process that is under way and not yet dominant. But if his prediction is to have any meaning, then it cannot be limited to a vague, vulgar Marxist "sooner or later" approach.

We would do well to quote McKinlay's own words (1978, pp. 157-58):

> As the result of the increasing bureaucratization which is being forced on medical practice as a consequence of the presence of the logic of capitalist expansion in the United States, physicians are slowly being reduced to a proletarian function and their formerly self-interested activities subordinated to the emerging broader requirements of highly profitable medical care production. . . . [Proletarianization is] *the process by which any occupational category is divested of control over certain prerogatives relating to the location, content, and essentiality of its task activities.*

McKinlay's prediction, then, is that the era of physician dominance and professional autonomy is drawing to a close. (For a more moderately formulated presentation of the "deprofessionalization hypothesis," see Haug 1987.) Light's (1986) recent paper on the growth of corporate medicine in the United States would seem to provide more evidence than McKinlay had a decade ago that the process of bureaucratization for profit is well under way.

But had McKinlay been familiar with the experiences going back to the beginning of the century, and particularly with European experiences, he would have been far more cautious in his prediction of only one possible historical development. Our review of doctors' strikes has, I believe, demonstrated that the medical profession is hardly on a unilinear, inevitable downward path to proletarianization. In country after country, it has faced and continues to face constantly emerging challenges to professional dominance and autonomy. The major challenge has been that of coming to terms with a variety of health insurance programs, and particularly with the increasing role of the state in such programs. The emergence of problems of access and equity, consumer demands, cost and efficacy, changing patterns of disease, the quality of life, and demographic changes—such issues seem to be universal. Similarly, the process of technological development and bureaucratization of medical care (though not necessarily for the reasons McKinlay gives) appears throughout the Western world. These are the challenges that I have called the developmental transition confronted by the medical profession and the societies in which it functions. All developmental transitions, as Erikson has pointed out, involve losses and gains, and compel reorganization. But if in regard to the course of the individual life cycle one might somehow see some substantive similarities among those who successfully meet the challenge (without forgetting the many who fail to do so), in historical developments, only the most superficial and meaningless analysis could fail to recognize profound differences among the various solutions that have been adopted.

A case in point is Taylor's (1984) detailed comparison of the very different paths followed by Britain and Italy in the field of preventive health care. As she puts it (pp. 109-10), a variety of factors must be taken into account "for any explanation of the content and direction of state responses to health problems . . . the struggle among different interests . . . the political, cultural and economic conditions . . . the structure of the state . . . the resources and organizational capacities of political actors." And hence the solutions adopted in each country will vary considerably.

What this study of strikes teaches us—I repeat my opening remark that my observations can only be considered tentative—is that while, on the one hand, there are commonalities that lead to doctors' strikes in different countries, the patterns and degrees of resolution of the underlying conflict, on the other hand, in both the short and the long run, will vary considerably. The Garden of Eden has been or is being left behind. What life on Earth is like differs from society to society.

One more word remains to be said. A full exploration of the scope of professional dominance and autonomy in the context of the varied structural and cultural solutions adopted in different countries (note, for example, that there has never been a strike in the Netherlands) would take another paper. Yet I cannot refrain from making one remark on the issue, having been so long immersed in thinking about doctors' strikes. Nowhere in the literature have I encountered the elementary, relevant fact that politicians, powerful entrepreneurs, and union leaders, no less than the rest of us (including medical sociologists), turn to doctors in hours of profound need. This is not the only reason to anticipate that professional dominance and autonomy, qualified and reinterpreted, will long be with us. But it cannot be ignored. The professional-proletarian bind exists. Nonetheless, I cannot see evidence that the bind is being resolved in the Western world in terms of the process predicted by McKinlay. (For more detailed support of this position, see Freidson 1986.) Or, as Glaser (1983, p. 360) puts it, in formulating his "Second Law of Medical Politics": "*In every system, the doctors get what they want; no NHI law can be enacted without nearly all the clauses demanded by the medical association.*" Perhaps Glaser has gone too far, particularly with respect to professional dominance on the national policy level. But thus far the historical evidence seems to be on his side.

I cannot refrain from including here, as an ironic footnote to history in reference to the Chilean strike recounted above, a paragraph from *The New York Review of Books* (June 25, 1987, p. 47), which I read after the chapter had been written:

> During the past few years, opposition to Pinochet has been led not only by such more or less predictable sectors of the middle class as the clergy, teachers, and university students, but by people who might seem unlikely participants in a struggle against a dictatorship, such as the doctors organized in the Chilean Medical Association (Colegio Medico). As a consequence, many doctors have been detained in Chile's prisons, including the president and secretary of the Medical Association, last year, and, currently, the director of the medical program of the Catholic Church's human rights organization, the Vicariate of Solidarity, along with a private physician who treated patients referred to him by the Vicariate.

REFERENCES

Alubo, S. Ogoh. 1986. "The Political Economy of Doctors' Strikes in Nigeria: A Marxist Interpretation." *Social Science & Medicine* 22:467-77.

Anonymous. 1975. "Damaging Action." *Lancet* 2(Dec. 6):1134.

Applebaum, Alan L. 1975. "The Meaning of the New York Strike." *Hospitals* 49(April 16):17a-17d.

Arnold, Peter C. 1984. "Australian Doctors on Strike." *British Medical Journal* 289(July 21):175-77.

Badgley, Robin F. 1975. "Health Worker Strikes: Social and Economic Bases of Conflict." *International Journal of Health Services* 5:9-17.

Badgley, Robin F. and Samuel Wolfe. 1967. *Doctors' Strike: Medical Care and Conflict in Saskatchewan*. Toronto: Macmillan.

Belmar, Roberto and Victor W. Sidel. 1975. "An International Perspective on Strikes and Strike Threats by Physicians: The Case of Chile." *International Journal of Health Services* 5:53-64.

Coburn, David, George M. Torrance, and Joseph M. Kaufert. 1983. "Medical Dominance in Canada in Historical Perspective: The Rise and Fall of Medicine." *International Journal of Health Services* 13:407-32.

Cronin, J. F. 1978. "Theories of Strikes." *Journal of Social History* 12:194-220.

Desky, Allan S., John R. McLaughlin, Howard B. Abrams, Kristan L'Abbe, and Frank M. Markel. 1986. "Do Interns and Residents Order More Tests than Attending Staff? Results of a House Staff Strike." *Medical Care* 24:526-33.

Editorial. 1964. "The Belgian Strike." *British Medical Journal*, April 11, 924-25.

Editorial. 1975. "Industrial Action by Doctors." *British Medical Journal*, December 6, 544.

Eldridge, J.E.T. 1972. "Explanation of Strikes." Chap. 1 in *Industrial Disputes*, edited by J.E.T. Eldridge. London: Routledge.

Ellencweig, Avi Y. 1983. " 'Caring' and 'Curing' in Modern Medicine: The Case of Doctors' Strike in Israel." Unpublished manuscript.

Freidson, Eliot. 1970. *Professional Dominance*. New York: Atherton.

———. 1986. "The Medical Profession in Transition." Pp. 63-79 in *Applications of Social Science to Clinical Medicine and Health Policy*, edited by L. H. Aiken and D. Mechanic. New Brunswick, NJ: Rutgers.

Friedenberg, Edgar Z. 1962. "The Gifted Student and His Enemies." *Commentary* 33:410-19.

Gamble, Stephen W. 1976. "Coping with a Strike by Doctors." *Hospitals* 50(17):61-64.

Gill, Derek G. 1980. *The British National Health Service: A Sociologist's Perspective* (NIH Pub. 80-2054). Washington, DC: Public Health Service.

Glaser, William A. 1983. "Lessons from Germany: Some Reflections Occasioned by Schulenberg's 'Report.'" *Journal of Health Politics, Policy and Law* 8:352-65.

Green, David and Peter A. Castaldi. 1985. "Special Report: A Crisis in Australian Medicine." *New England Journal of Medicine* 312(Jan. 3):62-63.

Greenberg, Daniel S. 1983. "Special Report: Health Care in Israel." *New England Journal of Medicine* 309:681-84.

Haug, Marie R. 1987. "Deprofessionalization Perspective." Paper presented at the annual meeting of the American Sociological Association, Chicago.

Heidenheimer, Arnold J. and Lars N. Johansen. 1985. "Organized Medicine and Scandinavian Professional Unionism: Hospital Policies and Exit Options in Denmark and Sweden." *Journal of Health Politics, Policy and Law* 10:347-70.

International Comments. 1964. *Journal of the American Medical Association* 188(June 1, June 8):839, 945; 189(July 20, Sept. 14): 250, 878.

Kuzmina, G. S. 1973. "From the History of the Participation of the Medical Intelligentsia in the First Russian Revolution: The Balashov Strike of Physicians in July 1905" (in Russian). *Sov.-Zdravookhr.* 32(8):67-71.

Light, Donald W. 1986. "Corporate Medicine for Profit." *Scientific American* 255:30-37.

Light, Donald W., Stephan Liebfried, and Florian Tennstedt. 1986. "Social Medicine vs. Professional Dominance." *American Journal of Public Health* 76:78-83.

Marcus, Sanford A. 1975. "The Purposes of Unionization in the Medical Profession: The Unionized Profession's Perspective in the United States." *International Journal of Health Services* 5:37-42.

McKinlay, John B. 1978. "The Changing Political and Economic Context of the Patient-Physician Encounter." Pp. 155-88 in *The Doctor-Patient Relationship in the Changing Health Scene* (DHEW Pub. no. [NIH] 78-183), edited by E. B. Gallagher. Washington, DC: Public Health Service.

———. 1984. *Issues in the Political Economy of Health Care*. New York: Tavistock.

McNamara, John J. and Michele Green. 1976. "An Evaluation of Emergency Room Services During the New York City House Officers' Strike." *American Journal of Public Health* 66:135-38.

Merton, Robert K. 1957. "Social Structure and Anomie." Pp. 131-60 in *Social Theory and Social Structure*, rev. ed. New York: Free Press.

Modan, Baruch. 1986. *Medicine Under Siege: The Doctors' Strike and the Crisis of Israeli Medicine* (in Hebrew). Tel Aviv: Adam.

Nesterenko, A. I. 1966. "The Struggle for the Establishment of Soviet Medicine: How the Strike of Moscow Physicians Was Broken (End of 1917-Beginning 1918) (in Russian). *Sov.-Zdravookhr.* 52(12):50-55.

Penchas, Shmuel. 1987. "Strikes in the Medical Sector: Past, Present and Future" (in Hebrew). *Harefuah* 112:100-2.

Pflanz, Manfred. 1978. "The Two Faces of the Patient-Doctor Relationship in a Changing Welfare State: Federal Republic of Germany." Pp. 45-55 in *The Doctor-Patient Relationship in the Changing Health Scene* (DHEW Pub. no. [NIH] 78-183), edited by E. B. Gallagher. Washington, DC: Public Health Service.

Phillips, Donald F. 1975. "The California Physicians' Strike." *Hospitals* 49(Aug. 1):49-52, 105.

Roemer, Milton I. 1979. "Doctor Slowdown: Effects on the Population of Los Angeles County." *Social Science and Medicine* 13C:213-18.

————. 1981. "More Data on Post-Surgical Deaths Related to the 1976 Los Angeles Doctor Slowdown." *Social Science and Medicine* 15C:161-63.

————. 1986. "Proletarianization of Physicians or Organization of Health Services?" *International Journal of Health Services* 16:469-71.

Ross, Arthur M. and Paul T. Hartman. 1960. *Changing Patterns of Industrial Conflict*. New York: John Wiley.

Scheler, Max. 1961. *Ressentiment*, edited by L. A. Coser. New York: Free Press.

Smelser, Neil J. 1963. *The Sociology of Economic Life*. Englewood Cliffs, NJ: Prentice-Hall.

Sorokin, Pitirim A. [1937-41] 1961. "5. The Principle of Immanent Change." Pp. 1311-21 in *Theories of Society*, edited by Talcott Parsons et al. New York: Free Press.

Stone, Deborah A. 1980. *The Limits of Professional Power: National Health Care in the Federal Republic of Germany*. Chicago: University of Chicago Press.

Taylor, Rosemary C.R. 1984. "State Intervention in Postwar Western European Health Care: The Case of Prevention in Britain and Italy." Pp. 91-117 in *The State in Capitalist Europe*, edited by S. Bornstein, D. Held, and J. Krieger. London: Allen & Unwin.

Twaddle, Andrew C. and Richard M. Hessler. 1986. "Power and Change: The Case of the Swedish Commission of Inquiry on Health and Sickness Care." *Journal of Health Politics, Policy and Law* 11:19-40.

von Moschke, Gerd. 1975. "Fight of the Leipzig Workers for a New Organization of Medical Care During the Physicians' Strike in 1904" (in German). *Zeitschrift Aertzliche Fortbildung* (Jena) 69(21):1141-43.

Warner, Ellen. 1984. "Israel's Troubled Health Care System." *Canadian Medical Association Journal* 130:454-63.

Yishai, Ram. 1986. *The Doctor's Strike: 2 March 1983-27 June 1983* (in Hebrew). Tel Aviv: Zamora, Beitan.

14

Action and Reaction:
An Integrated, Comparative Perspective on
Feminist and Antifeminist Movements

Janet Saltzman Chafetz
Anthony Gary Dworkin

In recent years, a substantial literature has arisen concerning the contemporary American New Right as a backlash or countermovement to feminism (e.g., Brady and Tedin 1976; Burris 1983; Conover and Gray 1983; Ehrenreich 1982; Gelb and Palley 1982; Luker 1984; Petchesky 1981; Tedin 1978; Tedin et al. 1977). The turn-of-the-century antisuffrage movements in the United States and Great Britain have also received attention (e.g., Banks 1981; Flexner 1975; Harrison 1978; Howard 1982; Marshall 1985; Marshall and Orum forthcoming). There is, however, scant literature on other backlash movements of any type, and even less that explores the theoretical relationship between change-oriented movements and those that arise in reaction to them (for exceptions, see Mottl 1980; Gale 1986). This chapter is a culmination of several years of work on women's movements and countermovements cross-nationally and historically (see Chafetz and Dworkin 1983, 1986, 1987). Demographic data utilized in this chapter to explore the structural variables affecting women's movements span a period from 1860 (as in the case of the First Wave of Women's movements in the United States) to 1970 (for all Second Wave feminist movements analyzed) for countries on six con-

AUTHORS' NOTE: *We wish to thank our former research assistant and thesis student, Stephanie Swanson, who, in both roles, helped to gather and analyze the data for the earlier projects on which this theoretical chapter is based.*

tinents. Organized countermovement activity was less pervasive, but we nevertheless relied upon as much cross-national data as were available. We integrate our conclusions from those two somewhat separate research endeavors into one process model, which is summarized in a chart presented later in the chapter.

Our use of a range of countries in the analysis was guided by two desires. First, we wanted to be able to demonstrate the ubiquitous nature of the influence of certain structural variables on movements and their countermovements. Second, we sought to disentangle idiographic cultural and historical explanations for the rise of movements and countermovements from their common structural basis. That is, when attention is focused upon only one or two societies, it is too facile to attribute the rise of a movement to unique events, or to attribute differences between movements to culture or history. When a number of societies are examined, structural commonalities can be isolated and, likewise, so can structural differences be ascertained that could account for the nature of movements and countermovements.

CONCEPTUAL DEFINITIONS

We define women's movements in a manner that includes both the nineteenth- and early twentieth-century ameliorative movements (termed First Wave) and the more ideologically radical, feminist ones that have emerged since about 1968 (Second Wave). Specifically, *we define women's movements as social movements consciously oriented to rectifying socially rooted disadvantages specific to females, which they experience on the basis of their gender*. This orientation constitutes their first (although not necessarily only) priority. They constitute a challenge to at least some aspect(s) of the status quo, and are thus change-oriented. Women's movements comprise at least one organization that is independent of control by governmental, political party, or other organizational entities that are in turn controlled by men (see Chafetz and Dworkin, 1986: chap. 1). The primary adherents to women's movements are women, but this does not preclude substantial male involvement as conscience adherents. Women's movements vary in time and space in many ways, including the scope and radicalness of their ideology, the number and specific types of goals or demands they seek on behalf of women, and their size.

Their opposition, when it emerges, should properly be termed "anti-woman's-movement movements." For the sake of sanity, however, we shall refer to such countermovements as "antifeminist movements." Also termed "backlash movements," countermovements represent "a conscious, collective attempt to resist or reverse social change" (Mottl 1980, p. 620). *An antifeminist movement is, therefore, defined as a social movement consciously oriented to preventing or reversing the gender-related changes sought by a women's movement.* Countermovements mobilize in response to a change-oriented movement that appears to be succeeding in achieving its goals. This means that, where a women's movement is small, weak, or appears to be unsuccessful, an antifeminist movement is unlikely to arise. We found some evidence of antifeminist movement activity in a group of nations; however, except for the United States during both waves and Great Britain during the First Wave of women's movement activity, the amount of information about these countermovements is very scanty. The three countermovements that have been described most fully represent responses to all but one case where a women's movement reached unambiguously mass proportions. Much of the information we present on countermovements is, therefore, based upon the experiences of the United States and Great Britain, but is also informed by available evidence from other nations.

Countermovements, when fully developed, consist of two very disparate kinds of groups. The first are vested-interest groups whose position in the society is threatened by the growing success of the change-oriented movement. *Vested-interest groups predate the change-oriented movement and have benefited from the relative disadvantages of the members of the social category whose movement they now oppose*, in this case, women. *They constitute the dominant elite against whom the change-oriented movement does battle* (see Castells 1983; Touraine 1981). Their motive for supporting or organizing a countermovement is to protect their dominance. Vested-interest groups have everywhere been primarily male-dominated and represent the core of a society's economic, political, religious, higher educational, and other central institutions. Organizations often employ people to monitor proposed legislation, current events, trends, and public opinion in order to learn quickly of impending threats to their interests. Control of organizational resources and networks with other organizational leaders, both formal and informal, permits quick mobilization. Antifeminist activism could begin as soon as the threat to their interests is perceived, but many organizations refrain from doing so. Organizational self-interest also entails the creation and maintenance of good public relations, at least with some specific constituency, if not the general public. Organizations and their leaders may not be in a position to publicly oppose the changes proposed by a threatening social movement (Gale 1986, p. 210). The perceived magnitude of the threat and the specific constituency to which an organization must appeal will strongly influence the extent and type (covert or overt) of action.

The second type of countermovement group is voluntary associations. These grass-roots groups are composed of individuals who may be drawn, at least in part, from the same social category as members of the movement they oppose, again in this case, women. *Members of countermovement voluntary associations fear that the new or proposed economic and structural patterns disrupt their social and/or economic status.* For them, the countermovement is "status politics" (Gusfield 1963). Unlike vested-interest groups, those who come to comprise the membership of backlash voluntary associations are typically slow to perceive threat from the change-oriented movement and, therefore, slow to organize in reaction. They must have their "consciousness raised"—much as change-oriented movement members must—before they become activists. Antifeminist vested-interest groups play a major role in the process of mobilizing and organizing countermovement voluntary associations.

WOMEN'S MOVEMENTS

The Dependent Variables:
Movement Ideology and Size

We began by thoroughly searching the scholarly, English-language literature produced by sociologists, historians, political scientists, and others, concerning women's movements and the organizations that constitute them.[1] We found descriptions of organizations that could reasonably be subsumed by our definition of women's movements dating back as far as the mid-nineteenth century and as recently as the 1980s. Movement ideology is conceptualized in terms of the extent to which the sex role and gender stratification system extant in the society is challenged. Earlier movements, termed First Wave, tended to be ameliorative and did not challenge male privilege; later movements, termed Second Wave, were uniformly feminist and did challenge such privilege. First Wave, primarily ameliorative, movements were documented in 31 different nations, five of which experienced two rather distinct movement phases. These movements only attempted to facilitate the role of women as wives and mothers. Neither the system of gender stratification nor the system of sex role definitions was challenged by the movements of the First Wave. By contrast, the social movements of the Second Wave challenged the privileged status of men and sought to alter the sex role definitions.

[1]. It is impossible to know whether nations not included in our sample lacked such a movement or merely lacked a scholar who wrote about it in English. After all, historians and social scientists do not usually study the nonoccurrence of a phenomenon.

Second Wave movements were documented in 16 nations. The nations, years of publicly visible movement activism (for First Wave only), maximum size to which they grew, and ideological scope of our total sample of movements are depicted in Tables 14.1 and 14.2. The nations listed in the tables represent every continent on the globe, especially in the First Wave.

First Wave movements focused on issues of women's rights, including educational opportunities; employment opportunities, primarily for single women; property rights; divorce reform, child custody and other legal changes, especially for married women; and, of course, suffrage. There was considerable similarity in the general issues raised cross-nationally, despite the fact that First Wave movements spanned a century and occurred in nations represented by a variety of different types of cultures, religions, and political forms. Education for women was uniformly the first issue raised, suffrage nearly always the last, economic opportunity and legal reforms coming in between. The precise nature of the legal reforms differed cross-nationally, depending on the precise nature of women's legal disabilities, but almost always referred to married women. Educational opportunity was a dichotomous demand, involving basic literacy for women in countries with high levels of illiteracy, and access to universities in already highly literate nations. Issues of temperance and the end of the sexual double standard, important in the United States, were widespread, including not only all Anglo-Saxon and most European nations, but China, Japan, Egypt, and several Latin American countries as well. Finally, the end of practices such as foot-binding, polygyny, or purdah was demanded in specific cases. Suffrage arose late as an issue because it was a response to the difficulties women faced in achieving other changes. Conceived as a tool to aid in gaining other changes, it frequently became the dominant movement goal, obscuring other demands. This was especially apparent in the United States and Great Britain, but not confined to them. The result was that, after suffrage was won, First Wave movements typically disbanded, with much of the rest of their agenda left incomplete.

What made First Wave movements almost entirely ameliorative, and distinguished them from Second Wave feminist movements, was their nearly universal acceptance of the idea that men and women are and ought to be fundamentally different; that each gender inhabits a separate sphere. Women were perceived as first and foremost mothers and wives; men, as public actors and breadwinners. Proposed changes were primarily justified in terms of the improvement of women's ability to perform their traditional obligations. Second, women could, because of their "special" virtues, presumably improve the moral tenor of public life, if granted the vote. The few instances where a more radical, feminist ideology emerged

TABLE 14.1: Estimates of Relative Size, Ideological Scope, and Approximate Dates of Independent First Wave Women's Movements

Country	Years	Size	Ideological Scope
United States	1848-ca 1870	incipient	feminist
	ca 1870-1920	mass	ameliorative
Great Britain	ca 1860-1900	incipient	ameliorative
	ca 1900-1918	mass and incipient	ameliorative and feminist
Canada	ca 1880-1918	intermediate	ameliorative
Australia	ca 1880-1901	incipient to intermediate	ameliorative
New Zealand	1885-1993	incipient to intermediate	ameliorative
Finland	ca 1880-1906	incipient	ameliorative
Norway	ca 1885-1913	incipient	ameliorative
Sweden	ca 1870-ca 1910	intermediate to mass	ameliorative
Denmark	ca 1870-ca 1910	intermediate to mass	ameliorative
Iceland	ca 1894-ca 1910	intermediate to mass	ameliorative
Holland	1894-ca 1910	intermediate	ameliorative
France	ca 1870-1900	incipient	feminist
	ca 1900-1914	intermediate	ameliorative
Russia	1905-1918	incipient	ameliorative
Germany	ca 1865-1914	incipient	ameliorative
	ca 1914-ca 1920	intermediate to mass	ameliorative
Italy	ca 1867-1914	incipient	possibly feminist
Austro-Hungarian Empire	1893-ca 1920	incipient	ameliorative
China	1911-1927	incipient	ameliorative
Japan	1880-1923	incipient	ameliorative
	1923-ca 1930	intermediate to mass	ameliorative
India	1917-ca 1950	incipient	ameliorative
Indonesia	1928-1942	?	ameliorative
Iran/Persia	1906-ca 1950s	incipient	ameliorative
Egypt	1919-ca 1935	incipient	ameliorative
Puerto Rico	1917-1936	?	ameliorative
Dominican Republic	1931-1942	incipient	ameliorative
Cuba	ca 1914-ca 1927	probably intermediate	ameliorative
Mexico	1904-ca 1940	intermediate and incipient	ameliorative and feminist
Argentina	ca 1900-ca 1930s	incipient	ameliorative
Brazil	ca 1920-1937	incipient	ameliorative
Chile	1915-1949	incipient	ameliorative
Peru	ca 1915-1925	less than incipient	ameliorative
Uruguay	1916-ca 1932	incipient	ameliorative

NOTE: Relative size refers to the largest size achieved by a movement during the time period in question. A question mark indicates that no estimate of size is possible.

were characterized by one of two phenomena: a small, feminist movement evolved into a more broad-based, ameliorative one (the United States and France); or a small feminist branch coexisted with a larger, ameliorative

TABLE 14.2: Estimates of Relative Size and Ideological Scope of Independent Second Wave Women's Movements

Country	Size	Ideological Scope
United States	mass	feminist
Great Britain	intermediate	feminist
Canada	intermediate to mass	feminist
Norway	probably intermediate	feminist
Finland	probably intermediate	feminist
West Germany	incipient to intermediate	feminist
Holland	mass	feminist
France	incipient to intermediate	feminist
Italy	intermediate	feminist
Spain	probably incipient	feminist
Portugal	incipient	feminist
Japan	incipient	feminist
India	incipient	feminist
Israel	incipient	feminist
Brazil	incipient	feminist
Puerto Rico	incipient	feminist

one (Great Britain, Mexico). By the Second Wave, namely, those movements that emerged after 1968, the ideology was uniformly feminist and the central demands were cross-nationally all but identical: reproductive freedom for women (including easy access to contraception and the right to abortion); government-funded child care; equal employment opportunity regardless of marital status; complete educational and legal equality; enhanced political power for women; and, most generally, the end of gender stereotyping and the idea of separate spheres. Issues of women's health, safety from male violence and harassment, homemaker rights, and lesbian rights also arose in nearly all cases. In essence, feminist movement demands involved a radical critique and called for the restructuring of all aspects of sociocultural life.

Aside from allowing us to dichotomize the ideology of women's movements, the descriptions we located have allowed us to establish a rough trichotomy of the maximum size to which each grew. We used a variety of types of data, depending upon what was available, to make the estimate: number of organizations and number of their members; number of public rally participants; number of petition signers; public opinion poll responses, especially response change over time; extent of geographic dispersal of movement groups; rallies or other activities beyond one or two cities in a country; number of movement publications and sales or subscription figures. In making use of these numbers to estimate relative movement size, we took into account the total size of a nation's population. A petition signed by 10,000 people in Iceland demonstrates a considerably larger movement than the same number of signers in China, India, or the United States. Total population size, however, was found to have no significant correlation with our final designation of movement size (in fact, we found a very small, negative correlation). A mass movement is defined as one in which a substantial proportion of the population, spread across a large number of towns and cities, was involved in some way, and/or in which public opinion changed to be strongly supportive of central movement goals. At the other extreme were incipient movements comprising one or two organizations, confined to one or two major cities, and involving only a small number of people who lacked broad-based support for their demands. Intermediate movements are those in between. The tables demonstrate the wide variation in movement size within the samples from both waves.

These basic descriptive cross-national data allow us to gain a perspective on the two waves of publicly visible women's movement activism in the United States that more richly descriptive studies of the U.S. movements alone do not. First, we see that in both time periods the United States experienced one of the largest movements. Mass women's movements have been rare; the United States has had two. Yet the ideologies of these movements, the kinds of demands made and the justifications used for them, have been nearly identical with contemporaneous movements elsewhere.

The Independent Variables:
Structural Change and Consciousness

We have developed our theory primarily on the basis of the social movements literature, incorporating resource mobilization theory, reference group theory, and older notions of strain into an eclectic model. When we examined the substantial *sociological* literature on women's movements, almost all of which pertains to the Second Wave in the United States, we found *historical accounts* of its origins but not coherent theoretical explanation (see Chafetz and Dworkin 1986, chap. 2). Rising divorce rates, falling birth rates, increased female education and labor force participation, "contagion" from the civil rights, student, and antiwar movements, Kennedy's Presidential Commission on the Status of Women, several specific books (e.g., Friedan's *Feminine Mystique*), a skewed sex ratio, and increased leisure constitute but a partial list of the things said to have "caused" the women's movement. Some of these phenomena are shared with other nations that experienced a women's movement; some are idiosyncratic; and some exist elsewhere where apparently no movement has arisen. We feel that it is the absence of a comparative perspective that has resulted in such a glaring absence of theoretical understanding.

In general, we posit that social structural changes associated with industrialization and urbanization serve as independent variables. These prompt certain social psychological responses among some women who are part of a larger pool of women similarly affected by the structural changes. These social psychological intervening variables, in turn, are of fundamental importance in producing a woman's movement, which is the dependent variable. The general process is the same for both waves. A critical variable, however, refers to expanded role opportunities for women, and it is the nature of these newly available roles that separates ameliorative from feminist movements. Using movement size as a proxy for whether or not a movement emerges,[2] we were able to test the relationship between the independent and the dependent variables, but could not measure the social psychological intervening variables. We hypothesize that the higher the levels of industrialization and urbanization, and the larger size of the middle class, the larger the size of the women's movement will be within each wave. We also hypothesize that these general structural variables are directly related to female role expansion, that is, the development of new opportunities for at least some proportion of women. In turn, the greater the female role expansion, the larger the size of the women's movement.

We have been able to locate census data for our sample nations that allow us to measure these independent variables in nearly all cases. For the First Wave we use census data for the closest available year to the end point of each movement, which approximately corresponded to the peak size of each movement. For the Second Wave cases we use 1970 census data uniformly. Because of the uneven quality and noncomparable measures of census data from so many nations, and especially from nearly 100 years ago, our measures are of necessity crude. Industrialization is operationalized as the proportion of the labor force employed in non-primary occupations. Urbanization is measured as the percentage of the total population living in cities of 100,000 or more. We use education as an indicator of the size of the middle class, arguing that this class legitimates its privileges using meritocratic criteria, chief among which is education. Given that children do not mount social movements, our measure of the size of the middle class refers to the percentage of children aged 5 to 19 who were in school twenty years prior to the year in which the other independent variables were measured. Role expansion for women for First Wave movements refers to two phenomena, only one of

---

[2.] We use movement size as a proxy, arguing that if the logic of our theory is correct concerning the variables that give rise to women's movements, then higher values on those variables should result in larger movements.

which was measurable using census data: increased educational opportunity. We measured this as the percentage of women aged 5 to 19 who
were in school twenty years prior to the peak movement year. The other
component of role expansion in that era refers to the entry of women into
nonemployment public roles, such as social, political, and moral reform
movement activism (e.g., abolition, temperance, socialism, nationalism);
philanthropy; and social welfare. As a probable rival hypothesis, we
explored the use of a labor force variable in the First Wave, but found that
no measure of women's labor force participation (women in the non-
primary, or manufacturing, or women in the tertiary, or service, sector)
could account for any variance whatsoever in movement size or movement ideology. For the Second Wave, female role expansion is measured
in several different ways pertaining to education and employment: the
proportion of women over 19 employed in nonprimary occupations; the
proportion in the tertiary sector; the percentage of females 5 to 19 enrolled
in school twenty years earlier; and the percentage of women aged 15 to 24
enrolled in college or university ten years earlier.

Because many of the variables used to explain both waves represented
assessments of educational and occupational participation over time,
there was extensive multicollinearity among the independent variables.
We were forced to select a severely trimmed model made up of only the
strongest predictors, despite the fact that many more variables had significant zero-order effects on movement size in each wave. While urbanization, industrialization, and size of the middle class account for 33%
of the total variance in the size of First Wave movements, to avoid the
multicollinearity problem, we have had to rely upon a single predictor—
industrialization—which explains 27.6% of that total variance. The model
presented for Second Wave movements includes only two variables, both
of which pertain to female role expansion: the percentage of women in
school twenty years earlier and the percentage of women in the tertiary
economic sector. This model explains 52.8% of the variance in the size of
Second Wave movements. Table 14.3 presents a summary of all of the
regression analyses presented throughout this section.

We have applied still another technique to the Second Wave data. We
regressed movement size on our two prior measures (percentage of
women in the tertiary sector and women in school twenty years earlier),
recomputed as residualized variables, and a residualized urbanization
variable (as before, the percentage of the population living in cities with
100,000 or more residents). Finally, we included our measure of the size
of the middle class (again, the percentage of the population between the
ages of 5 and 19 who were in school twenty years earlier). The other
variables were residualized by removing the influence of this education-
based variable from them. Each independent variable bore a very low

TABLE 14.3 Regression Models of the Size of First and Second Wave Women's Movements

Variable	Correlation Coefficients	b (se)	Beta
Size of first wave movement:			
industrialization	.526	.198 (.062)	.526
R = .526 R² = .276 F = 10.32 p = .003			
Size of second wave movement:			
female in tertiary	.421	.714 (.360)	.761
role expansion: school	.616	.479 (.147)	1.271*
R = .727 R² = .528 F = 6.71 p = .01			
Size of second wave movement (residualized):			
size of middle class	.323	.002 (.001)	.328
urbanization	.575	.006 (.001)	.785
role expansion: school	.343	.005 (.002)	.453
females in tertiary	.228	.002 (.001)	.371
R = .814 R² = .662 F = 14.27 p = .001			

*A beta this large suggests continued multicollinearity.

correlation with each other independent variable, but a significant correlation with the dependent variable—Second Wave movement size.[3] Urbanization bears the strongest effect on movement size, followed in order by female role expansion in school, women in the tertiary sector, and, finally, the size of the middle class. The revised model accounts for 66.2% of the variance in Second Wave movement size. As in the First Wave, urbanization and an expanded middle class enlarge the pool from which movement participants can be drawn. Second Wave movements differ from those of the First Wave, however, in their reliance upon female educational and labor market (tertiary sector) role expansions, as well. Thus a large middle class two decades prior to a movement, accompanied by substantial access to education among females, represents necessary

[3] The strategy we used to overcome the effects of multicollinearity is one recommended by Lin (1985, 1986). We regressed each of the independent variables upon the temporally earlier measure of the size of the middle class and computed the residuals, or parts not explained by that prior variable. This leaves each independent variable free from the effects of the educationally based measure. By definition then, each of the residuals bore a zero correlation with the size of the middle class. They also bore correlations of less than .10 with one another. They were only significantly correlated with the dependent variable, Second Wave size. Conceptually, the residualized variables remained as they were, but freed from that which they shared with size of the middle class.

TABLE 14.4 Discriminant Function Analysis of Ideological Scope:
First Versus Second Wave Movements

Variable	Unstandardized Canonical Discriminant Function Coefficient	Standardized Canonical Discriminant Function Coefficient
Urbanization	.044	.537
Size of middle class	−.026	−.474
Females in tertiary sector	.236	.903

preconditions for a large Second Wave movement. When that generation of females grows up in a society with high rates of urbanization and substantial female participation in the tertiary economy, the pool of potential movement participants is greatly expanded.

Does it then follow that a different set of variables explains the ideological score of the two waves? Which variables explain the ameliorative ideology of the First Wave and the feminist ideology of the Second Wave? Our discriminant function analysis demonstrates that labor force participation, especially percentage of women in the tertiary sector, and, to a lesser extent, urbanization differentiates between the ameliorative First and the feminist Second Waves, as we had hypothesized. We conclude, therefore, that the First Wave was created mainly by the effects on women's nonemployment roles of the growth of the middle class, while the Second Wave was created by further economic expansion and urbanization, which resulted in large numbers of women gaining access to labor force roles requiring advanced education. Table 14.4 presents the final results of the discriminant function analyses.

From the vantage point of these comparative data, we can see that the United States is relatively unique only to the extent that it became extensively industrialized earlier than most other nations in the nineteenth century, and has undergone more growth in the post-World War II era than most other nations in especially those tertiary sector jobs normally filled by women. As a result, during both eras larger numbers of women in the United States experienced expanded role opportunities than in most other countries, providing a larger pool from which activists for women's movements could be drawn. Many of the specific historical factors encountered in the literature on women's movements thus appear to be either irrelevant as causal factors or correlates of the very same macro processes that produce such movements. Given the same levels of urbanization and industrialization and the same size of the middle class, nations appear to have produced the same sized ameliorative movements earlier in this century. Given the same level of enhanced educational and employment opportunities for women, contemporary nations produce the same sized feminist movements. In fact, when one of the independent variables measured for a nation does not covary with the others, as, for example, in Japan, where labor force participation on the part of women outstripped educational opportunities for women, the size of the feminist movement is attenuated proportionately. There are, however, some cases where political factors obstruct this process, reducing the size of the movement from that predicted by the structural variables enumerated. These cases will be discussed later in this chapter.

ANTIFEMINIST MOVEMENTS

In the process of examining descriptions of women's movements, we ran across a number of usually brief discussions of countermovements. Aside from the United States and Great Britain, First Wave countermovements, of apparently small size, were documented in France, Italy, New Zealand, Jewish Palestine, Germany, Canada, and Australia. We found at least some evidence of Second Wave countermovements in Australia, Italy, France, Britain, and Germany, in addition to the United States. The vast majority of the *sociological* literature pertaining to antifeminist movements concerns the contemporary U.S. case. After we reviewed all the scattered information available, we began to see some emerging patterns, although there were too little data to analyze in any systematic fashion. The patterns we saw were as follows:

(1) With the exception of the antisuffrage movements in the United States and Great Britain, clergy from major orthodox, conservative, or fundamentalist religions play a central, overt role in organizing and supporting antifeminist activism. In the two exceptional cases, clergy were somewhat active and economic interest groups, very active. We interpreted the involvement of clergy as a type of vested-interest group activism, whose antifeminism reflects a sense of threat to their moral authority and possibly even to the male monopoly on clerical roles.

(2) Vested economic interests play an important role, often covertly, in funding and organizing antifeminist voluntary associations and lobbying politicians to fight measures proposed by a women's movement. Lobbying appears to be the first response to a women's movement, and to the extent that it is successful, further antifeminist organization typically does not occur.

(3) Antifeminist voluntary associations arise significantly after the start of women's movements (as many as 50 years later in the First Wave), at a point when many of the original demands for change have already

been met. Often they arise only in time to enter a last-ditch fight over the most radical of the proposed changes, such as suffrage in the First Wave or the Equal Rights Amendment (ERA) in the contemporary United States.

(4) Antifeminist voluntary association activists are characterized by one or more of the following traits: (a) married women encapsulated in traditional roles at a time when other women are assuming new roles; (b) male or female members of families undergoing class or status threats from other societal groups, and especially from the incursion of female labor into heretofore male jobs; (c) male or female members of elite families who profit most from the status quo.

(5) Regardless of time, place, or the specific demands and ideology of the women's movement they oppose, antifeminist movements develop an ideology that defines women's functions in terms of the care of family members and home; men's, as the economic support of their family; the family, as central to national well-being; and women's movements, as destructive of the family. Religious and patriotic symbolism are characteristically important elements of antifeminist rhetoric and ideology (see Chafetz and Dworkin 1987 for more detail about these findings).

Despite the relative paucity of information concerning organized antifeminism outside the United States, this study serves to cast doubt upon the usual sociological interpretation of contemporary antifeminism, especially of the New Right, in the United States. Because of the conspicuous—but, as we found, by no means unusual—role of conservative clergy in the contemporary American antifeminist movement, countermovement activists have been defined as engaged in a fundamental value conflict. Presumably, religiously based values concerning gender and family are perceived as threatened by a set of secular, individualistic values propounded by feminists (e.g., Harding 1981; Petchesky 1981; Luker 1984; Conover and Gray 1983). In this battle, the ERA and abortion have served as symbols of a fundamental and deep ideological disagreement. Our comparative information and perspective suggest that despite the obvious rhetoric of value conflict, and regardless of the almost omnipresent role of conservative clergy in such countermovements, the major sources of threat for antifeminists are, in fact, threats to class and status interests. Evidence for this assertion exists in the contemporary U.S. case, but is usually overlooked. When a variety of cases across time and space are examined, it is impossible to overlook the role of both economic vested-interest groups and of individuals whose jobs, or whose husbands' jobs, are threatened. Nor can one ignore threats to women's status as traditional wives and mothers, and men's, as family patriarchs. It takes no great imagination to understand that, to legitimate their sense of threat, an ideology or rhetoric of religion and patriotism is developed that

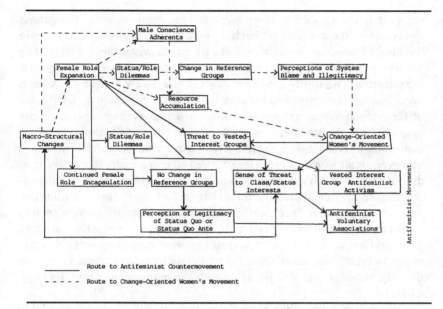

Figure 14.1: Basic Elements in an Integrated Theory of the Emergence of Change-Oriented Women's Movements and Countermovements: A Process Model

masks more direct self-interest. By and large, working only from one case, American sociologists have taken the mask too seriously.

AN INTEGRATED PROCESS MODEL OF THE EMERGENCE OF WOMEN'S MOVEMENTS AND COUNTERMOVEMENTS

Obviously, by definition, a countermovement emerges in response to a movement. In the remainder of this chapter we will explore the major elements of this process as it applies to the emergence of change-oriented women's movements and the backlash antifeminist movements they sometimes spawn. We will move from left to right in Figure 14.1.

It should be noted that, in our original model of the development of women's movements (Chafetz and Dworkin, 1986, chap. 3), we included a political variable as a control. We argued—and found supporting evidence—that change-oriented movement development is retarded or altogether thwarted by either of two extreme governmental responses: repression or co-optation. Repression exists when the government does not permit the existence of grass-roots organizations other than those sponsored by the government itself, or by the party in a one-party state. In the case of women's movements, it also exists where laws specifically prohibit political activity for women, in a system otherwise open to male organization. The ability of governments to effectively repress grass-roots organizations has improved substantially during this century. By the era of the Second Wave, nations with totalitarian governments were simply omitted from the sample, inasmuch as their women's organizations are controlled by a male-dominated party or government. In the First Wave, however, small women's movements often emerged under repressive conditions and later, with the end of repression, sometimes grew to substantial size. At the time their movements began, Germany, Russia, China, and Japan had laws that specifically restricted the right of women to join political organizations, attend political meetings, or publicly discuss political issues. At some point in their histories, ongoing women's movements in France, Russia, China, Japan, Persia/Iran, Brazil, and Peru were directly, although temporarily, repressed—sometimes quite brutally (e.g., China).

Co-optation exists when powerful male political leaders move quickly to grant some of the demands made by a movement, thereby *appearing* to render the movement moot. By granting the vote quickly and early (pre-World War I), New Zealand, Australia, Norway, and Finland effectively co-opted their First Wave women's movements, which never developed to their maximum potential size. Only where governments permit the free expression of grass-roots movements for women, and where they do not quickly act on one or two movement demands, will a woman's movement develop to the level predicted by the model. In this theoretical model we will simply presuppose this intermediate level of governmental response. We might add that, in the absence of a comparative study, as Americans we would have simply taken this intermediate level of governmental response for granted.

The primary impetus for the development of a women's movement is to be found in macro-structural changes, namely, increases in urbanization, industrialization, and the size of the middle class, as discussed earlier in our review of findings. The precise nature and relative importance of the structural changes that trigger the remainder of the process differ somewhat according to whether the focus is upon First or Second Wave movements. The critical theoretical point is that these structural changes permit or induce the emergence of new role opportunities for women, which we term "female role expansion." As discussed earlier, in the First Wave the new roles were primarily social movement roles, such as anti-slavery, temperance, socialist, and nationalist movements; philanthropy;

social welfare; and educational opportunity. In the Second Wave, the employment of married women, including mothers of young children, constituted the major form of role expansion, along with expanded educational opportunities. The impact of structural change upon individuals, however, is always uneven. Many women will be unable or unwilling to take advantage of the new opportunities, because of an insufficient amount of opportunity or human capital; familial obligations; or religious or other types of normative constraints. Therefore, many women will remain encapsulated in roles traditional for their gender.

The assumption of new roles by women creates status/role dilemmas for them. By this we mean contradictions between socially defined ascribed gender expectations and those associated with their newly emerging social roles. Women may find themselves treated according to traditional gender norms inappropriate to their achieved status/role, or they may be expected to behave in inappropriate or contradictory ways. As more and more women assume the new roles, those who remain in encapsulated roles begin to encounter status/role dilemmas of their own, involving their "failure" to assume the new, but increasingly normative, roles. For instance, today in many nations women who are not in the labor force are increasingly defined by societal members as the anomalies who need to "explain" their behavior.

Women who experience status/role dilemmas arising from role expansion are likely to change their comparative reference group from other women to the men with whom they are now in contact. These men have roles, competencies, or credentials that are equal—even inferior—to theirs, yet their opportunities and rewards are typically greater. In turn, women are likely to experience a sense of relative deprivation. Moreover, in their newly expanded roles they are likely to come into contact with one another, sharing and refining their sense of deprivation. As a result, at least some members of this growing pool of women will come to develop a perception that their disadvantages are not individually caused but are shared on the basis of their gender and produced by the social system; that the opportunity and reward systems are unfair and illegitimate; that, therefore, social change is a goal to be pursued. In short, some women experiencing role expansion and status/role dilemmas are likely to develop a gender consciousness analogous to the class consciousness of which Marx spoke. This is a necessary (but not sufficient) condition for the formation of a women's movement. It provides the motivation and ideology to pursue collective goals, but does not address the question of resources. In the process of consciousness development and the first stirrings of movement organization, such women are also likely to change their normative and gatekeeping reference groups. In this case, other women who, like themselves, have entered newly expanded roles come to replace men as reference groups. This reinforces their willingness to question the legitimacy of the existing gender system.

Women who experience status/role dilemmas arising from continued role encapsulation in an era of female role expansion undergo an analogous, yet very different social psychological process. They tend to maintain their traditional reference groups. Other women who, like themselves play traditional roles, continue to constitute their comparative reference group. Males, including especially their husbands, continue to constitute their normative and gatekeeping reference groups. In turn, these reference groups encourage a perception of the legitimacy of traditional gender arrangements. Such perceptions are necessary but not sufficient for the formation of antifeminist voluntary associations. They provide the ideology, but neither the motivation nor the resources, for acting. The motivation is a sense of threat to the class interest of their family and/or to their personal status as incumbents of traditional, encapsulated roles. Such a perception results in part from the increasing visibility of a women's movement. The very rhetoric that raises the gender consciousness of potential recruits to the movement functions over time to create for other women a sense that their values, and especially their status, are threatened. As they experience new social definitions that question the legitimacy of traditional commitments and create for them the status/role dilemmas of which we spoke, at least some are likely to conclude that the women's movement is causing a decline in their personal status. To the extent that a husband perceives economic or status threat from the women's movement, that will enhance the woman's own sense of threat, especially if she is economically dependent on his income.

Social movements require resources (Gale 1986; Gamson 1975; Jenkins 1983; Jenkins and Perrow 1977; McCarthy and Zald 1977; Tilly 1978; Zald and McCarthy 1979). A social psychological proclivity on the part of many women, while necessary, is scarcely sufficient to produce either a women's movement or an antifeminist one. Female role expansion provides, at least for some women, access to resources and skill development not previously available. These mostly elite women can accumulate the tangible and intangible resources (e.g., money, public speaking and organizational skills, networks with other women, contacts in the media and government, and so on) to mount a movement. Our data on women's movements depict virtually all of them in both waves as fundamentally comprising urban, educated, middle- to upper-middle-class women, precisely the group most likely to develop access to resources through expanded roles.

Additional resources may be provided to women's movements by male conscience adherents. Often, these are men who benefit in some way from the general social structural changes and/or changes in women's roles that are occurring. In our research on First Wave women's movements, for instance, we found that in those societies where women were traditionally most suppressed (e.g., China, Persia, Indonesia, India, Japan), the first stirrings of movement development were prompted by men. Specifically, groups of elite men, who were actively pursuing the modernization and Westernization of their societies, encouraged women to organize to enhance their status, in the belief that this was necessary for general social development. Contemporary male feminists are likely to have female partners who are labor force participants and whose income and promotion opportunities have been thwarted because of their gender.

Role encapsulated women are likely to have far less direct, personal access to either the tangible or the intangible resources required to organize antifeminist voluntary associations. Their husbands and fathers, however, may have such access. It should, therefore, come as no surprise that many antifeminist voluntary associations, especially during the First Wave, were exclusively male or comprised both sexes but initiated and led by men. Where male conscience adherents take a decided back seat in the functioning of women's movement organizations, men are often conspicuous leaders, public speakers, and organizers of antifeminist voluntary organizations. Such men may be motivated by threats to the status of male as superior to female, but mostly by threats to their economic interests. We found both elite men, whose business or political interests were threatened by the demands of the women's movement, and lower-middle- and working-class men whose jobs or wages were threatened by the incursion of female labor, to be active in antifeminist voluntary organizations. Often these men responded both as individuals and as members of vested-interest groups, and their wives constituted the core of the female membership in voluntary associations.

The primary impetus behind, and source of resources for, the development of antifeminist voluntary associations appears to be vested-interest groups. Their sense of threat arises potentially from two sources. The first is expanded roles for women, which may bring them into competition with men. For instance, organizations of male clerks and secretaries were very actively involved in First Wave antifeminism in some nations, in response to the increasing incursion of females into their occupation. The second source of threat is the demands made by the movement itself. For instance, as we noted earlier, First Wave movements, especially in Anglo-Saxon societies but elsewhere as well, were closely allied with—often indistinguishable from—temperance movements. It is, therefore, not surprising that the liquor interests were among the most important and conspicuous economic vested interests involved in many antisuffrage movements.

Recall that a very important source of both tangible and intangible resources is one or more conservative or orthodox religious institutions. The threat to them mainly is to their moral authority, inasmuch as women's movements question the God-givenness of the gender system, as propounded by the conservative religions. Major ways they aid antifeminist movements are to organize their own committed congregants into grass-roots associations and to develop and publicly proclaim an antifeminist rhetoric. They may also provide funds for antifeminist voluntary associations. Other types of interest groups often cannot directly organize a constituency. Moreover, they may be loath to be publicly associated with an antifeminist rhetoric, for fear of offending real or potential constituents. In fact, most often economic interest group activism is relatively covert and publicly invisible (e.g., lobbying, provision of funds). Vested-interest groups are unlikely to go to the effort and expense of organizing at the grass-roots level if they are able to use their preexisting political networks and influence to thwart the aims of the women's movement. Only if the movement becomes large and/or successful do we expect to see antifeminist voluntary associations arise. When they arise, they constitute a good indicator of the substantial nature of change in the gender system.

CONCLUSION

Women's movements emerge and grow when a sufficiently large number of women, drawn from a yet larger pool who have experienced role expansion, develop a gender consciousness and accumulate needed resources. They are aided in mostly minor ways by male conscience adherents. If they begin to become successful, vested-interest groups will perceive a threat and often take action to influence the political system. At the same time, women encapsulated in traditional roles gradually come to perceive a threat as well, in part because of the rhetoric produced by the women's movement, in part because of their increasing status/role dilemmas, and in part because of threats to their husbands' economic interests. They will be organized and led primarily by men, acting both individually and as representatives of vested interests, who provide the resources and ideology necessary to mount countermovement voluntary associations. The two movements thus develop dialectically, primarily in response to basic social structural changes that have very different impacts on different segments of the society.

The theoretical model presented in this chapter is the result of comparative research both cross-nationally and historically. We found that in the absence of such comparison, there simply was no *theoretical* explanation of why women's movements emerge when and where they do, and why they develop a characteristic ideology. In terms of the particular dimensions we examined—size and ideology—the two waves of U.S. movements have in no way been unique. But who could know this without comparison? Many of the factors widely cited in the existing literature were, however, relatively or completely idiosyncratic to our cases. Our research questions their causal relevancy. When we examined antifeminist movements, again we found that the U.S. cases were scarcely unique. Widespread interpretation, especially of our contemporary case, however, has been flawed precisely by the absence of a comparative perspective. Clearly, there were many aspects of antifeminist, and especially women's movements, that our analyses did not systematically address (e.g., relative success in goal attainment, organizational forms, relations with other social movements). We cannot know to what extent there is diversity across time, and especially across nations, on such dimensions. Nor can we know to what extent the U.S. experiences are generalizable to other movements on the dimensions we failed to examine. Our research strongly suggests, however, that the idiosyncratic cultures and histories of individual nations are probably of minor importance, relative to the more global variables concerning socioeconomic structure, in understanding social movements—or at least women's movements and their organized opposition.

REFERENCES

Banks, Olive. 1981. *Faces of Feminism: A Study of Feminism as a Social Movement*. New York: St. Martin's.

Brady, David and Kent Tedin. 1976. "Ladies in Pink: Religion and Ideology in the Anti-ERA Movement." *Social Science Quarterly* 59:198-205.

Burris, Val. 1983. "Who Opposed the ERA? An Analysis of the Social Bases of Antifeminism." *Social Science Quarterly* 64:305-17.

Castells, Manuel. 1983. *The City and the Grassroots: A Cross-Cultural Theory of Urban Social Movements*. London: Edward Arnold.

Chafetz, Janet Saltzman and Anthony Gary Dworkin. 1983. "Macro and Micro Processes in the Emergence of Feminist Movements: Toward a Unified Theory." *Western Sociological Review* 14(1):27-45.

———. 1986. *Female Revolt: Women's Movements in World and Historical Perspective*. Totowa, NJ: Rowman and Allanheld.

———. 1987. "In the Face of Threat: Organized Antifeminism in Comparative Perspective." *Gender & Society* 1(1):33-60.

Conover, Pamela J. and Virginia Gray. 1983. *Feminism and the New Right Conflict over the American Family*. New York: Praeger.

Ehrenreich, Barbara. 1982. "Defeating the ERA: A Right-Wing Mobilization of Women."
    Journal of Sociology and Social Welfare 9(3):391-98.
Flexner, Eleanor. 1975. *Century of Struggle: The Woman's Rights Movement in the United
    States*. rev. ed. Cambridge, MA: Belknap.
Gale, Richard. 1986. "Social Movements and the State: The Environmental Movement,
    Countermovement, and Government Agencies." *Sociological Perspectives* 29:202-40.
Gamson, William A. 1975. *The Strategy of Social Protest*. Homewood, IL: Dorsey.
Gelb, Joyce and Marian Palley. 1982. *Women and Public Policies*. Princeton, NJ: Princeton
    University Press.
Gusfield, Joseph. 1963. *Symbolic Crusades: Status Politics and the American Temperance
    Union*. Urbana: University of Illinois Press.
Harding, Susan. 1981. "Family Reform Movements: Recent Feminism and Its Opposition."
    Feminist Studies 7:57-75.
Harrison, Brian. 1978. *Separate Spheres: The Opposition to Women's Suffrage in Britain*.
    London: Croom Helm.
Howard, Jeanne. 1982. "Our Own Worst Enemies: Women Opposed to Woman Suffrage."
    Journal of Sociology and Social Welfare 9:436-74.
Jenkins, J. Craig. 1983. "Resource Mobilization Theory and the Study of Social
    Movements." *Annual Review of Sociology* 9:527-53.
Jenkins, J. Craig and Charles Perrow. 1977. "Insurgency of the Powerless: Farm Worker
    Movements (1946-1972)." *American Sociological Review* 42:249-68.
Lin, Nan. 1985. *Social Support and Health: New Directions for Theory Development and
    Research*. University of Rochester Doctoral Program in Nursing and *Sigma Theta Tau,
    Epsilon Xi* Chapter.
———. 1986. "Psychological Resources, Social Support, Life Events, and Depression:
    Models and Evidence." Paper presented at the American Sociological Association
    Meetings, New York.
Luker, Kristin. 1984. *Abortion and the Politics of Motherhood*. Berkeley: University of
    California Press.
Marshall, Susan. 1985. "Ladies Against Women: Mobilization Dilemmas of Antifeminist
    Movements." *Social Problems* 32:348-62.
Marshall, Susan and Anthony Orum. Forthcoming. "Opposition Then and Now: Countering
    Feminism in the Twentieth Century." In *Research in Politics and Society*. Vol. 2, edited
    by G. Moore and G. Spitze. Greenwich, CT: JAI.
McCarthy, John and Meyer N. Zald. 1977. "Resource Mobilization and Social Movements."
    American Journal of Sociology 82:1212-41.
Mottl, Tahi L. 1980. "The Analysis of Countermovements." *Social Problems* 27:620-35.
Petchesky, Rosalind. 1981. "Antiabortion, Antifeminism, and the Rise of the New Right."
    Feminist Studies 7(2):206-46.
Tedin, Kent. 1978. "Religious Preference and Pro/Anti Activism on the Equal Rights
    Amendment Issue." *Pacific Sociological Review* 21:55-66.
Tedin, Kent, D. Brady, M. Buxton, B. Gorman, and J. Thompson. 1977. "Social Background
    and Political Differences Between Pro- and Anti-ERA Activists." *American Politics
    Quarterly* 5:395-408.
Tilly, Charles. 1978. *From Mobilization to Revolution*. Reading, MA: Addison-Wesley.
Touraine, Alain. 1981. *The Voice and the Eye: An Analysis of Social Movements*, trans. by
    Alan Duff. London: Cambridge University Press.
Zald, Mayer N. and John D. McCarthy. 1979. *The Dynamics of Social Movements*.
    Cambridge, MA: Winthrop.

Part VI
Nation as "Unit of Analysis" and Transnational Analysis

15

The Other Working Class: Uncommitted Labor in Britain, Spain, and Mexico

Bryan R. Roberts

One of the most striking challenges for class analysis in recent years, and particularly for the analysis of the working class, has been the increase in the members of the labor force who do not fall into the category of full-time wage earners in regular employment, and who provide what, adapting Standing (1981, pp. 3-6), I call uncommitted labor. By uncommitted, I mean uncommitted to full-time employment either because of the nature of the contract (unprotected, part-time) or because the workers are unemployed or self-employed. The use of the term "uncommitted" has other implications to which I return in the conclusions. It implies a lack of commitment on the part of the employer, but also, frequently, on the part of the worker who shifts from one job to another that requires low levels of skill and provides few intrinsic rewards.

This phenomenon has been noted in the persistence of the informal economy in cities of developing societies, and is present in the advanced industrial countries and even in the socialist block (Mingione 1987; Portes and Sassen-Koob 1987; Grossman 1986). Uncommitted labor is not only provided by workers in informal enterprises, but includes the growing

AUTHOR'S NOTE: *I would like to thank Harley Browning, Joe Feagin, Elizabeth Jelin, and Guy Standing for their comments and insights. Also, I owe a considerable debt to Ubaldo Martinez Vega for introducing me both to Madrid and to the anthropological studies of the Madrid working class based at the Universidad Autonoma de Madrid.*

numbers of workers who are self-employed, are part-time workers, or are employed full-time in legal enterprises without contract or social security. These categories have been called atypical or nonstandard employment, and their significance documented for the European countries and Latin America (Cordova 1986; Marshall 1987). They constitute the basis for "awkward classes" who do not fit easily into, or confound, the classic divides of proletarian and bourgeoisie, as Portes (1985) has argued for Latin America and Pahl (1984, 1987) for Britain.

To explore the significance of this worldwide trend, I will look at how it varies between countries occupying different positions in the world economy: core, semiperiphery, and periphery.[1] I choose this basis for cross-national comparison because each position signifies historical differences in the formation of a proletariat and in the forms that uncommitted labor takes, making, for instance, informal economic activities more widespread in one context than in another.[2] Core nations, as the most highly urbanized and industrialized countries, have the longest and most universal tradition of full-time wage labor in both agricultural and nonagricultural activities. Semiperipheries are uneven in their development with economically advanced industrial and commercial regions in which wage labor predominates contrasting with economically backward regions of peasant farming and estates of low productivity. Peripheries, whose primary role in the world economy has been that of providing raw materials and agricultural products, have a weak development of the internal market and, until recently, a predominance of nonwage forms of labor.

Also, the processes that contribute to the making of "cores," "semiperipheries," and "peripheries" result in contrasts in the organization of the state and of civil society, two further variables that I see as crucial to understanding differences in labor commitment. The strong states of the core and their organized citizenry contrast with the weak states of the periphery whose population has little tradition of independent association in political parties and professional or trade associations.

My examples of core, semiperiphery, and periphery—Britain, Spain, and Mexico—are intended to be representative of their type. Britain represents the countries of "organized capitalism," in which capital is both vertically and horizontally integrated; full-time wage labor has been,

[1.] I use Wallerstein's (1974, p. 349) categories. For a more extensive discussion of the urban and industrial processes that sustain these positions, see my paper (Roberts 1981) in which the contrast is between Britain, Spain, and Peru.

[2.] Mingione (1987) makes a similar contrast, showing the differences between the countries of northern Europe, southern Europe, and the developing world in the organization of the informal economy.

until recently, the normal activity of the vast majority of the labor force; private or public expenditures on welfare are extensive; and classes have been mobilized on a national scale through political parties and trade and professional associations.[3] The semiperiphery is Spain, whose role in the making of the modern world resulted in a highly uneven pattern of development in which a large military, ecclesiastical, and civil bureaucracy and some nodes of outward-looking commercial and industrial prosperity, such as Catalonia, contrasted with the generalized poverty of rural and small-town Spain and the weakness, nationally, of representative civil associations. Spain's economic integration has come mainly in the post-World War II period through rapid industrialization, massive urbanization, and the consequent development of the internal market. The periphery, Mexico, represents those countries that have not yet experienced organized capitalism, and they are not likely to do so. It contains a large residue of peasant farmers and cities in which the fastest-growing employment opportunities are in self-employment or in small service enterprises with only a minority, and that mainly in recent times, employed in large-scale manufacturing enterprises. Mexico has few effective and independent forms of civil association that mediate between state and population.

Indicative of these differences in structural position in the world economy are the patterns of employment in the three countries. Britain, a mature industrial society, had, in 1965, 3% of its labor force working in agriculture compared with 47% in industry (manufacturing, construction, mining, and utilities); the proportions for Spain in the same year are 34% in agriculture and 35% in industry; and for Mexico, they are 50% in agriculture and 22% in industry (World Bank 1987, Table 32). Central government expenditures for 1972 on welfare services (education, health, housing, social security) show a similar pattern with the core country, Britain, spending a higher proportion of its gross national product (13.5%) on such services than either Spain (11.7%) or Mexico (5.6%) (World Bank 1987, Table 23).

I shall be concerned with both similarities and differences between the three countries. I focus on similarities to explore how pervasive the trend to uncommitted labor is. Similar economic trends do not necessarily have similar consequences, however, and I focus on differences to examine how historical contrasts in world position modify the forms that uncommitted labor takes in national societies. In the final sections of the chapter,

---

[3.] Lash and Urry (1987, pp. 17-83) emphasize the differences between core countries in terms of state intervention and in, among other factors, the strength of workers and employers associations. Compared to semiperipheral and peripheral countries, all core countries are highly organized economically, have powerful civil associations independent of the state, and have high public and private welfare expenditures.

I pursue this theme in terms of the ways in which the growing importance of uncommitted labor affects class relations in Britain, Spain, and Mexico. There are similarities, but also differences, because of the specific ways uncommitted workers are enmeshed with those in regular employment.

I take a relational approach to class analysis, seeing class as the emergent property of conflicts between groups over mutually valued resources. As Przeworski (1977) puts it, classes are the effects of struggles as various entities, such as political parties, unions, business, or neighborhood associations, compete to define the class interest and the groups to be included within it. Consequently, classes are historically and situationally defined, depending, as Stark (1980) shows for the United States, on the success of organizations in enforcing claims for a privileged position for their members, and in persuading other relevant actors, such as the state, to recognize these claims. I will use a similar approach in examining the "classness" of uncommitted workers, looking at how community organization and state regulations unite or polarize different types of workers in Britain, Spain, and Mexico.

ECONOMIC RESTRUCTURING AND
THE LABOR MARKET

One assumed consequence of the core-periphery continuum is a difference in the relative position of labor, with peripheral countries providing the cheap uncommitted labor that, in part, makes possible the higher pay and benefits of the labor of the core countries. Any evidence for similarities in the trend to uncommitted labor challenges this assumption. In this section, I will consider the evidence for a relatively clear and similar trend in Britain, Spain, and Mexico toward the preponderance of uncommitted labor. I will also explore the reasons why, in terms of the labor market, cores may be turning into peripheries.

In the three countries, there has been both an absolute and proportional increase since 1970 in the self-employed and family worker component of the nonagricultural labor force. In Britain, the self-employed, excluding unpaid family workers, rose as a proportion of the employed population from 8.6% in 1972 to 8.8% in 1980 and 12.3% in 1985 (Standing 1986, Table 23). The trend in Spain, which saw an increasing concentration of population in the large cities in this same period, is less consistent: in 1970, 21.2 of the nonagricultural population in work was self-employed or unpaid family workers; in 1980, the proportion was 20.8%; and in 1985, 22.4% (OECD 1987, pp. 374-75). The equivalent figures for Mexico, which also experienced rapid population concentration, are 19.6% in

1970, 26.7% in 1980, and an estimated 29% in 1985 (Dirección General de Estadística, 1972, 1986, Cuadros 40, 25).[4]

The trends for unemployment are also upward. In Britain, unemployment increased from 2.3% in 1970 to 5.8% in 1980 and 11.9% in 1985 (OECD 1987, pp. 450-51). In Spain, the increase has been more spectacular, from 1.9% in 1970 to 12.3% in 1980, to 21.5% in 1985 (OECD 1987, pp. 374-75). Only in Mexico has the rise been modest, from 4.9% in 1970, in Mexico City, where a quarter of the Mexican population lives, to 5.7% in 1985. There is no national system of unemployment insurance in Mexico, and, as we will see, other forms of uncommitted labor are more significant.

The potential historical significance of these figures should be noted. They show the reversal of what is often seen as a key component of economic modernization, the massive and continuous concentration of the labor force in full-time employment following industrialization and urbanization. In the three countries, this trend has been a clear one, beginning at the end of the eighteenth century in Britain and ending in the 1960s, whereas in both Spain and Mexico, the trend appears mainly in this century, beginning in the 1940s and ending in the 1970s.

This evidence must be treated with some caution. The current significance of self-employment, part-time work, or unemployment may reflect the temporary effects of economic cycles rather than a permanent restructuring. Moreover, estimating trends is made difficult by the relative lack of comparable and reliable figures on the various categories of uncommitted labor. Unprotected labor is submerged and escapes most surveys, while many countries do not publish data on the extent of part-time work. Even unemployment is, in some places, an ambiguous category meaning quite different situations in countries in which unemployment pay is given as compared with those where to be unemployed is to starve unless help can be obtained from family or friends.

There is a stronger reason than the available statistics for suggesting that the reversal of proletarianization is a permanent one, and represents a general trend shared by countries of different levels of economic development. Enterprises in both the developed and the developing world appear to be introducing more flexible working practices in the face of international competition and the possibilities created by current technological changes (see Portes and Sassen-Koob 1987). The emphasis on flexibility is reinforced by the shift from manufacturing to the services as sources of employment. Service enterprises, such as retail stores and

[4.] The Mexican census of 1980 used a different definition of employment from that of 1970, which is likely to exaggerate the numbers of self-employed and unpaid family workers. From 1982, however, the trend to increased self-employment is documented as government surveys of the urban labor market, and my 1985 estimates are based on these (INEGI 1986).

many financial and technical services, are often based on personal contact with the client and a customized service, requiring flexible labor time and working practices. Personal and even many producer services do not require much capital and can be efficiently provided by small-scale enterprises or individually.

The use of labor in more flexible ways occurs in a broad range of enterprises and industries, responding to different exigencies: those lines in which labor is a significant cost, in which the demand for labor fluctuates over the year, in which the small size of enterprise gives greater flexibility in meeting client demand than does the assembly line, and in which there is sharp competition from cheap producers at home and abroad. Flexibility can be attained by persuading workers to vary their hours and to take on a variety of tasks; but it can also be achieved by hiring labor casually without protection of contract or social security, by going underground, or by subcontracting (Michon 1987a).

The increase in the proportions of labor working flexible hours and under temporary contract also reflects changes in the supply. In both developed and underdeveloped countries, the economic participation rates of the adult population have fallen as greater proportions of the young population remain in education and greater proportions of the elderly retire from the labor market. This trend has been partly offset by substantial increases in adult female participation rates. The increasing costs of urban subsistence in both developed and underdeveloped countries, with the move toward consumption-orientated economies, have led women to complement the household income by paid work.

Women provide an available source of flexible labor, being prepared to work at times that allow them to fulfill other domestic obligations and with low earnings that even in Britain are often regarded by employers, other family members, and even the women themselves as only complementing the household income (Brannen and Moss 1987). Increases in the female labor supply and the substantial migrations of workers from underdeveloped to developed countries mean that firms in core countries can easily obtain "cheap" labor at home. One result, then, of current economic restructuring is a considerable heterogeneity of labor conditions within core countries and their regions, as Feagin (1987) shows for the United States.

These changes in demand and supply have been reinforced, in recent years, by a widespread tendency of governments to deregulate labor markets on the grounds that greater flexibility would foster more rapid economic growth. In the three countries, government, through withdrawal of job protection or through lack of enforcement of labor legislation, has been a major factor in the growth of self-employment and part-time employment. In both Britain and Spain—though the former country is

TABLE 15.1: Estimates of Nonagricultural Labor Force That Is Uncommitted: Britain, Spain, and Mexico: Circa 1985 (percentages)

	Unprotected Workers[a]	Part-Time Workers	Self-Employed & Family Worker	Unemployed	Total %
Britain	4	19	9	12	45
Spain	10	6[b]	16	20	52
Mexico[c]	18	12	28	6	64

SOURCE: Britain, adapted from Central Statistical Office (1987, Tables 4.7-4.11, 4.21); Spain, adapted from Benton (1987, Table 2.2) and INE (1984, pp. 21,28); Mexico, adapted from *Censo de Población 1980* (Tables 25, 35), INEGI, 1986, (Table 3.5), Guadalajara labor force survey.
a. Unprotected workers are *full-time employees* who are not covered by social security, with insecure contracts.
b. The estimate for part-time workers in Spain is not based on any statistical source.
c. The Mexican estimates for unprotected workers and the unemployed are based on labor force surveys in Guadalajara and Mexico City, respectively.

governed by a conservative party and the latter, by a socialist one—changes in labor legislation in the 1980s in government attitudes and the weakness of trade unions in the face of industrial reorganization have made it easier for employers to take on people casually, have reduced obligations of employers to part-time workers, and have diminished the protection for low-paid workers (Cordova 1986; Standing 1986; Michon 1987b; Sagardoy 1987). In Mexico, deregulation is less evident, but it has occurred as in the agreements with the new "in-bond" industries established on the U.S.-Mexican border and in certain interior locations. State regulation of the labor market in Mexico, such as a minimum wage, social security obligations, and different types of labor contract, is not onerous when compared to regulation in Britain or Spain, giving little or no protection to workers on temporary contracts, and is not strictly enforced.

THE FORMS OF UNCOMMITTED LABOR

There are important differences between the three countries in the forms that uncommitted labor takes (Table 15.1). It is these differences and the relation of the various types of uncommitted worker to those in full-time, stable employment that, as we will see in the next section, lead to contrasts in class relations. In the final part of this section I indicate some of the historical experiences associated with core, semiperipheral, and peripheral positions that help explain the differences in uncommitted labor. The exercise that follows is only a first step in disaggregating the various categories of labor that fall outside stable full-time employment.

There is considerable heterogeneity, even within these categories, which needs research, especially in light of the general significance of the phenomenon it represents: Remember that, in the three countries, uncommitted labor is now almost half or more than half the labor force.

In Britain, part-time employment and open unemployment are the most important components of uncommitted labor. Britain is the only one of the three countries in which these two categories constitute a greater proportion of the population than the unprotected and the self-employed, though the absolute levels of open unemployment are higher in Spain (Table 15.1). Britain not only has the lowest levels of self- and family employment, but informal enterprise, or informal employment, is not a significant feature of the labor market. The growth of an informal economy is severely restricted by an efficiently administered tax and social security system, an active industrial inspectorate, and, not least, the propensity of neighbors to report noncompliance with social security legislation or zoning ordinances. Two relatively large-scale surveys of different British labor markets—the Isle of Sheppey in Kent and Macclesfield, near Manchester—found participation in the informal economy to be very small and usually in addition to work in the formal economy (Pahl 1984, p. 241; Laite 1986). My estimate for unregulated workers is based on the figures for temporary workers whose numbers have grown substantially in the first years of the 1980s.[5]

Part-time jobs increased as a percentage of employment from approximately 15% in 1971 to over 20% in 1984. They accounted for almost three-quarters of the overall increase in employment in the service industries in this period, and without them the overall decline in employment in Britain, particularly marked in manufacturing, would have been severe. There is a high degree of segmentation in the part-time labor market. Most part-time jobs are held by women and are mainly in the service industries, with, for example, married women with young children working evening shifts, students working on weekends, and married women with children in school working at lunch hour peaks.

Spain has high reported levels of unemployment, but as striking is the fact that over a quarter of the Spanish nonagricultural labor force was reported by government surveys as self-employed, family labor, or unprotected workers. A recent government-sponsored survey reported high levels of unprotected workers, mainly among the self-employed but also among full-time employees—the basis for my estimate in Table 15.1 (Benton 1987, p. 45). Other evidence supports this indication of the

[5.] Temporary workers are often hired out through agencies with whom they have contracts, though benefits are low; unregulated homework has been reported in Britain, and is a growing but still relatively minor part of employment (Marshall 1987; Standing 1986, pp. 115-20).

growth of an informal economy. Ybarra (1988) uses survey evidence to show the substantial informalization of the Alicante economy that has occurred in recent years. Alicante is responsible for 49.7% of employment in the footwear industry and 48.8% of employment in the toy industry in Spain. In the survey of the province's labor force, it was found that 54.8% of footwear employment and 45.4% of toy employment was informal in that it was unprotected by labor legislation or social security. A high proportion of textile employment was also informal. This informal employment was predominantly full-time and was the only source of income of the mainly female labor force.

There are no comparable statistics for Spain on part-time work. It is likely, however, that part-time work is less significant than in the British context because the flexibility offered by part-time work is likely to be provided by informal employment, much of which is paid by the piece. Until 1985, employers in Spain were discouraged from using part-time labor by legislation that made the social security obligations to such labor similar to those for full-time labor (OECD 1986, p. 57).

Mexico has small relative and absolute levels of unemployment. Even during the recession years, mainly because of the absence of unemployment insurance, reported unemployment has remained low in the main urban areas of Mexico. In 1986, rates of open unemployment of 2.6% were reported for Guadalajara, of 4.9% for Mexico City, and 5.0% for Monterrey (INEGI 1986, pp. 55-70). The estimate for unprotected workers in Table 15.1 is based on a labor force survey of registered enterprises in manufacturing, construction, and some government services in the metropolitan area of Guadalajara, Mexico's second largest city (Escobar 1986, pp. 32-42). Even the largest enterprises employ workers without providing them with contractual or social security. Guadalajara has an economic structure that probably contains proportionately more small-scale and "informal" enterprises than do Mexico City and Monterrey (Arias and Roberts 1985). Other case studies, however, indicate that unprotected labor is common in the large cities (Benaria and Roldan 1987).

These differences between the three countries are based on contrasts in social security and labor legislation that have resulted from the experiences of urbanization and industrialization associated with contrasting positions in the world economy. The British urban working class was formed by the beginning of the twentieth century, mainly on the basis of large-scale industrial employment, and became settled in residentially stable, homogeneous neighborhoods. This context produced a highly organized working-class movement and political struggles, which resulted in a pervasive state regulation of both the urban environment and the labor market, and a universally available system of social security. Little space has been left for an informal economy, and other forms of uncommitted labor predominate.

Spain has only recently become a predominantly urban country, mainly from the 1950s onward. Employment growth was originally based on medium and large-scale enterprises in manufacturing and construction. The working class is more socially heterogeneous, with less urban work experience than is the case of Britain, and is made up of migrants from many parts of Spain. The organized sector of the working class was strong in the 1970s and, under the conditions of the transition to democracy, had considerable political weight; but its coverage of the urban work force was partial and its successes in gaining concessions were, almost exclusively, in protecting jobs in formal enterprises, rather than in securing a general improvement in urban labor or living conditions. The result was a continuing high rigidity in real wages and escalating wage costs, leading to substantial layoffs, and encouraging the growth of an informal economy (OECD 1986; Benton 1986). There is entitlement to unemployment pay, but for a limited period only, and, unlike the British case, there is no guarantee of a minimum subsistence payment to families.

In Mexico, rapid urbanization has created jobs in small as well as large enterprises, and in the services more than in manufacturing and construction. The urban labor force is the least stable of the three countries, with an ongoing movement of people from rural to urban areas, return migration, urban to urban migration, and international migration. Urban living conditions are rudimentary, with a substantial part of the working class having to build its own housing and the lack, in many cities, of basic infrastructure, such as a domestic water supply and sewage. Apart from a rudimentary system of health care, there is no universally available social security. The ruling party, the PRI, has had a monopoly of political power since the Mexican Revolution of 1910, and has not had to take account of any effective organized opposition. Organized labor, part of PRI, has, in comparison with Britain and Spain, little bargaining power. Its successes have been concentrated in a few key industries, such as petroleum, and mainly in securing contractual security for relatively small groups of workers. The state's regulation of the labor market is generally ineffective, and an abundant labor supply has allowed employers considerably flexibility in their employment strategies, including low wages for most categories of workers and an extensive use of unprotected labor and subcontracting.

CLASS RELATIONS AND UNCOMMITTED LABOR

In this section, I shift attention to the some of the general implications of uncommitted labor for class relations in the three countries. My account is speculative, aiming to raise questions for research, because this kind of labor has only infrequently been subject to systematic study in either class or stratification analysis.

The increase in uncommitted labor is likely to introduce a greater volatility into class relations in the advanced industrial world, and reinforce an existing volatility in the developing world. The class relations of those whose labor is uncommitted are specific to particular contexts and inherently changeable given that they can be viewed as competitors, parasites, or allies by full-time workers, depending on the dynamics of the economy, state welfare policies, and social and community networks. There is volatility at the individual level also, because workers are likely to change job statuses during the life cycle so that their degree of work commitment varies according to different moments in the life or household cycle. Economic conjuncture and government policy likewise determine whether the various categories of uncommitted labor are seen as social and economic threats or assets to employers.

As uncommitted labor grows as a proportion of the labor force, so it is likely to introduce a more marked heterogeneity into the heart of working-class communities, in terms of work statuses and in terms of the economic and political factors that influence economic well-being and life chances. In neither Britain, Spain, nor Mexico are the providers of uncommitted labor a homogeneous group of the poor and exploited. Indeed, the general categories that I am using—self-employment and family labor, part-time work, unprotected employment—would need to be disaggregated even further in empirical research. There are contrasts between the high incomes that the owners of small-scale enterprises often earn and the low incomes of their employees (Portes et al. 1986). Female home-workers or the unemployed on welfare payments usually receive a pittance compared to skilled craftsmen working informally as freelance workers in construction or in small shoe or repair workshops.

Motivations for taking up the different forms of uncommitted labor vary, as do the aspirations associated with these jobs. Some people take up these kinds of jobs because there is no alternative, and whatever they get is better than nothing; others, especially those with some capital or special expertise, see in it the opportunity to make money more easily and quickly than through full-time employment in the formal sector.

Part of what is happening is a subtle change in the way in which the working class relates to the labor market. The increasing importance of uncommitted labor entails a shift from individual to household characteristics in determining the labor market status of both individuals and their families. Because uncommitted workers usually receive low incomes, they are often part of a forced household strategy of diversifying work roles to maximize income, increasing the numbers of household members who work for pay. They inevitably make the household's experience of the labor market more heterogeneous and less determined by one occupational culture than is the case when a family's life chances are determined by the occupational position of the full-time "breadwinner." One tentative conclusion is that the growing importance of uncommitted labor, either as a permanent work status or a temporary one, is likely to make the kind of job that an individual does a less significant determinant of life chances than other factors such as household composition and cycle, gender, and age.

A further similarity between the three countries is that uncommitted labor is likely to reinforce the local dimension of class relations. Involvement in the informal economy, for example, means an intensification of local relationships as a means of obtaining information about jobs. Gimeno et al. (1986) describe how those in their Madrid sample who are totally involved in the informal economy are the most active in seeking and maintaining social relationships. Men looking for casual work in construction meet, for example, at bars to hear about possible job sources. Harris et al. (1985), describing the situation of redundant steelworkers, in South Wales, also emphasize that informal contacts are the main means by which small-scale subcontractors recruit casual labor. These subcontractors have taken over some of the work that was formerly done by the large steel enterprise. In his national study of the unemployed in Britain, White (1984, pp. 101-5) shows that the major source of jobs for the recurrently unemployed are personal contacts. These account for 40% of jobs, which were mainly in small-scale service enterprises. In contrast, the government employment service accounted for only 20% of new jobs.

In Guadalajara, Mexico, natives of the city find their first jobs in small informal establishments, learning a skill, which later they may use to obtain work in a large-scale enterprise. The informal enterprise is an important source of social as well as economic activity in the Guadalajara neighborhoods.[6] A dramatic example of how uncommitted labor enforces local relationships comes from a recent study of working-class neighborhoods in Santiago, Chile (Rodríguez 1987; Tironi 1987). There, the average journey to work of residents has dropped sharply since the late 1960s when a comparable survey was carried out. Rising levels of unemploy-

---

[6.] Escobar (1986, p. 129), in an analysis of the informal enterprise and the local labor market in Guadalajara, comments: "The successful [small-scale entrepreneurs] rarely move to live away from the working-class districts, given the need for local labor and their local contacts. . . . Their economic mobility—generally small—brings benefits for neighbors and friends."

ment and the elimination of formal sector jobs, especially in manufacturing, as a result of the policies of the military junta, have focused economic life on the neighborhood. The result, it must be noted, is not high levels of cohesion or cooperation. Instead, there is considerable economic competition and increasing social isolation as people are deprived of the work relationships they once had in large-scale enterprises.

The increasing importance of uncommitted forms of labor is thus likely to make people unusually dependent on community ties for meeting their economic needs. Social isolation for those who are unprotected workers, are self-employed, are unemployed, or are part-time workers is likely to be more costly than for those in full-time, formal work who can draw on workplace relations. Incomes from uncommitted labor are generally so low that family and community relationships are important means of making these incomes stretch, either through diminishing dependence on the market by exchanges of goods and services, loans and aid in emergency, or through income pooling strategies within a household. Family and community relationships also provide information about informal job opportunities, sources of cheap supplies, and so on. As Mingione (1987) points out, community relationships can protect people against the competitive pressures of the labor market, where other forms of protection, such as labor unions or government social security legislation, are not developed. There is, however, an ambivalence in this dependence on community. Tensions both within and between households may increase as people compete, as well as cooperate, to obtain scarce resources.

An increasing social heterogeneity and sense of localism are likely to reinforce the spatial factor in the class relations of the working class. The geography of class becomes more complex as differences in the local context make for variations in the salient issues around which classes form. Labor markets become more local, and contrast in their consequences for class relations with the national ones that they are replacing. Nationally organized labor markets reinforce work identity as the salient basis of class interest and action, unifying geographically dispersed workers in a common set of demands and complaints. Local labor markets make salient community and neighborhood issues—the common interest of people who otherwise are fragmented by the small scale of enterprises, self-employment, and different work schedules. Issues of housing, social infrastructure, and communal welfare, and the solidarities and divisions generated by these, become the bases of class action.

These trends are part of a larger economic and political process based on new communication technologies and new spatial patterns of industrial organization. The city is reshaped by these developments, resulting in the fragmentation of social communities and the increasing importance of spatial organization in class relations.[7] The change in working patterns toward greater job instability, the fragmentation of working relations, and a lower commitment to an occupational culture is a fundamental aspect of these general processes.

UNCOMMITTED LABOR AND
WORKING-CLASS POLARIZATION

Finally, I explore the differences in class relations produced by the specific forms taken by uncommitted labor and by contrasts in state regulation of the labor market. I will limit my contrasts to national differences, though taking my examples from case studies of particular localities. National contrasts are not, however, the only interesting ones because regions and localities are also likely to differ from each other depending on the particular local mixes of work statuses, and their significance for the local economy.

An important source of variation are the different ways in which informal workers, part-timers, and the unemployed relate to the rest of the working population. Uncommitted labor has, potentially, diverse implications for the connectedness of intraclass social relationships, whether fostering exchange and cohesiveness among the working class, whether leading to social isolation, or creating new class divides by differentiating the coping patterns of one section of a community from another.

Where state regulation of the labor market is pervasive, as in Britain, uncommitted labor appears to polarize the working-class population into segments differentiated by access to employment or dependence on state welfare. In Britain, poverty is an administrative category defined, basically, by eligibility for supplementary benefit. For those at the poverty line, there is relatively little incentive to take up paid work, because benefits will be lost. Surveys indicate that, in the case of households of unemployed men, wives are less likely to work for pay than in the cases of households where husbands are in full-time employment (Hakim 1982; Laite 1986).

Pahl (1984, pp. 198-231) argues that it is the number of earners in a household, and stage in household cycle, that makes the most difference to what a family is able to do—what equipment it has, what self-provisioning it can do, and what it can afford to buy on the market. Employment brings cumulative advantages in the British case, providing access to resources, social contacts, and so on. In the Isle of Sheppey,

---

[7.] See Soja's (1986) analysis of Los Angeles and Feagin's (1987) general account of American cities.

where Pahl carried out his study, the poorest members of the population did not have sufficient resources to engage in remunerative informal activities, lacking the equipment to do maintenance and repair work and the capital to buy it.

In Spain, the mixed case in which state regulation of the labor market is only partial, the situation appears to be different in that putting more labor into the market is a resource of the poorest—those involved in the informal economy. Those families totally involved in the formal economy have less people working, normally only the male breadwinner. In the Madrid working-class suburb of Leganes, studied by Gimeno and his colleagues (1986), those working formally have stable jobs with adequate social security coverage for themselves and their families.

Differentiation in Spain is based on the distinction between households whose members work formally, and have few adults working, and those whose members work informally and all work who can. This differentiation may have consequences for the education of children, making it more difficult for those in the informal sector to obtain education, but it does not appear to polarize the local community as in the British case. The informally employed are socially active, in making contacts and doing whatever jobs they can find. The formally employed are also active, though in the types of activities that provide communal services. There are no reports of the moral opprobrium of being poor and not having a regular job that surround the unemployed in Pahl's study.

Women have less chance of surviving outside the household than in Britain, and less support from the state to do so. On the other hand, the fieldwork of the Madrid group suggests that household survival strategies entail less pressure on women than we will see to be the case in Mexico (Gimeno et al. 1986). Women also appear to be more closely involved in community relationships than appears to be the case in Britain. Among those totally involved in the informal economy, there is the most flexible distribution of domestic work among males and females and the greatest economic decision making by women, while the more involved the household is in the formal economy, usually implying that the male is the only full-time worker, the more traditional is the division of labor, with domestic tasks falling on the woman, who has little say in economic matters.

Mexico represents the extreme case of a competitive labor market in which there is little state regulation. In the absence of an effective welfare system, and low pay even in the formal sector of employment, there is little differentiation within the working class. The informal sector is considerably larger than in Britain and offers full-time employment to a large section of the urban population. This population is not set apart by poverty or style of life from the rest of the working class for two reasons. First, differences in pay and conditions of work in formal and informal employment are not markedly different. In our Guadalajara study, we found an average difference of 18% in favor of those formally employed. Second, those informal workers in Mexico whose wages are markedly lower than the minimum wage—mainly female home-workers—are often members of households in which other members (the male head, the children) are employed in formally registered enterprises (Benaria and Roldan 1987). Working-class subsistence in Mexico is necessarily based on the pooling of household resources because even pay in large-scale enterprises is insufficient to maintain a family. Thus the combination of jobs in formal and informal sectors is a common pattern of working-class employment.

In this Mexican context, the community and its relationships are the major resource available to the working class, and the main basis for collective action. Exchanges with neighbors are important for surviving crises and for the information that will gain supplementary work for a household. The economically worst off in the Mexican situation are those who are isolated from community relations—single-parent families, although many of these develop close exchanges with neighbors and kin, and "living-in" domestic servants (Gonzalez 1986). The quality of the environment is important to these survival strategies. Being able to obtain cheap housing through self-construction and having access to water and sewage facilities are some among the many interests that the Mexican urban working class have in common. Job-related issues are less relevant: the minimum wage affects few workers, while conditions of work either in formal or in informal enterprises do not appear to concern workers. There is a considerable job mobility within and between cities and careers in any one place are short.

The implications for household organization contrast with both Britain and Spain. The nature of job opportunities has contradictory implications: They are essential to household survival and, so, it is important that members of a household pool budgets and stay together; yet, these opportunities place an increasing burden on the women, especially the wives who do not have access to the kind of labor-saving devices that their counterparts have in the other two countries or to an adequate urban infrastructure. These women must often undertake a "double day," working at home-work or in domestic service and returning home to do the household chores.

Conflict within households is common, indicating that household strategies of survival do not imply consensus, and that much of household solidarity is based on coercion and lack of alternative possibilities of survival outside the household. Women as single-parent families have a difficult time surviving in Mexico. In this situation, women are more committed to the neighborhood and their networks than are the men. In terms of neighborhood issues, they are often more active and more pragmatic.

CONCLUSION

Two somewhat contradictory processes are affecting labor markets throughout the world. One is the continuing expansion of job opportunities, particularly marked among women. The absolute numbers of people in the labor market are substantially greater in the 1980s than they have been in any other period of history. At the same time, the proportion of people in full-time employment has declined substantially in recent years. The economically active population, both in the advanced industrial countries and in the developing countries, contains substantial numbers—in developing countries often a majority—who either are in nonstandard employment or are unemployed. The two processes are connected by technological changes and by international economic competition leading to a stable, and at times declining, demand for permanent labor, and an increasing demand for labor that can be used flexibly by the enterprise.

Uncommitted labor has significant consequences for class relations, differentiating the working population into those who are full-time employed and those whose working careers are more unstable or intermittent. Making ends meet often depends on state welfare payments, as in the case of the unemployed, or on the earnings of other household members, as in the case of part-time and family workers. Uncommitted labor thus adds further dimensions along which the class identity of the working population can be forged: the nature and quality of public services, the extent of state welfare payments, the quality of the urban infrastructure.

These dimensions may or may not reinforce class identities based on conflicts over wages and conditions of work, but they introduce new and often more localized sources of social differentiation. Local facilities and local social networks become more crucial to an individual's or a household's capacity for economic survival and improvement. The organization of the household in terms of the household division of labor, and the management of consumption through, for example, lessening dependence on the market through self-provisioning and other strategies, can affect life chances as powerfully as occupation or income. Sources of identity other than work-based ones become more salient for class relations, depending on whether uncommitted labor concentrates among certain types of households or among certain categories of members such as women, the young, or the old.

This argument is speculative, and depends, to a considerable extent, on whether uncommitted labor is uncommitted in the deeper sense of being occupationally unstable and having a purely instrumental view of work. I have not been able to explore this theme adequately, because it requires systematic work histories of the uncommitted as well as data on work attitudes and aspirations. But two hypotheses are suggested. One is that there is greater job instability among the uncommitted, with more frequent changes in jobs and in types of work than is the case for those in regular full-time employment.[8] The second, related, suggestion is that uncommitted workers identify less with their work than is the case for full-time workers, having proportionately fewer work-based social relationships and generally deriving less job satisfaction.

If these suggestions are true, then as uncommitted labor grows in importance for both individuals and households, work is likely to become a less significant source of personal and collective identity. The impact of occupational cultures on working-class communities is likely to be less, and other sources of identity are likely to be stronger bases for association. The working class effectively disappears from class analysis.

Such a direction of change also means that the job that an individual has will be a less useful indicator of levels of family income, of patterns of expenditure, of aspirations for the children, and even of social and political attitudes. In short, many of the proven assumptions of stratification research may need to be rethought as, and if, uncommitted labor becomes the norm, not the exception, in the labor market.[9]

The consequences of uncommitted labor for class relations are not, however, uniform. Different historical positions in the world economy continue to leave a legacy for labor. The core country, Britain, developed the most complete regulation of the labor market and the most extensive protection of the working population. The periphery, Mexico, has the least regulation and protection; while the semiperiphery, Spain, is intermediate. In Britain, uncommitted labor occurs primarily through part-time work and unemployment; in Spain, through informal employment, including self-employment, and unemployment; and in Mexico, through informal employment.

[8] The differences may not be great because both part-time work and self-employment can be relatively stable. The OECD figures (OECD 1986b, p. 19) for Britain show that part-timers stay on average six years in their jobs, compared with nine years for full-timers, and have a higher job turnover.

[9] Sullivan (1988) makes the related argument that it is the firm and industry sector—the characteristics of the job—rather than an individual's occupation that is becoming the most significant predictor of life chances, as occupational skills cease to guarantee stable employment.

There are important differences between the countries in the degree of dependence that those providing uncommitted labor have on public, private, or community means of obtaining income and welfare. These differences account for the contrasts in the patterns of differentiation among working populations noted in the three countries: In Britain, where the informal economy is not extensive, but public welfare is, there is a polarization of the working population between those with paid employment and those who depend on state subsidies. Patterns of consumption increasingly differentiate this working population. In Spain, where there is a substantial informal sector, but also considerable state protection for those in formal employment, there is an income and status differentiation according to the degree of involvement in the formal or informal economy, but common dependence on the labor market and being subject to its volatility still appear to provide a stronger shared identity for the working class than is the case in Britain. In Mexico, where wages are low and state protection inadequate even for those in formal employment, there is little differentiation among the working population because of the need of households to obtain whatever income they can get from whatever source. Uncommitted labor appears, then, to erode working-class identity most at the core—where, historically, it had developed most—and least at the periphery.

Despite these differences, uncommitted labor means that the issues around which classes form are likely to be more locally and regionally specific than is the case where full-time employment is the norm and the labor market is a nationally regulated one. Countervailing this potential spatial fragmentation of class organization, however, is the emergence of new bases for collective action as the increasing heterogeneity of job positions reinforces gender and age identities, creating special interests and potential political divisions. These research questions are as relevant in the advanced industrial world as in the developing world. They require detailed work on the implications of employment trends for household and community organization. It is at this level that the dynamics of class organization are increasingly likely to be shaped.

REFERENCES

Arias, P. and B. Roberts. 1985. "The City in Permanent Transition." Pp. 149-75 in *Capital and Labor in the Urbanized World*, edited by J. Walton. London: Sage.

Benaria, L. and M. Roldan. 1987. *The Crossroads of Class and Gender*. Chicago: University of Chicago Press.

Benton, L. 1986. "The Role of the Informal Sector in Economic Development: Industrial Restructuring in Spain." Ph.D. dissertation, Johns Hopkins University.

———. 1987. "Invisible Factories: The Informal Economy and Spanish Industrial Development" (Mimeo). Cambridge: MIT.

Brannen, J. and P. Moss. 1987. "Dual Earner Households." Pp. 75-95 in *Give and Take in Families*, edited by J. Brannen and G. Wilson. London: Allen & Unwin.

Central Statistical Office. 1987. *Social Trends 17*. London: HMSO.

Cordova, E. 1986. "From Full-Time Wage Employment to Atypical Employment: A Major Shift in the Evolution of Labor Relations." *International Labor Review* 125(6):641-58.

Dirección General de Estadistica. 1972. *Censo General de Población, IX. 1970*. Resumen General. Mexico, D.F.: Author.

———. 1986. *Censo General de Población X, 1980*. Resumen General. Vols. 1, 2, Inegi. Mexico, D.F.: Author.

Escobar, A. 1986. *Con El Sudor de tu Frente*. Guadalajara: El Colegio de Jalisco.

Feagin, J. 1987. "Cities and the New International Division of Labor: An Overview." Pp. 3-36 in *The Capitalist City*, edited by J. Feagin and M. P. Smith. Oxford: Basil Blackwell.

Gimeno, J., M. Hurtado, P. Monreal, J. Perez, B. Ruiz, and C. Zlolniski. 1986. "Economia sumergida y organización familiar." Paper presented at the 2nd Symposium on the Informal Sector, Johns Hopkins University, October.

Gonzalez de la Rocha, M. 1986. *Los Recursos de la Pobreza*. Guadalajara: El Colegio de Jalisco.

Grossman, G. 1988. "Informal Incomes and Outlays of the Soviet Urban Population." In *The Informal Economy*, edited by A. Portes, M. Castells, and L. Benton. Baltimore: Johns Hopkins Press.

Hakim, C. 1982. "The Social Consequences of High Unemployment." *Journal of Social Policy* 2(4):433-67.

Harris, C., R. Lee, and L. Morris. 1985. "Redundancy in Steel." Pp. 154-66 in *New Approaches to Economic Life*, edited by B. Roberts, R. Finnegan, and D. Gallie. Manchester: Manchester University Press.

INE (Instituto Nacional de Estadística). 1984. *Encuesta de Población activa: Principales resultados*. Madrid: Author.

INEGI (Instituto Nacional de Estadística Geografía e Informática). 1986. *Cuaderno de Información Oportuna Regional* No. 7. Mexico. D.F.: Author.

Laite, A. J. 1986. *The Social Implications of Changing Patterns of Work and Employment*. ESRC Final Report No. G00232051. British Library Document Center.

Lash, S. and J. Urry. 1987. *The End of Organized Capitalism*. Madison: University of Wisconsin Press.

Marshall, A. 1987. *Non-Standard Employment Practices in Latin America*. Discussion Paper, DP/6/87. Geneva: International Institute for Labor Studies.

Michon, F. 1987a. "Time and Flexibility: Working Time in the Debate on Flexibility." *Labor and Society* 12(1):3-17.

———. 1987b. *La segmentation 15 ans apres*. Working Document. Paris: Universite de Paris, Seminaire d'Economie du Travail.

Mingione, E. 1987. "Economic Development, Social Factors and Social Context." Paper presented at the annual meeting of the American Sociological Association, Chicago.

OECD. 1986a. *Economic Surveys, 1985/1986: Spain*. Paris: Author.

———. 1986b. *Employment Outlook* (September). Paris: Author.

———. 1987. *Labor Force Statistics, 1965-1985*. Paris: Author.

Pahl, R. 1984. *Divisions of Labor*. Oxford: Basil Blackwell.

———. 1987. "The Distributional Consequences of Informal Work." Paper given at the 6th Urban Change and Conflict Conference, University of Kent, England.

Portes, A. 1985. "Latin American Class Structures." *Latin American Research Review* 20(3):7-39.
Portes, A., S. Blitzer, and J. Curtis. 1986. "The Urban Informal Sector in Uruguay." *World Development* 14:727-41.
Portes, A., M. Castells, and L. Benton, eds. 1988. *The Informal Economy*. Baltimore: Johns Hopkins Press.
Portes, A. and S. Sassen-Koob. 1987. "Making It Underground." *American Journal of Sociology* 93(1):30-61.
Przeworski, A. 1977. "Proletariat into a Class." *Politics and Society* 7(4):343-401.
Roberts, B. 1981. "Migration and Industrialising Economies: A Comparative Perspective." Pp. 192-219 in *New Perspectives in Urban Change and Conflict*, edited by M. Harloe. London: Heinemann.
Rodríguez, A. 1987. "Veinte años de las poblaciones de Santiago." *Proposiciones* 14:24-43.
Sagardoy, J. A. 1987. "Labor Market Flexibility in Spain." *Labor and Society* 12(1):55-67.
Soja, E. 1986. "Taking Los Angeles Apart." *Environment and Planning D* 4:255-72.
Standing, G. 1981. *Unemployment and Female Labour*. New York: St. Martin's.
———. 1986. *Unemployment and Labour Market Flexibility: The United Kingdom*. Geneva: International Labour Office.
———. 1986. "Meshing Labor Flexibility with Security." *International Labor Review* 125(1):87-106.
Stark, D. 1980. "Class Struggle and the Transformation of the Labor Process." *Theory and Society* 9(1):89-130.
Sullivan, T. 1988. "The Decline of Occupations." Paper presented at Notre Dame Conference on Changing Social Institutions, March.
Tironi, E. 1987. "Pobladores e inegración social." *Proposiciones* (Santiago, Chile) 14:64-84.
Wallerstein, I. 1974. *The Modern World-System*. New York: Academic Press.
White, M. 1984. *Long Term Unemployment and Labor Markets*. London: Policy Studies Institute.
World Bank. 1987. *World Development Report 1987*. New York: Oxford University Press.
Ybarra, J.-A. 1988. "Industrial Informalization in the Valencian Economy." In *The Informal Economy*, edited by A. Portes, M. Castells, and L. Benton. Baltimore: Johns Hopkins Press.

16

Educational and Occupational Attainment in 21 Countries

Donald J. Treiman
Kam-Bor Yip

The process by which social status is transmitted from generation to generation has long been of interest to students of society, both in the United States and abroad. Indeed, research on social mobility and status attainment has had a lively international flavor at least since the 1950s, when the ISA Research Committee on Social Stratification first became active. Large-scale studies were conducted in many countries, often borrowing from and partially replicating other studies. In this way a collection of more or less comparable data was built up for a substantial number of nations throughout the world. Moreover, studies conducted for other purposes, such as the eight-nation Political Action Survey and national election studies modeled on the University of Michigan U.S. election

AUTHORS' NOTE: *The data utilized in this chapter were compiled or analyzed under grants from the National Science Foundation to the University of Wisconsin (GS-2487), to Columbia University (28050), and to UCLA (SES 83-11483); from the National Institute of Mental Health to the Center for Policy Research (MH 26606); and from the John R. and Dora Haynes Foundation to UCLA. The chapter was put in final form while Treiman was an ASA/NSF/Census Fellow. Jan Dronkers, Harry Ganzeboom, Robert Hauser, Michael Hout, Jonathan Kelley, Mel Kohn, and Judah Matras provided useful comments on an earlier version. We are grateful to Rudolf Andorka, Archibald Haller, John Jackson, Jonathan Kelley, Vered Kraus, Ken'ichi Tominaga, Kyrzstof Zagorski, Alice Robbin of the Data and Program Library Service, University of Wisconsin; Elizabeth Stephenson of the UCLA Social Science Data Archive; and the staff of the Inter-University Consortium for Political and Social Research at the University of Michigan for assistance in securing the data utilized here, and to the staff of the UCLA Social Sciences Computing Facility for support in data processing.*

studies often included data of interest to students of social stratification and social mobility.

The increasing availability of suitable data has given rise to a long series of increasingly sophisticated cross-national comparative studies of occupational mobility. Important recent studies include Tyree et al. (1979), Grusky and Hauser (1984), Erikson and Goldthorpe (1985a, 1985b, 1986), Treiman and Kelley (1986), Ganzeboom et al. (forthcoming), and Yamaguchi (1987); for a review of earlier studies, see Ganzeboom et al. (forthcoming). An important issue addressed by these studies, which is still not resolved, is whether there is a common "social fluidity regime"—or pattern of social mobility—that characterizes industrialized societies (or perhaps all complex societies) or whether, alternatively, there are systematic national variations in mobility rates and mobility patterns.

The liveliness and vigor of recent cross-national comparative research on *occupational mobility* is not matched by comparative research on *status attainment*. Despite a thriving tradition of research, initiated by Blau and Duncan (1967), on the factors that contribute to educational, occupational, and income attainment in specific countries, mainly the United States, attempts to compare the status attainment process across countries are very sparse. Comparisons have been limited mainly to studies of small numbers of countries (e.g., Jones 1971; Kerckhoff 1974; Lin and Yauger 1975; Treiman and Terrell 1975; Pontinen 1976; Boyd et al. 1980; Zagorski 1984) or else have involved rather casual juxtaposition of the coefficients of published models with little attention to problems of measurement comparability (e.g., Heath 1981). Virtually the only systematic large-scale comparisons are those undertaken by Treiman and Roos (1983) and Roos (1985) of gender differences in the process of status attainment.

The reason for this is, in fact, quite straightforward: The data comparability requirements for comparative studies of status attainment are much more stringent than for comparative occupational mobility studies. Mobility studies are, after all, restricted to the analysis of a single cross-tabulation, relating father's occupation to son's occupation.[1] By collapsing mobility tables into a small number of categories, analysts have achieved at least nominal comparability across countries. Thus a substantial portion of the comparative mobility analysis to date has been conducted using published mobility tables, often collapsed to a 3 by 3 classification. Only recently, as interest has grown in analyzing more detailed mobility tables, have researchers gone to the effort of construct-

---

[1] Most analyses of occupational mobility tables have been limited to men, as have most analyses of status attainment. Below we discuss some of the reasons for this.

ing new mobility tables from unit data in order to enhance classification comparability (e.g., Erikson and Goldthorpe 1985a, 1985b, 1986; Treiman and Kelley 1986; Ganzeboom et al., forthcoming). But even this effort is much less demanding than what is required to create comparable measurements of education, occupation, and income from unit data originally coded in a variety of schemes—an effort that has engaged us and our associates for more than 10 years. No one else has been foolish enough to undertake such a task.

Theoretical Developments

Although there has been little comparative research on status attainment processes, a number of hypotheses have been advanced regarding the sorts of differences across countries that might be expected were comparable data available for analysis. These derive from two sources: theoretical arguments pertaining to the process of status attainment per se and arguments made in the context of comparative analyses of occupational mobility that would pertain to the status attainment process also. In the present chapter we are concerned with only two of the several hypotheses that have been put forward. These are very general hypotheses, which apply to all countries, capitalist and socialist alike.

Hypothesis 1. *Industrialized societies will tend to be more open than nonindustrialized societies.*

and

Hypothesis 2. *Societies in which the degree of status inequality is high will tend to be less open than societies in which the degree of status inequality is low.*

Industrialization. Let us consider the industrialization hypothesis first. In the course of a synthetic review of the comparative literature on social stratification and mobility some years ago, Treiman (1970) advanced several propositions relating the status attainment process to the level of industrialization. In particular, he proposed (1970, p. 221):

(1) *The more industrialized a society, the smaller the direct influence of father's occupational status on son's occupational status.*
(2) *The more industrialized a society, the greater the direct influence of educational attainment on occupational status.*
(3) *The more industrialized a society, the smaller the influence of parental status on educational attainment.*

The main basis for the claims regarding occupational allocation was that with industrialization there is a greater bureaucratization of work, which results in a shift away from the direct inheritance of jobs and an increase in the role of formal education as a vehicle for learning occupationally relevant skills. Moreover, as Treiman (1970, p. 218) noted, "the demand of highly industrialized societies for a mobile and adaptable labor force likely results in a shift from ascriptive to universalistic achievement criteria as a basis for occupational role allocation." The main basis for the claim regarding the influence of parental status on educational attainment was that free education is more readily available in industrialized societies and hence in particular is more readily available to those from low status origins.

Status inequality. The arguments just offered are reasonable so far as they go. But they neglect what is perhaps the most important concomitant of industrialization—the reduction in the degree of status inequality, a point Kelley has developed at length (Kelley 1978; Kelley et al. 1980; Kelley and Klein 1981, pp. 16-21; Kelley et al. 1981; see also a similar argument by Tyree et al. 1979). Consider what it is that gives those from high status origins an advantage in the pursuit of socioeconomic success. These resources are of three kinds: material capital, human capital, and social capital. Wealth and income are important in paying for schooling, permitting a child to continue in school rather than enter the labor force early, and, in some instances, providing the funds to set up a business, trade, or professional practice. Skills, knowledge, information, and attendant aspirations and expectations, which are strongly implicated in differential educational and occupational success, tend to be transmitted to children even when material resources are depleted or lost, as the success of various immigrant and refugee groups attests. Finally, social capital, the contacts and connections of fathers, can be helpful to their sons in securing jobs or developing business opportunities.

It follows that where differences in parental resources are large, their impact on the achievements of sons should be large. For example, in a society in which fathers who are professionals have an average of fourteen years of education and fathers who are unskilled laborers have an average of four years of education, it is likely that the difference in achievement between the sons of professionals and those of unskilled laborers will be greater than in a society in which fathers who are professionals have an average of sixteen years of school and fathers who are unskilled laborers have an average of twelve years of school. In the latter system the social distance between the two sons is much smaller and the likelihood that they are exposed to the same opportunities, particularly the same educational opportunities, is much larger; hence, the likelihood is much greater that the ultimate status positions of the two sons will depend mainly upon their own talents rather than on their fathers' positions.

Although the level of status inequality tends to decline as countries industrialize, mainly because free education becomes widespread and because of concomitant shifts in the nature of occupational systems, industrialization and inequality do not move in perfect concert. Hence, it is useful to consider the effects of these two factors separately. Moreover, other factors, such as whether a country has a state-socialist system, may affect the degree of inequality, but an analysis of the determinants of societal variations in inequality is beyond the scope of this chapter. In what follows, we will investigate Treiman's three specific hypotheses regarding the effects of industrialization that we quoted above and also a parallel set of three hypotheses regarding the effects of inequality.

DATA AND METHODS

Data

The analysis reported here is based on representative samples of the male labor force aged 25-64 in 21 countries. These data sets cover nearly all the countries for which surveys of representative national samples containing detailed (three-digit) information of father's occupation exist. Our data sets are restricted to males both because data on females are available for a much smaller sample of countries and because the inclusion of women in status attainment models greatly increases their complexity because of the sporadic labor force participation of women in most societies. For cross-national comparisons of gender differences and similarities in status attainment, see Treiman and Roos (1983) and Roos (1985). The age restriction is imposed both to minimize bias resulting from the exclusion of those still in school in their early twenties, who typically will attain high status occupations, and to avoid distortions resulting from the instability in the early parts of the socioeconomic career. Although this never occurs in practice, because the loss of data would be too great, in principle analyses of intergenerational mobility and status attainment should be restricted to samples of men in midcareer, say aged 35-54, in order to measure the characteristics of fathers and sons at similar stages of their careers.

The choice of data sets. For many of the 21 nations included here, several data sets containing the appropriate variables are available. In the interest of simplicity, however, we have restricted the present analysis to a single data set from each country. Our choice of data sets to include in the present analysis was based on three factors: First, we did not have access to all of the extant data sets for each country or have not yet completed the necessary preparatory work. Second, where there was a clear difference in the quality of available data sets (as indicated by the size of the sample, its representativeness, the completeness of the variable set, or the precision with which information was obtained), we utilized the highest-quality data set. Finally, all else being equal, we opted for a data set collected in the early 1970s. Although in some sense there is no particular reason to insist that cross-national comparisons be based on data collected at the same time, given that each data set can be analyzed "in the ethnographic present" by constructing measures of societal characteristics from the variables in the data set or choosing measures for appropriate dates from other sources, our task is simplified if we do not have to entertain the possibility that time is a dimension of variability between data sets. That is, by choosing data sets from a small range of years, we automatically control for the effect of variations in the world economy. We also, of course, simplify the task of constructing appropriate societal variables. Table 16.1 describes these data sets.

Individual-Level Variables

As we noted above, the major hindrance to cross-national comparisons of status attainment has been the difficulty of achieving comparability of measurement. Because the coefficients of status attainment models are known to be quite sensitive to variations in measurement procedures (Treiman 1977, chap. 8), cross-national comparisons make little sense unless the variables included in the models are measured in a genuinely comparable way across countries. For this reason, we decided to restrict our attention to very simple models specifying the relations among four variables that we think we can measure comparably across countries— father's education and occupation and son's education and occupation.

For both generations *education* is measured by years of school completed. For many countries (the United Kingdom is a particularly striking case in point), this is a rather crude measure of educational attainment because the advantage that education confers depends as much on the type of schooling one attains as on the amount of schooling. But for the purposes of cross-national comparisons, there are no obvious alternatives. The measurement of educational attainment is curiously crude in most sample surveys. With few exceptions (e.g., the Oxford Mobility Survey for England and Wales), the complexity of educational systems is not adequately reflected in the way education is ascertained in sample surveys. Thus for most countries we have only a single question about amount or type of schooling that at best can be transformed into a measure

TABLE 16.1: Description of Data Sets Analyzed

Country	Year of Survey	Name of Survey and Principal Investigators	Number of Cases[a]
Capitalist industrialized countries:			
Australia	1967	Australian National Political Attitudes Study (Aitkin, Kahan, and Stokes)	677
Austria	1973	Political Action: an 8-Nation Survey, 1973-76 (Barnes, Kaase et al.)	397
Denmark	1972	Scandinavian Welfare Study (Allardt)	149
England and Wales	1972	Oxford National Occupational Mobility Inquiry (Goldthorpe and Hope)	7,469
Finland	1972	See Denmark	266
German Federal Republic	1976	ZUMABUS (Wildenmann, Mayer, and Mueller)	567
Ireland	1973	Determinants of Occupational Mobility (Jackson)	1,645
Israel	1974	National Labor Force Survey (Matras)	2,922
Italy	1973	See Austria	512
Japan	1975	1975 Social Stratification and Mobility Survey (Tominaga)	1,703
Netherlands	1973	See Austria	257
Northern Ireland	1973	Determinants of Occupational Mobility (Jackson and Miller)	1,721
Norway	1972	See Denmark	282
Sweden	1972	See Denmark	342
United States	1973	Occupational Changes in a Generation II (Hauser and Featherman)	16,422
Socialist-bloc countries:			
Hungary	1973	Central Statistical Office Social Mobility Microcensus (Andorka)	10,366
Poland	1972	Central Statistical Office Mobility Survey (Zagorski)	27,630
Developing capitalist countries:			
Brazil	1973	Brazilian Institute of Statistics, IBGE (Haller and Pastore)	5,198[b]
India	1971	Cross-national Program in Political and Social Change (Verba, Nie, and Kim)[c]	1,540
Philippines	1972	Philippine National Demographic Survey (Concepcion)	3,605
Taiwan	1970	Value System of Taiwan (Grichting)	741

a. Males aged 25-64 with no missing data.
b. A 10% sample of all cases surveyed.
c. Not a national sample; restricted to four Indian states: Andra Pradesh, Gujerat, Uttar Pradesh, and West Bengal.

of years of school completed (by assigning a score that in our judgment represents the midpoint of years of school completed by those in each category).

Occupational status is measured by the Standard International Occupational Prestige Scale (Treiman 1977). This scale has been shown to replicate closely the occupational prestige hierarchies of most countries in the world for which local data exist and also has been shown to produce scores that are highly correlated (on the order of .8-.9) with scales based on the socioeconomic characteristics of occupations, such as the Duncan Socioeconomic Index (Treiman 1977, chap. 8) and Kelley's International Socioeconomic Status Scale (Kelley et al., 1980). The main difference between prestige and socioeconomic status scales is in the position of farm owners, which tends to be near the mean of the distribution on prestige scales but near the bottom of socioeconomic scales. In consequence, results obtained in analyses of those from nonfarm origins tend to be quite similar regardless of which sort of scale is used, whereas intergenerational correlations of occupational status for samples that include the agricultural labor force tend to be higher when computed using socioeconomic status scales than when using prestige scales (the difference typically being on the order of .1).

While prestige is a central feature of occupational rewards, and is probably the best summary measure of occupational *status* (understood in its classical, Weberian, sense), it is not a particularly good indicator of occupational *resources* of the sort that will provide sons with a competitive advantage. For this purpose, a socioeconomic status scale might be a better choice, particularly because the two major components of most occupational socioeconomic status scales are the average education and the average income of incumbents, which Treiman has argued are important indicators of differences in occupational resources (1977, chaps. 1 and 5). It is awkward, however, to measure occupational status differently in the two generations. Moreover, occupational socioeconomic status scales have a serious drawback in their own right: The fact that a component of occupational SES is education while education is the other major variable in the model produces a part-whole artifact of an unknown degree. For these reasons, we decided for the present analysis to use prestige as our measure of the occupational status of fathers as well as respondents.

Societal Variables

As noted above, our main hypotheses about societal variations in the process of status attainment concern the effects of the level of industrialization, on one hand, and the degree of status inequality, on the other. To test these hypotheses, therefore, we need appropriate indicators of industrialization and inequality.

Inequality of father's education. To test the claim that the greater the inequality of socioeconomic resources held by fathers, the greater the dependence of status attainment on social origins, we needed to measure the inequality of socioeconomic resources in the fathers' generation. Given the limitations of data, this was possible only for fathers' educational attainment. We constructed two measures of the degree of inequality in the years of schooling obtained by fathers in each country, standardized them to a mean of zero and a standard deviation of one, and averaged them. The two measures were (1) the ratio of the mean years of schooling obtained by fathers who were high-prestige professionals to the mean years of schooling obtained by fathers who were low-prestige production process workers[2] and (2) the coefficient of relative variability of the years of schooling obtained by fathers (the standard deviation divided by the mean). The correlation between the two components is .89, computed over the 19 countries for which they could be constructed (father's education was not ascertained in Australia and Brazil). Both of the component measures and the derived composite are shown in Table 16.2, as are the other societal measures and their components.

Income inequality. Because we have no measure of fathers' incomes, we constructed a measure of income inequality for the respondents' generation. To do this, we utilized information on the income of respondents from our data plus a measure of income inequality derived from other sources. The income inequality measure from our data is the ratio of the mean income of high-prestige professionals to the mean income of low-prestige production process workers. Some evidence that this measure closely approximates what we would have obtained if we had information on fathers' income is to be found in the extremely high correlation (.99) between the educational inequality measure computed for fathers and respondents. The second measure of income inequality is the proportion of income held by the top 10% of families. The correlation between the two measures, for the 15 countries for which both are available, is .89. Again, we created a composite measure by standardizing each of the components and averaging the standardized scores. In cases where one

[2.] These categories are those used in Treiman's 14-category International Standard Classification of Occupations (Treiman 1977, chap. 9). "High-prestige professionals" are those in the ISCO category "Professional, Technical and Related Workers" (International Labour Office 1968) with a prestige score of 58 or greater. "Low-prestige production workers" are those in the ISCO category "Production and related workers, transport equipment operators and labourers" with a prestige score of less than 26.

TABLE 16.2: Selected Characteristics of the 21 Countries

Country	Percentage Distribution of Father's Occupation[a]			Percentage in Agriculture 1960[b]	Energy Consumption per Capita 1960[c]	Percentage of Income Held by Top 10% 1970[d]
	Nonmanual	Manual	Farm			
Capitalist industrialized countries:						
Australia	30	47	22	11	3918	24
Austria	20	44	36	24	2155	–
Denmark	17	42	41	18	2829	26
England & Wales	22	67	11	4	4907	24
Finland	11	31	58	36	1650	33
Germany	27	52	21	14	3673	30
Ireland	15	36	49	36	1844	–
Israel	48	38	14	14	1243	–
Italy	22	46	32	31	1135	31
Japan	31	22	47	33	1166	27
Netherlands	35	48	17	11	2691	28
Northern Ireland	20	50	30	4	4907	24
Norway	21	39	40	20	2740	22
Sweden	17	49	34	14	3491	21
United States	28	47	25	7	8047	27
Socialist-bloc countries:						
Hungary	10	38	52	38	2080	19
Poland	8	31	61	48	3097	21
Developing countries:						
Brazil	12	16	71	52	337	51
India	14	22	64	74	140	35
Philippines	10	13	77	61	143	37
Taiwan	28	12	59	45[k]	–	25

a. Computed directly from our survey data.
b. Taylor and Jodice (1983, Table 6.1).
c. Taylor and Jodice (1983, Table 3.7). Kilograms of coal per capita or equivalent.
d. Taylor and Jodice (1983, Table 4.1). Percentage of income received by top 10% of households.
e. Computed directly from our survey data: ratio of mean income of those in high-prestige professional occupations to the mean income of those in low-prestige production process occupations.
f. Computed directly from our survey data: ratio of mean years of school completed by fathers who are in high-prestige professional occupations to mean years of school completed by fathers who are in low-prestige production process occupations.

measure was available but not the other, we used the standardized score for the available measure. In this way we were able to create an income inequality measure for all countries included in the analysis except Israel.

TABLE 16.2 (continued)

Income Inequality[e]	Father's Educational Inequality[f]	Father's Educational Variability[g]	Industrialization Index[h]	Income Inequality Index[i]	Father's Educational Inequality Index[j]
2.6	1.9	–	.78	-.38	–
1.8	1.6	.29	-.01	-.61	-.45
3.1	2.2	.18	.32	-.12	-.60
2.2	1.5	.12	1.22	-.48	-.69
2.9	1.7	.35	-.45	.32	-.40
2.1	1.7	.23	.64	-.09	-.52
3.7	1.7	.29	-.40	.39	-.45
–	2.8	.80	.01	–	.30
–	1.9	.70	-.45	.39	.18
1.8	1.5	.34	-.50	-.38	-.40
2.6	2.1	.41	.46	-.10	-.29
2.4	1.7	.28	1.22	-.43	-.47
1.7	2.0	.32	.25	-.73	-.42
2.0	2.0	.34	.60	-.74	-.39
2.2	1.7	.49	1.97	-.28	-.22
–	2.5	.44	-.39	-1.24	-.24
–	2.0	.44	-.38	-.97	-.29
10.1	7.6	–	-1.20	3.38	–
3.3	10.3	2.07	-1.81	.53	3.49
3.8	2.4	1.19	-1.48	.81	.60
2.2	3.4	1.43	-.84	-.41	1.28

g. Coefficient of relative variation: ratio of the standard deviation of father's years of school completed to the mean of father's years of school completed.
h. Mean of percentage in agriculture and per capita energy consumption, where both variables are converted to standard form (mean = 0 and standard deviation = 1). If the value of one of the component variables was missing, the value of the other component was used.
i. Mean of percentage of income held by top 10% and income ratio, constructed following the same procedure as for h.
j. Mean of the two measures of educational inequality, constructed following the same procedure as for h.
k. Estimated by regressing percentage in agriculture on "farm."

Level of industrialization. To measure the level of industrialization, we averaged standardized indicators of the level of per capita energy consumption and the percentage of the labor force not in agriculture, both measured as of 1960.[3] These measures seem to us to be conceptually better indicators of aspects of development that affect the stratification system than are measures such as GNP per capita, which are distorted by idiosyncratic features such as oil production and also are not generally available for socialist-bloc countries. The correlation between our two measures is .75.

Characteristics of the Countries

Table 16.2 gives selected characteristics of the countries for which we have data. It is not surprising that most of the available data sets are from industrialized capitalist nations. But the socialist bloc is represented by two countries—Hungary and Poland—and nonindustrialized nations by four countries—Brazil, India, the Philippines, and Taiwan. Moreover, there is substantial diversity within the industrialized capitalist nations, as can be seen from the coefficients in Table 16.2. In particular, Finland, Israel, Ireland, Italy, and Japan all had much lower levels of per capita energy consumption than the remaining capitalist industrial nations and all but Israel had substantially higher proportions of the labor force in agriculture. Still, these nations are clearly in a qualitatively different position in the world economy from the countries labeled "nonindustrialized."

Of greater interest in the present context are the various measures of the degree of status inequality. In general, inequality is high in the developing countries and low in the socialist-bloc countries. Among the developed capitalist countries, income inequality is relatively high in Finland, Ireland, and Italy, and fathers' educational inequality is relatively high in Israel and Italy. Thus we have reason to expect substantial inter-country variability in the degree of openness of the status attainment process.

Table 16.3, which shows means and standard deviations for the variables included in the analysis, reinforces our impressions of differences among these countries and yet, at the same time, reveals some notable similarities. The mean level of educational attainment is very similar

[3.] Although societal forces probably have their greatest impact on career beginnings, and hence are best measured at the beginning of the career, the relative position of nations with respect to the kinds of indicators we utilize here tends to change very slowly over time. For example, for the 21 countries included here, the correlation between per capita energy consumption in 1960 and 1975 is .93 and the correlation between the percentage in agriculture in 1960 and 1977 is .95. Hence our measures of these characteristics as of 1960 (and of income inequality as of 1970) are unlikely to misrepresent seriously the relative position of the various countries with respect to these factors at the time the men in our samples were beginning their careers.

TABLE 16.3: Means and Standard Deviations for Variables in the Status
Attainment Model, 21 Countries

Country	Means				Standard Deviations			
	E_f	P_f	E	P	E_f	P_f	E	P
Capitalist industrialized countries:								
Australia	–.–[a]	42.3	9.7	43.5	–.–[a]	14.8	3.8	14.4
Austria	7.2	37.3	10.0	39.4	2.1	10.3	2.2	12.2
Denmark	7.3	37.2	8.0	39.6	1.3	9.9	2.1	12.0
England and Wales	8.3	36.0	10.4	39.9	1.0	11.1	2.2	12.8
Finland	6.0	37.9	7.8	39.1	2.1	8.8	2.1	11.5
German Federal Republic	9.9	41.7	11.1	44.8	2.3	11.2	2.4	12.2
Ireland	8.6	38.6	10.2	39.1	2.5	11.3	2.6	12.2
Israel	4.9	38.8	9.5	40.8	3.9	12.1	4.4	14.1
Italy	5.0	37.0	7.8	38.6	3.5	8.9	4.4	11.5
Japan	8.0	39.1	10.9	41.0	2.7	10.6	2.9	11.9
Netherlands	7.5	40.0	10.0	44.8	3.1	13.6	3.2	14.3
Northern Ireland	8.1	37.0	10.1	39.3	2.3	11.5	2.5	12.7
Norway	7.6	38.9	9.0	43.1	2.4	10.0	3.0	13.3
Sweden	7.1	37.1	8.7	41.1	2.4	10.0	2.8	13.6
United States	8.4	38.2	12.0	42.1	4.1	11.1	3.2	12.8
Socialist-bloc countries:								
Hungary	6.4	30.3	8.1	35.1	2.8	8.3	3.3	12.4
Poland	6.2	36.5	8.8	37.9	2.7	7.6	3.1	10.4
Developing countries:								
Brazil	–.–[a]	28.1	3.7	33.0	–.–[a]	11.6	3.8	12.8
India	1.4	40.9	2.5	40.7	2.9	11.9	3.7	11.9
Philippines	3.2	38.6	6.2	37.7	3.8	8.3	4.5	9.6
Taiwan	2.3	40.2	6.0	40.4	3.3	9.1	4.3	11.7

a. Not ascertained. Question not included in survey.

among all the industrialized capitalist countries (the mean of the means is
9.7 and the standard deviation of the means is 1.2). The level of schooling
is somewhat lower in the two socialist countries and still lower in the
developing countries. In every country in our sample the average number
of years of schooling is larger in the sons' generation, by an average of 2.3
years. It is not surprising that the intergenerational increase in education
is greatest in two of the developing countries—the Philippines, where
sons have nearly twice as many years of schooling as fathers, and Taiwan,
where sons have more than twice as many years of schooling as fathers. It
is interesting that the one other country with a substantial increase in the
number of years of schooling—in absolute although not in percentage
terms—is the United States, where the average man in the labor force has

12 years of schooling, about a year more than men in the other two industrial leaders, Germany and Japan.

In contrast to schooling, which has increased substantially nearly everywhere, the average level of occupational status has increased only slightly in most countries and is actually slightly lower in the sons' generation in India and the Philippines. Moreover, there is very little variability across countries in the mean level of occupational prestige. The main reason for this is that farm owners, with a prestige score of 38, are near the mean of the distribution in most countries, so that the shift out of agriculture does not affect the mean level of prestige.

ANALYSIS

Modeling Educational Attainment

We begin by considering a simple model of educational attainment, by estimating for each country an equation of the form

$$\hat{E} = a + b(E_f) + c(P_f) \qquad [1]$$

where E = years of school completed by the respondent, E_f = years of school completed by the father of the respondent, and P_f = the prestige of the respondent's father's occupation. Table 16.4 presents these results.

On average, the process of status attainment in the 19 countries for which complete data are available (father's education was not ascertained in the Australian or Brazilian surveys) is similar to what we would have expected from earlier studies, particularly in the United States: Father's education is much more important than father's occupational status (on average, the ratio of size of the standardized coefficients is nearly 8 to 1); and these two variables together account for more than a quarter (29%) of the variance in the years of schooling attained by the men in our samples.

Yet there is considerable diversity around this average pattern. In England and Wales, Ireland, and Northern Ireland, in particular, years of schooling are not well predicted. This may, however, be as much an artifact of deficiencies in measurement as a reflection of the educational openness of British and Irish society, given that these places all have multidimensional educational systems that are not well captured by a unidimensional measure such as years of school completed. Evidence

TABLE 16.4: Coefficients of a Model of Educational Attainment, for 19 Countries[a]

Country	Metric Regression Coefficients			Standardized Coefficients		
	E_f	P_f	Constant	E_f	P_f	R^2
Capitalist industrialized countries:						
Austria	.48	.019	5.8	.45	.09	.24
Denmark	.94	.016	.6	.56	.07	.35
England and Wales	.53	.065	3.7	.23	.32	.20
Finland	.51	.026	3.8	.47	.10	.26
German Federal Republic	.41	.030	5.8	.39	.14	.23
Ireland	.40	.018	6.0	.38	.08	.16
Israel	.57	.027	5.6	.49	.07	.28
Italy	.71	.019	3.6	.58	.04	.36
Japan	.41	.060	5.2	.40	.22	.28
Netherlands	.58	.025	4.7	.56	.11	.38
Northern Ireland	.39	.034	5.7	.36	.16	.18
Norway	.44	.074	2.8	.35	.25	.29
Sweden	.58	.050	2.7	.49	.18	.37
United States	.33	.040	7.8	.42	.14	.24
Socialist-bloc countries:						
Hungary	.42	.090	2.8	.35	.22	.27
Poland	.60	.004	4.9	.52	.01	.28
Developing countries:						
India	.81	.027	.3	.65	.09	.46
Philippines	.68	.016	3.4	.57	.03	.33
Taiwan	.59	.093	.9	.45	.20	.31

a. Australia and Brazil are excluded because no data on fathers' education are available for these countries.

supporting this possibility is to be found in Treiman and Terrell's (1975) analysis of status attainment in the United States and Britain.[4]

Although father's occupational status has only weak effects on son's educational attainment in most countries, England and Wales, Japan, Norway, Hungary, and Taiwan are exceptions, judging from the standardized coefficients, which are greater than .2 in these countries. The reason fathers' occupational status affects educational attainment in these countries in particular is puzzling, because there is nothing obviously

[4.] That analysis, based on data from a 1963 national representative sample of males in England, Scotland, and Wales, included information on father's occupation but not father's education. The correlation between father's occupational prestige (measured as it is here) and the school-leaving age of sons was .25, whereas the correlation between father's prestige and an effect-proportional measure of educational achievement of sons that took account of type as well as amount of schooling was .34.

distinctive about the set of countries for which fathers' occupational status has a nontrivial effect independent of fathers' education.

Societal variation in educational openness. We now reach the central concern of the chapter—assessment of our hypotheses regarding societal variations in the status attainment process. We first consider the impact of societal factors on the extent to which education is dependent on social origins. Specifically, we test the hypotheses that (1) the more industrialized a society, the smaller the influence of parental status on educational attainment; and (2) the greater the degree of educational inequality, the greater the influence of parental status on educational attainment.[5] We do this by estimating a regression equation in which the observations are the 19 countries for which we have complete data (recall that no fathers' education measure is available for Australia or Brazil), the dependent variable, C, is the coefficient of determination shown in the right hand column of Table 16.4, $R^2_{E(E_fP_f)}$, and the independent variables are the measures of educational inequality, EI, and industrialization, D, shown in Table 16.2 (in the right-hand column and the third column from the right). That is, we estimate an equation of the form

$$\hat{C} = a + b(EI) + c(D) \qquad [2]$$

with 19 observations, which yields, in standardized form,

$$\hat{c} = .53(ei) - .14(d) \qquad [3]$$

with $R^2 = .40$ and Adj. $R^2 = .33$.

From these results there is some indication that, as we hypothesized, educational attainment is more heavily dependent on social origins in countries in which the degree of status inequality is high (the standardized coefficient is .53). There is, however, little support for our other main hypothesis. The dependence of educational attainment on social origins is not substantially related to the level of industrialization, once account is taken of the degree of status inequality (the standardized coefficient is .14). Although, as we see in Table 16.5, our measure of the dependence of education on social origins, $R^2_{E(E_fP_f)}$ (= C), is substantially correlated with both the educational inequality index (.63) and the industrialization index (−.49), the net effect of industrialization is very small. It is evident

[5] We omitted the income inequality variable from this analysis because its correlation with our measure of the dependence of education on social origins was weak (.26). This is not particularly surprising. We would expect the effect of social origins on education to depend much more on the level of *educational* inequality, particularly as measured in the father's generation, than on *income* inequality. After all, it is human capital acquired at home that is most likely to create an advantage in the competition for educational success.

TABLE 16.5 Correlations Among Societal Variables[a]

Variable	(2)	(3)	(4)	(5)	(6)	(7)	(8)	(9)
(1) Educational inequality	.41	−.65	.63	.46	.02	−.24	.62	−.67
(2) Income inequality		−.42	.26	.38	−.52	−.38	.55	−.48
(3) Industrialization			−.49	−.46	.09	.31	−.53	.64
(4) $R^2_{E(E_f P_f)}$ (= C)				.74	−.10	.23	.11	−.20
(5) $b_{EE_f.P_f}$					−.34	.23	.22	−.06
(6) $b_{EP_f.E_f}$						−.01	−.20	−.02
(7) $R^2_{P(E_f P_f E)}$							−.35	.75
(8) $b_{PP_f.E_f E}$								−.59
(9) $b_{PE.E_f P_f}$								

a. Correlations based on 18 countries for which information is complete.

that, although educational opportunities are more open in more industrialized societies, this is because such societies tend to have less status
inequality; net of the level of status inequality, the level of industrialization has little impact on the openness of educational opportunities.
Together, however, the degree of educational inequality and the level of
industrialization of countries account for at least a third of the variance
across countries in the degree of openness of the educational system.[6]

Modeling Occupational Attainment

Occupational status is known from studies of single countries to be
heavily dependent upon education and moderately dependent on father's
occupational status. In general, father's education has been shown to have
no direct effect on son's occupational status; the correlation between these
two variables, which generally is moderately strong, arises entirely from
the effect of father's education on father's occupation and of father's
education on son's education. For this reason, and also because information on father's education is not available for two of our countries, we
model the dependence of occupational status on two variables only:
father's occupational status and respondent's education. To do this we
estimate, for each country, an equation of the form:

$$\hat{P} = a + b(P_f) + c(E) \qquad [4]$$

6. Although the coefficient of determination, R^2, is .40, it is more appropriate to consider
the adjusted R^2, .33, which takes account of the small number of observations relative to the
number of variables.

TABLE 16.6: Coefficients of a Model of Occupational Attainment, for 21 Countries

Country	Metric Regression Coefficients			Standardized coefficients		
	P_f	E	Constant	P_f	E	R^2
Capitalist industrialized countries:						
Australia	.28	1.3	19.5	.28	.33	.23
Austria	.15	3.0	3.8	.13	.54	.35
Denmark	.19	4.0	.7	.15	.70	.58
England and Wales	.21	2.4	7.6	.18	.41	.26
Finland	.19	2.3	13.8	.15	.42	.23
German Federal Republic	.14	2.9	6.5	.13	.58	.40
Ireland	.38	1.5	8.6	.35	.33	.27
Israel	.11	1.9	18.8	.10	.58	.38
Italy	.07	1.5	23.9	.05	.59	.37
Japan	.18	1.5	17.5	.16	.37	.21
Netherlands	.20	2.3	14.1	.19	.51	.36
Northern Ireland	.27	2.2	7.3	.24	.43	.30
Norway	.22	2.7	9.9	.17	.62	.50
Sweden	.05	3.1	12.3	.04	.64	.43
United States	.13	2.2	11.3	.11	.54	.34
Socialist-bloc countries:						
Hungary	.16	2.4	11.1	.11	.63	.47
Poland	.18	1.8	15.7	.13	.53	.32
Developing countries:						
Brazil	.17	1.8	21.6	.16	.52	.38
India	.50	.6	18.8	.50	.17	.33
Phillipines	.39	.5	19.9	.33	.22	.18
Taiwan	.20	.9	26.8	.15	.35	.18

where P is the prestige of the respondent's occupation at the time of the survey, P_f is the prestige of the father's occupation when the respondent was about 16 years old, and E is the years of schooling obtained by the respondent. Table 16.6 shows the results. Again, as in our analysis of educational attainment, we have a picture of a generally similar pattern of occupational attainment across all countries but of marked variations across countries around the general pattern. Let us begin with the overall pattern. Two main points emerge. First, on average, about a third (.34) of the variance in the occupational status of individuals can be accounted for by their years of schooling and their fathers' occupational status. Second, education is a much stronger determinant of occupational status than is father's occupational status (the average ratio is greater than 4:1).

Still, there is substantial variability in the process, even among in-dustrialized countries. Again, the results may in part reflect differences in measurement quality given that four of the six industrialized countries for which the standardized coefficient for education is less than .5 are or were British (Australia, England and Wales, Ireland, and Northern Ireland), as are all three countries for which the standardized father's occupation coefficient is greater than .2 (Australia, Ireland, and Northern Ireland). But this cannot be the entire explanation because the education coefficients are low for Finland and Japan as well. Clearly, we need to know a good deal more about how fathers transmit occupational status to their sons other than by encouraging (or not encouraging) them to do well and go far in school. One possibility is that the net effect of father's occupational status is entirely restricted to cases in which sons go into the same line of work as their fathers (say, as indicated by identical codes in a detailed occupation classification) and that, for those who go into different occupations than their fathers, the effect of father's occupation operates entirely through education.

Societal variations in the occupational attainment process. Let us turn now to hypotheses regarding the determinants of societal differences in the process of occupational status attainment. Recall that we posited that education should be a stronger determinant of occupational status in relatively egalitarian systems than in systems with great status inequality and that the effect of social origins should be stronger in systems with a high degree of status inequality than in relatively egalitarian systems. We also posited a stronger effect of education and a weaker effect of social origins in industrialized societies. To test these hypotheses we estimate two regression equations for the 18 societies for which we have complete data:

$$\hat{B}_E = a + b(EI) + c(II) + d(D) \qquad [5]$$

and

$$\hat{B}_{PF} = a' + b'(EI) + c'(II) + d'(D) \qquad [6]$$

where B_E is the metric regression coefficient relating occupational status to education,[7] from Table 16.6; B_{PF} is the metric regression coefficient relating occupational status to father's occupational status, also from

---

[7] It could be argued that standardized coefficients should be used as indicators of the relative importance of education and social origins in each country rather than metric coefficients. Standardized coefficients are sensitive to differences in the variances of the variables in the model, however, and hence metric coefficients are more appropriate for cross-population comparisons. Fortunately, in practice it makes little difference. We have carried out a parallel analysis using the standardized coefficients and the results lead to similar conclusions.

Table 16.6; EI is the measure of educational inequality described above; II is the corresponding measure for income inequality; and D is the measure of industrialization described above. The results, expressed in standard form, are

$$\hat{b}_e = -.39(ei) - .19(ii) + .31(d) \qquad [7]$$

with $R^2 = .55$; Adj. $R^2 = .46$; and

$$\hat{b}_{pf} = .39(ei) + .32(ii) - .15(d) \qquad [8]$$

with $R^2 = .49$; Adj. $R^2 = .39$.

Inspecting these coefficients, it is evident that our hypotheses are generally supported; the size of the coefficient relating education to occupational status increases with industrialization and decreases as inequality increases. And the size of the coefficient relating father's occupational status to respondent's occupational status decreases with industrialization and increases as inequality increases. Second, more than 40% of the variance across countries in the size of each of these coefficients is explained by inequality and industrialization. Third, the degree of educational inequality in the father's generation dominates these equations. In both equations it is the largest coefficient, whereas the relative size of the other two coefficients reverses for the two equations.

CONCLUSIONS

Although somewhat complex in their detail, the results presented here can be summarized quite simply. First, in most countries educational attainment is a much more important determinant of occupational status than is father's occupational status. Because education is largely independent of social origins, the consequence is that occupational status attainment is mainly a matter of achievement and not of ascription. Second, insofar as education does depend on social origins, it depends mainly on father's education rather than on father's occupational status. This suggests that the main advantage that fathers confer on their sons is one of human capital—the skills and habits and values that enable sons to do well in school. Third, there are strong and systematic societal differences in both the degree of openness and the nature of the status attainment process. Industrialized societies tend to be more open than developing societies, but this is mainly because there tends to be less status inequality, particularly inequality in father's education, in industrialized societies. And both industrialization and status equality promote achievement at the expense of ascription, as measured by the increased effect of education and the decreased effect of father's occupation on occupational status attainment. The strongest effect on the achievement-ascription mix is the level of inequality of father's education, which once again suggests the importance of human capital, and differential access to human capital, as the driving force in stratification.

REFERENCES

Blau, Peter M. and Otis Dudley Duncan. 1967. *The American Occupational Structure*. New York: John Wiley.

Boyd, Monica, David L. Featherman, and Judah Matras. 1980. "Status Attainment of Immigrant and Immigrant Origin Categories in the United States, Canada, and Israel." *Comparative Social Research* 3:199-228.

Erikson, Robert and John H. Goldthorpe. 1985a. "Commonality and Variation in Social Fluidity in Industrial Nations: Some Preliminary Results." CASMIN Working Paper 4.1. Mannheim: University of Mannheim.

———. 1985b. "A Model of Core Social Fluidity in Industrial Nations." CASMIN Working Paper 5.1. Mannheim: University of Mannheim.

———. 1986. "National Variation in Social Fluidity." CASMIN Working Paper 9. Mannheim: University of Mannheim.

Ganzeboom, Harry B. G., Ruud Luijkx, and Donald J. Treiman. Forthcoming. "Intergenerational Class Mobility in Comparative Perspective." *Research in Social Stratification and Mobility*, Vol. 8, edited by Arne Kalleberg. Greenwich, CT: JAI.

Grusky, David B. and Robert M. Hauser. 1984. "Comparative Social Mobility Revisited: Models of Convergence and Divergence in 16 Countries." *American Sociological Review* 49:19-38.

Heath, Anthony. 1981. *Social Mobility*. Glasgow: Fontana.

International Labour Office. 1968. *International Standard Classification of Occupations*. rev. ed. Geneva: International Labour Office.

Jones, F. Lancaster. 1971. "Occupational Achievement in Australia and the United States: A Comparative Path Analysis." *American Journal of Sociology* 77:527-39.

Kelley, Jonathan. 1978. "Wealth and Family Background in the Occupational Career: Theory and Cross-Cultural Data." *British Journal of Sociology* 29:94-109.

Kelley, Jonathan and Herbert S. Klein. 1981. *Revolution and the Rebirth of Inequality: A Theory Applied to the National Revolution in Bolivia*. Berkeley: University of California Press.

Kelley, Jonathan, Robert V. Robinson, and Herbert S. Klein. 1981. "A Theory of Social Mobility, with Data on Status Attainment in a Peasant Society." *Research in Social Stratification and Mobility* 1:27-66.

Kelley, Jonathan, Robert V. Robinson, Patricia A. Roos, J.L.P. Thompson, and Donald J. Treiman. 1980. "Social Stratification in Cross-Cultural Perspective: A Preliminary Analysis of Survey Data from Fourteen Societies." Paper given at the annual meetings of the American Sociological Association, New York, August 27-31.

Kerckhoff, Alan C. 1974. "Stratification Processes and Outcomes in England and the U.S." *American Sociological Review* 39:789-801.

Lin, Nan and Daniel Yauger. 1975. "The Process of Occupational Status Achievement: A Preliminary Cross-National Comparison." *American Journal of Sociology* 81:543-62.
Pontinen, Seppo. 1976. "Patterns of Social Mobility in the Scandinavian Countries." Licentiate thesis, University of Helsinki, Institute of Sociology.
Roos, Patricia A. 1985. *Gender and Work: A Comparative Analysis of Industrial Societies.* Albany: State University of New York Press.
Taylor, Charles Lewis and David A. Jodice. 1983. *World Handbook of Political and Social Indicators.* Vol. 1, *Cross-National Attributes and Rates of Change.* 3rd ed. New Haven, CT: Yale University Press.
Treiman, Donald J. 1970. "Industrialization and Social Stratification." Pp. 207-34 in *Social Stratification: Research and Theory for the 1970s,* edited by Edward O. Laumann. Indianapolis: Bobbs-Merrill.
———. 1977. *Occupational Prestige in Comparative Perspective.* New York: Academic Press.
Treiman, Donald J. and Jonathan Kelley. 1986. "Is There a World Wide Social Fluidity Regime?" Paper presented at the meeting of the ISA Research Committee on Social Stratification and Mobility, Rome, April 3-5.
Treiman, Donald J. and Patricia A. Roos. 1983. "Sex and Earnings in Industrial Society: A Nine Nation Comparison." *American Journal of Sociology* 89:612-50.
Treiman, Donald J. and Kermit Terrell. 1975. "The Process of Status Attainment in the United States and Great Britain." *American Journal of Sociology* 81:563-83.
Tyree, Andrea, Moshe Semyonov, and Robert W. Hodge. 1979. "Gaps and Glissandos: Inequality, Economic Development, and Social Mobility in 24 Countries." *American Sociological Review* 44:410-24.
Yamaguchi, Kazuo. 1987. "Models for Comparing Mobility Tables: Toward Parsimony and Substance." *American Sociological Review* 52:482-94.
Zagorski, Krzysztof. 1984. "Comparisons of Social Mobility in Different Socio-Economic Systems." Pp. 13-41 in *International Comparative Research: Social Structures and Public Institutions in Eastern and Western Europe,* edited by Manfred Niessen, Jules Peschar, and Chantal Kourilsky. Oxford: Pergamon.

17

Conceptions of Christendom: Notes on the Distinctiveness of the West

John W. Meyer

In recent comparative work on the distinctiveness of the West, the core explanatory problem seems to be to account for the rise of a system that both encouraged strong local social mobilization and linked this mobilization to very general and universalistic long-distance relationships. One crucial aspect of this is the interpenetration of organizational arrangements and institutional or ideological ones. It is understandable that the recent literature gives explanatory attention to the polity and culture of Christendom as the frame within which this took place.

BACKGROUND

In much comparative research, general civilizational properties do not come up or are left in the background of the analysis. In comparisons of groups or societies within a generally Western frame, for instance, or of time periods all of which are covered by the Western trajectory, it seems reasonable to take for granted the civilizational situating conditions as invariant. If we want to know why early capitalist institutions appeared in Northern Italy or the Netherlands rather than elsewhere in Europe, or why

AUTHOR'S NOTE: *I am indebted to my continuing collaboration with John Boli, Ronald Jepperson, Francisco Ramirez, and George Thomas. Ideas here are taken from Thomas et al. (1987) and Jepperson and Meyer (1988). The chapter also benefited from suggestions by S. N. Eisenstadt, and by members of the State and Institutions Seminars at Stanford (1986-87).*

strong national states appear in England and France, it may not help much to think about the civilizational context.

On the other hand, ignoring such conditions may lead to a kind of reductionism in which we treat forces and relationships within the Western situation as natural or universal, ignoring their sociocultural constitution. We are thus likely to overstate the importance of the factors that vary locally—such as economic, military, political, cultural, ecological, or even personal properties—and to understate the importance of factors that are more systemic. Sociologists tend to be especially conscious of this problem when they see the naïveté of the economists or occasional psychologists approaching comparative work with heroic rather than contextual assumptions. They may be less conscious of the problems when the heroic assumptions are more sociological ones. Specific social structures and relationships might generate the consequences we attribute to them only when they have the meanings and supports created in the wider Western system. We are likely to discover this, or even think about it, only when we make broader comparisons and are forced to discover more about the conditions under which our propositions might be true.

Consider examples: (1) It is common among both economists (e.g., North 1981, North and Thomas 1973) and sociologists (recently and dramatically, Wallerstein 1974, 1980) to see the extraordinary expansion of the Western economy as having developed out of high levels of competition among states and their subunit property-holders. A key feature of the system thus distinguished is the absence of effective political regulation of the whole economy, or the absence of an overall "state" in the West. This is a comparative point of some importance, given that civilizations integrated in imperial forms (e.g., China) clearly do not generate the same continuing expansion. On the other hand, a great many large-scale trading systems (e.g., in the Mediterranean or in the Indian Ocean) have operated without politically integrating empires, but also without generating property-holding, rationalization, or long waves of expansion either. It may be necessary to look beyond putatively universal principles of competition to understand what about the Western frame set such mechanisms in place.

(2) It is now also common to see the Western state system as expanding externally and internally as a result of the opportunities, pressures, and strains of interstate competition (Tilly 1975, 1984; Skocpol 1979; Evans et al. 1985). Again, the absence of systemic political integration becomes the key independent variable. Why it was possible to build up such extraordinary integration at the subunit (i.e., national state) level becomes

unclear—after all, many centerless political systems engender competition without creating national organizational integration among their subunits. Further, why did the forces constructing integration at the level of large-scale subunits not continue to operate at the system level? Ex post facto, arguments about political returns to scale are made, but these are not very convincing—especially late in the twentieth century, when it is hard to see state size as in any way linked to efficiency. It may be necessary to look beyond supposed natural competitive forces to find a richer set of civilizational properties that might account for the long-term rise and maintenance of the competitive nation-state system.

These considerations arise from problems in the internal analysis of the evolution of the West. When the research agenda becomes explicitly comparative across civilizations, of course, civilizational properties move to the center of the stage. Taking this perspective, the recent literature returns to the classical issues of the distinctiveness of the West as a matter of course (e.g., Jones 1981; McNeill 1963; Anderson 1974; Mann 1986; Hall 1986; Eisenstadt 1982; and elsewhere).

It is interesting and important that the issues here, which are the focus of this chapter, do not for once come down to questions of definition. "The West" refers to the social, political, economic, and religious arrangements of Western Europe and Latin Christendom and the areas of its modern expansion. By most useful accounts, this system now extends around the world (within which a new notion of the West as one element of world society now emerges—a definition not employed here). There are questions about whether and when particular territories and populations were incorporated into the West, but they are not central. There are many crucial questions about how autonomous the development of West has been, or how derivative from peculiar circumstances of its origins, or from cultural and economic transactions with its social environments. These are closely related to the issues discussed below: conceptions of just what is distinctive about the West.

As in many cases in the social sciences, the definition of the West is relatively unproblematic not because political or economic transactional boundaries are so clear but because the historical participants themselves tended to have rather clear notions of the boundaries of their own world. Their conceptions, relabeled, become social scientific. The same situation may hold with "civilization," which is another intrinsically—but not in use—problematic term. Attempts at definition are much less convincing than the practical consensus, which tends to be shared with the participants as they define their own history and boundaries.

WHAT IS TO BE EXPLAINED?

An intellectual generation or two ago, there would have been much more ambiguity about the distinctive features of the historic Western system that require explanation. Isolated institutions of various sorts would have been selected as central, in analyses that varied sharply from theory to theory: some general values—technical arrangements and economic growth, political organization (bureaucracy, democracy)—perhaps even properties of personality and child rearing. Functional analyses of society, both on the left and the right, all reduced social life to an organizational system with perhaps a culture on top and personality below. Theories that deemphasized culture or personality developed special conceptions of almost demonic forces of social organizational integration or interdependence (and sometimes exploitation).

A generation of macro-sociological research has led to conceptions that are less vulgar—less likely to reify social organization, and thus to leave culture, religion, and law disembodied ideas or ideals. As a consequence, intellectual syntheses that may start from widely varying ideological or metatheoretical postures in fact reach a working agreement on core features of the Western system.

First, there is general awareness of the importance of the organization of the West around externally and ideologically validated social units in complex relationships—nation-states, firms, groups, individuals. These units not only gain strength but are also involved in reciprocal recognition, and often are recognized as partially autonomous by higher authorities. They thus have some symmetry. They variously compete, conflict, cooperate, and copy each other in patterns that are often of considerable stability organizationally and legitimacy culturally (as, for instance, in rules of sovereignty, responsibility, and property). The stability and legitimacy require explanation. Contemporary theorizing is less likely to treat such units as the nation-state, the firm, or the modern individual citizen and person as having naturally evolved out of micro-level transactions or their supposed functional requirements.

Second, the collectivities so constructed are unusually highly integrated or intensified (Mann 1986). They are more active and more mobilized for purposive action than similar units in other systems. Individual purposiveness and responsibility are more developed, along with group capacities to act. Individuals and their activities are tied closely to the collectivities and collectivities to their subunit components. This is both an organizational matter (as in bureaucracies, national markets, or individuated nuclear family systems) and an institutional or cultural one (as with democracy, nationalism, welfare states, highly social definitions of progress, or educational and religious systems built around the integration and control of individuals and their activities). The penetrative linkages involved—found in states, but also in business, military, political and cultural, or religious organization—constitute "rationalization," the term so often used to describe the internal organization of the units of the Western system (Jepperson and Meyer 1988).

In the modern period, individual economic activity, for instance, is tightly linked by rules of accounting to the budget and welfare of the family, the firm, and even the national GNP. Reproductive activity is similarly accounted, recorded, and managed at all sorts of policy levels. But this is not only a "top-down" matter of organizational control: persons at the bottom of modern ladders mobilize around abstract rights and duties for all sorts of reasons. It all requires better explanation: We still do not understand quite why modern people vote, or participate so cooperatively in mass military action in the modern crusades, or submit their children so eagerly to decades of baptism in national schooling systems. We think we understand why elites want them to, but we are wrong: Our analyses do not explain why almost all the other elites in human history regarded such arrangements (e.g., arming, consulting, and schooling the peasantry) with horror.

Third, the social units that arise and intensify in the Western system are supported and validated by elaborate external linkages, both organizationally and culturally, and tend to take forms highly standardized and legitimated in terms of these linkages. There are the ties of economic, military, and political exchange, cooperation, and conflict, all organized in universalistic frames around very general and elaborately discussed principles. The rules of the proper exercise of violence or exchange are set out in very general and symmetrical ways. Culturally, definitions of goals such as progress and justice—very widely shared—are standardized, but so are scientized definitions of appropriate means and resources. Thus local economic activities and human reproduction are not only integrated in immediate control systems, but are now reported in standard ways around the world.

Western units, from individuals and groups and organizations to national societies, exist in a system Mann (1986) calls extensive, and are supported and legitimated by external meanings and relationships. These permit and encourage the broadest set of standard long-distance exchanges, worldwide political arrangements, and a world culture of standard goals and sciences (Meyer 1980).

EXPLANATORY MODELS

There is something of a resurgence of explanations of the West in what were once considered materialist terms (e.g., Jones 1981; McNeill 1963). The ecology of Western Europe created decentralized units; the discovery of rich overseas possibilities encouraged further fragmentation. New technical devices (e.g., plows, guns, and navigation) encouraged intensification and extensification. Population expansion also encouraged intensification and, through conflict, extensification. There may be less inclination than formerly, given a worldwide system that is racially pluralistic, to use racial theories.

A number of these traditional theories can account for the politically fragmented character of the West—ecological constraints, technical developments outrunning social control possibilities, and so on. They have much more difficulty explaining why intensively organized societies were possible, and why these societies were involved in such high levels of continuous interdependence with each other—in other words, our second and third issues above. A great many social systems become fragmented without generating nation-states as a competitive mechanism.

In classic agrarian societies (e.g., China or India), long periods of decentralization are typical, with one or another competitor rising to dominance but with dominant entities moving quickly to segmentation rather than mobilization and intensification. And much fragmentation can occur without generating the high levels of interdependence (culturally, politically, economically, and militarily) so characteristic of the Western system of competitive isomorphism.

What is the source of the West's capacity to develop and sustain orderly long-distance linkages beyond its political control system, and to penetrate society with collective meanings, rights, and powers without collapsing in chaotic and segmented power systems? One can run these two questions through any list of social sectors or institutions one likes. Militarily, for instance, we are looking for the source of the West's capacity to organize worldwide missions, and for the source of its capacity to mobilize massive internal military participation without inevitably endangering the regime (contrary to the wisdom of state-builders over the millennia, who knew better than to arm their subjects overmuch—Thomson and Krasner 1987). Economically, politically, religiously, the same questions arise.

The obvious answer, to which the current literature returns, has to do with the unique structures of Christendom. The West had no integrating imperial frame after Charlemagne, but it had an institutional structure carrying a high culture with integrating possibilities. And this institutional system maintained a hegemony, not only over the whole West but to a degree unusual in such societies, one that penetrated local social life down to, in principle, the individuals and families and communities involved. All of this was relatively integrated in one general polity, or model of collective life.

There is a good deal of consensus that the structures of Christendom were central factors helping to determine the great distinctive Western, and now world, outcomes. There is less consensus on the specific properties of Christendom that were important and on how they worked. Thinking on the issue has been limited by tendencies to think in terms of differentiated variables and categories that arose later in Western history. There is a tendency to think of Christendom and the Church as what we would now call a religious system, reading back into history the more specialized notions we now attach to the term "religion." This, further, leads to a sharp differentiation between religious ideology and religious organization, and to a tendency to reify both abstractions. It also leads to a tendency to distinguish sharply between religious and social history, and to keep the two fields of inquiry separate and in rather limited contact.

There is also a related tendency to treat the history of Christendom as an elite enterprise, and to treat more local political and economic organization (e.g., feudalism) as distinct from it—a tendency that systematically underemphasizes the local social roles of Christendom in organizing society.

It thus comes as a recurrent shock to rediscover how much European (and later American) local social and economic organization was and is in the hands of components of the Church and its successors. American scholars have to struggle to remember that in the later Middle Ages perhaps a third of the land in Europe was in the hands of the organizations of the Church—and that, despite lack of individual interest and participation, surprising social resources still are in those hands. European scholars tend to forget that a continuingly important feature of the American polity is individual religious participation and highly personal religious commitment. In both cases, scholars have a tendency to treat such Western features as anachronistic survivals or as derivative reflections of tension and alienation.

Christendom, more reasonably, is seen through earlier (and probably modern) Western history as a much less differentiated, specialized, and organizationally structured system: more a polity than a "religion" (in the modern sense), less articulated organizationally and ideologically and with less differentiation between the two. And it should be seen as involving great interpenetration between the elite, or universal, and the local, or situated—one can argue that precisely this quality of Christendom, and the mobilization, structuration, and liminality involved, were the core distinctive properties building the special Western dynamic and precipitating all the main elements we now see as so crucial. Thus we have the individual as member (and democracy), the individual as property-holder (and the market economy), society as a project, the nation-state and nationalism, and science with the interpenetration and tension between the mundane and the transcendental, and so on.

SOME MEANINGS OF CHRISTENDOM

The theoretical reluctance to see Christendom as a general civilizational frame has led to a tendency to see some isolated variables as playing a central role. We can distinguish four types of theoretical reasoning depending on whether Christendom is seen as (1) more organizational or more ideological and (2) more elite and central or more mass and peripheral (or local).

(1) Elite and organizational Christendom. One of the oldest lines of social scientific thought has emphasized the role of Christendom as a systemwide organizational structure. The elites of the Church were all linked, functioned in a common and written language, and shared a common authority context. This facilitated mobilization around systemic conflicts and possibilities, whether military, political, or religious. It gave national power an unusually potent set of functionaries for local control and mobilization, but also a set of functionaries tied into a common culture. Thus much more law- and rule-based political integration was possible. They structured much more potential for long-distance relationships than might ordinarily characterize such simple agrarian societies. Elite competence and integration facilitated thus all three of the distinctive Western properties noted earlier: long-distance integration, local mobilization, and the linkage of the two in models of society (e.g., the nation-state).

This line of thought tends to remove the Christianity from Christendom, emphasizing the literate competence of the elite functionaries and the commonality of the organizational frame holding them together rather than the substantive content of the literate tradition in question or the substantive rules of the organization linking the elites (Collins 1986). Christendom thus becomes an accidental resource at the hands of local power mobilizers and at the hands of those segments (e.g., economic, military, or political) of society benefiting from the availability of long-distance connections. There is, at bottom, no explanation of the success of the organizational system.

Further, this line of thought has difficulty explaining why, if Christendom as a system was so organizationally powerful, it could not become a complete and dominant political organization of its own. Why would so dominant a network fail to successfully create its own imperial center? And why instead did dominant subunits arise using the facilities of this putatively powerful system? Perhaps the forces of economic and political chaos determined this, putting power in the hands of decentralized locals. But in this case, why the successful utilization of the system by the long-distance traders, cultural elites, and political claimants?

The notion of economic and social lags decentralizing Christendom also does not well explain the success of the system as a network. One can ex post facto create precious theories that define the system as having been just a bit too decentralized to permit political unification, but just a bit too integrated to allow complete fragmentation—this is the route taken in the academic field of international relations, with its "balance of power" theories. It is unconvincing that such a tenuous equilibrium accounts for a millennium of Western distinctive history. We need theories that depict the West as both centralized and decentralized at the same time.

(2) Christendom as penetrative peripheral social organization. Another line of theory stresses the importance of the Church as a major component of local society in the West. It provided a closer cultural tie than obtained in other agrarian systems between peripheral life (both in distant corners of the world and in local villages and towns) and great cultural centers. In contrast to most agrarian societies, most of the local elites were in this organization, and it constituted, throughout Europe, most of the local government. (Later on, in America, "religious" organization also provided the main fabric of local social organization.)

This means that to a much greater extent than elsewhere, the institutional structure of local life was in the hands of the partially standardized rules and perspectives that were in principle universalistic and system-wide. Individual persons had souls, which means that they were part of, subject to, and entitled directly in, a wider standard cosmos. Functional groups (agricultural workers, landowning elites, occupational specialists, age and gender groups, the military, and local ceremonial leaders) were all occupants of roles acknowledging regulation by this structure, and derived their meaning and status from it. Gradually, the family—even the local peasant family—was penetrated by its rules, with marriage becoming a sacrament, and the membership and status of children certified by the Church. In contrast to other agrarian societies, both local and long-distance trade were also under the regulation of this structure, and derived status and rights and obligations from it. Unlike other agrarian macro systems, in which the military elites but not the traders have sacralized status, in Christendom both did.

The significance of this system for later Western development can be seen as great and lasting. As opportunities for political and economic mobilization arose, the organizational and normative possibilities for mobilization incorporating local social life directly in wider systems were greatly facilitated. Military, economic, and political conscription were plausible given populations already structured as available members. On the other side, the perspectives, rights, and demands of the locals had much more general standing in the emergent larger collectivities. In the typical Western development, one can see this either as exploitation from above or as mobilization from below: elites using their claims to functional authority in the collectivity to control the masses, or masses using their membership status to impose demands on elites. The real point—the real genius of the arrangement—is that it is both, and continuously supports mobilization.

Even in our own time, most of what is called "modernization" can be seen as an organizational expansion of this aspect of Christendom. The microscopic economic activities of persons are structured in terms of great laws and forces, and evaluated in terms of their contribution to national GNPs. Political systems penetrate individual life with their laws and depend on the myths and rituals of individual choice. Wars mobilize commitments and participation. Culture—even much of high or religious culture—is to penetrate and control individual action and depends on the "opinions" of individuals organized in publics.

Local life, in other words, is structured in terms of large-scale organizations and rules—even family battles over mundane domestic activities are fought out in terms of general norms, with the aid of religious, scientific, and therapeutic agents of great rules and now with the increasingly active participation of the state. It would be hard to imagine another civilization in which so many authorities using so much high culture would address such issues as who is to do the housework, or schemes for controlling and rewarding laborers, or the rights of fetuses.

On the other hand, a narrowly organizational analysis of all this—in previous periods as well as now—is clearly very incomplete. Given the obvious organizational decentralization and decoupling of the system, how is it possible that local life could be structured in this way, under claims of generality and universalism? There is no organizational explanation of what kept and keeps the system together, avoiding the descent into local parochialism so characteristic of other civilizational systems. What keeps so many obviously peripheral matters (local work practices, or housework, or the instruction of local children) linked so tightly to great centers, and discussed at the world level by scientists and policymakers and record-keepers? Why has the system been so strong; and, if strong at the local level, why has it remained relatively culturally integrated?

Some analysts see world society as now held together by the power of centers, whether political or economic, but it is very difficult to find in earlier Western history forms of organizational power that kept myriad local activities tied in to the greater Western cosmos. Every empirical examination of Western history (and also contemporary world society) finds ample evidence of practical organizational decentralization that would be sufficient to generate a chaos that is not there in reality. Even in hegemonic America, one of the continuing intellectual puzzles is the historic maintenance of a highly integrated and homogeneous society of organizationally rather autonomous local structures. Social scientists attempt weak organizational explanations (high mobility, economic interdependence, common religious origins) but ultimately throw up their hands and refer the mystery to Tocqueville (1969).

Briefly, it is clear that the causal linkages holding the West together as a cultural system, and now integrating the world society, are more than a set of organizational links of power and interest embedded in a structure of explicit authority and compliance.

(3) Christendom as mass ideology. In *The Protestant Ethic,* Weber saw Christendom as having evolved a set of widely shared religious doctrines that in substance (not organizationally) helped impel economic modernization. Related arguments linked this religious system, itself devolved from the Church and especially from its monastic traditions and their Protestant generalization, to such modernizing institutions as democracy (Butterfield 1950), science (Merton 1970), nationalism (see Anderson 1983 for a recent interpretation), and secular or materialist individualism in general (Engels).

Disputes over the narrower role of Protestantism itself should not obscure the broader understanding that the substantive ideologies of Christendom were deeply involved. Indeed, one main trend since Weber, and also found in other aspects of his own work, has been to trace the same causal connections further back into Western religious history, as in Collins's (1986) discussions of earlier Western economic expansion and as in the conventional discussion (also noted by Collins 1986) of the importance of the monastic traditions, and the contrasting instances of monasticism in other civilizations in which it was transcendentalized or destroyed by political assault (as in both China and Japan).

In these theories, the core ideas see Christendom as quite distinctive as an ideological system. It carried, first, an integrated and universalized transcendental cosmos separated rather sharply from ongoing social life. Second, it had a rationalist and demystified view of nature, less interpenetrated with transcendental forces on an ongoing basis (though operating under their timeless charter). Third, it contained a conception of humans (even individual souls) and society as involved in a project linking universal moral forces with particular and real natural reality. The parallels between these ideological conceptions and the social features we noted earlier as distinctive to the West are obvious.

The vision of Christendom as mass ideology, like other versions of reductionist thinking, relies heavily on conceptions of society as arising and changing out of individual (or subgroup) beliefs and action: Stinchcombe (1968) calls the line of theory involved "demographic explanation." A model of persons as heavily socialized is involved, along with a model of activity as resulting from individual choice and thus motivation and perception. Weber's conception of the workings of the Protestant ethic, for instance, is filled with imagery about the impact of the ideas involved, as individual beliefs, hopes, and fears, on the economic mentality or spirit of the individuals themselves, and presumably thus on their behavior as individual social action. In a period in which social theory is more attentive to social organization, structure, and legitimation as a collective process, the "Protestant ethic" now reads dated. And it seems now to overemphasize the uniqueness of later periods of Western history (Collins 1986).

(4) Christendom as elite ideology. In interesting reinterpretations of Weber's arguments, Swanson (1967) put forward notions of Christendom as an ideological system legitimating changes in the elite organizations of the Western system. The lines of thought involved have been developed by Wuthnow (1987). Related ideas, treating Christendom as something of a legal system, are developed by Anderson (1974; see also Collins 1986).

The core themes here mirror ideas about Christendom as mass ideology. They see individual behavior as a moral project in nature linked to great collective goods. Elite ideology in Christendom legitimates this in terms of more explicit models of this collective good, and in terms of models of elite authority and responsibility both for individuals and for the collective good. Notions of the rights and responsibilities of the (absolutist) state are involved, and also of the authority and responsibility of economic power under various forms of collective regulation. The welfare, progress, and justice of society as a project are ultimate goals, and the authority of elites derives from their legitimate role in managing these. Welfare, justice, and progress also explicitly incorporate the roles of the masses—both rights and obligations—in society.

This subjection of elites to common systemic norms can help account for the overall integration of the Western world-system. Purely organizational power has always been weaker in the West than theorists like to believe, and is inadequate as a complete explanation. There is the rise of highly legitimated national sovereignty, and the highly collective organization of economic life in worldwide flows. There are surprisingly common notions of both the social functions of the national collectivities and the rights and duties of the souls (now citizens) in the Western world-system throughout its history (Thomas et al. 1987). The extraordinary inclination to copy—or thus for new models of progress, welfare, and justice to diffuse rapidly—can better be accounted for in substantive rather than purely organizational terms. Western society is, and has always been, theorized: a system so theorized, and in such universalistic terms, can engender a great deal of diffusion. In our own world, even vaguely scientized innovations (Japanese employment arrangements, American educational peculiarities) can flow extremely rapidly: similar but less professionalized processes occur throughout Western history.

SOME NEEDED REVISIONS

The intellectual tendency to emphasize specialized conceptions of the aspects of Christendom most relevant to the direction of the West has some obvious costs, and may leave in the background dimensions that should be taken as central.

First, the tendency to separate elite and mass aspects of Christendom, both in considering organizational structure and in taking into account ideology, ignores what may be the most distinctive aspects of the West. A crucial Western property seems to be the interpenetration, both organizationally and ideologically, of the same general systemwide culture. Exactly this, it is easy to argue, accounts for the high interpenetration of the macro, "public" or central, with the micro, or "private" and peripheral: the standardization and disciplining of local political, economic, and cultural activity in terms of general substantive and organizational rules. It can also account for the construction of the great collective structures around the rights and duties and participation of such peripheral subunits as individuals.

Thus each Western farmer plants under universalistic substantive rules and conceptions (some scientific, some legal), and under some sort of general organizational regulation (e.g., state prescriptions and constraints): the farmer's output is similarly evaluated in terms of collective standards (measures of product and value) and enters directly into collective measures of product and progress. The GNP is made up of the products of such farmers, and justice comprises assessments of the equality of their earnings and conditions. Their obligations to the collectivity are also, correspondingly, close.

In short, the interpenetration of mass and elite elements, constructing an integrated model of society as a project, may be what is distinctive about the West, rather than the mass or elite elements alone. The point is made most forcefully by Mann (1986), that Christendom was unusual in combining structures that were systemic and extensive with highly intensive ones. Other recent work makes similar points (e.g., Eisenstadt and Sachar 1987).

Second, it may be even more problematic to separate organizational and ideological matters, in considering Western distinctiveness. There is a great intellectual desire to do so—whole lines of thought consider only organizational linkages making up state and society without regard to any content as a matter of principle, relegating ideological matters to the arcane and segregated domain of religious or "Church" history. In many fields (e.g., economic history, international relations, the theory of the state) there is a great faith in the possibilities of purely organizational analyses, and a sort of reiterated emphasis on the need for a study of formal relationships apart from social content, of interested functionaries and bureaucrats, of exploitative insiders and controllers, and so on (Skocpol 1985; Tilly 1984; see Evans et al. 1985 for a general review).

The weakness of the rhetoric behind the appeals to a purely "organizational" conception is revealed when one examines the actual academic field concentrating on the study of organizations (see Scott 1987 for a review). It turns out that modern organization theorists do not believe in pure formal organization dominated by imperative authority and efficient and formalized divisions of labor: Modern organizations are not like this, it is discovered, but are highly infused with institutional content and meaning—and indeed function only because of this (March and Olsen 1984; Meyer and Scott 1983). Systems that operate entirely in terms of formal authority and hierarchy, it turns out, tend to be highly ritualized and segmented (in classic imperial, not Western, forms)—effective coordination requires much more of a common institutional frame (in short, ideology).

Contrary to the dreams of the more fanatic organizational realists, an assembly line that was only an assembly line would not work very well (or, probably, at all). Similarly for the lateral aspects of the division of labor—coordination cannot be effectively achieved only from above, but always requires much more by way of an institutionally supported set of shared lateral commitments of a broadly substantive or ideological sort.

In other words, part of the distinctive character of the West may lie neither with the Western ideology nor with the Western organizational forms but with the ongoing interpenetration and interdependence between the two. Western organization can get so extensive and complex precisely because it is infused with meanings that glue together in understandings the elements that tend to be fragmented or decoupled organizationally (Meyer and Scott 1983) and because it props up a system of shared meanings with extraordinarily potent organizational weapons. The fact that Western organizational life may combine both ideal and transcendental elements with mundane and real ones, in a way that runs against the inclinations of most agrarian systems toward sharp separation (for an extreme example, see Geertz 1980), may be a core property.

THE SOCIAL CONCEPTS OF
SOCIETY AND SOCIAL ACTION

If it were true that Christendom reflected a tendency to integrate mass and elite (or peripheral and central) organization and culture, and also to integrate organizational and ideological models, it might be useful to try to find more descriptive imagery to capture the modes of thought involved.

One conceptual suggestion would be to propose that Western Christendom evolved, to a distinctive degree, a conception of society as a system both bounded from and also linked to a natural cosmos and a transcendental one. This society, in the Western conception, is indeed a system of interdependent internal components, not simply a communal entity or point in cosmic space. Not only society but the people and/or groups making it up are entities with moral standing—and the two are linked together through reciprocal rights and obligations that must fit together. Beyond being simply a system, this society is an action system with its own purposive actor (e.g., the state) or is made up of such purposive and responsible actors as individuals and interest groups (Jepperson and Meyer 1988; Thomas et al. 1987). Both centers and the peripheral masses are part of this society or social system, bound together in common and interdependent relation both transcendentally (the souls in a Christian community) and in the natural world. And because this social system is linked to both a transcendental cosmos and a natural one, it is conceived to have both ideal or ideological elements and also real or organizational ones, tightly integrated. Thus the peculiar Western social scientific inclination to see a tension between, yet an integration of, the "ideal" and the "material" may best be seen as an intrinsic structural property of Western society.

From this point of view, the Western cultural inclination to conceive of a human society, right down to the individual soul (later citizen, now human personality), and to define it as a universal moral project in a very real (and ultimately orderly and lawful) natural world, accounts for both the tendency to integrate centers and peripheries (in a conceived "society") and the tendency to link abstract ideological principles to concrete social activities (in theories of "action," for which the West is so notorious, both in its pure ideologies—such as economics—and also in its social sciences).

A good many agrarian systems develop conceptions of society, but less mobilized or complete ones—a fragmentation between centers (linked to transcendence, often) and peripheries (seen as linked to the animal world)—develops; or a distinction between transcendental and mundane, in other terms. Even in the West, variants arise: (1) society as a cow to be developed or exploited by supermen of one sort or another, such as parties, states, or religious elites; (2) society as the world of the privileged, resting on the backs of human animals; (3) society as a corrupt city of man, divorced from the sacred ideal; or (4) society as a spiritual community to be achieved only through separation from the real world through devices like celibacy or exotic forms of education.

In the West, the variants do not win out—both centers and peripheries are incorporated into society, as are both ideal models and real-world organization and activity. Over time, the familiar institutions accomplishing these integrations, and the dynamic tensions associated with them, come into place. Structures like democracy and legitimated movements incorporate masses into centers, and produce citizens and persons capable of the astonishing modern feats of opinion and participation. Ideologies and organizations discipline centers to reduce all goals to the welfare and progress of society through the organized nation-state. The natural world comes under the greatest and grandest ideological scrutiny, so a system that once asked the young to calculate the number of angels who could dance on the head of a pin can ask them now, in utter seriousness, to calculate the number of grains of sand in the Sahara. Serious modern adults can spend proper (and respected and paid) lives studying the reproductive behavior of, say, ants. On the other side, practical activity is similarly to be disciplined by general ideology—unlike the peasant, the modern Western artisan is to control behavior in terms of all sorts of general ideological principles (both scientific and legal or moral).

Much of what we call social structure is made up of the treaties articulating the oppositions incorporated into the Western definition of society—between public and private, collective and individual, ideal and material, and so on (Alford and Friedland 1985). This civilization is renowned for its creation of differentiated structure, though this is as much a property of the Western theory or ideology as a matter of actual social activity. The Western system cannot easily sustain real communities, with sovereignity and purpose—but with unanalyzed interiors—because it celebrates both human society and the human individual as its constitutive element. Society is a rationalized purposive system: a project in time and space. The success or failure of this social project must be seen in terms of its relation to the activities and progress of individual souls.

There is thus not simply a doctrine or conception of society, but an analysis of this society as an action system. The ideology involved (and, of course, most of Western social theory) thus comprises an action theory. Many modern social scientists cannot imagine an alternative, but the doctrines and analyses generated in most civilizations have almost none of the properties of action theory, either in depicting persons or in analyzing society.

Western society and ideology (the two are intertwined) are filled with highly articulated and analyzed normative and cognitive notions of action. There are economic and psychological theories of individual action, and the associated legal and cultural efforts to enact these in practice. There are political theories of the linkage among the individuals making up society, and legal and moral efforts to put these in place. And there are organizational theories of proper action by collectivities within society; and a variety of theories of the state as an actor for society against nature or other societies. All these theories have the most peculiar status—they are both scientific and normative in character, and drift back and forth between depictions of natural and transcendental law.

Theories of action imply that subunits, as well as society itself, have the moral or spiritual qualities of sovereignty and purpose and internal discipline in some sort of transcendental frame, the scientific competence at means-ends calculation, the legal standing to hold resources, and other depicted properties. But it is also supposed that all of these properties are not simply ideal or abstract, but are also true in the real empirical world. Private property and what in California is called personality—including all sorts of goals, all sorts of competencies and calculations—are all natural empirical properties of individual human beings or can and should be made such. Human actorhood is both universal and spiritual and local and immediate and concrete.

At the least, we need social theories of inaction, nondecision, and otherhood, to go with our theories of action, decision, and the self. Better still would be analyses more useful for civilizational comparisons, less entrapped in Western categories.

CONCLUSION

The close linkage of society as project, sharply differentiated from both the gods and nature, to its individual human actor components, similarly endowed, obviously gives Western society a good deal of dynamic potential under favorable conditions. Resources or gains that pile up in centers are a little less likely than elsewhere to be burned off in building either a transcendental or a real world of elite exotica, but end up empowering society. The enhanced power of ordinary human peripherals, because they are legitimated as standard "actors," becomes more available for mobilization in great systems, as in Tocqueville's (1969) account of American stateless nation-building, rather than ending in segmenting wars of each against all. Organizational expansion turns to cultural and ideological ends (the power of now-hegemonic America is used to sustain not American capitalism but various world cultural doctrines); but also religious, legal, and scientific ideological developments are put quickly to organizational service.

All these are elements of what Mann (1986) calls intensification—the Western interpenetration of organization and ideology, state and society, center and periphery. But one can make the same points about the external linkages and expansiveness of the Western system (Mann's "extensification"). The linkage of universal and abstract with local and concrete provides many devices for the rapid flow of all sorts of institutions and links around the whole known world and for the legitimated expansion of that world.

REFERENCES

Alford, Robert and Roger Friedland. 1985. *Powers of Theory*. Cambridge: Cambridge University Press.

Anderson, Benedict. 1983. *Imagined Communities*. London: Verso.

Anderson, Perry. 1974. *Lineages of the Absolutist State*. London: New Left Books.

Butterfield, Herbert. 1950. *Christianity and History*. New York: Scribner.

Collins, Randall. 1986. *Weberian Social Theory*. Parts 1 and 2. Cambridge: Cambridge University Press.

Eisenstadt, S. N. 1982. "The Axial Age: The Emergence of Transcendental Visions and the Rise of Clerics." *Archives Europeennes de Sociology*, pp. 294-314.

Eisenstadt, S. N. and A. Sachar. 1987. *Society, Culture, and Urbanization*. Newbury Park, CA: Sage.

Evans, Peter, Dietrich Rueschemeyer, and Theda Skocpol. 1985. *Bringing the State Back in*. Cambridge: Cambridge University Press.

Geertz, Clifford. 1980. *Negara*. Princeton, NJ: Princeton University Press.

Hall, John. 1986. *Powers and Liberties*. New York: Penguin.

Jepperson, Ronald and John Meyer. 1988. "Polities, Actors, Functions, and Organizing." In *The New Institutionalism in Organizational Analysis*, edited by W. W. Powell and P. J. DiMaggio. Chicago: University of Chicago Press.

Jones, E. L. 1981. *The European Miracle*. Cambridge: Cambridge University Press.

Mann, Michael. 1986. *The Sources of Social Power*. Cambridge: Cambridge University Press.

March, James and Johan Olsen. 1984. "The New Institutionalism." *American Political Science Review* 78:734-49.

McNeill, William. 1963. *The Rise of the West*. Chicago: University of Chicago Press.

Merton, Robert. 1970. *Science, Technology and Society in Seventeenth-Century England*. New York: Harper & Row.

Meyer, John. 1980. "The World Polity and the Authority of the Nation-State." Pp. 109-37 in *Studies of the Modern World-System*, edited by A. Bergesen. New York: Academic Press.
Meyer, John and W. R. Scott. 1983. *Organizational Environments*. Newbury Park, CA: Sage.
North, Douglass. 1981. *Structure and Change in Economic History*. New York: Norton.
North, Douglass and Robert Thomas. 1973. *The Rise of the Western World*. Cambridge: Cambridge University Press.
Scott, W. Richard. 1987. *Organizations*. 2nd ed. Englewood Cliffs, NJ: Prentice-Hall.
Skocpol, Theda. 1979. *States and Social Revolutions*. Cambridge: Cambridge University Press.
———. 1985. "Bringing the State Back in." Pp. 3-43 in *Bringing the State Back in*, edited by P. Evans, D. Rueschemeyer, and T. Skocpol. Cambridge: Cambridge University Press.
Stinchcombe, Arthur. 1968. *Constructing Social Theories*. New York: Harcourt, Brace & World.
Swanson, Guy. 1967. *Religion and Regime*. Ann Arbor: University of Michigan Press.
Thomas, George, John Meyer, Francisco Ramirez, and John Boli. 1987. *Institutional Structure*. Newbury Park, CA: Sage.
Thomson, Janice and Stephen Krasner. 1987. "Global Transactions and the Consolidation of Sovereignty." Workshop on International Theory, Bad Homberg.
Tilly, Charles, ed. 1975. *The Formation of National States in Western Europe*. Princeton, NJ: Princeton University Press.
———. 1984. *Big Structures, Large Processes, Huge Comparisons*. New York: Russell Sage.
Tocqueville, Alexis de. 1969. *Democracy in America*. New York: Doubleday, Anchor.
Wallerstein, Immanuel. 1974, 1980. *The Modern World-System*. Vols. 1 and 2. New York: Academic Press.
Wuthnow, Robert. 1987. *Meaning and Moral Order*. Berkeley: University of California Press.

Index